*The Unfolding
of* The Seasons

The Unfolding
of The Seasons

Ralph Cohen

ROUTLEDGE & KEGAN PAUL
London

First published 1970
by Routledge and Kegan Paul Ltd
Broadway House, 68–74 Carter Lane
London EC4
Made and printed in Great Britain
by C. Tinling and Co. Ltd
London and Prescot

ISBN 0 7100 6612 0

To my wife
Libby Okun Cohen

CONTENTS

CONTENTS

ACKNOWLEDGEMENTS

In writing this book, I had before me an audience composed of those teachers and friends who shared my belief in the value of *The Seasons* and others whose criticism I respect, but who differ from me on the value of this poem. Marjorie H. Nicolson first drew my interest to the poetic incorporation of science in the poem and Geoffrey Tillotson's essays on eighteenth-century poetic diction suggested to me the need to probe the artistry of the poem. My friend and former colleague, John Espey, helped me to see the poem afresh through his wise and thorough knowledge of Thomson's poetry. Reuben A. Brower's reservations about the poem's 'unified vision' forced me to provide answers that I might otherwise have neglected; I hope he will be persuaded by what follows.

I wish to thank Marjorie H. Nicolson, John Espey, Martin Battestin, David Morris and Charles Peake for reading various versions of the manuscript and for their valuable suggestions. Thomas Clayton helped me prepare a concordance and discussed with me the various uses to which it could be put. My wife, to whom this book is dedicated, urged me to keep in view the larger implications of this study; from the beginning she saw its relation to the critical ideas expounded in *The Art of Discrimination*. If others are persuaded to accept these larger implications, especially those regarding Augustan poetic style and culture, she is largely responsible. I am indebted to the Center for Advanced Studies of the University of Virginia for the opportunity to complete this study and to Frances Lackey and Donald Gwynn Watson for help with the proof-reading. I have, of course, sought to avoid errors, but those that remain are my own responsibility.

BIBLIOGRAPHICAL NOTE

The text for my explication is the 1746 edition of *The Seasons*. All quotations are taken from this edition, but with the numbering corrected. The line numbers now correspond with those in the readily available *Oxford Standard Authors* series, *The Complete Poetical Works of James Thomson*, ed. J. Logie Robertson (1908). Whenever I refer to earlier versions of *The Seasons*, I use Otto Zippel's *Thomson's Seasons Critical Edition*, Berlin, 1908, *Palaestra* (LVXI). Since there is no definitive edition of Thomson's works, I have used Patrick Murdoch's reliable 1762 edition of the plays and Alan Dugald McKillop's fine edition of *The Castle of Indolence and Other Poems*.

INTRODUCTION

A number of critics[1] have sought to teach us how to read *The Seasons*, but their efforts still meet the determined resistance of such careful readers as F. R. Leavis and Reuben A. Brower. In *Revaluation* F. R. Leavis wrote: 'when we think of Johnson and Crabbe, when we recall any example of a poetry bearing a serious relation to the life of its time, then Gray, Thomson, Dyer, Akenside, Shenstone and the rest clearly belong to a by-line. It is literary and conventional in the worst sense of those terms.'[2] And there is a more recent attack on the artistry of *The Seasons* by Reuben A. Brower, who like another critic who guarded our tender sensibilities from Milton, warns against a Thomson revival on the grounds that Thomson lacks a 'unifying vision active in the separate descriptions.'[3]

When such warnings are issued, it is necessary not to heed them, but to test them. Now is the time to examine the poetry of *The Seasons* not only because we have been warned not to do so, but because the poem obviously possesses sufficient 'life' to merit attention and attack. Perhaps, then, a study of the poem ought to begin by answering the assertion that it bears no 'serious relation to the life of its time.'

First and foremost, *The Seasons* is an Augustan poem, sharing with the major poetry of the period an awareness of the valued past, the corruption of this past in the present, the limited nature of human life, and the faith that a better life exists beyond 'this dark State.'[4] When a recent critic contrasts the Augustan 'humanist' satiric tradition which 'is convinced that human nature, for all its potential dignity, is irremediably flawed and corrupt at the core'[5] with the nonsatiric which 'tends to draw its real strength from the new industrial and commercial evidence of the validity of the idea of progress,'[6] he is perpetuating a misinterpretation that even a perfunctory reading of *The Seasons* refutes.

Not only does Thomson propound the 'humanist' view of the limitation of man, but he sees man surrounded and often overwhelmed by natural forces. If in *Spring* God smiles upon man and brings him into a Golden Age. He also ceases to smile and brings destruction

1

upon this peaceful haven. Thomson's poem is identified with the life of its time by revealing that the natural environment no less than human environment possesses beauty, awe as well as destructive powers. For if man can control the garden, he cannot control the storm, if he can plant in spring, he cannot be sure that he will be able to reap in autumn. Thomson's poem reveals an awareness of simultaneous and often contradictory actions in space, of joy in one place and sadness in another. It urges upon the reader the need to understand the environment by plunging into it not merely by seeing, but by tasting, smelling, hearing and touching it.

Thomson accepts the constant change governing his world, and this is why the turning of the seasons is the professed subject of the poem. By definition the seasons are cyclical, not progressive, and although chronologically seeds grow, men grow and states grow, they also decline. Only in heaven, where the good arrive, can inevitable progress be found. For the rest, British commerce may thrive while British culture declines, primitive people may exist in Africa while a civilized society exists in Britain. Thomson neither proposes nor defends 'the validity of the idea of progress.'[7]

Thomson recognized the fragmentariness of man's experience, knowledge and happiness. He wrote of moments of harmony and of a limited ideal in nature and in man's rural retreats from nature, harmonious moments that provided a union with the past or a hopeful prospect for infinity. But such moments and places were necessary relief from the anxiety and uneasiness of actual human experience. The model people and places are necessary in *The Seasons* because they affirm the possibility of temporary relief from anxieties and disappointments and the hope of a future life. In the inevitable turning of time and fortune all retreats have to be abandoned. As Thomson wrote to Elizabeth Young upon the death of her sister, 'true Happiness is not the Growth of this mortal Soil, but of those blessed regions where she is now.'[8]

The Seasons, with its awareness of limitations and change, urges upon man a participation in the environment, an awareness of it that provides unexpected delights together with expected sadness, destruction and the need to trust in God. And it does so by developing techniques for revealing the past in the present, the individual in the general the sadness in the joy. Brower's reference to 'separate descriptions' assumes, if I interpret it correctly, that the descriptions have no 'vital poetic connection' with other passages, but at least one modern critic claims to have found such connection. Patricia M. Spacks points out that 'Even the passages of *The Seasons* most famed as descriptive set-pieces reveal the same preoccupation [as the non-descriptive passages] with emotional and intellectual significance rather than merely appearance.'[9] The 'unifying vision' is that God's love and wisdom, only fragmentarily perceptible in the beautiful and dangerous aspects of man and nature, will become fully perceptible in a future world. Thomson's 'vision' evokes sentiments of beauty, sublimity, benevolence, fear and anxiety so that the reader may be led to believe in, to love, to trust, and to fear God's power.

This vision controls the descriptions as it does every aspect of the poem. It can be discovered in the overall unity where what is dominant in one season is converted into a subordinate role in another. The idea of love in *Spring*, for example, is subordinated to that of light and power in *Summer*; and this power is subordinated to the tempered atmosphere, the mists and declining sun of *Autumn*. The seasons follow a cyclical rhythm: gentle *Spring*, potent *Summer*, declining *Autumn*, destructive *Winter*. And yet each of these seasons contains, though it subordinates, opposing forces, and all are governed by the secret-working hand of God. Thus, though each season is rhythmically, associatively, and thematically connected with the preceding and following, the whole reveals the inevitable fragmentation of man's knowledge of the world. Each season is intertwined with a natural element and a human responsiveness so that as the earth opens, love flowers. And the fire of the sun brings enlightenment and oppressiveness followed by *Autumn* harvests which are like life-giving or saddening waters. The *Winter* tempests with their invigorating as well as destructive powers close the cycle in which *Spring* seeds lie dormant.

The sources and models for *The Seasons* are *Job*, the *Georgics*, *De Rerum Natura*, *L'Allegro*, *Il Penseroso* and *Paradise Lost*, and these do not lead to a new genre called 'descriptive poems.'[10] Rather, *The Seasons* is a religious didactic poem, and its 'unifying vision' appears in the manner in which it joins eulogies, elegies, narratives, prospect views, historical catalogs, hymns, etc. Even if these are at times artistically ineffective, the point is that they are subsumed under a conception in which they are associatively clustered to indicate the limited feature of each season. Thus even if, when removed as set-pieces, some parts are organic in themselves, their place in each season is inorganic or associative, so that organicism becomes merely another type of fragment.

The interpretation of a world where man and nature become part of a family of which God is the Father in no way implies that they uniformly reflect each other. Most men are dominated by selfish rather than benevolent desires and there are in nature 'vindictive' and 'jealous'[11] forces; although love and benevolence are desirable, man and nature only occasionally achieve harmony. If, as a sympathetic critic of *The Seasons* writes, Thomson's 'internal moral world and the external world were intended to be in complete harmony,'[12] then in Thomson's world such completeness is impossible, and his 'intention' unfulfilled. The realms of man and nature sometimes touch and sometimes clash, sometimes one forms an ironic or sentimental commentary upon the other, but the underlying conception is that neither one is complete nor are they together an illustration of the meaning of the world. They may create momentary harmonies or disharmonies, but they make clear that only God can explain the way of His wisdom and love.

Thomson adjusted contemporary practices to his own purposes and fashioned a language for his encompassing vision. He found continuities from the past in the present, different perspectives of the same or similar events, value and impressiveness in the objects and actions of nature. His adaptations included a private use of Latinate terms, the mixing of present with past participles, the introduction of scientific terms in religious passages, the use of general terms with specific implications. Thus the language of the poem reflected the 'vision' since terms possessed different perspectives, and at different times the same word occurs in varied, even contrary contexts.

Thomson's innovations are particularly noticeable in his use of periphrasis. This image was what critics referred to when they attacked the literariness or conventionality of his poetry. R. D. Havens in 1922 declared that Thomson 'delighted in unnatural and inflated circumlocutions, like "the household feathery people" (hens), "the copious fry" or "the finny race" or "the glittering finny swarms".'[13] Such objections have been answered extensively, and John Butt's comments can stand for numerous others: 'Thomson's Latinisms came naturally to a lowland Scot writing Southern English, and his periphrases were used not to escape vulgarity, but precisely and evocatively.'[14] Thomson's precision, achieved by converting periphrasis to a combination of personification and scientific classification, interpreted nature accurately, scientifically and humanistically in order to illustrate the relation between the realms of man and animal.

4

Thomson's general terms, decried as turgid and repetitive, function not as flabby general terms, but as forms of metonymy in which the whole stands for a part and in different contexts for different parts, so that the fragmentation of the world is always conceived as a class or ideal term comprehending a variety of individual members. In connecting pastoral conventions to a comic conception of contemporary rural life, he developed a linguistic procedure (I have called it 'illusive allusion') in which he playfully ridiculed the convention and parodied its applicability to the present. He was not unwilling to burlesque the convention of the hunting scene or to mock the convention of pastoral love. Since he sought a perspectival interpretation of human experience as well as of art, he could include two versions of the same genre or convention with contrasting implications.

But varied meanings of the same word or convention in no way led Thomson to relativism, for he accepted the belief in God's wisdom and love. He accepted some aspects of literary continuity by incorporating Biblical, classical and Miltonic allusions into his vision. These became a basis for his interpretation of the simultaneity of past and present. And the virtues of the heroic, political, and literary heroes of the past find a place in his catalogs because they represent values that the virtuous moderns also possess. Despite changing particulars, there were virtues that endured exactly as there were evils that endured. When Hoxie N. Fairchild writes that in *The Seasons* God is social and smiling, that 'All of Him has faded away except the cosmic grin,'[15] he completely ignores Thomson's repeated assertions of human pain and suffering: 'the thousand nameless Ills,/That one incessant Struggle render Life,/One Scene of Toil, of Suffering, and of Fate' (*Winter*, 349–51).

Thomson converts conventional figures such as repetition or metaphor to his own vision of a brilliant and dangerous spatial world in change. Thus repetition as epizeuxis defines intensity by spatial movement or extent. His use of metaphor that shifts between natural description and personification relates felt particularity to a parallel human order and reaffirms the human feeling necessary to the interpretation and appreciation of nature. Another aspect of Thomson's use of metaphor contrasts man's imperfection with God's perfection by illustrating the dependence of man's imagination upon God's creativity. The same term is, in one instance, literal, and, in another, metaphoric. The deluge is an actual deluge in one season, a deluge of light or earth in another. The elements themselves are converted into aspects of each other, and the implications of this precedure are both scientific and religious. There is nothing that man can imagine or discover which God has not already created in the universe. Man can occasionally discover what he never knew before, but it was always there, and it supports the interpretation of man's knowledge as fragmentary and God's power as omnipresent.

In this world in which nature is often puzzling, anxiety is no stranger to man. Geoffrey Tillotson notes that '*anxious* was a favourite Augustan epithet,'[16] and Thomson's poem adjusts a common term and idea to his own ends. The wandering narrator observes uncertainty, harmony and disharmony. But these lead him to a recognition of his own limitations. Critics have objected that Thomson often shifts from one place to another without explanation, what Reuben A. Brower calls 'the bald lack of transitions,' yet this practice is consistent with his vision. Logical and reasonable explanations will not do; good men die and evil ones live on, and no rationalizing will explain God's wisdom. Time and again the ironic silence indicates the need for faith and the failure of reason to understand God's ways. Indeed, when the individual feels most at one with God, silence is the only answer, and the last line of the 'Hymn' is, 'Come then, expressive Silence, muse his Praise.'

With the varied uses of genres and figures, Thomson necessarily combined poetic tones appropriate to them. In his depiction of rural workers his language is occasionally sensual, aware of the pleasure in sexual play and healthy sexual appetites. To talk of Thomson's bad taste is to disregard the fact that in the poem sexual pleasures are a genuine part of the transient joys of rural man. Thomson had a fine sense of playing off one style against another to illustrate the unexpected collocation of joy and suffering, and his letters reveal that the poetry expressed deep-rooted human values, pertinent to his comic and ironic as well as to his serious tones.

> It is always a maxim with me, [he writes in a letter of 1742]
>> To honour humble worth, and, scorning state,
>> Piss on the proud inhospitable gate.
> For which reason I go scattering my water every where about Richmond.[17]

Throughout the poem Thomson attacks courtiers and aristocrats and all others who in pride and viciousness pursue their selfish interests. These Thomson sees as never entering the kingdom of heaven, but his sympathy for the poor and the weak does not lead him to a revolutionary position. He opposes the vicious jailers, the mean squires, the cruel bird-killers, but he adheres to a conventional class structure. His view of change operates within the given natural and institutional boundaries.

The estates with their prospects constitute a middle place between earth and heaven from which one can view infinity. Thomson establishes a typical eighteenth-century cluster of peace, prosperity, patriotism, and plenty, and the estates are the sources of wealth and the basis for Britain's power, This means that the poem is often fulsome in its praise of aristocrats; often the dreariest passages are those in which the ideals of the squirearchy are identified with those of the Horatian contented man, and complacence is substituted for composure.

In *The Seasons* Thomson undertook a series of experiments that led him to new uses of imagery, to trials in word combinations, to incorporation of scientific with classical and Biblical language in order to express his poetic vision of the world. The traditions of word order, sentence structure, diction and subject that he inherited he sought to use for his own new purposes. He developed techniques of recurrence to express subtle temporal and spatial changes; he used the inherited figures of paradox and irony to express scientific ideas in which minute space contained worlds and silence roared. Within the view of successive space, he saw a constant shifting and interrelating of men and nature in which objects were transformed, as were the words that Thomson used to express them. His poem moved within a classical and religious tradition that was connected with an exhilarating sense of the present, scientifically and precisely felt. Thomson used nature to develop a 'new-creating Word' and 'a heightened Form.' The new word and form expressed, within a great tradition of English poetry, the fragmentary perception of the beauty, sublimity, benevolence and destruction that man experienced, but only God fully understood.

In arguing for *The Seasons* as a work with a 'unified vision' and a relevance to its own period and thus to ours, I have had to become detailed and precise. A consequence of this has been my decision to curtail discussion of the blank verse, not a matter of much disagreement, in order to concentrate on what has been overlooked, misconceived, or misinterpreted. I have not sought to overlook Thomson's faults or to apologize for them. If my explanation is persuasive, the values of the poem will sustain it.

INTRODUCTION

NOTES

[1] Alan D. McKillop, *The Background of Thomson's 'Seasons,'* Minneapolis, 1942, ed. *James Thomson* (1700–1748) *Letters and Documents*, Lawrence, 1958, and ed., *The Castle of Indolence and Other Poems*, Lawrence, 1961; D. Nichol Smith, *Some Observations on Eighteenth Century Poetry*, London, 1937; Marjorie H. Nicolson, *Newton Demands the Muse*, Princeton, 1946; Geoffrey Tillotson, *Augustan Studies*, London, 1961; John Butt, *The Augustan Age*, London, 1950; Martin Price, *To the Palace of Wisdom*, Doubleday, 1964; Josephine Miles, *Eras and Modes in English Poetry*, Berkeley, 1957; Patricia Meyer Spacks, *The Poetry of Vision*, Cambridge, Mass., 1967; Douglas Grant, *James Thomson*, London, 1951; C. V. Deane, *Aspects of Eighteenth Century Nature Poetry*, Oxford, 1935.

[2] F. R. Leavis, *Revaluation*, London, Peregrine Books, p. 90.

[3] Reuben A. Brower, 'Form and Defect of Form in Eighteenth Century Poetry: A Memorandum,' *College English*, 29 (April, 1968), 538.

[4] *Summer*, 1800.

[5] Paul Fussell, *The Rhetorical World of Augustan Humanism*, Oxford, 1965, p. 8.

[6] *Ibid.*, p. 22.

[7] R. D. Havens, 'Primitivism and the Idea of Progress,' *SP* (1932), 41.

[8] *Letters*, p. 170.

[9] Patricia M. Spacks, *The Poetry of Vision*, Cambridge, 1967, p. 19.

[10] For 'descriptive poem', see *The Art of Discrimination*, London, 1964. See pp. 132–39.

[11] 'Vindictive' nature, *Spring*, 308.

[12] Maren-Sofie Röstvig, *The Happy Man*, Oslo, 1958, II, 265.

[13] Raymond D. Havens, *The Influence of Milton on English Poetry*, Cambridge, Mass., 1922, p. 138.

[14] John Butt, *The Augustan Age*, London, 1950, p. 93. D. Nichol Smith, *Some Observations on Eighteenth Century Poetry*, Geoffrey Tillotson, 'Augustan Poetic Diction, II,' *Augustan Studies*, London, 1961, p. 81.

[15] Hoxie N. Fairchild, *Religious Trends in English Poetry*, New York, 1939, I, 519.

[16] Tillotson, *Augustan Studies*, p. 79.

[17] *Letters*, December 7, 1742, p. 142.

I

SPRING

THE LOVE SONG OF JAMES THOMSON

i. Rhetorical Techniques of Harmony and Disharmony (1-233)

When James Thomson published *Spring* in 1728, he had already published *Winter* (1726) and *Summer* (1727). This poem, therefore, took for granted the descriptions of the previously published seasons, and sought to present the 'softer Scenes':

> But chief
> In Thee, Boon Spring, and in thy softer Scenes,
> The Smiling God appears.
>
> (*A*, 821–23)

Thomson had earlier written of 'Winter' in which the scenes were not 'soft' and God not 'smiling':

> Dread Winter has subdu'd the Year,
> And reigns, tremendous, o'er the desart Plains!
> How dead the Vegetable Kingdom lies!
> How dumb the Tuneful! Horror wide extends
> His solitary Empire.
>
> (*Winter*, *A*, 359–63)

And when he revised *Winter* (1744), he distinguished among the many muses that dictated the poem: the 'happy Muse' (691), the 'Tragic Muse' (342), the 'sage Historic Muse' (587), the 'Comic Muse' (650), and the '*Rural Muse*' (663).

The *Hymn* to *The Seasons* refers to 'the *varied* God' (2) and in *Spring* Thomson refers to his 'varied Verse' (578); the variety that he brings to his blank verse parallels the variety that God gives to the universe. In this respect, to study Thomson's activity is to study what he himself quite consciously insisted upon: 'His [Aikman's] Reflections on my Writings are very good; but He does not, in Them, regard the Turn of my Genius' enough. Should I alter my Way, I would write poorly. I must chuse, what appears to me the most significant Epithet or I cannot, with any Heart, proceed.'[1] If the letter insists only on his epithets, his repeated efforts to correct, revise and amplify the poem refer to the whole range of his poetic activity.

No poem of the eighteenth century reveals as many continuing revisions as *The Seasons* issued in that name in 1730. *Winter* was first issued in 1726, *Summer* in 1727, *Spring* in 1728, *Autumn* in the first edition of *The Seasons*. The whole was revised in 1730, in 1744, in 1746.[2] None of Thomson's other works show this devotion to revision, and many of them cast some light upon this, the major poem of his life.

The Seasons may be important to some critics because of its philosophical or historical sentiments, but I wish to argue for its artistic validity. Thomson introduced into English poetry a number of techniques to express his Augustan version of man, nature and God, techniques that permitted him to describe nature in observed, sometimes even scientific detail, while relating it to a classical tradition and a religious belief. He was not always successful in presenting it, but he found a style for expressing changes in man, nature and society while holding to the orthodox belief in God's love and wisdom.

This can be seen in the very opening of *Spring* when '*Spring*' is identified as 'Ethereal mildness,' a personification that is mixed with natural description and addressed in the vocative, as is the Countess of Hertford, to whom the season is dedicated.

> COME, gentle SPRING, Ethereal Mildness, come,
> And from the Bosom of yon dropping Cloud,
> While Music wakes around, veil'd in a Shower
> Of Shadowing Roses, on our Plains descend.
>   O Hartford, fitted, or to shine in Courts
> With unaffected Grace, or walk the Plain
> With Innocence and Meditation join'd
> In soft Assemblage, listen to my Song,
> Which thy own Season paints; when Nature all
> Is blooming, and benevolent, like thee.
>
>   (1–10)

Spring is the only season dedicated to a woman, and like the first book of *De Rerum Natura*, dedicated to Venus, it deals with love. *Spring* presents the rebirth of nature, of love in birds, animals and man in three stages: (1) the unfolding of love in the reanimation of the earth, (2) the aerial love song and mating of the birds, followed by reference to the bull, stallion, sea monsters and domestic fowl, (3) the 'infusive force of Spring' on human love. But throughout this and other seasons, there is the love of God. Thomson identified in his 'Argument' to *Spring* only the progressive part of the total order, but even in this season he describes not only 'the wild and irregular Passion of Love' but the fall from the Golden Age, and the destruction of the world by the Flood.

This season opens and closes with the descent and ascent of conventionalized visions, *Spring* being personified and men and women idealized. But within this encompassing cycle in which nature is reduced to social order and man to the recurrent natural rhythm, there enters at once the Countess of Hertford. The season arrives in a spatial concert or concord image of shadowy (foreshadowy) fulfillment; while music wakes 'around', 'Spring' descends from the cloud to the plain. The sexual possibilities of the image to which Thomson returns later in the poem are muted when reference is made to the Countess of Hertford, who, as innocence and meditation, personified and joined in 'soft Assemblage,' is implored to 'listen to my Song' and is exaggeratedly compared to nature. Here, as in other eulogies, the provocativeness of an image is lost because the conventional praise avoids the charged implications of the comparison.

The personified 'gentle SPRING' and its appositive, the naturalistic 'Ethereal Mildness,' are surrounded by the vocative of movement, 'come.' The poet calls upon 'Spring' to descend amid a concert of senses—of hearing, sight, smell, even touch—that suggest the future in the present. This simultaneity of senses as well as of time and motion sets the tone for the transformation of the earth through the beauty of blossoming, of 'Spring's' rebirth with its synonyms, 'waking,' 'kindling,' and 'love,' and its nourishment of the earth.

Since this image is one of extension, of concerted movement through space from heaven to earth, Thomson apparently considered a more regular, less complicated image. But he abandoned this alternative, keeping the sensuous interplay. What he considered was:

Come, gentle Spring, fair Queen of Seasons, come,
And from the Bosom of yon dropping Cloud,

11

With the glad Hours, the Zephirs, Loves, and Joys
Gay-fluttering round thee, on our Plains descend.

(MS, 1–4, p.8)

This revision, more paintable though it was, altered the transforming images of sound, sight and smell that were to unify the responses to 'Spring,' and Thomson rejected it in favor of the original.

The poet does not connect the two formal addresses—one to personified 'Spring' and the other to the Countess of Hertford—but they are joined analogically and although the song that paints is conventional Thomsonian synaesthesia, the hyperbolic 'Nature all/Is blooming, and benevolent, like thee' (9–10) is obvious flattery.

The image of birth, love and nourishment—of '*Spring*' descending from the bosom of the cloud followed by the renewal of nature and man—is the central image of the season, a season which deals with man's loss of innocence from the Golden Age (pure birth and its destruction), the sensuous birth of spring flowers, the love of birds and animals, the joy, pain, the ideal of human love. Thomson deliberately sought to make the music of the induction with its varied vowel range, its resonance and alliteration part of his meaning. For he was to present the sounds as a significant part of the season. It was John Clare who recognized the subtlety of these lines and who wrote in his *Journal* that they 'made my heart twitter with joy.'

The imagery of diffusive movement in the following description (11–47)—'Dissolving Snows' (16), 'trembling Year' (18), 'driving Sleets' (20), 'sounding Marsh' (23)—contrasts a temporal, bound world with an unbound one. The 'moving Softness' (33) being 'unconfin'd' (32), leads to 'unbinding Earth' (33), a relief from the *Winter* stiffness and crampedness of nature, for the 'unconfinedness' is an expanding, though not an absolute space. The space of *Spring*, from earth to ether, can 'grow' or 'blossom,' but it is successive and limited. As *Winter* departs, there occurs freedom of expansion, release from obstruction, so that the sower who 'liberal, throws the Grain' (45) sows love and expansion, the fertility of space.

'Unconfin'd,' 'unbinding' are terms that by their negation suggest a limit—nature is no longer confined or bound as it was.[3] 'Unconfin'd' (32) and 'unbounded' (70) apply to spatial phenomena but they also apply to feelings and music—'unbounded Passion' (*Winter*, 340), 'the Love of Nature unconfin'd' (*Autumn*, 1020), 'this Joy o'erflows/ In Music unconfin'd' (*Spring*, 589–90). 'Unbounded' can, therefore,

12

refer to unleashing dangerous passions as well as pleasant ones, and the breaking of 'bounds' is only an exceeding of limits, not an abandoning of them.

Early in the poem, Thomson implies by his use of negative prefixes that the cycle of nature exists in some neutral way from which *Spring* releases the earth that had in the previous season been bound and that, as the poem advances, is bound again. The same stem, 'bound,' acquires both negative and positive directions, and from the outset Thomson plunges into a typical procedure of varied, even contradictory contexts that develop in depth in this and subsequent seasons.

By the time Thomson was writing this season, he had begun to increase the personifications in the poem, and when he published a revised *Winter* in *The Seasons* of 1730, he was seeking to establish a kingdom of nature that was a kingdom of the world. He began to include hostile descriptions—'surly Winter,' Winter bidding 'his driving Sleets/Deform the Day delightless' (20–21)—which were to permit him in each of the four seasons to suggest the conflicts and clashes, the chaotic disorder, formlessness, to be set against absence of conflict in the peaceful or retired life.

The observational description and the moralizing passage represent, in the first invocation to 'Heaven' and 'Britons' (48–77), the speaker as an observer of nature, recording the observations with care, and as a Christian moralist singing hymns to his readers. '*Spring*' descends from the open 'Bosom' (2) of the cloud but paradoxically the grain is thrust into the 'Bosom' (46) of the 'Earth,' which is then shut; but open or shut the *Spring* cloud and earth mingle their elements to create expansiveness, flowers and harvest, in a particular Thomsonian evocation of expansiveness by harmonious actions. Thus, 'The Harrow follows harsh and shuts the Scene' (47) indicates growth because the harshness of the harrow is part of the harmony of cultivation, and is not the end or final shutting of the scene. But in *Winter* Thomson writes:

> And pale concluding Winter comes at last,
> And shuts the Scene.
>
> (1032–1033)

Here mortal life ends; the second birth is beyond this world.

The laboring farmer with his 'well-us'd Plow' (36) naturalistically loosens the soil, but he is also idealized by being placed within a tradition of the warrior-king as farmer:

13

In antient Times, the sacred Plow employ'd
The Kings, and awful Fathers of Mankind.

(58–59)

In rebuking the wealthy 'who live/In Luxury and Ease, in Pomp and Pride' (52–53) for rejecting as unworthy the themes of rural life, the poet holds up the model of Augustan Rome that admired the pastorals and georgics of Virgil, and places himself within the Virgilian tradition. Yet the veneration of the plough is no mere rural idealization; it becomes the basis for British wealth and commerce. The laboring farmer, therefore, becomes in *The Seasons* a political figure, not merely uncorrupted by ease, but generous to his country and to the world at large. In *Spring*, the other elements, air, water, fire (aspects of nature), are invoked to bring the planting of the earth to fruition:

Ye fostering Breezes, blow!
Ye softening Dews, ye tender Showers, descend!
And temper all, thou influential Sun,
Into the perfect Year!

(49–52)

These planted treasures then become part of the commercial interchange: as the pomp of life is wafted to Britain so British earth becomes like the flowing sea:

Nature's better Blessings pour
O'er every Land, the naked Nations cloath,
And be th' exhaustless Granary of a World!

(75–77)

In the examples of reciprocal imagery that Thomson develops, the 'well-us'd Plow' is associated with the 'sacred Plow' and, in a metonymic image, the Britons are exhorted to 'cultivate' (67) the plow. The luxuriant proud, on the other hand, become 'Insect-Tribes' that seek to destroy the cultivation. Since cultivation becomes a political act, the imagery reveals a transformation from the individual to the country, and expansiveness joins countries by making the earth flow. This spatial, commercial, political harmony is not, however, the totality of *Spring*. For although the poet sings of Spring causing nature to relent (35) (the softening of the earth), of Spring green as 'smiling Nature's universal Robe' (89), of 'Harmonious Nature' (258), meaning the concord of sky, wood and sun in the Golden Age, yet this very

14

Golden Age is followed by 'Nature' disturbed, even deemed 'vindictive' (308), and the *Spring* lover, musing on his absent love, sees Spring itself and nature decline:

> The rosy-bosom'd Spring
> To weeping Fancy pines; and yon bright Arch,
> Contracted, bends into a dusky Vault.
> All Nature fades extinct.
>
> (1010–1013)

In this poem the term 'nature' or 'nature's' (with a single instance of 'natural') occurs 92 times: *Spring*, 24; *Summer*, 26; *Autumn*, 22; *Winter*, 17; *Hymn*, 3. It is used repeatedly throughout each of the seasons, and it is not only positive or negative depending upon the context, it can mean rural economy, the animals that inhabit the countryside, the forces that are subservient to God, the forces that God uses to shape man. 'Nature' can be kind, vindictive, jealous, graceful, bountiful. In fact, the variations on nature reflect the variations that God has, since the fall, given to the world.

When Wordsworth declared that Thomson was fortunate in his title,[4] he implied that a poem called *The Seasons* had a subject of enduring, archetypal interest. Certainly the four elements are never far from the observational level of the narrator, and although each season deals with the blending or clashing of earth, air, water, and fire, in actual or analogous form, each season possesses a dominant element. *Spring*, because it deals with fruition, love, the expansion of natural and human forces, gives dominance to the earth, whose secret workings and flowerings exemplify the expansive (love) mood.

> NOR only thro the lenient Air this Change,
> Delicious, breathes; the penetrative Sun,
> His Force deep-darting to the dark Retreat
> Of Vegetation, sets the steaming Power
> At large, to wander o'er the vernant Earth,
> In various Hues; but chiefly thee, gay *Green*!
> Thou smiling Nature's universal Robe!
> United Light and Shade! where the Sight dwells
> With growing Strength, and ever-new Delight.
> FROM the moist Meadow to the wither'd Hill,
> Led by the Breeze, the vivid Verdure runs,
> And swells, and deepens, to the cherish'd Eye,
> The Hawthorn whitens; and the juicy Groves

15

Put forth their Buds, unfolding by Degrees,
Till the whole leafy Forest stands display'd,
In full Luxuriance, to the sighing Gales;
Where the Deer rustle thro the twining Brake,
And the Birds sing conceal'd. At once, array'd
In all the Colours of the flushing Year,
By Nature's swift and secret-working Hand,
The Garden glows, and fills the liberal Air
With lavish Fragrance; while the promis'd Fruit
Lies yet a little Embryo, unperceiv'd,
Within its crimson Folds. Now from the Town
Buried in Smoke, and Sleep, and noisom Damps,
Oft let me wander o'er the dewy Fields,
Where Freshness breathes, and dash the trembling Drops
From the bent Bush, as thro the verdant Maze
Of Sweet-briar Hedges I pursue my Walk;
Or taste the Smell of Dairy; or ascend
Some eminence, AUGUSTA, in thy Plains,
And see the Country, far-diffus'd around,
One boundless Blush, one white-empurpled Shower
Of mingled Blossoms; where the raptur'd Eye
Hurries from Joy to Joy, and, hid beneath
The fair Profusion, yellow Autumn spies.

(78–113)

The rebirth of nature, described in personification that has sexual overtones—'the penetrative Sun,/His Force deep-darting to the dark Retreat/of Vegetation' (79–81)—arises from the secret-working power of the sun, and the growth of nature takes place before the narrator's eye that responds to the sights, sounds, smells, tastes, touch of nature.

The technique for achieving this sensuousness includes the use of verbs and participles to indicate spatial and temporal movement: 'deep-darting,' 'wander,' 'growing,' 'runs,' 'swells,' 'deepens,' 'whitens,' 'Put forth,' 'rustle,' etc. This movement gradually leads to the moment of completion—'At once, array'd/In all the Colours of the flushing Year.' Another is to suggest in the same passage the process and the product, to discover the completion as extension of color, of sound, of smell, see the extension as one moment in space and time, 'one boundless Blush': to interpret harmony as extension and variety in unity. This latter harmony deserves, perhaps, the name of the spectrum technique, a method by which the objects of extended nature appear, but merely appear, to fuse into one when observed as part of a prospect view.

The 'steaming Power'—moving sap—gives the flowers their diverse and vivid colors and 'wanders,' like the narrator, over the earth; it is like the hidden force that drives the speaker, and the consequence is love, a 'united Light and Shade,' a spatial phenomenon observable in extent. But the idea of space should not be confused with the idea of sight. Space is the arena in which events are observed; and such observation suggests a blending of all senses, sight, sound, touch, etc., with faith. Thus the image of the running 'Verdure' that 'swells, and deepens, to the cherish'd Eye' conveys growth, movement, color and intensity. The 'cherish'd Eye' sees and hears and smells. The eye, of course, does not 'see' the 'Buds, unfolding by Degrees,' but is aware of the totality of the process in examining a part. The effect of the whole is not mere vision:

> the whole leafy Forest stands display'd,
> In full Luxuriance, to the sighing Gales;
> Where the Deer rustle thro the twining Brake,
> And the Birds sing conceal'd.
>
> (92–95)

The narrator smells the 'Freshness' of the fields, touches the trembling drops, tastes 'the Smell of Dairy.' These are acts achieved in successive movements, but they form a concert, an act of harmony that, in rural nature, is an act of love. And as he observes the scene from an eminence, the diffused countryside appears one, the different elements are now 'seen,' having individually been felt and sensed and touched. The flowers blend into 'One boundless Blush, one white-empurpled Shower/Of mingled Blossoms' (110–11). But even here the Eye 'yellow Autumn spies' and sees the future harvest in the present.

The *presentness* is evoked by the narrator's direct address:—'but chiefly thee, gay *Green*!' (83)—by his personal flight from the buried city and his touching of and wandering through nature. The wandering not only relates the personal speaker to the moving power that colors the flowers but also locates him within the concord of the general view. Thus the view at hand—'dash the trembling Drops/From the bent Bush'—and the view of the country 'far-diffus'd around' identify the part in the prospect, the individual in the natural range, the present

17

in the cycle of the past. And this is one of the typical Thomsonian strategies of relating the actual to the ideal.

The transition from the fine growth passage to the insect plague is made by reference to autumn in spring, for here is the return of 'Untimely Frost' (117). This was a section (114–36) which Thomson revised; in 1744, he removed 33 lines and placed them, with alterations, in *Summer*. The flatness of this didactic passage is evident, and yet terms common to *Spring* are repeated—'cutting Gale,' 'breathe,' 'wide-dejected *Waste*,' 'wasteful'—and these are connected with a high increase in periphrasis: 'Insect-Armies,' 'feeble Race,' 'sacred Sons of Vengeance,' 'a frosty Tribe.' The 'smoking,' too, is seen as a positive act in contrast to the smoke-buried town and its noisome damps. And he sought too, in 1744, to connect the insects threatening the harvest with the prideful men ('Insect-Tribes') who threatened England's 'Granary,' changing 'You're but the Beings of a Summer's Day' to 'And some, with whom compar'd, your Insect-Tribes/Are but the Beings of a Summer's Day' (60–61).

The original (1728) passage that was transferred, revised, to *Summer* in 1744 did, indeed, contain admission of a conflict between animals, a conflict that explained the passage more effectively than anything in the revision:

> Even Animals subsist
> On Animals, in infinite Descent;
> And all so fine adjusted, that the Loss
> Of the least Species would disturb the whole.
>
> (*Spring, A*, 155–58).

It is unnecessary to assume that Thomson did not know what he was doing—that he could not tell good lines from bad—when he transferred the passage and thus emphasized the fault of the remainder. Throughout the revisions there is an intelligent artistic consciousness, and in this instance some possible reasons for the transfer, for the elimination of this Great Chain reference, and the addition of a didactic address to the 'Swains,' can be suggested: (1) the plenitude of the passage was more consistent with *Summer*; (2) the implicit recognition of the presence of secret evil was inconsistent with *Spring*; (3) the constant presence of insects was incompatible with the growth and process he sought; (4) the didactic address was an attempt to explain away evil in the wrong season since Thomson wished to retain the duality of nature but not give *Spring* a wrong emphasis. The revision gained consistency at the cost, however, of artistic effectiveness.

The shower (143–233) resumes the theme of the birth of the spring flowers (78–113), and it explores the relations between love and birth. The narration, told from the observational view, moves from the sun's force (fire and heat) to that of the clouds (water), and provides two perspectives from which to view earth's relationship to heaven. Each, being an aspect of present nature, stresses the cyclical quality with its difference in sameness. Thus repetitiveness occurs, present time being considered simultaneous, and each event being seen from two perspectives. In line 88 'Led by the Breeze, the vivid Verdure runs,' but in lines 155–56 the breeze is no longer the leader: 'Gradual, sinks the Breeze,/Into a Perfect Calm.' While spring is displayed 'In full Luxuriance, to the *sighing Gales*' (93), before the shower 'not a *Breath*/Is heard to quiver thro the closing Woods' (156–57) [my italics]; while the sun darts into the earth in one moment, after the storm the mountain is lit up: 'The rapid Radiance instantaneous strikes/Th' illumin'd Mountain' (192–93) and the landscape erupts in laughter.

These aspects convey the spatial and temporal variety of the present, and the technique demands that, by means of the apparent repetitions, discriminations be made in the use of the same or similar words and actions. Thus 'Breeze' which 'leads' in the first section is led in the second; the sounds of the wind, the deer, and the birds— hidden and accidental at first—are also seen as part of a harmony. The principle underlying this reversal is that of the expanding present: the same scene or action is treated from another point of view in order to expand the range (space and time): the reversal is not an instance of contradiction but of reciprocity. Thomson's opposites are chaos and harmony, and these are not reconcilable. But harmony can be expressed by blending, reciprocity, successions, versions of perspective. The reciprocal actions are indicative of the love implicit in nature, but it is a love acknowledged as two-sided. For the romantic poets, as M. H. Abrams has pointed out, the 'correspondent breeze' is correlated with a complex subjective process: 'the return to a sense of community after isolation, the renewal of life and emotional vigor after apathy and a deathlike torpor, and an outburst of creative power following a period of imaginative sterility.'[5] But for Thomson the breeze is indicative of the changing variety of nature, its rich responsiveness to different elements at different moments, its limited transitory quality within recurrent cycles:

THE North-East spends his Rage, and now, shut up
Within his iron Caves, th' effusive South
Warms the wide Air, and o'er the Void of Heaven
Breathes the big Clouds with vernal Showers distent.
At first a dusky Wreath they seem to rise,
Scarce staining Ether; but by fast Degrees,
In Heaps on Heaps, the doubling Vapour sails
Along the loaded Sky, and mingling deep
Sits on th' Horizon round a settled Gloom.
Not such as wintry Storms on Mortals shed,
Oppressing Life, but lovely, gentle, kind,
And full of every Hope and every Joy,
The Wish of Nature. Gradual, sinks the Breeze,
Into a perfect Calm; that not a Breath
Is heard to quiver thro the closing Woods,
Or rustling turn the many-twinkling leaves
Of Aspin tall. Th' uncurling Floods, diffus'd
In glassy Breadth, seem thro delusive Lapse
Forgetful of their Course. 'Tis Silence all,
And pleasing Expectation. Herds and Flocks
Drop the dry Sprig, and mute-imploring eye
The falling Verdure. Hush'd in short Suspense,
The plumy People streak their Wings with Oil,
To throw the lucid Moisture trickling off;
And wait th' approaching Sign to strike, at once,
Into the general Choir. Even Mountains, Vales,
And Forests seem, impatient, to demand
The promis'd Sweetness. Man superior walks
Amid the glad Creation, musing Praise,
And looking lively Gratitude. At last,
The Clouds consign their Treasures to the Fields,
And, softly shaking on the dimpled Pool
Prelusive Drops, let all their Moisture flow,
In large Effusion o'er the freshen'd World.
The stealing Shower is scarce to patter heard,
By such as wander through the Forest-Walks,
Beneath th' umbrageous Multitude of Leaves.
But who can hold the Shade, while Heaven descends

In universal Bounty, shedding Herbs,
And Fruits, and Flowers, on Nature's ample Lap?
Swift Fancy fir'd anticipates their Growth;
And, while the milky Nutriment distills,
Beholds the kindling Country colour round.

(143–85)

The response of one element of nature to another, of air, water and earth to each other, is suggested by the use of 'Breathes' (146), 'Breath' (156) and 'Breadth' (160). For the 'effusive South' (144), which 'blows,' 'inspires' and imagistically 'exhales' the rain clouds, is compared with the woods' readiness to receive the 'heavenly' rain (blessing)—'not a Breath/Is heard to quiver thro the closing Woods' (156–57). Silence in nature is described in terms of cessation of motion as well as of sound, so that the 'uncurling Floods, *diffus'd*/In glassy Breadth' (159–60) [my italics] are spread out in glassy motionlessness in contrast to the 'effusive' (not 'diffusive') south wind which 'poured out' the rain clouds. And the 'effusive' wind is eventually compared with the clouds that 'let all their Moisture flow,/In large Effusion' (175–76). Describing cessation of motion in *Summer*, Thomson wrote:

The very Streams look languid from afar;
Or, thro th' unshelter'd Glade, impatient, seem
To hurl into the Covert of the Grove.

(448–50)

The *Spring* and *Summer* images are both instances of illusion in which the personification is clearly separated from the natural description by 'seem.' In *Spring* the 'seeming' creates a visual motionlessness, separating the 'glassy Breadth' from the personified 'delusive Lapse.' *Summer*, however, distinguishes the distance involved in the prospect view from the sudden and contrasting close action of the stream hurtling into the grove. The first expresses the quiet and motionless time of expectancy and new beginnings; the second expresses the contrasting forces of peace and power, light and heat.

The soundlessness and motionlessness are achieved by the use of present participles implying action but supporting its opposite. This lexical procedure in which *no* 'rustling' turns the 'many-twinkling Leaves' and the 'uncurling Floods' are uncurled and glassy, corresponds to the harmony technique of negative terms explained above.

C   21

Motion is described as simultaneous rather than successive to convey blending of behavior. Wind and cloud, for example, fructify earth, and their correspondence suggests a relation not only between elements of nature but between differences within the very language itself. For the passage has a considerable number of Latinate terms that have come to be identified with the artificiality of Thomson's diction: 'delusive,' 'Verdure,' 'lucid,' 'consign,' 'Prelusive,' 'elusive,' 'diffusive,' 'Effusion,' 'umbrageous,' 'Nutriment,' 'distil.' The lines which contain such terms contain them in considerable frequency, so that 'effusive,' 'diffusive' and 'Effusion' connect actions to show relationships that play within a common range of language and nature. This can again be observed in 'delusive' and 'Prelusive' in which the water is first seen as playfully deceived ('thro delusive Lapse') and when the rain falls, the pool receives the 'Prelusive Drops'—the awakening introductory drops which disturb the 'glassy Breadth' by creating a 'dimpled Pool' and an end to deception.

Geoffrey Tillotson has pointed out the Virgilian echoes of this diction in which borrowed language complicates the respected past with present time.[6] It should also be added that in *The Seasons* such diction becomes a form of linguistic nationalism supporting and expressing the author's patriotism. This diction can also express the complex quality of an action, as in 'Thro splendid Kingdoms now devolves his Maze,/Now wanders wild' (*Summer*, 816–17). 'Devolves' implies the intricate, complex, but organized ('Maze') passages through which the Nile flows, and is contrasted with 'wanders wild,' a simple, even though unrestricted movement, though neither is chaotic.

Thomson not only uses a Latinate diction in conventional Miltonic ways, but he learns from Milton (and probably Ovid) to play upon variations of the same term either by changing the prefix ('delusive', 'Prelusive') or the suffix ('effusive,' 'Effusion'). But where Milton establishes a coherence of implication, Thomson's changes support harmony or a blending of apparently contrary actions—the wind 'breathes' the clouds over the heavens, moving them with rapidity, whereas not a 'Breath' is heard to quiver in the woods. Contrary actions in *The Seasons* are not, therefore, necessarily inharmonious since they can lead to common effects; but chaos, defined as clashing antagonisms, or formlessness, the loss of locatable boundary in this world—these are versions of disharmony.

In addition to the Latinate diction, Thomson uses scientific terms and scientific knowledge to supersede or extend the knowledge of the past, thus making his poem temporally continuous. He also combines scientific or literal description with metaphor to create inconsistent images as a means of expressing human order coexisting with wantonness. Thomson moves from personification to natural description to connect the scientific, reality level of the poem with the implied maze-like unity of the world. The contrary technique (I propose to call it 'naturalization') is to conceive of human beings in terms of nature, to compare Lavinia and her mother, for example, to 'the gay Birds that sung them to Repose' (*Autumn*, 190).

If one considers the mixed image as personification coupled with natural description, then periphrasis, in much of *The Seasons*, becomes personification and scientific description, a variant of this mixed image. And this image functions as a harmonizing feature, relating man with nature, society and God. The fish are the 'finny Race' (395), bees 'busy Nations' (150), flowers 'Tulip-Race' (539), birds 'gay Troops' (584), 'glossy kind' (617), 'soft Tribes' (711). The personification is implicit in the substantive, and the natural description in the adjective. Man and nature can also be recognized as forming parts of a single classification. The adjective or noun that precedes the image indicates the group within the large classification, and as John Arthos has pointed out, different characteristics of the group permit differing adjectives to modify 'Nations.' There is no reason to believe that such personifications are substitutions for particulars; they are often followed by listings of particulars that are supposed to contrast with group terms. There are more examples of this type of periphrasis in *Spring* than in any other season.

Connected with periphrasis of nations, tribes, etc., that imply personifications is the prevalent social family metaphor, images of parents and children. Nature is called 'great Parent' (*Winter*, 106), and the sun is called 'Parent of Seasons' (*Summer*, 113), the river, as a source, is the 'Parent-Main' (*Autumn*, 754), the love of birds for their young, 'Parental Love' (*Spring*, 733) and 'fond parental Soul' (*Autumn*, 1344), the onset of the storm, 'the Father of the Tempest' (*Winter*, 72), the flying pollen, the 'Father-Dust' (*Spring*, 541). In *The Seasons*, family metaphors (family, parent, mother, father, infant, child, and their variants) add up to eighty: family (7), parent (17), mother (13), father (10), infant (14), child (11), brother (7), sister (1).

The frequent use of the extensive family metaphor seems the consequence of a social order in which the family becomes a much more significant unit than it was previously. The eighteenth-century novels, like this poem, give a centrality to the family rather than to the court, and nature is seen to possess family characteristics because it represents both the work of God and the model of social change. For nature and the family are seen as unfolding, as growing, changing, or in scenes of 'sad Presage' (see Chapter II) as troubled and uneasy at the cessation of action.

Nature and man, with God as father, are seen in a family image that tends to relate all of nature analogically: Thomson accepts the hierarchy of a rising chain, but adds to it the horizontal chain of a spreading family. And, while retaining allegorical personifications, Thomson mixes them with literal descriptions. For example, in *Autumn*, the general fog sits 'Unbounded o'er the World' (730), as does 'black Night' in *Winter* (158), and both are positional personifications mixed with natural description. This figural personification is part of the personifying technique in *The Seasons* (and in Augustan poetry in general). Chapin[7] and other critics have suggested that the purposes of such personifications are to dramatize the abstract, to make generalizations amenable to a theory that emphasized sight, to humanize the abstract in a society that found mankind the proper study of man. Thomson's poetry individualized this general tendency by using personification as a form or order while shuttling between the personification and disordered nature, by converting periphrasis into a form of personification, making nature part of God's family. This family is identified not merely by parental imagery, but by political personifications. Thus kingship is attributed to rivers, lions, the sun, man and God: The Nile, 'Rich King of Floods!' (*Summer*, 805), the Thames, 'Large, gentle, deep, majestic, King of Floods!' (*Autumn*, 122), the lion, 'shaggy King' (*Summer*, 925), GOD, 'Nature's KING' (*Winter*, 197) and, literally, 'The Kings, and awful Fathers of Mankind' (*Spring*, 59).

There is, also, an additional explanation for the prevalence of personification in *The Seasons*. The figure distances the poet's self from nature, yet provides neutral, generalized human features to express his involvement in it. Since the figure moves between human and natural characteristics, the poet can use scientific knowledge humanistically. At the same time the distancing of the poet is necessary to avoid any implication of judging nature by his values, to avoid, that is, the sin of pride. What this device generalizes, therefore, are relations between man and nature, and what it seeks to avoid is the imputation of singularity in the person of the personification.

24

The varieties of personification in the poem other than periphrasis, not unlike the varieties in Pope's poetry, include (1) allegorical personification, (2) pictorial or figural (other than allegorical) personification, and (3) mere metaphoric personification. The first use is exemplified by the introductory allegorical figures of each season. The figural personifications include the fog quoted above, and the metaphoric personifications include all the humanized natural actions: the sighing breeze, trembling leaves, bending sky, etc. Almost all of these personifications become, in *The Seasons*, part of Thomson's mixed form, but since their mixtures have different implications, they should be distinguished.

The allegorical personifications of *Spring* and *Summer*, for example, are mixed with natural description, *Spring* being described as 'Ethereal Mildness' (1) and *Summer* as 'In pride of Youth, and felt thro' Nature's Depth' (3). *Autumn* is a conventionalized reaping figure, and *Winter* is 'Sullen, and sad' (2) and later, king of misrule. There is little reason to believe that these personifications are equally effective: *Spring* and *Summer* indicate, by their mixed form, the continuity of the seasons and the conversion of *Spring's* sexual love into other types of heat. The alternation of personification with natural description gives the images a transitional quality, converting the convention into a nature conjoined and intertwined with human attributes. Patricia M. Spacks writes, with reference to 'surly Winter' (11), that 'Nature is personalized without being quite personified, through such modifiers as *howling, ravaged, kind*.'[8] The formal images are less effective because they separate the traditional personifications from moving nature. The personification of *Winter*, while insisting on the formal properties of King Winter and his court, illustrates the dislocating, false-appearing power because the winds of misrule blow through the court of supposed justice (898).

The pictorial or figural or positional personifications are described as sitting, standing, lying, ruling—human positions of order, comfort, authority. Thus one of the functions of this device is to give human or recognizable order to nature. This is Thomson's praise of Newton— he 'saw/The finish'd University of Things/In all its Order, Magnitude and Parts'[9] (139–41, *To the Memory of Sir Isaac Newton*, 1727). Newton was heroic; he divined the secrets of nature. Pictorial imagery serves to relate the present to the Virgilian past just as do the techniques of Latinate terms and word order, by placing personified qualities in a spatial environment. The '*Power of Cultivation*' lies upon the vales and hills he fructified:

> O Vale of Bliss! O softly-swelling Hills!
> On which the *Power of Cultivation* lies,
> And joys to see the Wonders of his Toil.
>
> (*Summer*, 1435–37)

So, earlier, Pope in *Windsor Forest* personified Industry, Peace and Plenty:

> Rich Industry sits smiling on the Plains,
> And Peace and Plenty tell, a Stuart reigns.
>
> (41–42)

For Thomson the image of '*Power of Cultivation*' is an attempt to merge the idea of men's industry with the secret-working powers of nature; the pictorial personification represents an effort of fusion in contrast to the idea of blending, an attempt in this image to present nature's force in human terms although man's efforts and nature's were responsible for the harvest. In this respect, therefore, Thomson was using classical imagery and experimenting, not very successfully, with new meanings.

The dramatizing function of the personification can be seen by comparing Pope's personification of melancholy with Thomson's. Pope writes in *Eloisa to Abelard*:

> Black Melancholy sits, and round her throws
> A death-like silence, and a dread repose:
> Her gloomy presence saddens all the scene,
> Shades ev'ry flow'r, and darkens ev'ry green,
> Deepens the murmur of the falling floods,
> And breathes a browner horror on the woods.
>
> (165–70)

Thomson writes:

> HE comes! he comes! in every Breeze the POWER
> Of PHILOSOPHIC MELANCHOLY comes!
> His near Approach the sudden-starting Tear,
> The glowing Cheek, the mild dejected Air,
> The soften'd Feature, and the beating Heart,
> Pierc'd deep with many a virtuous Pang, declare.
>
> (*Autumn*, 1004–9)

Thomson's passage is a sudden shift from declaration to exclamation.

26

The power of philosophic melancholy is personified but the personification is developed by effects on human beings, the catalog of responsive tear, cheek, air, etc. The purpose of the image is to dramatize an action by making it appear as a presence before the listeners. This was the technique Thomson employed in *Agamemnon* when he had Cassandra describe the advent of the not-yet-arrived Agamemnon:

> He comes, he comes! the hapless victor comes!
> Even now his trophy'd vessel streaks the main,
> And plows the billows with triumphant prow.
>
> (I, iii)[10]

But Cassandra's exclamation is not personification; 'he' refers to Agamemnon, a prophetic statement of his actions. The use of this expression in the drama is simple demonstration that Thomson considered it dramatic. Since the literal and metaphoric are expressed in identical spatial terms, one premise is that he sought to make invisible feelings visible. Another is that he is both describing an experience and placing it within the cosmic order; I would insist on separating experience from cosmic order, though A. D. McKillop believes that in *The Castle of Indolence* Thomson 'is both recording and creating the experience. The images are in the landscape and in the mind, and perception and creation merge.'[11]

Pope's description of melancholy proceeds by a catalog of effects upon nature; Thomson's upon man. But melancholy appears suddenly in both instances; there is no gradual development of depression of which melancholy is the climax; the surrounding objects or the varied features of man become changed by its presence. The need to see it as human is to attribute to the feelings an authority recognizable by analogy to human power in the social or political realm.

Thomson's revisions of the shower passage reveal the self-consciousness of his style and his extremely subtle use of biblical with scientific language to produce an imagery combining motion, extent, and natural change, and future with present time. This harmonic blending is one of Thomson's important contributions to the poetic expression of Augustan ideas.

The shower passage in *Spring* is based on a distillation image of the relation between the sky and the earth; it originally read:

> But who would hold the Shade, while Heaven descends
> In universal Bounty, shedding Herbs,
> And Fruits, and Flowers, on Nature's ample Lap?

Imagination fir'd prevents their Growth,
And while the Verdant Nutriment distills,
Beholds the kindling Country colour round.

(Spring, A, 205–10)

In the 1746 version *(Spring,* 180–85) Thomson revised 'would' to 'can,' 'Imagination' to 'Swift Fancy' and 'Verdant' to 'milky.' The first two changes stress present time and movement; 'milky,' however, represents a more subtle technique. At the time that Thomson made these changes, he added one line to the bird passage of the shower enclosed in brackets:

Hush'd in short Suspense,
The plumy People streak their Wings with Oil,
[To throw the lucid Moisture trickling off;]
And wait th' approaching Sign . . .

(Spring, 164–67)

'Verdant' formed part of the original passage and was used to refer to the promised grass. It was part of the Psalmist's language of rain as 'Herbs,/And Fruits, and Flowers.' The addition of the scientific line established a close relation between it and the distillation image, for 'to distil' is, in eighteenth-century usage, 'to trickle off.' Thus the 'trickling off' of the rain from the birds who did not use it was compared with the rain 'distilled' upon the landscape, a rain fruitful with nourishment. 'Lucid,' therefore, was compared not with a color but with a non-lucid appearance, 'milky' (life-giving), at the same time that elimination of 'Verdant' removed the repetition of 'falling Verdure' (164).

The scientific image combined religious with scientific language, and 'milky Nutriment'[12] contributed to this combination of past with present at the same time that it supported the birth imagery. The distillation image uses science to create an emergent landscape. The light of the fancy sees the rain dripping down ('distilled'), and this distillation is a 'milky Nutriment' which paradoxically colors ('inflames') the whole countryside. It seems likely, too, that there is a double implication in 'kindles,' since it means 'to give birth,' and this is exploited by the revision as well as by 'milky.' Thus the rain provides nourishment that causes the blossoming of flowers. The fancy or imagination which is inspired ('fir'd') can be understood as paradoxically distilling, by its fire, the falling rain, and, simultaneously beholding it. The power of the imagination anticipates because it

28

imitates existing nature, becoming a heat, inspiration, color image; what it imagines is what has time and again come to pass. Science is used to support the religious interpretation of harmonious blending and the merger coincides with Thomson's view of *Spring* as earth responding to the powers of nature in a burst of growth, color, and interaction of present with future.

The lines (186–88) lean heavily on the preceding terms 'full-distended,' 'genial' (fruitful, gentle), 'Stores' (treasures), 'well-shower'd Earth' in order to introduce the vividness of motion in the sunset. Here the concert of nature is both seen and heard in the imagery of color and sound. In the first part of the shower passage the poem dealt not with the destructiveness or force of a shower, but rather with its communal relation to nature and to man, who was 'superior' to nature's impatience. But the conclusion develops the quickness and brightness and noisiness of the sunset so that 'Indulge,' the complacent term, is contrasted with 'effulge'—the flashing, momentary brightness, and one of the frequent terms for the *Summer*, not the *Spring*, sun —in a play on common sounds with contrary meanings that is characteristically Thomsonian.

The sun image proceeds from the concluding fire metaphor and offers a variant description of the budding flowers. There, the secret powers of spring growth were stressed, with colors and smells; here the love, joy and concerted elation of one part of nature to another, the gaiety of the different aspects of nature after the shower. Thus the motion of the heavens (clouds 'gay-shifting') and the break-up of the clouds are seen as responsive to the sun's beam. The beam 'strikes,' 'streams,' 'Shakes,' 'lights'—images of motion, light, sound and action that suggest the reverse of the earlier picture of a smoking city, for now the setting sun

> in a yellow Mist,
> Far smoking o'er th' interminable Plain,
> In twinkling Myriads lights the dewy Gems.
>
> (194–96)

The concert is established by contribution of different members; the action is divided by phrases each of which identifies a place or manner. The instantaneousness is achieved by the collection of fragments into tens of thousands ('Myriads') of lights; the generality is then expressed in sentences in which the laughter—in addition to the radiance just described—now returns to some of the areas, the forest, woods, mountains and vales.

> Full swell the Woods; their every Musick wakes,
> Mix'd in wild Concert with the warbling Brooks
> Increas'd, the distant Bleatings of the Hills,
> The hollow Lows responsive from the Vales,
> Whence blending all the sweeten'd Zephyr springs.
>
> (198–202)

The 'swelling' of the woods is the awakening to varied music—the swelling therefore announces the expansiveness of spring, its sounds and motion—the 'Increas'd' warbling of the brook, the responsive answers of the vales to the hills. Swelling is also a motion: it gives sweetness, 'love,' to the wind (Zephyr) which now carries the consequences of the shower. Not only does this passage return to the induction—'While Music wakes around, veil'd in a Shower/Of shadowing Roses' (3–4)—it provides a definition of how music 'wakes,' and 'waking' is a song of love, of expansive forces. The repetition and amplification, therefore, become organizing devices.

The awakening of music occurs simultaneously with the spreading rainbow and implies that the sounds connect variety on earth as well as earth with the heavens. The rainbow is 'refracted' from the 'eastern Cloud,' and in answer to the golden gem-like quality of the sun's rays, the clouds counter with the multi-colored rainbow. The colors are unfolded from the 'white mingling Maze' and thus light shoots up and 'runs' from one color to another, becoming analogous to the colored countryside kindled by the rain, the 'milky Nutriment,' and both are instances of the full spectrum unfolded from 'white.' There is, thus, in terms of color, still another harmonizing device.

The 'sage-instructed' eye and the 'Swain' sum up the difference in interpreting the rainbow, the first accepting and understanding nature's variety and its transience, the other enchanted and delighted by it without understanding how the 'Arch' eludes him. The nature which the narrator describes expands upon the sight. The 'Swain,' enchanted, but uninformed, is not unlike the botanist, informed but not able to cope, as 'awful NEWTON' did, with the variety and extent of nature. For the mixing of seeds and soil creates a fertility beyond man's power to assess.

This view of sensuous, creative nature beyond the ability of man even to catalog is a consequence of the fall of man. In the Golden Age, spring was eternal, and there was no need to stress the fleeting quality of the moment because time was irrelevant. In those days time went cheerfully along and harmony reigned; now harmony has to be sought and seized—and if, in *Spring*, it can be found, it can also be lost. Then man was the 'Lord, and not the Tyrant of the World' (241).

ii. Illusive Allusion and the Themes of Harmony (234–571)

The movement from *Spring* profusion to the virginal profusion of the Golden Age is made by reference to the mystery of the 'secret Stores/Of Health, and Life, and Joy' (235–36), a conventional pastoral association in which the original profusion and innocence exceed that in *Spring*. 'Innumerous' thus recalls the former time when it referred to everything in life, not merely to the multitudinous present. But neither in the past nor in the present can the narrator explain the 'secrets' of the Golden Age or the reasons for the loss of 'Concord of harmonious Powers' (276). When, therefore, he moves from the Golden Age to its loss, he operates associatively; that is, movement from one condition to its opposite is not explained as necessarily derived from the original condition. In *The Seasons*, opposites become merely an associative device, more prominent in some seasons (*Summer* and *Winter*) than in others; they remain perspectives without fusing, illustrating man's incapacity to penetrate the power and mystery of God's apparent paradoxes.

In the 'Golden Age' passage (242–71), dealing with the innocence (or spring) of man and referring to activities and scenes already created, Thomson's poetic powers falter. The sense of growth, motion and time has, in the Golden Age, no proper alternative. The Golden Age appears as a series of assertions; its cheeriness arises from kind, even dormant orderliness, not from a blended variety or a love that is exercised. The language of ideal time demands a positive vision of heavenly glory, but Thomson seems unable to make the ideal interesting. He resorts to a language not governed by poetic diction, but by synonyms of consonance and gladness, enough to make a boring hell of heaven. The language that identifies the ideal differs from his sensuous vocabulary, and Thomson, who originally had such a vocabulary (*A*, 296–323), omitted this passage in 1744. (He included a similar section in the addition of the torrid zone passage to *Summer* (629 ff.).)

The causes of the loss of man's innocence elude Thomson. He turns not to the reasons for its loss but to the present turmoil.

> Now the distemper'd Mind
> Has lost that Concord of harmonious Powers,
> Which forms the Soul of Happiness; and all
> Is off the Poise within: the Passions all
> Have burst their Bounds;
>
> (275–79)

Reason, Anger, Envy, Fear, Love and Grief are known only by their excesses; here where Thomson has an opportunity to become iconographic in the way that Pope, and later Collins, did in their musical odes, he prefers personifications that define states of feeling rather than express visual attitudes. Thus 'Convulsive Anger storms at large' (282) or 'Desponding Fear . . . loosens every Power' (286–87). C. V. Deane refers to these correctly as 'Thomson's list of merely melodramatic personifications'.[13] These human emotions

> From ever-changing Views of Good and Ill,
> Form'd infinitely various, vex the Mind
> With endless Storm.
>
> (298–300)

Emotions that fail to mix harmoniously, that vary but have no consonance, are antithetical to the *Spring* shower which creates harmony by blending elements. Thomson's description of the excesses of the passions neglects the causes for loss of concord and uses personifications to avoid the clash between ideal passions and their corrupters. When he pursues the corresponding corruption (or deluge of nature (309–16)), the effectiveness of this event rests upon a different use of diction.

> HENCE, in old dusky Time, a Deluge came:
> When the deep-cleft disparting Orb, that arch'd
> The central Waters round, impetuous rush'd,
> With universal Burst, into the Gulph,
> And o'er the high-pil'd Hills of fractur'd Earth
> Wide-dash'd the Waves, in Undulation vast;
> Till, from the Centre to the streaming Clouds,
> A shoreless Ocean tumbled round the Globe.

The passage originally (1728) read:

> Hence in old Time, they say, a Deluge came;
> When the dry-crumbling Orb of Earth, which arch'd
> Th' imprison'd Deep around, impetuous rush'd,
> With Ruin unconceivable, at once
> Into the Gulph, and o'er the highest Hills
> Wide-dash'd the Waves, in Undulation vast:
> Till from the Centre to the streaming Clouds
> A shoreless Ocean tumbled round the Globe.

(A, 354–61)

The revisions add to the consistency and enforce the 'fractur'd' quality of earth, tighten the correspondence between broken earth and undulating waves, eliminate a wrong implication in 'imprisoned Deep,' heighten the contrast between the explosive submergence of the earth and tumbling waves. Here the Latinate diction creates a sense of formal distancing (the 'old dusky Time') and it develops the interrelatedness of earth and ocean so that 'deep-cleft' and 'disparting,' 'impetuous' and 'rush'd,' 'wide-dash'd' and 'Undulation vast' and 'tumbled' contain connotative meanings that repeat and discriminate continuing and contrasting elements. The destroyed earth that depends upon the obvious allusion to God's wrath has a traditional base from which to fall, but not the description of the excessive passions. The technique, moreover, is that which became apparent in earlier passages: the submergence of one kind of nature which only appears to have (in contrast to actually having) a reciprocal relationship to that which overwhelms it. The explosive burst of the event, narrated in a single sentence, reveals that submergence, the loss of shape ('deep-cleft,' 'disparting' and 'fractur'd') of the earth, destroys its wholeness, its beauty and its once-possessed paradisial boundlessness. The order of the clauses and phrases suggest by their modification and qualification the fragmentariness of the earth and its infinite submersion. The earth is submerged and the elements—earth, fire ('Burst'), air ('Clouds')—are overturned; *Spring*'s order in which the earth is dominant becomes a watery chaos.

The excessive passion which, in man, was an indication of the fall is analogically related to the fragmentation of nature—'the deep-cleft disparting Orb.' The break-up of the globe and its inundation is another type of excess and the difference between the passages lies in the vision of interrelated yet clashing elements. The waves rise above the globe and tumble around it; between sinking and rising an analogy occurs, an analogy that counterpoints the ideal descent of 'Spring' and the sentimentalized fantasy concluding *Spring* in which the lovers 'sink' in final sleep to rise to immortality (1174–76). But no such contrast occurs between the extravagant and controlling passions in man. Thomson's plays, it might be noted, seem to founder on emotional crises as do his descriptions of the passions, whereas the natural environment provided him with a specifically controlled reference.

This difference can, perhaps, be further explained by the concept of physical space in this passage. The deep-cleft earth rushing explosively into the gulf suggests a changing space; in previous growth descriptions this unfolding formed spring's expansiveness. Here expansiveness—the roused waves—is a loss of innocence and permanence; the fragmented seasons are the result. Each season, therefore, in its own way seeks to achieve—though it can no longer do so—the stable, permanent and absolute space that once existed. The changing space and time are signs of this great loss. The unfinished quality of Thomson's space—prospects that fade into the distance, and changes in nature that are unfinished—implies a world in which 'unfinished' means, so far as man's sight or knowledge can discover, incomplete or unstable or un-self-contained. The very seasons themselves are instances of a broken world, and the full understanding of nature or of man can be achieved only by an act of faith.

> THE Seasons since have, with severer Sway,
> Oppress'd a broken World: the Winter keen
> Shook forth his Waste of Snows; and Summer shot
> His pestilential Heats. Great Spring, before,
> Green'd all the Year; and Fruits and Blossoms blush'd,
> In social Sweetness, on the self-same Bough.
> Pure was the temperate Air; an even Calm
> Perpetual reign'd, save what the Zephyrs bland
> Breath'd o'er the blue Expanse: for then nor Storms
> Were taught to blow, nor Hurricanes to rage;
> Sound slept the Waters; no sulphureous Glooms
> Swell'd in the Sky, and sent the Lightning forth;
> While sickly Damps, and cold autumnal Fogs,
> Hung not, relaxing, on the Spring of Life.

But now, of turbid Elements the Sport,
From Clear to Cloudy tost, from Hot to Cold,
And Dry to Moist, with inward-eating Change,
Our drooping Days are dwindled down to Nought,
Their Period finish'd ere 'tis well begun.

(317–35)

This is a passage of considerable importance because it relates the ideal to the actual in a traditional interpretation of man's fall. The sway—the revolutions of the seasons—oppresses a broken world, and when winter falls, it brings 'A heavy Gloom oppressive o'er the World' (*Winter*, 58). The poem does indeed deal with *Winter*'s 'Waste of Snows' although it is a 'dazzling' as well as a 'wild' waste (*Winter*, 239), and *Summer* does indeed create 'pestilential Heats' that poison the 'sickening City' (*Summer*, 1053), but it also illuminates the landscape 'Fervent with Life of every fairer kind' (*Summer*, 780). In this age 'drooping days' are 'of turbid Elements the Sport' (*Spring*, 331), tossed from one extreme to the other, just as in *Winter*, Leviathan and 'his unwieldy Train, in dreadful Sport,/Tempest the loosen'd Brine' (1015–16), disregarding man and his suffering. The *Spring* passage suggests the irony with which to read the subsequent fishing scene, since in it man, who can be the 'Sport' of the elements, to his 'Sport' repairs (396).

Thomson raises the question whether man ought to kill even for food, though the passage is a form of playful speculation. The wolf and tiger attacked household animals, but man ought not to become like these vicious predators. Yet this vegetarian view is expressed with considerable tentativeness.

shall he, fair Form!
Who wears sweet Smiles, and looks erect on Heaven,
E'er stoop to mingle with the prowling Herd,
And dip his Tongue in Gore? The Beast of Prey,
Blood-stain'd deserves to bleed: but you, ye Flocks,
What have you done: ye peaceful People, What,
To merit Death?

(354–60)

Man, 'Who wears sweet Smiles, and looks erect on Heaven,' is capable of excess of passion but also of control, of piety and kindness, of ideal behavior, not 'pure' perfection, but more perfection than man's animal killing indicates. This entire passage, however, must not

be taken as more than an exercise of the sentimental sublime—and
one which inartistically imitates the biblical convention of 'you' and
'ye'—a risk in 'the bold presumptuous Strain':

> but 'tis enough,
> In this late Age, adventurous, to have touch'd
> Light on the Numbers of the *Samian* Sage.
> High HEAVEN forbids the bold presumptuous Strain,
> Whose wisest Will has fix'd us in a State
> That must not yet to pure Perfection rise.
>
> (371–76)

This completed the passage, and it was not until 1746 that Thomson
added:

> Besides, who knows, how *rais'd* to higher Life,
> From Stage to Stage, the *Vital Scale ascends*?
>
> (377–78)

This revision seems to call into question the assurance with which
he had treated the Samian Sage in Part III of *Liberty* (1735). In lines
32–70 he touched, without lightness, on the doctrines of Pythagoras:

> He taught that life's indissoluble flame,
> From brute to man, and man to brute again,
> For ever shifting, runs the eternal round;
> Thence tried against the blood-polluted meal,
> And limbs yet quivering with some kindred soul,
> To turn the human heart. Delightful truth!
> Had he beheld the living chain ascend,
> And not a circling form, but rising whole.
>
> (63–70)
>
> (And form a rising not a circling Whole. 1738)[14]

What Thomson added in 1746, therefore, implied that man's state of
imperfection was achieved in no way known to man. It served to
reinforce the hesitancy surrounding the whole 'adventure.'

The fishing scene is among the best-known passages of *Spring*, but
it was not introduced until 1744; it is a comic description of an action
ironically commenting on 'pure Perfection' (376). As a 'Digression,'[15]
it represents a typical spring activity, and this was Thomson's justification for inserting it. But by inserting it here, the poet creates a
characteristic relation between heaven and earth, ascent and descent,

in order to deal, playfully, with the limitations of man. The preceding Pythagorean verse paragraph concludes with the lines about the vital scale ascending; the digression opens with a description of the purified stream descending (581–82). The transition leads to a sport that is not quite innocent, so that even in man's simple pleasures, he is not without his imperfections. These imperfections can be detected in the tone of some parts of the passage and the comic devices for describing the sport. There is a mock-heroic tone in the reference to the fish as the 'little Naiads' (403) who 'love to sport at large' (403) in the ample wave. After the fall, man and the days themselves because of 'turbid Elements the Sport' (331), whereas the fish who are in their proper element become a 'Sport' for man.

> And, whitening, down their mossy-tinctur'd Stream
> Descends the billowy Foam: now is the Time,
> While yet the dark-brown Water aids the Guile
> To tempt the Trout. The well-dissembled Fly,
> The Rod fine-tapering with elastic Spring,
> Snatch'd from the hoary Steed the floating Line,
> And all thy slender wat'ry Stores prepare.
> But let not on thy Hook the tortur'd Worm,
> Convulsive, twist in agonizing Folds;
> Which, by rapacious Hunger swallow'd deep,
> Gives, as you tear it from the bleeding Breast
> Of the weak helpless uncomplaining Wretch,
> Harsh Pain and Horror to the tender Hand.
>
> (381–93)

The principle of reversal, treating the same scene or action from another point of view to suggest reciprocity or harmony, can be used, as it is here and elsewhere, to illustrate contrasting intents. Thus, a reference to Pythagorean doctrine—what 'the feeling Heart/ Would tenderly suggest' (370–71)—is warningly converted into injunctions against worm-fishing because of concern for the bleeding worm, then for the fish, and then for the fisherman whose hook gives 'Harsh Pain and Horror to the tender Hand.' The use of live worms is cruel, and the shift from the colloquial to the pathetic directs the reader to the uncertain tone of this apparently playful, yet actually cruel act. Fly-fishing becomes the playful counterpart of the insect plague, substituting the attitude of a game for the serious one of deliberate (though necessary) extermination, of the war within nature, and this treacherous playfulness will further be seen as self-defense in the behavior of the Heath-Hen—'pious Fraud' (*Spring*, 700).

The techniques of playfulness include deliberate—even extreme—distortion of sentence structure, extravagant, violent, mock-heroic, even burlesque language of sentimental exaggeration ('the weak helpless uncomplaining Wretch'), and serious terms placed in a light or gay context. Thus the potent rays of the sun which penetrated the earth pierce the stream and rouse the 'finny Race.' The 'Breezes curling play' (earlier the waters had 'uncurled'), the shadowy clouds are lightly borne 'o'er Ether.' The stream itself 'plays in undulating Flow' (407) and becomes part of the game.

I have been describing a conscious play element, but there is, in this passage, an unconscious element. Thomson's language, with its allusiveness and multiple references, often possesses unexpected, probably unintended, internal associations that support and extend the implications of a passage, though they sometimes can, as in the eulogy of Chesterfield in *Winter* or in the description of 'Dew-dropping *Coolness*' in *Summer* (206), parody the effect needed.

Thus the poet writes that now is the time 'To tempt the Trout' (384) and the trout 'attempts to seize' (427) the fly. The principle of reciprocal action, moving from the fisherman to the trout, is developed by the 'tempt'—'attempts' relation. The temptation is carried on by a rod 'with elastic Spring' (385) and when the fisherman throws his line he 'marks' the fish, the 'springing Game' (410)—where the literal spring quality of the rod by which the fish is caught is seen to possess the same quality as the fish itself. 'The floating Line' used to capture the fish results, when the fish is caught, in making him resemble the object that has tamed him for he is now 'floating broad upon his breathless Side' (440). And although the fisherman is advised, 'to thy Sport repair' (396), the objects of his sport, the fish, are described as engaged in sport as well—the 'little Naiads love to sport at large' (403) —they are both players and the object of play. This interplay between fisherman and fish establishes a contest linguistically bound together by plays on words in which the former wins; his instruments possess the powers necessary to subdue the fish.

Even though Thomson wrote of fishing as a sweet and innocent country sport in 'Of a Country Life' (1720), it is, in *The Seasons*, an exercise in guile, in which the expansive *Spring* waters, 'Swell'd' (380) with rains, create the proper time for fishing, and the sun pierces the waters and the breezes 'curling play' (397). This playful quality is carried even to the contest of the fisherman and the monarch of the brook, for when the trout is caught, 'to the Shore/You gaily drag your unresisting Prize' (441–42). But the playfulness is not without its serious undertones about nature as puzzle, for the shadowy clouds borne 'high to their Fount' (399), become the occasion, by shading the sun, for the monarch's 'sullen Plunge' (429–31). Nature helps man to trick the fish, and spatial expansiveness is suddenly reduced to the fish inactively being dragged to shore.

This scene, with its oddly victorious human triumph, is Thomson's version of a special quality in Augustan poetry. Thomson achieves a sense of the comic by what might be called the procedure of *illusive allusion*.[16] Augustan poetry is marked by frequent allusions, but in Thomson playfulness calls forth submerged puns, parodies, verbal transformations, and other types of Augustan wit. In Thomson this procedure results from moving between the literal and the metaphoric. His conscious language often leads to unconscious transformations that are not exploited, but are nevertheless present. C. V. Deane hints at this procedure when he remarks of the *Autumn* lines, 'The Stork-Assembly meets; for many a Day,/Consulting deep, and various' (853–54), that 'authors of phrases of this type not only show a connoisseur's relish in the amenities of a settled style; they illuminate the object from a fresh angle by revealing its unconscious humour.' And Reuben A. Brower refers to this aspect of Thomson's individual idiom as 'the slightly parodic, etymological wit of his style.'[17] This use of submerged allusion need not, of course, be confined to the comic.

Thomson's conscious allusions to earlier passages and words in the poem appear in the *Spring* coquetry of the barnyard, and in the numerous passages that seem to refer to one another. This procedure appears also in *The Castle of Indolence* where in Canto I, iv, the poet puns on 'heard' and 'Herds' to connect those who hear with the animals that make the heard sounds:

> Join'd to the Prattle of the purling Rills,
> Were heard the lowing Herds along the Vale.[18]

Or in Canto I, xxxiii, where an epic and mock-epic rhetorical figure of repetition is converted into a witty device of spatial extension:

> Soft Quilts on Quilts, on Carpets Carpets spread,
> And Couches stretch around in seemly Band;

And endless Pillows rise to prop the Head;
So that the spacious Room was one full-swelling Bed.[19]

There are numerous instances in his letters to show that Thomson delighted in puns, word-play, and allusions, and this procedure, conscious and unconscious, is present in his writings from the 1720's to the 1740's.[20]

By alluding to conventional pastoral situations, fishing, bathing, or sheep-shearing, Thomson gives to *The Seasons* lines that are linguistically ambiguous, containing submerged puns, paradoxes and ironies of transformation. Such passages are not without playful irony toward the convention, although such 'wit' is muted, but the passages combine accurate natural description with highly conventionalized activities and figures, and this very comparison is witty. For Thomson is parodying the convention. The procedure connects the poem to the contemporary wit or satiric tradition and gives a liveliness and humour to Thomson's treatment of conventional pastoral scenes.

In *Spring*, this technique is connected with the expansiveness of the season and with man's love for a sport that leads to an ambiguous harmony. The unambiguous and rapturous harmony with nature is developed in the climax to the first part. There, with artistic success, the description of the mixture of natural and human forces at increasing intensity brings to bear the sum of Thomson's techniques for conveying the sensuousness of growth and love. The narrator starts as a reluctant spectator hesitant to proceed, but with the aid of his beloved, he begins to grasp the meaning of love, ultimately bursting into an invocation. What he achieves is a description of love among the flowers, the sensuous description of sexual activity concealed in the imagery of nature—the development, in other words, of a language that refers to nature, but with scientific accuracy refers to sexual processes of the season.

The fishing episode is followed by an imperative to the reader to seek rest and ease; just as the sun wishes to be free to express its languor at noon, so, too, should the reader. The poet urges the reader ('Then seek the Bank' 446) to surround himself with the elders, lilies, cowslips and violets, or, if reclining under the ash overhanging the cliff, to spy the culver 'shoot' and the hawk build his nest. In both situations man is placed within nature while being able to recreate, by the reading of Virgil or by his own observing, other rural scenes

Or by the vocal Woods and Waters lull'd,

40

And lost in lonely Musing, in a Dream,
Confus'd, of careless Solitude, where mix
Ten thousand wandering Images of Things,
Soothe every Gust of Passion into Peace,
All but the Swellings of the soften'd Heart,
That waken, not disturb, the tranquil Mind.[21]

(460–66)

The entire passage (443–66), added in 1744 along with the fishing episode, relates the active deceptive engagement of fisherman to the passive but true engagement of poet or of reader, the delusive physical action and the tranquillizing rest with its active musing. In the fishing episode the sun 'pierc'd the Streams, and rous'd the finny Race' (395); in the following sequence the sun paradoxically shoots 'listless Languor thro the Deeps' (445). The bank to which the fish had been lightly tossed or slowly dragged is equivalent to the bank to which, in the heat of noon, the reader is urged: 'Then seek the Bank.' But as the reader lies down and becomes part of nature, his fancy expands and his imagination is full of soothing motion. This added passage repeats again the cycle of *Spring*: the penetrative force of the sun followed by inner growth that leads to participation in or awareness of harmony. The climax moves from 'musings' to the actual vividness of nature.

BEHOLD yon breathing Prospect bids the Muse
Throw all her Beauty forth. But who can paint
Like Nature? Can Imagination boast,
Amid its gay Creation, Hues like hers?
Or can it mix them with that matchless Skill,
And lose them in each other, as appears
In every Bud that blows? If Fancy then
Unequal fails beneath the pleasing Task;
Ah what shall Language do? Ah where find Words
Ting'd with so many Colours; and whose Power,
To Life approaching, may perfume my Lays
With that fine Oil, those aromatic Gales,
That inexhaustive flow continual round?

(467–79)

The language, the finished mixture of sight, sound, smell, taste of blossoming spring, the synaesthetic imagery, mixing sight and smell, are the poet's attempt to meet nature's challenge to the senses by capturing these in words. In *Summer* I shall discuss Thomson's views

41

of poetry; I wish here to analyze some of Thomson's procedures for achieving a sensuousness of language appealing to a diversity of senses. It remains one of the triumphs of the poem. The experiment took love for its subject, and Thomson developed a language that, by accurately describing nature's awakening, conveyed sexual implications. That love is a human version of expansion by union need not be stressed, and its relation to the growth of flowers in this procedure gives added coherence to the seasons. And it is appropriate that Thomson introduced an address to Amanda (Elizabeth Young) in 1744, the woman with whom he was in love.

The suggestive language includes repetitions and synonyms with altered meanings, images of interrelations between man and nature, Biblical and Latinate words to suggest ongoing change. In this section the mixing, breathing, blushing, blossoming of flowers imply sexual bevavior. Thus the mixture of Latinate terms with Anglo-Saxon ones, 'the Lily drinks/The latent Rill' (495–96), of scientific terms with non-scientific, 'with inserted Tube,/Suck its pure Essence' (511–12), creates distancing in the language, disguising the implicit personifications that are mixed with natural description. The imagery of drinking, of smelling that 'takes the ravish'd Soul' (502), of sucking and pollination ('loading') has intense sexual implications, and the deletion in 1744—when he included Amanda—of a too specific sexual image tends to confirm this view.[22] To observe an act and its consequences simultaneously, a variant of the procedure of describing objects in terms of what they will become or are capable of creating—describing 'rain' as 'promised Sweetness' or 'milky Nutriment'—is, of course, a Biblical procedure that Thomson applied to spatial extension.

The Amanda lines follow from the query, 'But who can paint/Like Nature?' (468–69). The poet undertakes the deception by appealing to virgins and youths, 'whose Hearts/Have felt the Rapture of refining Love' (481–82). Of these Amanda is foremost, 'Pride of my Song' (483), who by wearing flowers improves them. Thus with her physical and moral beauty at his side, the poet is prepared to see the sensuous and moral beauty of the flowers:

> Oh come! and while the rosy-footed May
> Steals blushing on, together let us tread
> The Morning-Dews, and gather in their Prime
> Fresh-blooming Flowers, to grace thy braided Hair,
> And thy lov'd Bosom that improves their Sweets.

(489–93)

The address to the Countess of Hertford described her as 'blooming' and 'benevolent,' a model for the season, but Amanda with her 'braided Hair' and 'lov'd Bosom' is a sensuous May virgin matching blushing May.

The poet urges Amanda to accompany him on a walk in which the odors take 'the ravish'd Soul' (502). Just as the looks of Amanda 'deeply pierce the Soul' (486) and just as Amanda is 'Form'd by the Graces, Loveliness itself!' (484), so nature spreads 'Unbounded Beauty to the roving Eye' (507):

> Nor is the Mead unworthy of thy Foot,
> Full of fresh Verdure, and unnumber'd Flowers,
> The Negligence of *Nature*, wide, and wild;
> Where, undisguis'd by mimic *Art*, she spreads
> Unbounded Beauty to the roving Eye.
>
> (503–7)

This procedure with 'Soul' referring to his beloved, to flowers and to bees, permits Thomson to identify degrees of variation in his version of human or natural behavior. At the same time the technique of illusive allusion used for tonal effects in the fishing episode creates transferable implications between the natural and human realm. In this respect Thomson is not unlike Pope, who, in *Windsor Forest* and *The Temple of Fame*, moves from one realm to another.

The water image (494–98), the breeze image (498–502), the earth or flower image (503–7) are all sexual images of intermixture and exposure, and the 'fervent Bees' (508), burning with activity, suck the juices and pollinate the flowers. It need not be pointed out that the 'fervent Bees' are the 'busy Nations' two lines below, and that 'fervent' describes their swarming, socially ardent condition and 'Nations' the ordered carrying out of their mission.

The sweeping catalog that follows the sexual involvement is, with regard to the narrator, marked by heightened excitement. It is a view of a 'finish'd Garden', that in its bounded or organized plan—in comparison to the 'Negligence of Nature' (505)—also conveys the inexpressible beauty of nature:

> AT length the finish'd Garden to the View
> Its Vistas opens, and its Alleys green.
>
> (516–17)

In the survey of the 'vivid Verdure' at the opening of *Spring*, the poet surveyed the groves, forest and garden, and of the latter he remarked:

> At once, array'd
> In all the Colours of the flushing Year,
> By Nature's swift and secret-working Hand,
> The Garden glows, and fills the liberal Air
> With lavish Fragrance.
>
> (95–99)

And in exploring the garden here he returns, in a unifying procedure, to the 'lavish Fragrance,' writing of the 'lavish Stock that scents the Garden round' (534). Reclining, walking, 'distractedly wandering' are three movements of increasing excitement and inspiration, leading to an invocation to God, the creator. They are types of mingling or a mixing with nature, beginning with establishment of distance, then walking amidst nature as an equal participant, and then swept up by the force and attractiveness of nature.

In *The Seasons* Thomson was engaged in a number of language experiments that I have been describing, and, here, he created the intermingling of the elements as a form of mixed personification and natural description relevant to human sexual behavior. Those critics who have found Thomson's descriptions of the 'Auriculas, enrich'd/ With shining Meal o'er all their velvet Leaves' (535–37) precise and particular, are not incorrect, only irrelevant. For Thomson's precision is not part of a view that the particular is preferable to the general, but that the particular is as much a 'mixture,' a 'mingling' as the general. This mixture is a composition of spatially observable elements that exist together; they are not fused so that they have lost individual identity, but rather each retains its separateness. For articulas are not only ear-shaped but contain shiny meal, have velvet textures (touch) and are, indeed a mixture. Here, too, one should point out that the 1744 revision did not create greater abstractness, for the above passage remained to 1744 as

> Auriculas, a Tribe
> Peculiar powder'd with a shining Sand,
> Renunculas, and Iris many-hued.
>
> (*A*, 492–94)

The revision rendered the flowers more precisely, presented a clearer description of mingled characteristics. The whole passage (516–55) expresses this sensuous richness of nature in the garden approximating

'Negligence of *Nature*, wide, and wild.' In the Lyttelton passage
Thomson returns again to nature's expansiveness and grace by
referring to 'the Shade/Of solemn Oaks that tuft the swelling
Mounts/Thrown graceful round by Nature's careless Hand' (914–16).
The expansiveness is envisioned first in a long view, then in a close one:

> Snatch'd thro the verdant Maze, the hurried Eye
> Distracted wanders; *now* the bowery Walk
> Of Covert close, where scarce a speck of Day
> Falls on the lengthen'd Gloom, protracted sweeps;
> *Now* meets the bending Sky, the River *now*
> Dimpling along, the breezy-ruffled Lake,
> The Forest darkening round, the glittering Spire,
> Th' etherial Mountain, and the distant Main.
>
> (518–25) [my italics]

The distraction, in which the narrator is pulled *at once* in all directions
by the astounding mixture of nature—'now,' 'Now,' 'now'—evokes
a series of elliptical clauses in which 'the hurried Eye,' although
understood as subject, is too hurried to complete the grammar. The
sentence enacts the distraction, the eye 'meeting' one extensive object
after the other, each demanding a different response to the elements
of nature—the 'dimpling' river or the 'ruffled Lake'—and the narrator
realizes that such mixtures are not merely 'so far excursive' but exist
at the reach of his hand:

> at Hand,
> Along these blushing Borders, bright with Dew,
> And in yon mingled Wilderness of Flowers,
> Fair-handed Spring unbosoms every Grace:
>
> (526–29)

Reuben A. Brower, discussing a section of the flower passage
(526–54), remarks that:

> The reader of these lines wanders in a pleasant, faintly amusing
> stream of almost pure delights of vision, smell, and touch. But they
> do loosely compose a metaphor—of Spring, and beyond that of
> the vaguely benign Thomsonian Nature. How loose it is we
> may see by examining the metaphorical gesture with which the
> passage opens,

> Fair-handed Spring unbosoms every Grace . . .

45

'Fair-handed' and 'unbosoms' and 'Grace' ought to invite us to look for links in the lines that follow, but they most certainly do not. The lady Spring is overlooked like a piece of garden sculpture, while a lazy, hazy sense of springtime serves to connect almost anything. All of the flowers are of a 'springiness,' even to an American reader who ordinarily does not associate the daisy or wallflower or stocks with spring. The failure of much of eighteenth-century poetry, we might note in passing, is not due to over-generality but to the lack of a metaphorical sense which connects and gives meaning to detail.[23]

This is an intelligent version of the argument that Thomson's diction is loose and hazy, and Brower has selected for examination a passage that is normally praised for its description. But the argument that Thomson's metaphoric structure is loose cannot, I believe, be sustained by this example; on the contrary, the passage has an un-usually complex and consistent, even tight, structure characteristic of Thomson's poetic vision. 'Spring unbosoms every Grace' provides 'links' with what follows, and what precedes. It is a line that looks back as well as forward; indeed, it is peculiar to assume that such an image only looks forward, since 'Spring' is being compared to Amanda in the preceding verse paragraph. Amanda, 'Formed by the Graces' (483), is urged by the poet to join him in gathering

> Fresh-blooming Flowers, to grace thy braided Hair,
> And thy lov'd Bosom that improves their Sweets.
>
> (492–93)

Just as the poet gathers flowers to grace Amanda's bosom, so 'Spring' removes from the bosom of the earth ('unbosoms') every 'Grace,' every flower that attires in loveliness the female beauties that gather them. 'Spring' is 'Fair-handed' because it hands the flowers from its bosom to the beholder's sight (makes them grow and gives them beauty); it is also a pun on 'at hand,' meaning 'nearby', as well as the capacity to make the nearby surroundings beautiful.

> But why so far excursive? When at hand,
> Along these blushing Borders bright with dew,
> And in yon mingled Wilderness of Flowers,
> Fair-handed Spring unbosoms every Grace.

'Unbosoms' is defined by the next line, for 'Spring' 'throws out' (or causes the earth to 'throw out') the snowdrop, crocus and other flowers. The metaphor of 'Spring' not only looks immediately back and forward; it also recurs to the continuing image of the induction in which 'Spring' descends from the bosom of the cloud, bringing showers that will turn the earth into a flowering harmony image.

How consistent, precise, and functioning is Thomson's catalog can be seen by a study of the passage in which Reuben A. Brower finds only a 'list of flowers with the heading, "spring-blooming" . . . the only connection we need make in reading the list is one of time: we recall that the flowers indeed do "bloom in the spring." '[24]

The flower names—the crocus, polyanthus, anemones, auriculas—function like the subtle Latinate terms: to create distance despite closeness, to create rhetorical impressiveness while evoking simple colors and forms, to create a sense of derivation or allusion, e.g. ranunculas (flowers like frogs), anemones (sea and land flowers), the ox-eye daisy, wallflowers, etc., and thus of mixture in the very naming. If in line 504 the narrator saw unnumbered flowers, now a single flower—the polyanthus—has 'unnumber'd Dyes' (532). The 'Tulip-Race' is defined in family terms, a personification of pollination:

> from Family diffus'd
> To Family, as flies the Father-Dust,
> The varied Colours run.
>
> (540–42)

And in a burst of *negation*, which *positively* describes the bloom of spring as foreshadowing summer, with only a single verb to control the catalog—combining sexual reference to inner purity, the smells, the derivative implications of floral names and the concluding shower allusion to *Spring*, 'Nor, shower'd from every Bush, the Damask-rose' (552)—the narrator finally abandons his effort and calls on God. The use of negative terms for positive assertion, the use of language with illusive allusions, the combination of details for harmonic blending by degree—all represent notions of artistic harmony. The negation suggests the multitude of flowers not included, concluding with the realization that merely noting some of those not to be omitted makes clear how many more have been, and how impossible it would be to convey the variety of hues, colors, smells of all. Not only does the word order with its appositives create the multiplicity and mixture characteristic of the season (supported by the naming of the flowers), but the sentence structure with its phrases and nouns finally reaches the negative admission of the poet's own incapacity to convey the beauty of the flowers: 'With Hues on Hues Expression cannot paint' (554).

> No gradual Bloom is wanting; from the Bud,
> First born of Spring, to Summer's musky Tribes:
> Nor Hyacinths, of purest virgin White,
> Low bent, and blushing inward; nor Jonquils,
> Of potent Fragrance; nor Narcissus fair,
> As o'er the fabled Fountain hanging still;
> Nor broad Carnations; nor gay-spotted Pinks;
> Nor, shower'd from every Bush, the Damask-rose.
> Infinite Numbers, Delicacies, Smells,
> With Hues on Hues Expression cannot paint,
> The Breath of Nature, and her endless Bloom.
>
> (545–55)

The passage together with the preceding (530 ff.) does convey the 'gradual' bloom by means of the spectrum range, by the analogical qualities of the flowers, and by the fact that each flower appears in its proper order, its *gradus*, as spring advances into summer. Thus, the innocent hyacinth, 'Low bent, and blushing inward' (548), is seen with the narcissus which over 'the fabled Fountain' (550) hangs—neither modest nor blushing. And the 'gradual Bloom' describes the white hyacinth, the yellow jonquils, the white and yellow narcissus, the flesh-colored carnations, the 'gay-spotted Pinks' (551), and the deep damask-rose. The sentence moves to a climax of color and sensuousness, the achievement of 'Bloom' that begins as 'gradual' and comes to be seen as 'endless' (555) because it is an expression of God's varied presence, an ever-flowering creation, a harmony of color.

The technique of the spectrum is a characteristic example of Thomsonian harmony, and Marjorie H. Nicolson has documented such passages in *The Seasons* in *Newton Demands the Muse*.[25] The technique, as I have indicated, is a spatial blending of sexual and sensual features in *Spring*. Such blending involves the wholeness implicit in the spectrum at the same time that it indicates only partial color change and transformation, for the poet cannot describe the infinite colors, let alone the infinite fragrance of nature. The spectrum can, however, suggest the multiplicity of nature's hues. Each individual flower forms part of a brilliant harmony image illustrating colors, smells, and life (blossoming). Just as earlier Thomson had described the sight of the flowers from a height as 'One boundless Blush, one white-empurpled Shower/Of mingled Blossoms' (110–11), resulting from unfolding 'The various Twine of Light' (211), so each particular feature was representative of a plenitude existing in extent. The kinds of harmony, therefore, were the result of a blending of particulars that were either derived as a whole from white light (or God) or were mixed 'in wild Concert' (199), or were soothed into peace in the mind of man:

> All but the Swellings of the soften'd Heart,
> That waken, not disturb the tranquil Mind.
>
> (465–66)

The *Spring* concept of harmony, therefore, does not involve tension or clash, but rather the blending of gentle responses in agreeable order. The chords of disharmony, as in the destruction of the world, result from clashing and unresolvable tensions. Thomson's order involves movement that awakens a responsive sense of life and awareness, but does not disturb the tranquil mind. This is the position Thomson expressed to Lyttelton, July 14, 1743, using terms at times identical with those in the poem. Referring to Hagley, he writes that he expects that there the 'Mind will not only be soothed into Peace, but enlivened into Harmony.'[26]

It is possible for harmony to reach a sublime rapture even in *Spring*, and this occurs when the love of nature leads to love of God—as in the Lyttelton passage.

> By swift Degrees the Love of Nature works,
> And warms the Bosom; till at last sublim'd
> To Rapture, and enthusiastic Heat,
> We feel the present DEITY, and taste
> The Joy of GOD to see a happy World!
>
> (899–903)

Sublime harmony occurs in the religious context where man feels God's presence and tastes His joy, though earlier in *Spring*, when the speaker tastes 'the Smell of Dairy' (107) or looks at the mingled blossoms, there is only the harmony of the beautiful.

Marjorie H. Nicolson has suggested that Thomson's ideas of the beautiful and the sublime have their source in Addison's *Pleasures of the Imagination*, in which Addison associates 'color' with the beautiful, for Thomson associates 'color' with the 'beautiful' and 'light' with the 'sublime'. She writes: 'Thomson's important distinction between the "beautiful and the sublime", so far as light and color were concerned, occurred in "Spring" and "Summer". That the distinction was self-conscious and not merely fortuitous, and that it had been made even more clear to Thomson by the Newtonian discoveries, certain chronological facts would seem to indicate.'[27] *Spring*, she explains, is filled with color; *Summer* with light,[28] a view that my own findings support.

These harmony procedures need to be contrasted not only with disharmonious chaos but with the unbeautiful deforming of the world, with the narrative of 'sad Presage' in which the cycle of action is forever incomplete. The limited completeness of the spectrum leads to a hymn of thanksgiving for the God-given beauty. The description is spatially extended, forming a family of gradual distinctions, 'unfolding by Degrees' (91), while, by negation, suggesting the incompleteness of the whole. Thomson developed this technique of limited completeness, which I call the 'completed fragment', to express the common Augustan conception of limited nature. Thus together with reciprocal harmony (the movement from passive to active) he uses the idea of nature in transition to express attitudes he shares with his contemporaries.

The hymn concluding this part (556–571), summarizes in language and in thanksgiving, the activities of *Spring* to this point. And although the narrator addresses God who, with a 'Master-hand/ Hast the great Whole into Perfection touch'd' (559–60), 'Perfection' does not refer to man's view of nature, but to God's, for man's state 'must not yet to pure Perfection rise' (376); for man the seasons are fragments the meanings of which he can only partially perceive; man's understanding of 'Perfection' is limited and although God is perfect, man is not.

Beginning with the induction, the poem moves from the heavens to earth and back; just as personified *Spring* descends at the beginning and the happy lovers ascend at the conclusion. This movement reflects the co-operation among the elements as it reflects the constant state of motion in the universe. By means of the prospect view, the spectrum view, the reciprocity of elements, it places man and nature within the larger perspective of the heavens. Since the speaker sees the precise, at-hand description as well as the infinite expanse, he places himself between the precise and the general, the finite and the infinite, and is thus a middle man whose precise observation is followed by contemplation and reflection. His address to God belongs with recognition of man's limitations, yet he is grateful even for these limitations because they give life to the senses and the mind; they make man the explorer and the scientist, ever intent upon the pursuit of knowledge and wisdom through space.

iii. The Pathetic and Comic Passions of Birds and Beasts (572–866)

The second of the three parts of *Spring* begins with a return to the unifying idea of ascent: 'My Theme ascends, with equal Wing ascend,/My panting Muse' (573–74). The poet begs for his winged muse to borrow the song of the nightingales as earlier the sight of the 'breathing' prospect had bid his Muse to 'Throw all her Beauty forth.'

> Lend me your Song, ye Nightingales! oh pour
> The mazy-running Soul of Melody
> Into my varied Verse!
>
> (576–78)

And the narrator announces a theme consciously new: to 'touch a Theme/Unknown to Fame, *the Passion of the Groves*' (580–81). The first 'Theme' (573) dealt with birth, breath and bloom of spring, with the earth and its floral products; the second deals with the air and the sounds and objects of the air. The 'ascent' is thus literal, not philosophic, and when the narrator turns to the third part of *Spring*, he undertakes a 'nobler' note, an attempt by heaven and earth to 'raise his [man's] Being, and serene his Soul' (870). The physical ascent, applied to the birds, becomes metaphoric and metaphysical when applied to man.

The note will be 'nobler' because man can express in language his love of God, because man can be a spokesman for the ideal. *Spring* is the only season in which there exists this progressive unity, 'ascending from the lower to the higher,'[29] because it is the time of hope, rebirth. The other seasons also deal with a world in which man, bird, beast and flower are seen as coextensive, but they are progressive in a chronological scheme rather than a metaphysical one; each season is cyclical; it recurs.

The first part of *Spring* dealt with space as the surface of the earth, so that even the sun's penetration had as its end the bringing of plant life to the surface. Thus location, particulars of color and growth, the sense of nature as mixture in the earth led to the innumerable variety of flowers, of kinds and of the same kind. In the second part, space is seen as extension in air, not on earth; and since music is carried in the air, it becomes characteristic of this section. In both parts, the sense of the unfinished world, the uncountable infinitude of nature, is an inheritance of seventeenth-century views of an imperfect world.

I do not wish to strain the element of earth beyond its confines, but I suggest that the passion of the groves is consistent with this elemental dominance. For the passage is called '*the Passion of the Groves*' (581), a metonymical image in which the groves represent the birds. Metonymy functions for Thomson as an example of the whole used to represent individual aspects, qualities or feeling. Metonymy is thus a figure which reflects the poet's conception of a whole unchanging though with constantly changing parts or perspectives. Thus the term 'Passion of the Groves' (*Spring*, 581) refers to the loves of the birds in the grove, 'autumnal Prime' (*Autumn*, 697) refers to the ripe grapes and 'crystal Treasures of the liquid World' (*Autumn*, 824) refers to the clear waters that prove valuable to nature and man; 'rigid Influence' (*Winter*, 742), a periphrasis for snow, is also a type of metonymy in which the effect is used to define the cause.

Metonymy is the technique used to make every copse and bush 'prodigal of Harmony' (598). So, too, 'the waste of music' combines a visual image of extent with aural lavishness and prodigality. The birds in their behavior in the groves are a continuation of the birth of the groves themselves, and the birds are thus artistically and meaningfully related to the expansion of nature. In the previous section this spatial imagery operated in terms of sight; here it functions in terms of sound.

The 'Soul of Love' wafted to the birds seizes them, and they burst into song.

> Up-springs the Lark,
> Shrill-voic'd, and loud, the Messenger of Morn;
> Ere yet the Shadows fly, he mounted sings
> Amid the dawning Clouds, and from their Haunts
> Calls up the tuneful Nations. Every Copse
> Deep-tangled, Tree irregular, and Bush
> Bending with dewy Moisture, o'er the Heads
> Of the coy Quiristers that lodge within,
> Are prodigal of Harmony. The Thrush
> And Wood-lark, o'er the kind contending Throng

Superior heard, run thro' the sweetest Length
Of Notes; when listening *Philomela* deigns
To let them joy, and purposes, in Thought
Elate, to make her Night excel their Day.
The Black-bird whistles from the thorny Brake;
The mellow Bullfinch answers from the Grove:
Nor are the Linnets, o'er the flowering Furze
Pour'd out profusely, silent. Join'd to These
Innumerous Songsters, in the freshening Shade
Of new-sprung Leaves, their Modulations mix
Mellifluous. The Jay, the Rook, the Daw,
And each harsh Pipe discordant heard alone,
Aid the full Concert: while the Stock-dove breathes
A melancholy Murmur thro' the whole.

(590–613)

The whistling, answering, modulations form a 'Concert' ('symphony')
—and the passage constitutes an achievement in the particularity of
sounds, and all 'This Waste of Music is the Voice of Love' (615). The
'Concert' belongs with the blending, concord, commerce cluster of
The Seasons. By derivation, 'concert' comes from the Latin 'to
contend,' and, in Thomson's use, it is a contention that has become a
harmony, an interpretation that supports Thomson's view of poetry
as a competition with nature. So, too, 'commerce' is a mixing on the
economic level that involves spatial exchange. The harmonious
musical mixing becomes the vocal equivalent of the color spectrum,
and both are part of the spectrum technique. Just as the flowers form
an harmonious sexual unfolding so the songs of the birds reveal the
vocal beauty of sexual behavior.

The description of the flowers is here matched by the sexual antics,
the mating dance and nesting of the birds. The theme, as Thomson
states it, is '*the Passion of the Groves*' (581). In this respect, he wishes
to establish the analogical relation among flowers, birds, animals
and man: the blending that creates the harmony of God's universe.
But Thomson does not hesitate to describe precise mating practices.

First, wide around,
With distant Awe, in airy Rings they rove,
Endeavouring by a thousand Tricks to catch
The cunning, conscious, half-averted Glance
Of their regardless Charmer. Should she seem

Softening the least Approvance to bestow,
Their Colours burnish, and by Hope inspir'd,
They brisk advance; then, on a sudden struck,
Retire disorder'd; then again approach;
In fond rotation spread the spotted Wing,
And shiver every Feather with Desire.

(620–30)

The sexuality includes the initiation of the bird family, and the entire passage (614–765) deals with the organization of family, the concern for children and the ultimate dissolution of parental love (732–33) when it becomes needless.

The description of bird love mixes the scientific with the ideal, permitting the poet to descend to minute particulars while retaining the personification of sacrificial parents: they multiply (expand) in accordance with God's commands. But even in this season of love, it is apparent that man is often hostile to the birds, killing them and caging them, and it is ironic that after man's viciousness the poet should offer as explanation: 'Unlavish *Wisdom* never works in vain' (734). There are men subject to tyrannical impulses, men moved by evil and barbarous forces even in *Spring*, but the origin of wickedness is never clear. After the Golden Age men in some way became evil, and in *Winter* the poet suggests that some men are governed by the 'Lust of Cruelty' (372) or 'fell Interests.' Whatever the origin, there is no doubt in *The Seasons* of the reality of destructive and wicked human actions. Whether nature in its deluge is destructive is a question that must be answered by religious faith.

The concert of the birds and the exposition of nesting describe instinctive behavior, but although both involve the intermixing of nature, the first is exciting and the second tame. The choral passage has a sense of flight, posture (or ascension), an inner-outer relationship, a responsive chorus and a musical range that conveys the meaning of music and motion as love. The trite image of 'pouring' the soul of melody (577) or the more daring image of the linnets 'o'er the flowering Furze/Pour'd out profusely' (606–7) conveys the literal-metaphoric mixture of the vibrating air 'pouring' sounds or the linnets as the embodiment of sounds. The vocal-visual expansiveness implicit in the concert, even to the paradoxical description of the 'kind contending' throng and the responsive choral exchange between the blackbird and the bullfinch, captures the sexual outburst. In this way

54

the sounds of love 'their Modulations mix/Mellifluous' (609–10). Even 'The Jay, the Rook, the Daw' (610), discordant alone, aid 'the full Concert' (612).

Hypothetically, there is no reason why the description of nesting and egg-sitting as an expression of familial love should not be effective, but because the narrator wishes to emphasize the ideal behavior of the birds—('kind' (648) and 'Pious' (670))—while describing nesting habits accurately, he creates a separation between the obvious human analogy and the realistic detail. One can grant the readiness to minimize the natural world in which birds eat insects, even though such insects are destructive, as those in the plague passage; but the retreat of the birds is not seen in terms of departure from the space to which they ascended. The birds are personified and sentimentalized as sympathizing lovers (665), as 'Parents' (676), and the female is a pious toiler.

Thomson deliberately sought to press the sentimentalizing in making his revision. Originally it read:

> So pitiful, and poor,
> A gentle Pair on Providential Heaven
> Cast, as they weeping eye their clamant Train,
> Check their own Appetites, and give them all.
>
> (A, 633–36)

This was expanded in 1744 and 1746 to read:

> Even so a gentle Pair,
> By fortune sunk, but form'd of generous Mold,
> And charm'd with Cares beyond the vulgar Breast,
> In some lone Cott amid the distant Woods,
> Sustain'd alone by providential HEAVEN,
> Oft, as they weeping eye their infant Train,
> Check their own Appetites and give them all.
>
> (680–86)

The metaphor of the gentle bird 'Parents' was compared to the human parents 'by Fortune sunk.' The added lines, stressing isolation and loneliness in the 'distant Woods' as a test of sacrifice and virtue, correspond to those in *Autumn* that describe Lavinia and her mother, comparing their life with that of the birds.

She with her widow'd Mother, feeble, old,
And poor, liv'd in a Cottage, far retir'd
Among the Windings of a woody Vale;

(181–83)

....
Almost on Nature's common Bounty fed,
Like the gay Birds that sung them to Repose,
Content, and careless of to-morrow's Fare.

(189–91)

The relation between man and birds is interpreted as one of separate but parallel realms although both are part of a larger natural family, in which man's conscious powers entail obligation to weaker members of the family. The past participles—'sunk,' 'form'd,' 'charm'd,' 'Sustain'd'—coupled with 'Sweeping' and followed by the present tense, 'Check' and 'give,' show past and present mingling in the description of actions such as sacrifice or discipline ('Check,' 686) and consequent generosity and blessedness ('give,' 686). And in this passage there is present, too, the characteristic Thomsonian paradox 'charm'd with Cares' in which one welcomes the anxieties or sacrifices ('Cares,' 682) as well as the children for whom one makes sacrifices: the process and the product. The tortured lover leads a life 'Of fevered Rapture, or of cruel Care' (1110). He is neither charmed by his anxieties nor does he feel 'melting Sentiments of kindly Care' (675). But even the nightingale feels the cruelty of 'Her ruin'd Care' (715), the fledgling ruined by being caged.

The structure of this retirement image—the gentle pair is sustained in its isolation by trust in divine providence—fits into the structure of prospect images which move from the individual object to the distant ones and the merging of these with the clouds and heavens. It belongs with images of God's love in contrast to those of chaotic isolation and fragmentation or of stiffness and death suffered for no known reason (innocent Amelia, the frozen swain, etc.). The point is, however, that, operating within the norm of his retirement imagery, the poet here deliberately prettifies experience, deliberately presses emotive explanations upon the reader, instead of giving him (as in his best passages) scope for responses.

The bird sounds of *Spring* are not without their playful and mournful notes, and in this part evil can be defined as lack of love. If the image of the sacrificial parents applies to bird and man, the 'unfeeling School-Boy' (694), the 'tyrant Man' (703), the 'unrelenting Clowns' (719) create suffering and pain among the birds. Here Thomson avoids the issue of the birds of prey that necessarily attack other species, but since the birds are referred to as 'Brothers' (703) of the muse, the hawks would not, of course, be singing birds. The pain or evil which the birds feel is an uneasy concession in *Spring*, for despite the season of love, acts of 'unlove' continue. The season stresses expansiveness and love, but it is not to be assumed, as many critics have assumed—indeed, some have gone so far as to suggest that evil is unacknowledged in the poem as a whole—that evil does not exist in *Spring*.

Evil actions deprive the birds of their liberty or of their loved objects. The acts and the men who perform them are vicious and cruel—'unfeeling,' 'Tyrant,' 'unrelenting.' The three verse paragraphs that deal with evil (687–728) treat it in different tones. The first parallels the fishing episode in its playfulness and deception, except that here the birds deceive man in self-protection; for with whirring, wheeling flights of deceptive fluttering, the birds distract the attackers. The sounds of playful deception 'o'er the trackless Waste/ The Heath-Hen flutters (pious Fraud!)' (699–700), are replaced in the succeeding paragraph by the moral declamation of the narrator bemoaning the caging of the nightingale. The final paragraph pathetically describes the bird whose nest has been robbed.

The first part of *Spring* described the progressive stages of involvement of the narrator in the catalog of flowers to explain the mingling or mixing in movement. But the stages here can be described as the cessation of movement, as increase of isolation. The bird first flutters away and plays, then her fledgling is caged and, finally, her nest is robbed and she remains 'abandon'd to Despair' (723). The disengagement from movement, from the normal process of change, is the result of a sudden and brutal transformation. Man who destroys love in nature destroys, too, the normal growth of nature; and the sounds of joy become the sounds of sadness.

> . . . all abandon'd to Despair, she sings
> Her Sorrows thro the Night; and, on the Bough,
> Sole-sitting, still at every dying Fall
> Takes up again her lamentable Strain
> Of winding Woe; till wide around the Woods
> Sigh to her Song, and with her Wail resound.
>
> (723–28)

This elegiac tone is contrasted with the stock-dove's melancholy murmur that forms part of the harmony of song (612–13) at the opening of the section. The rise and fall of sorrow is a lonely cry, and the echoing woods create no harmony but merely the rhythm of loneliness. Thus the difference between the sounds of love and despair is a difference between harmony and its absence. Despair, suffering, the opposite of love is the absence of harmony; not disharmony necessarily but the unvaried rise and fall of a single lamentable strain. The rise and fall of sound, the rise and fall of harmony, the rise and fall of love, the rise and fall of men—this literal and imagistic movement in *Spring* suggests the double view that Thomson possesses of man's joy and suffering, and although this season deliberately avoids stressing the destructive powers, it does not deny the actuality of suffering.

In this part the musical reference in the image—while 'Music wakes around' (3)—is developed, indicating that the 'waking' of music is not only the outburst of spring sounds; it is also the sound of the bird's 'lamentable Strain/Of winding Woe.' And in the following section on human love, the original image is again recalled by its perversion, indicated by the depravity implied by 'inglorious laid' amidst the luxury of perfumes and oils: 'EVEN present, in the very Lap of Love/Inglorious laid; while Musick flows around,/Perfumes, and Oils, and Wine, and wanton Hours' (996–98). Only at the conclusion of the poem, in the idealized description of the lovers, is *Spring* again recalled in its proper terms of hope—'veil'd in a Shower/Of shadowing Roses' (3–4). For their virtuous love is untouched by the jarring world and 'consenting SPRING/Sheds her own rosy Garland on their Heads' (1168–69).

The organizational procedure of recurring to the induction to *Spring*, amplifying and applying it, gives this season a coherent development. And it does so by the eighteenth-century procedure of perspectives by which the knowledge of the season is unfolded. Thus it is completely appropriate that the poet should turn from the loss of freedom in the 'feather'd Youth,' to a freedom encouraged and, in the nature of behavior, desirable. Parental love demands that the young birds be taught to take their liberty and to fly from parental care, even if they have to be chided, exhorted, commanded, or compelled (744–46). The colloquial passage of love through release becomes a prelude to a sublime passage of the behavior of eagles and their young.

HIGH from the Summit of a craggy Cliff,
Hung o'er the Deep, such as amazing frowns
On utmost *Kilda*'s Shore, whose lonely Race
Resign the setting Sun to *Indian* Worlds,
The royal Eagle draws his vigorous Young,
Strong-pounc'd, and ardent with paternal Fire.
Now fit to raise a Kingdom of their own,
He drives them from his Fort, the towering Seat,
For Ages, of his Empire; which, in Peace,
Unstain'd he holds, while many a League to sea
He wings his Course, and preys in distant Isles.

(755–65)

The imagery of parenthood is compared with the sublime imagery
of royalty—the eagles now prepared to raise a kingdom of their own.
The tone of the passage rests on a sense of the grandeur of moving
through space, and hidden in the conclusion is the unexpected menace
of 'preys in distant Isles' (for man as 'destin'd Prey' of the plague, see
Summer, 1059). Sublime power is not without sublime violence, and
like the fruitful autumn spied amidst the *Spring* flowers, there is
future, menacing, destructive sublimity spied amidst undestructive
sublimity.

This revised passage is an instance of repetitive alteration, for earlier
the narrator had reclined under the spreading ash which overlooked
the 'Steep' in a language almost identical with this, 'Or lie reclin'd
beneath yon spreading Ash,/Hung o'er the Steep' (451–52). The
earlier passage used the reclining narrator to observe motion and
distance, comparing the sense of ease and comfort of place with that
of space and vigor ('beetling Cliff'), an inclosed place with an open
exposed one. But the eagle passage uses a very similar description,
moving from the summit of the cliff into the world space, and the
loneliness of the royal eagle is made more lonely by the idea of a
'Race' that 'resign' the 'setting Sun to *Indian* Worlds.' The eagle,
however, is a powerful figure, unresigned, flying to distant isles and
exercising his royal prerogative of 'preying.' Indeed, it is the eagle who
will in *Summer* become the sublime muse of the poet and who should
be compared with the tender or beautiful nightingale.

The poet descends from the sublime heights of the eagle's flight to
observe the rook who builds his 'airy City' (769) high amid the boughs
and to survey 'the various Polity' (771) of the 'mixt Household-Kind'

59

(772). There, in order, he describes the hen, the cock, the duck, the swan, the turkey, the peacock and the 'cooing Dove' (786). This entire passage belongs within the range of what Burke later called the 'beautiful.' It describes the domestic posturings of the animals that appear in literal description and, yet, have comic undertones by comparison with the sublime and powerful eagle. Here again the undertones belong to the illusive allusion procedure. Thus the 'fearless Cock,/Whose Breast with ardour flames, as on he walks,/Graceful, and crows Defiance' (774–76) is implicitly compared with the royal eagle 'ardent with paternal Fire' (760). The eagle 'preys in distant Isles' (765) whereas the 'stately-sailing Swan' (778) 'guards his Osier-Isle' (781). The 'royal Eagle' (759) is alluded to in the peacock who 'swims in radiant Majesty along' (785). Such descriptions of family protection and personal pride establish a correspondence between the beautiful domestic kingdom, the sublime family of the eagle and the human family.

The comic undercurrent flows from the implied bursting of barriers, so that the eagle's ardor and the cock's, the eagle's majesty and the peacock's, while analogical, imply a somewhat exaggerated relation—because of the use of similar terms. Thus, while Thomson illustrates the appropriateness of each group in protecting the home, his recognition of similarity establishes parallels among different groups in nature, and delights in the consequent disproportions. When Thomson seeks to establish two versions within the same natural range, he provides variants of the same behavior. Thus the mating dance of the forest birds and the behavior of the cooing dove are both forms of 'amorous Chace' (787), but in the latter there is a mocking tone by which the passion of the groves becomes the coquetry of the barnyard:

> O'er the whole homely Scene, the cooing Dove
> Flies thick in amorous Chace, and wanton rolls
> The glancing Eye, and turns the changeful Neck.
>
> (786–88)

Continuing his spatial excursion from the doves, the narrator moves from the gentle tenants of the shade to the 'rougher World/Of Brutes, below' (790–91). He grants their violence, brutality and lust, but resists embellishing this theme, continuing his descent through spring by describing the 'broad Monsters of the foaming Deep' (822). Their flouncing and trembling contrast with the order of the duck

60

'before her Train' (777) and the stately-sailing swan that 'Bears forward fierce' (781), providing a ludicrous undertone of varieties of
lovemaking.

This language procedure in which literal terms seem to allude to
situations that possess a comic quality or a range of association
results, in the fishing episode, from Thomson's self-reflexive or allusive vocabulary. Here, it results from the juxtaposition of orders of
nature different in kind but similar in detail—in addition to which
there is present the Virgilian source of the description. With a series
of paradoxes, 'cruel Raptures' and 'Savage Kind' (826), Thomson
turns to the wild animals who 'growl their horrid Loves' (830). The
entire sentence (825–30) with its originally serious Virgilian imitation
omitted, stresses the grotesque viciousness of the beasts aroused by
love. It brings this passage into association with Thomson's views
of the contrary possibilities of any action, even though the 'sublim'd'
wrath, the 'fiercer' bands and 'horrid' loves give the lines a somewhat
burlesque tone, almost a parody on rather than an achievement of
disorder.

Rejecting this violent love, the narrator returns to an idyllic pastoral
scene, ascending from the ocean depths to the 'Mountain-brow' (832).
The sun becomes again a 'healthful' force and the lambs gleefully
play. The hill around which they innocently run is the symbol of a
Britain which was once disunited (deformed) but has now become the
island in which the subjects harmoniously love. Thus the scene moves
through the pastoral paradise to patriotic praise of country:

> To this deep-laid indissoluble State,
> Where *Wealth* and *Commerce* lift the golden Head;
> And, o'er our Labours, *Liberty* and *Law*,
> Impartial, watch, the Wonder of a World!   (845–48)

The movement from pastoral to patriotic love is, if one wishes to
pursue it, a fiction for the 'BRITISH FAIR,' or, at best, a censored
message for their ears presenting the possibility of ideal love. Thomson sees the image of lifting as a form of thanksgiving with the state
as recipient of God's beneficence—'the mountains lift their green/
Heads to the sky,' 'Sickness lifts her languid head.' Thus nature, man,
and national commerce are, when successful, indebted to God for
their success, but there are those scenes in which man and ships are
buried or sunk, not lifted but interred.

Thomson wrote of the iron time in which men lived, and he

notes the cruel raptures of love among the brutes. But with a rhetorical flourish he stops himself from pursuing these, though he does pursue the evils or pains caused by nature in *Summer* and *Winter*. When, therefore, he moves in *Spring* from country to God, he is in a Virgilian, tradition-old orbit of enhancing the present powers.

In observing the flowers, the narrator tried, though he acknowledged the impossibility of success, to match the actuality by words; it was, indeed, a contention testable by looking upon nature. But in moving to the ideal country house, he writes of a visible world as an 'Emblem' (*Summer*, 465), not in process of change or in blended harmonious and sensuous activity, but as an Edenic model which, for all its immediate visibility, is an idealized haven outside time and change. In describing this ideal, Thomson uses a vocabulary, a cluster of terms that he applies to the land, to the state, to social behavior and to art. These terms form a family of related meanings so that the sower 'liberal, throws the Grain' (*Spring*, 45) and nature is called 'liberal' in blowing the seeds abroad.

> With such a liberal Hand has Nature flung
> Their Seeds abroad, blown them about in Winds,
> Innumerous mix'd them with the nursing Mold,
> The moistening Current, and prolifick Rain.
>
> (*Spring*, 230–33)

There the relation is made between man and nature, both being able to act in a 'liberal' or generous way, though man can behave as a tyrant to birds and animals; he cages the nightingale, 'in the narrow Cage/From Liberty confin'd, and boundless Air' (*Spring*, 704–5). In *Autumn* the husbandman is urged to fling the grain with a liberal hand for the gleamers: 'fling/From the full Sheaf, with charitable Stealth/The liberal Handful' (167–69). Being 'liberal,' free or generous, is identified with a natural process of generosity or plenitude, and the distinction (as well as similarity) between 'liberal' and 'lavish' can be noted in the following lines:

> At once, array'd
> In all the Colours of the flushing Year,
> By Nature's swift and secret-working Hand,
> The Garden glows, and fills the liberal Air
> With lavish Fragrance.
>
> (*Spring*, 95–99)

Here the harmony produced by the 'secret-working Hand' results in a 'glowing' garden that sends into the air the moist fragrance of the flowers. In Thomson the 'liberal' free-moving air is complemented by the lavish—freely outpouring—scent. Another context clarifies these particular usages by incorporating elemental interchanges into the terms for 'generous,' 'loose,' 'free.'

> These [the seasons], in successive Turn, with lavish Hand,
> Shower every Beauty, every Fragrance shower,
> Herbs, Flowers, and Fruits.
>
> *(Summer*, 126–28)

But if in these contexts 'liberal' and 'lavish' support one another, Thomson recognizes that man can be selfishly 'lavish,' just as God can be wisely 'unlavish': 'Unlavish Wisdom never works in vain' (734). In the *Spring* passage rejecting such unfeeling behavior on the part of the wealthy, he refers to the

> sordid Sons of Earth,
> Hard, and unfeeling of another's Woe,
> Or only lavish to yourselves; away!
>
> (875–77)

And he contrasts with these the 'generous Minds' (878) in whom creative bounty 'burns' (879) and appears in the 'liberal Eye' (881). 'Liberal' and 'lavish' become aspects of nature and behavior that move between a proper harmony and a disharmony. Liberty, being liberal, then becomes identified with the reciprocal harmony of nature and of man. Thus Britain, when it is identified with liberty, creates vigor and reciprocal activity on the part of all inhabitants:

> Happy BRITANNIA! where the QUEEN OF ARTS,
> Inspiring Vigor, LIBERTY abroad
> Walks, unconfin'd, even to thy farthest Cotts,
> And scatters Plenty with unsparing Hand.
>
> *(Summer*, 1442–45)

The prospect view which immediately precedes this last quotation— 'HEAVENS! what a goodly Prospect spreads around' (*Summer*, 1438)— is Thomson's method of placing the country estates as look-out points from which one sees the world extending from immediate surroundings to infinity. In this way the estate becomes an ideal point from which to conceive of a future eternity. The estates therefore are physical entities that permit views into the past and future. As retreats they function to make past time simultaneous, that is, they make possible the looking back into history as though it is laid out before the contemplator. The prospect view provides an uninvolved way of being involved in the past. But the difficulty with Thomson's view is his tendency to overlook, in a political and social sense, the difficulty of attaining liberty. He is cognizant, however, that 'looseness', 'lavishness,' 'luxury' can be governed by false or inadequate limits and thus become corrupting. Referring to Lord William Russell, executed in 1683, Thomson writes of the

> giddy Reign;
> Aiming at lawless Power, tho meanly sunk
> In loose inglorious Luxury.
>
> (*Summer*, 1525–27)

If 'looseness' can be a virtue, as when the zephyrs, 'floating loose' (*Summer*, 123), complement the other elemental forces in the turning of the seasons, or when women are praised as their limbs 'Float in the loose Simplicity of Dress' (*Autumn*, 590), it nevertheless demands bounds that provide harmonious reciprocity; it is a concept of the environment, of man's relation to the state, even a concept of art. For although Thomson refers to nature spreading 'Unbounded Beauty to the roving Eye' (*Spring*, 507), he means that in the particular scene there is beauty wherever the eye turns; in *Winter*, the exile roams 'the Prison of unbounded Wilds' (799).

The revised hortatory passage about God as the source of love nevertheless insists that the 'SMILING GOD' is chiefly seen in 'Spring' and its soft scenes (861–62).

> Chief, lovely Spring, in thee, and thy soft Scenes,
> The SMILING GOD is seen; while Water, Earth,
> And Air attest his Bounty; which exalts
> The Brute-Creation to this finer Thought,
> And annual melts their undesigning Hearts
> Profusely thus in Tenderness and Joy.
>
> (861–66)

But did not the 'raging Passion' (793) of the bull lead to violent battle when confronted by his rival?

> Their Eyes flash Fury; to the hollow'd Earth,
> Whence the Sand flies, they mutter bloody Deeds,
> And groaning deep th' impetuous Battle mix.
>
> (804–6)

Critics have taken the unfortunate figural personification, 'SMILING GOD' to represent Thomson's view of the deity in the poem, though the evidence that he finds man proud as well as benevolent, violent as well as peaceful, evil as well as good is amply spread out; and God's love and wisdom must be taken on faith. The term 'smile,' with its variants—'smiling,' 'smiles,' 'smil'd'—occurs 39 times in the poem (*Spring* (7), *Summer* (15), *Autumn* (7), *Winter* (7), *Hymn* (3)) and is Thomson's translation of the Latin *laetus*, the meanings of which range from 'joyous' and 'pleased' to 'fertile,' 'rich,' 'abundant.' In remarking on the use of 'smiling' in 'The Pride of smiling GREECE, and Human-kind' (*Winter*, 452), E. E. Morris notes that it is a 'translation of Gr. λιπαρός (lit. shining), an epithet which the Athenians were especially fond of applying to the splendour of their city. It describes both the purity of the air, and the sun always shining on their many marble buildings. Cf. Eur., *Alc.*, 452. It is very common in Pindar.'[30] Professor Tillotson remarks that '*Smiling*, a common word in eighteenth-century pastoral, may be considered the equivalent of *laetus*, which Virgil constantly applied to crops.'[31] The 'SMILING GOD' (862) of the soft *Spring* scenes creates the 'gay *Green*' grass, 'smiling Nature's universal Robe' (84), an image in which 'smiling' means fertile and colorful. In describing the Golden Age, Thomson writes, 'Harmonious Nature too look'd smiling on' (258), using 'smiling' as a personification implying nature's mildness. But 'smiling' can be used literally in the line, 'Mean-time a smiling Offspring rises round' (1145); 'smile' is also, even in *Spring*, used negatively to describe deceptive female behaviour, as when the poet warns the youth to beware of 'Th' enticing Smile' (990).

When Thomson refers to God's 'single Smile' (*Summer*, 179), the sending of joyful light to the world, or when he describes the look of love in the eyes of British women, with beauty sitting 'high-smiling' the image is unfortunate:

> The Look resistless, piercing to the Soul,
> And by the Soul inform'd, when drest in Love
> She sits high-smiling in the conscious Eye.

> (1592–1954)

But even with such a term as 'smile,' Thomson recognizes contrary contexts. He refers in *Autumn* to the 'lying Smile' (1297) of courtiers, and in the turn of fortune narrative of Lavinia, he remarks, 'Fortune smil'd, deceitful, on her Birth' (178), though Lavinia herself goes to

65

glean in the fields 'With smiling Patience in her Looks' (216), where 'smiling' means a willing acceptance of necessity's command.

Not only does 'smiling' occur in contexts that warn against the smile, but the term must be understood as one part of a world view, in which 'rage' and its variants ('raging,' 'rages,' 'rag'd') form an antithetis to 'smiling,' etc. They occur 49 times in the poem (*Spring*, 8; *Summer*, 19; *Autumn*, 12; *Winter*, 10). In *Spring* the North-East wind 'spends her Rage' (143) or the caught trout exhausts 'his idle Rage' (439), but in the love passages the bulls kindle up 'their Rage' (808), and the jealous lover is seized with 'consuming Rage' (1096). If the soft scenes of *Spring* tend to minimize the rage of nature, *Summer* stresses it. There the torrid zone rages, the 'rending Lightnings rage' (799), and the rage of the torrid skies 'starve the blasted Year' (1094). Even in the temperate zone, lightning 'fires the Mountains with redoubled Rage' (1149), though the sun, too, can lose his rage (1371), and rage can become a literal instead of a metaphoric term: Thomas More 'Withstood a brutal Tyrant's useful Rage' (1490). These are not isolated instances but characteristic procedures by which apparently opposing terms like 'smiling' or 'Rage' can sometimes oppose and sometimes support one another. Still, the narrator provides each season with a dominant mood, and though he admits other moods, he minimizes them. *Spring* is the season of love, of expansiveness, of tender growth; this does not mean that violence and 'cruel Raptures' do not exist in this season, but rather that the narrator prefers not to dwell on them.

iv. The Contrary Contexts of Language and Love (867–1176)

When the narrator undertakes to 'sing th' infusive Force of Spring on Man' (868), he must reject the sordid, unresponsive men upon whom *Spring* has no such force.

> Hence! from the bounteous Walks
> Of flowing Spring, ye sordid Sons of Earth,
> Hard, and unfeeling of another's Woe,
> Or only lavish to yourselves; away!
> But come, ye generous Minds.

(874–78)

Artistically, this passage (867–903) fails as poetry, and its failure is instructive. It is built upon personified abstract nouns—not unlike the catalog of corrupt passions (282–87). Here the listing becomes prolific: 'CREATIVE BOUNTY' (879), 'Goodness' (883), 'Sickness' (892), 'Health' (893), 'Contentment' (894), 'Serenity' (897). The narrator seeks to personify ideal *Spring* states of mind and body, though only the good men, of whom Lord Lyttelton is a model, possess them. Such abstract qualities—marked predominantly by single adjectives to provide only a degree of a whole as in 'CREATIVE BOUNTY,' 'restless Goodness,' 'Reviving Sickness,' and 'young-ey'd Health'—are always available, but are achieved only by the active search of the good man. Badness, therefore, is the non-seeking, or the seeking of luxury for one's own purpose—'only lavish to yourselves,' a luxury denounced at the beginning of *Spring*.

What the narrator, in his address to the 'generous Minds' implies, is that such men are like flowers—'Ye Flower of human Race!'—and that the earth's expansiveness typifies their generous character as it does the birth of nature. But the narrator is unable to describe goodness in the interrelated way that he wishes. The images become either trite or syntactically tortured.

> But come, ye generous Minds, in whose wide Thought,
> Of all his Works, CREATIVE BOUNTY burns,
> With warmest Beam; and on your open Front,
> And liberal Eye, sits, from his dark Retreat,
> Inviting modest Want.
>
> (878–82)

'Creative Bounty' and 'modest Want' form part of a typical Thomsonian image of the sun penetrating the 'dark Retreat' of retiring need, of generous minds seeking out the needy and aiding them. The image has its heavenly parallel, too, in 'silent-working HEAVEN, surprising oft/The lonely Heart with unexpected Good' (885–86). But the passage is overloaded with personifications and movement, shifting too rapidly from the human to the natural to the divine; such speedy shifts result in the paradoxical hyperbole of 'CREATIVE BOUNTY' that 'burns' and 'sits.' Despite the consistency of this passage with Thomson's own poetic procedures, it does not achieve the skilful expression he can manage elsewhere. The external forces of spring suddenly serve only the good men.

67

For you the roving Spirit of the Wind
Blows Spring abroad; for you the teeming Clouds
Descend in gladsome Plenty o'er the World;
And the Sun sheds his kindest Rays for you,
Ye Flower of human Race!

(887–91)

The phrases which should serve, therefore, to show man as part of the natural cycle seem to have no more than formal unity. Thus 'Sickness' that 'lifts her languid Head' (892) or 'Contentment' that 'walks/The sunny Glade' (894–95) become spectators rather than the sought active agents: the expansion and fertility of nature have no counterpart in the abstract personifications that stand apart from rather than become a part of nature.

The insertion of the panegyric to Lyttelton in 1744 can now be seen as an attempt to give precision to the earthly ideal by naming a specific example. For this reason the conclusion of the abstract section relates the narrator to the good men by changing the form of address from 'ye' to 'we,' and illustrates the point about the relation of abstractions to the spectator. We feel the presence of God; indeed, we 'taste/The Joy of GOD' (902–3). Originally (up to 1744) Thomson retained a passage stressing the total harmony of 'all Beings,' thus explaining the 'universal Smile,' and the relation of nature to man's 'glittering Spirits.' For this generalization he substituted a very specific relation between place and response. The Lyttelton insertion serves to unite the last love section of the season while echoing with variation the verse praagraph following the fishing passage (443–66). This paragraph was added at the same time as the Lyttelton lines, and both passages embody the *Spring* cycle of penetration, enclosed inner growth, and the achievement of tranquillity.

In *Spring* the harmonies are preceded by moments of uneasiness: the tension before the storm is broken by the shower which by infusing nature with powers of growth creates a moving harmony of growth and color. And the contest with the fish is followed by a harmony in which man flees from the heat and finds tranquility amid nature. The first harmony results from nature infusing the earth (an earlier example is the sun causing the sap to run or the shower that kindles the country). It functions by having certain features of nature blend with others to create a concord, and the anticipation is an instance of nature's expectation, suspension, anxiety, an uneasiness

68

that man only occasionally reflects. There is, however, another type of harmony in which man does establish a consistency between his thoughts and nature's tranquil behavior. In the poem, these rare moments must be interpreted in the context of other passages in which nature's actions disregard or conflict with man's feelings.

This reciprocal harmony, occurring where nature's movements, smells, sights and sounds suspend the participant's awareness of present conflicts and passions, makes possible his movement into the past or into the eternal time of literature. Such moments in nature are temporary, although they give the reader a foretaste of paradisial harmony. But there is, in *Summer*, e.g., the realization that the achievement of angelic harmony must, for some, be preceded by pain and suffering:

> 'Once some of us, like thee, thro stormy Life,
> Toil'd, Tempest-beaten, ere we could attain
> This holy Calm, this harmony of Mind,
> Where Purity and Peace immingle Charms.'
>
> (548–51)

This holy calm, this sublime harmony—the other might be called the pathetic or beautiful—is what is in store for the good man after this world, and the conclusion to *Winter* urges him to endure this life, for in the next *Spring* will reign forever.

The fisherman-swain, whose passions were soothed by wild though lovely nature, is placed at ease 'With all the lowly Children of the Shade' (450). But in the third part of *Spring*, the generous aristocrat Lyttelton strays at ease within his landscaped estate, Hagley Hall—'Thy *British Tempe*' (909).

> There along the Dale,
> With Woods o'er-hung, and shag'd with mossy Rocks,
> Whence on each hand the gushing Waters play,
> And down the rough Cascade white-dashing fall,
> Or gleam in lengthen'd Vista thro' the Trees,
> You silent steal; or sit beneath the Shade
> Of solemn Oaks, that tuft the swelling Mounts
> Thrown graceful round by Nature's careless Hand,
> And pensive listen to the various Voice
> Of rural Peace: the Herds, the Flocks, the Birds,
> The hollow-whispering Breeze, the Plaint of Rills,

F

69

That, purling down amid the twisted Roots
Which creep around, their dewy Murmurs shake
On the sooth'd Ear.

(909–22)

This landscape was designed to provide a contemplative influence, and Thomson writes, 'thy Passions thus/And Meditations vary, as at large,/Courting the Muse, thro HAGLEY PARK you stray' (906–8). Its planned effect was to create an environment that did not depend upon the accidents of the season but provided the spectator with a continuing response, as if such landscapes influenced the onlooker to partake in harmony, regardless of his own feelings.

But the relation between nature and man is not as direct as this implies if one considers the poem as a whole. For not only do ungenerous men in *Spring* not respond to generous nature, but the hearts of lovers who dote on their beloveds or grow jealous of them use nature for their own purposes, responding to selected aspects such as gloom or the song of the nightingale without establishing any harmony. Even the innocent are destroyed by natural forces, Amelia being struck down by lightning and the noble expedition of Willoughby being immured in ice by 'jealous Nature' (*Winter*, 929).

Although in each season there are moments when a tranquil harmony is established, and man responds with a moral sympathy to nature, this is only one aspect of a relationship that rejects any simple, direct moral exchange between man and nature as a guide to understanding God's forces in the universe. Thomson admired Hagley Park, as his letter to Elizabeth Young (dated Aug. 29, 1743) makes clear. But, as he wrote her, if he had to choose between living in the 'finest Country Retirement' without her or in some other place with her, the choice would be simple:

This is the truly happy Life, this Union of Retirement and choice Society: it gives an Idea of that which the Patriarchal or Golden Age is supposed to have been; when every Family was a little State by itself, governed by the mild Laws of Reason, Benevolence and Love. Dont however imagine me so madly rural as not to think those who have the Power of Happiness in their own Minds happy everywhere. The Mind is it's own Place, the genuine Source of it's own Happiness; and, amidst all my Raptures with Regard to the Country, I would rather live in the most London corner of London with you, than in the finest Country Retirement, and that too enlivened by the best Society, without you. You so fill my Mind with all Ideas of Beauty, so satisfy my Soul with the present and most sincere Delight, I should feel the Want of little else. Yet still the Country Life with You, diversifyed now and then by the Contrast of the Town, is the Wish of my Heart. May Heaven grant me that favourite Happiness, and I shall be the happiest of men. And so much the happier as the Possession of you will excite me to deserve my Happiness, by whatever is virtuous and Praise-worthy.[32]

Thomson uses a Miltonic allusion, 'The Mind is it's own Place, the genuine Source of it's own Happiness,' to mean that the mind, when it is seized by an embracing influence, Elizabeth Young's beauty, is not readily made to respond to any other. In this respect Thomson's view of the mind is consistent with his interpretation of nature in which man, despite the hardships caused by violent storms or an inhospitable environment, nevertheless is imbued with the sub-lime awe and love of God, though he, too, would prefer to live without such hardships.

In *Spring*, Hagley Hall represents a model estate; it not only provides a landscape that creates harmony and private retreat; it also looks out, from a prospect, upon towns, mountains and the heavens. The Hall becomes a haven for the '*favour'd Few*' (949) as well as a look-out point for future harmony.

The disproportionate quality of this harmony view is apparent in the description of Lucinda and Lyttelton, with souls attuned. In describing the harmony between husband and wife, the imagery has the 'tender Heart' (941) pouring its copious treasures and Lyttelton drinking ethereal joy from Lucinda's eyes. This awkward use of nature to create blending in exaggerated rather than moving situations misuses the technique and seems almost to parody it, even though Thomson was writing from personal knowledge of Lyttelton and his wife.

The Hagley Hall prospect view climaxes the walk through the garden:

> Meantime you gain the Height, from whose fair Brow
> The bursting Prospect spreads immense around;
> And snatch'd o'er Hill and Dale, and Wood and Lawn,
> And verdant Field, and darkening Heath between,
> And Villages embosom'd soft in Trees,

And spiry Towns by surging Columns mark'd
Of houshold Smoak, your Eye excursive roams:
Wide-stretching from the *Hall*, in whose kind Haunt
The *Hospitable Genius* lingers still,
To Where the broken Landskip, by Degrees,
Ascending, roughens into rigid Hills;
O'er which the *Cambrian* Mountains, like far Clouds
That skirt the blue Horizon, dusky, rise.

(950–62)

As Lyttelton mounts the height, he surveys the surroundings beyond the garden from a 'fair Brow' (950) which is like the 'Mountain-brow' (832) of the shepherd and his ideal flock, and his role as shepherd-poet hero becomes clear. For although, as Hugh Miller and others have pointed out, this view is what one actually saw from Hagley Hall, poetically this passage with its catalog of 'Hill and Dale,' 'Wood and Lawn,' green field and darkening heath, conveys distance in space that absorbs the 'spiry Towns' as well as the village, suggesting the harmoniously ordered view that the landed aristocrat provides from his retreat. As space extends the 'broken Landskip,' unlike the 'disparting Orb' (310) or 'fractur'd Earth' (313), ascends by degrees and becomes part of that infinity of space which belongs to the ideal—so that the mountains (earth) rise like 'far Clouds' (airy moisture) and Hagley Hall becomes a unifying outlook from which the elements blend into one another.

In the earlier prospect view from the garden (516 ff) the poet contrasted the flower harmony with that of the distant spires and main. But Hagley Park, identified as it is with Lyttelton, becomes a model for the remembrance of the past, the life of the present and the glory of the future.

The prospect view in *Spring*, when compared with that in Coleridge's 'Reflections on having left a Place of Retirement,' indicates that for Thomson spatial extent suggests a view infinitely prolonged and relates the future to the past and present in a simultaneous existence. For Coleridge the prospect is a whole, a unified 'temple' that is itself an organized transcendental object, a beautiful unity and a religious symbol.[33] In *The Seasons*, even though Thomson in the 'Hymn' refers to 'the spacious Temple of the Sky,' nature beyond the finished garden implies, through extension, the infinity of the world. Although what one sees beyond the garden are the fragmentary forms of nature, what one believes in are God's power and love. When Thomson's discriminations are replaced by a Wordsworthian organic structure, as in *Tintern Abbey*, for example, a different kind of organization is imposed upon the poem, and, in consequence, different functions are given to rhetorical figures and pastoral conventions. The language of organicism tends to sweep all terms into a more consistent vocabulary stressing not the verbal, active function of qualities, not the life in things but the life of things, the felt and shared infusive force in all objects.

The observed agonies contrast with the ideal of love that concludes *Spring* and recall the implications of the loss of innocence after the Golden Age. Even in *Spring*, love can be a cruel sickness, and in the revision of this section in 1730 Thomson added a passage on the cruelty and pain of ungenerous love, its selfishness and private pleasure. Here are differences of degree, the language of nature for the human situation, the resumption of the theme of limitation. The contrary contexts of human love correspond with Thomson's imagistic techniques in which harmony and disharmony form necessary parts of the poem. Even in the season of love it is imperative that wrong love or brutality (bird-killing) be admitted.

The description of the virgin (963–70) in terms of the elements— flower (earth), fire (passion), air ('breathes of Youth,' 966), water (tears)—suggests intensity of disorder—'Palpitations wild' (969) and 'kind Tumults' (969).

> From the keen Gaze her Lover turns away,
> Full of the dear exstatic Power, and sick
> With sighing Languishment.
>
> (971–73)

Both the female and the male are subject to ecstasies beyond control. It is not unexpected that the narrator should interrupt the description, and function as moral commentator, warning the maid of the lover's guile (though such warnings seem simple-minded). But the unmarried virgin, described in the sexual language of expansive spring flowers—'fresher Bloom' (964), 'blush deeper Sweets' (966), 'shining Moisture' (967) and the heated language of 'her wishing Bosom' (968)—becomes, like the birds who 'shiver every Feather with Desire' (630), a creature shaken by the agonies as well as pleasures of love. For the bowers which were to Lyttelton a retreat, an occasion for recalling noble associations, can become a bed of treachery.

73

> Nor in the Bower,
> Where Woodbines flaunt, and Roses shed a Couch,
> While Evening draws her crimson Curtains round,
> Trust your soft Minutes with betraying Man.
>
> (979–82)

The two-sidedness of love is precisely what has been established, and the moral warning is not inconsistent but too obviously direct in an atmosphere of indirection, the woodbines, roses and evening encouraging by flaunting, couching and curtaining the seduction. It is rather the use of 'soft' as 'tender' or 'sexual' that calls attention to itself. 'Soft' is an emotionally weighted term in *Spring* announced in the eulogy to Hertford: 'With Innocence and Meditation join'd/In soft Assemblage' (7–8). The term and its variants—'soften'd,' 'softening,' 'softly'—occur thirteen times in the 1176 lines whereas in the 1805 lines in *Summer* (half as long again) it occurs only eleven times, of which one (125) is a reference to *Spring* and another (297) is a transfer from *Spring*.

Although *Spring* is characterized by love and tenderness, and 'soft' therefore refers to an emotive as well as tactile quality, there is more artistic justification for 'soft Minutes' in which time is made tactile and becomes part of the danger of seduction than for 'soft Assemblage' because 'Innocence' and 'Meditation' draw 'soft' into equal generality instead of being subdued by it.

In *Spring* 'soft' refers to all aspects of the season—sounds (268), sights (861), prospects (954), touch (711); in *Summer* 'soft' and its variants are almost completely confined to the moral voice of the narrator (853, 875, 891, 1379, 1435) or to passages about women (1354, 1580, 1694). The sole other reference is to 'soft fearful People' (378), a periphrasis for sheep. The point is that such terms have special reference to qualities of the particular season, and, although they may not always prove successful, they are not to be considered as trite and thoughtless.

'Soft' is also part of a dialectical relation involving 'hard,' 'frozen,' 'frosty' and their variants, and it is used in widely diversified contexts, blending the physical with the moral and allegorical—sheep are 'soft,' the arts of peace are 'softening' in a moral sense, and a 'soft Assemblage' composed of 'Innocence' and 'Meditation' is an allegorical personification.[34] The manner in which Thomson takes a term and converts it into a virtue or fault can be seen in his use of 'waste,' where his procedure clearly differs from that of Milton, who, according to Isabel MacCaffrey, typically uses 'wasteful' to

> add resonance rather than true ambiguity. The connotations *all point in the same direction*, toward destruction and dreariness, and Milton's habit on the whole was to choose words whose variant meanings would reinforce rather than balance or contrast with each other; contrast came between words, not within them. Other instances can be found among the Latinate words that are to be understood in both the root and derived sense, like the one describing the Angel Abdiel: *fervent*, at once burning 'in a flame of Zeale' and eager.[35] [my italics]

Thomson's inventiveness and originality lead him to his own version of the Augustan double view, *using the same term with contrary as well as with varied meanings*.[36] It is a linguistic procedure that reflects his perspectival or reciprocal view of experience. For example, the jealous youth, haunted by false love, is described in terms of extinction and emptiness: 'His brightest Aims extinguish'd all, and all/His lively Moments running down to waste' (1111–12). This use of 'waste' as a retreat from *Spring*'s love and expansiveness recalls the term in the plague: 'The full-blown Spring thro all her Foliage shrinks,/Joyless, and dead, a wide-dejected Waste' (118–19). But the plovers sing to the 'listening Waste' (25), the 'far-resounding Waste' (829) in which 'Waste' is not a desolate but a responsive wilderness. 'Waste' characterizes the desolation of spring and the fall of man in the conclusion to the false-lover section, in which the false lover is part of the decline of man, nature and the world. But 'Waste' also means prodigality and, in the passion of the groves, the narrator finds love as prodigal, 'Waste' ('vastness') as indicative of love: "Tis Love creates their Melody, and all/This Waste of Music is the Voice of Love' (614–15). The two uses distinguish between the 'listening,' 'resounding' waste and the dead or soundless waste, between a desolation that responds to and partakes of a harmony, and a desolation that is dead, isolated or infinite only in the sense of death. Thus even in *Spring* the element of earth can be unexpansive, and uncreating love like uncreating silence is part of its possibilities.

Even though Latin terms like *voluptas*, *ratio*, *semina* were used by Lucretius in widely different senses,[37] Thomson's extensive procedure is unique. For example, the Latinate 'inglorious' is used as a sexual pun referring to unceremonious as well as earthy behavior, 'EVEN present, in the very Lap of Love/Inglorious laid' (*Spring*, 996–97), but in *Autumn* the term retains its original Virgilian meaning of 'humble' in an address to nature, a usage that reverses the former context:

> under closing Shades,
> Inglorious, lay me by the lowly Brook,
> And whisper to my Dreams.
>
> (1369–71)

Other Latinate terms, like 'temper'd,' 'sublim'd,' 'refin'd,' 'luxuriant,' are used in contrary or widely varied contexts, sometimes with scientific as well as classical implications to provide a specific awareness of a world capable of change, even of contradiction. Thus the technique of repeating the identical term leads to differences within formal or formalistic identity.

'Sublim'd,' for example, is used in contexts of science, nature, manners, and rhetoric. Thus contemplation of nature by sublimation, by the heat of feeling, leads to rapture: 'till at last sublim'd/To Rapture, and enthusiastic Heat,/We feel the present DEITY' (*Spring*, 900–2), though the poet also refers to the savage race as sublimed not to rapture, but to violence, 'sublim'd/To fearless Lust of Blood' (*Summer*, 912–13). The mountain is characterized as 'horrid, vast, sublime' (*Autumn*, 711) and, referring to Milton's genius, Thomson writes:

> A Genius universal as his Theme,
> Astonishing as Chaos, as the Bloom
> Of blowing Eden fair, as Heaven sublime.
>
> (*Summer*, 1569–71)

'Beauty,' however, though not a scientific term, is also used in contexts of nature, manners, morals and art. Thomson describes nature spreading 'Unbounded Beauty to the roving Eye' (*Spring*, 507). Referring to the scenes in the torrid zone, he writes: 'Great are the Scenes, with dreadful Beauty crown'd/And barbarous Wealth' (*Summer*, 643–44); he refers to the leopard as 'the Beauty of the Waste' (*Summer*, 919). Musidora's body possesses beauty and grace (*Summer*, 1323–24). The 'Village-Toast' (*Autumn*, 1226) is described 'in native Beauty rich' (*Autumn*, 1227). Shaftesbury is described as one who sought 'To touch the finer Movements of the Mind,/And with the *moral Beauty* charm the Heart' (*Summer*, 1554–

55). It should be noted that in the contexts of beauty and the sublime Thomson makes only a rough distinction, with beauty referring primarily to familial virtues and graces, though he writes of 'dreadful Beauty' and 'Unbounded Beauty.'

And a term like 'deep(s)', which has extensive use as an adjective, can, even as a noun, refer to several different elements: the ocean depths (*Spring*, 822), the depths of the earth (*Spring*, 445; *Autumn*, 1358) and the recesses of time (*Winter*, 588). Indeed, using a term like 'prospect' to mean a specific scene, then a metaphor for ships' spires, then a general term for man's situation is a characteristically Thomsonian procedure, moving from the literal and scientific datum to a religious absolute, from the finite to the infinite while acknowledging that the known is only fragmentary and the unknown an act of faith. And a term like 'shoot,' for example, means 'to kill' in one context, and 'to grow' in another.

The criticisms of Thomson's 'empty rotundities'[38] often apply to his use of general terms, such as 'Soul,' 'Grace,' 'Love,' etc., but if his conception of language is understood, then the varied contexts provide the basis for the interpretation of similar terms. I have argued that Thomson's use of periphrasis and Latinate diction are consistent with his view of limited and fragmentary experience that, in different perspectives, provides aspects of an unattainable whole. And in pointing to his absolute terms, I have argued that these always imply limits and their purpose is the corollary of perspective uses; they imply a whole and a harmony that is deceptive because it is necessarily only a part of human experience.

This practice is apparent when, in warning the youth, the narrator uses terms that have positive meanings, most of them in earlier lines from *Spring*, with negative implications; he writes of the 'kindling' grace (989), 'inticing' smile (990), 'beauteous' beams (991), all of which conceal 'Cunning, Cruelty, and Death' (992). But earlier, the 'kindling' country bursts into color (185); there is the 'inticing' bud (798), and later—in *Summer*, 739—'beauteous' beams of day. As for the nouns, Hertford's 'Grace' was 'unaffected' (6), mild man had sweet 'Smiles' (355) and the sun's 'Beams' (354) bore ten thousand delicacies.

In a description conveying implications of the sexual situation while playing upon the corruption of the initial *Spring* image, the narrator talks of the pangs of conscience even while 'in the very Lap of Love.'

EVEN present, in the very Lap of Love
Inglorious laid; while Musick flows around,
Perfumes, and Oils, and Wine, and wanton Hours;
Amid the Roses fierce Repentance rears
Her snaky Crest: a quick-returning Pang
Shoots thro' the conscious Heart; where Honour still,
And great Design, against th' oppressive Load
Of Luxury, by Fits, impatient heave.

(996–1003)

The gentle image of *Spring* in the induction is transformed into the oppressiveness of luxuriant love, and the line 'While Music wakes around, veil'd in a Shower/Of shadowing Roses' (3–4) becomes 'while Musick flows around,/Perfumes, and Oils, and Wine, and wanton Hours;/Amid the Roses fierce Repentance rears/Her snaky Crest' (997–1000). Personified *Spring* becomes the wanton in whose love the young man is entangled, and the postures—'laid' and 'rears' —no longer depict the soft assemblages of innocence and meditation.

The imagined 'musings,' the bizarre responses to the absent love, become now the comparative basis for understanding the earlier retreats into the bower. The youth reclining under the ash from the hot sun (451) or Lyttelton sitting under the oak in the shade (914–15) blends with nature, and the past and present form a continuum. The enchanted lover, however, 'by restless Musing fed' (1005), rushes to the shades or the bank not to establish a rural accord, but to burden nature with his exaggerated and inharmonious cares (1030–32). The lover sits isolated among the social band, his acts and sentences unfinished. In the proper lover the thoughts swelled—'the Swellings of the soften'd Heart,/That waken, not disturb the tranquil Mind' (465–66)—but in the uncontrolled lover such swellings are fantastic wanderings. The imaginings of the ideal lover are temporal associations that create a continuity with the past, that fortify the motionlessness of the body with the motions of the mind, that intermix thought and feeling. The lover wrapped in visions of 'unreal Bliss' (988) creates a separation between his mind (his visions, his feelings and his thoughts) and body:

borne away,
On swelling Thought, his wafted Spirit flies
To the vain Bosom of his distant Fair;
And leaves the Semblance of a Lover, fix'd

> In melancholy Site, with Head declin'd,
> And love-dejected Eyes.

(1019–24)

The dreams and visions of the lover (1004–73) reveal some of Thomson's best qualities as a narrative poet: the use of cyclical themes to show alterations of attitude, the use of inversion and versification to support meaning, the use of the four elements to draw attention to distinctions within mixtures or 'minglings' so that inflations are distinguished from expansion, constriction from limitation. The above passage typifies the conversion of man into the spiritless statuesque by inappropriate motion and dissociation. The 'wafted Spirit' flies, borne away on the 'swelling Thought,' but the 'swelling' is a fantastic one and the journey is futile. As the lover's mind flies in vain, the lover's body 'fix'd/In melancholy Site,' mimics the posture of a lover, but is only a semblance, an incomplete fragment.

It is important to note here that *Sophonisba*, performed in 1729, and probably written in 1728 (the year *Spring* was published), contains the character of a doting and enchanted lover, Masinissa. His frantic, yet pathetic, passion is defined by lines that describe the *Spring* lover's infatuation:

> and she alone
> Heard, felt, and seen, possesses every Thought,
> Fills every Sense, and pants in every Vein.

(1013–15)

Masinissa's soliloquy in Act III, i, expresses his abandonment:

> 'Tis Love, almighty Love!
> Returning on me with a stronger tide,
> Come to my breast, thou rosy-smiling god!
> Come, unconfined! Bring all thy joys along,
> All thy soft cares, and mix them copious here.
> Quick, let me fly to her; and there forget
> This tedious absence, war, ambition, noise,
> Friendship itself, the vanity of fame,
> And all but love; for love is more than all![39]

This speech poses a false view by 'mixing' soft cares when hard ways are demanded; it requests love to come 'unconfined' when Sophonisba is a prisoner and love ought to be controlled, even 'confined.' It

79

presents a speaker ready to disregard the obligations to friend and country, one who strangely mixes 'noise' and 'Friendship' together as common nuisances. And this rejection of variety for the single-minded absorption becomes the cause of Masinissa's corruption.

The love-frenzy, though described in the 1728 poem, retains its validity in 1746 as a continuing aspect of Thomson's views on the longing lover. For in his letters to Elizabeth Young in 1743, he returns to those themes of retirement, anguish and personal indulgence: 'Let me hide myself again in the Country, more distressfully in Love than ever. There I shall better enjoy my Sufferings; there, without Interruption, indulge the melancholy Pleasure of continually musing on those Charms that have undone me.'[40] In 1730 Thomson added some lines on the absence of the loved one:

> But absent, what fantastic pangs arrous'd,
> Rage in each thought, by restless musing fed,
> Chill the warm cheek, and blast the bloom of life?
>
> (1004–6) (B, [918]–[20])

In his letter of April 19, 1743, he writes: 'All that an absent Lover can feel I feel in it's most exquisite and charming Distress. . . . Every thing I see puts me in Mind of you. Here you sat; there you walked; there Love first unloosed his Tongue, and with faultering Accents could scarce articulate his Words'.[41] Thomson writes (1728): 'She alone/ Heard, felt and seen, possesses every thought,/Fills every Sense, and pants in every Vein' (1013–15). And again, 'From the Tongue/Th' unfinished Period falls' (1018–19).

These valuable letters reveal the consistency of Thomson's responses to unreciprocated love; they also reveal the validity of his rhetoric so that in his letters as in his poetry, he expresses himself in a language of spatial movement though the poetry concentrates it with resultant intensity and makes apparent changes and transformations the lover undergoes, such as that of the flight to the 'glimmering Shades, and sympathetic Glooms' (1026).

There are several points to be made here regarding the language of the poem and the letters. In the 1743 letter Thomson describes his private feelings in the language of the poem he had previously written. He writes that he is continually 'musing' on charms that have undone him; in the poem he writes of the lover fed 'by restless musing.' In his letter he writes, 'Everything I see puts me in mind of you'; in the poem he writes,

>   she alone
> Heard, felt, and seen, possesses every Thought,
> Fills every Sense, pants in every Vein.
>
>   (1013–15)

Thomson writes of the time that 'Love first unloosed his Tongue, and with faultering Accents could scarce articulate his words' and in the poem the lover cannot finish his sentence: 'From the Tongue/Th' unfinish'd Period falls.' Thomson's description of his own condition in a language similar to that of *Spring* composed in 1728 reveals his consistency of feeling and thought in these matters. But it reveals also that the language of personal feeling as well as of description was not contrived for poetry but sprang from a consistent attitude to experience. Horace E. Hamilton has shown that the Hagley Park passage that Thomson added to the 1744 edition of the poem had numerous verbal correspondences with that of his letter to Elizabeth Young dated August 29, 1743 (quoted above).[42]

The language of Thomson's letters supports the view of a world in which benevolence and reward are only occasionally and fragmentarily present. And if it is suggested that the diction of *The Seasons* is not always present in the letters, the answer is that it is made consistent with what is. Thomson can fail to use his language effectively, but effectiveness is guided by the kind of view he seeks, and this is to be sought in and through the development of the poem. When the wild lover flees to 'glimmering Shades' (1026) or throws himself upon the bank (1030–31) and 'swells the Breeze/With Sighs unceasing, and the Brook with Tears' (1031–32), the exaggerated tone of this passage is detectable by the change in diction of the one immediately following:

> Thus in soft Anguish he consumes the Day,
> Nor quits his deep Retirement, till the Moon
> Peeps thro the Chambers of the fleecy East,
> Enlighten'd by degrees, and in her Train
> Leads on the gentle Hours.
>
>   (1033–37)

The gently playful personification of the moon introduces still another variation of anguish: the false identification with the moon, and the woes of the nightingale. Thus the wounded lover becomes the

self-tortured poet in whom 'Rapture burns on Rapture, every Line/
With rising Frenzy fir'd' (1046–47). The poet who had written of
swift fancy that 'fir'd' (183) the growth of spring flowers, whose
imagination operated properly in anticipating the future, becomes
sick when his sense of art is with 'Frenzy fir'd.'

This passage describes an aspect of love, of actual, existing human
behavior which is wrong, though not unmixed with charm or pleasure.
Unreal bliss possesses an intensity, variety and excitement that can
give pleasure—though the pleasure proves morally unsatisfactory.
Yet, artistically, Thomson's description of this kind of love is more
convincing than his praise of Lyttelton and Lucinda, the model
lovers. It is clear that for Thomson the tortured lover does not possess
the harmony shared by this ideal pair; he exalts one emotion, not
shared by the beloved, at the expense of all others; thus his feelings
become a form of chaos. But Thomson was able to make the tortured
lover more sympathetic than the ideal, perhaps because he recognized
the overwhelming presence of anxiety in the world in which man-made
evil and pain exist, and their sources are in the heart of man—'let
th' aspiring Youth beware of Love' (983). Only a few can resist
temptations, although to succumb is to suppress the variety of nature,
for the lover does not see nature as it is in all its sights and sounds:
'All Nature fades extinct' (1013). He interprets nature as a form of
private responsiveness, disregarding all aspects which do not suit
his own emotions. He assumes a correspondence between himself
and nature that is non-existent and self-deceiving. The tortured lover
ignores the multiplicity of nature and so, too, the value of visions—
these become deliriums and frenzies: not fulfillment but exhaustion,
not composure but suffering. Yet Thomson seems to have shared
such feelings in his private life, for he expresses them in his letter to
Elizabeth Young, March 10, 1743:

But why should I teaze you with a Subject about which I have
Reason to suspect you are quite indifferent, my Hopes and Fears,
what will make me happy or unhappy? Tho' I could dy for you,
there is little, I am afraid, you would do for me: not even take the
least unformal Step to deliver me from this miserable Anxiety,
this unsupportable Fear of losing all that is dear and excellent to
me in the World, the Life of Life, the Soul of Happiness. What
signifies my languishing here in this tiresome Town, where I
seldom see you, and which is utterly disagreeable to me in every

Respect but that you are in it? Let me hide myself again in the Country, more distressfully in Love than ever. There I shall better enjoy my Sufferings; there, without Interruption, indulge the melancholy Pleasure of continually musing on those Charms that have undone me. You cannot deprive me of That; and if I am to be unhappy it will give a Sort of Relish to my Misfortunes that I am unhappy by the Means of you—But I will not yield to so dispirited a Thought. Surely Nature is too just and benevolent to suffer a Passion like mine to be in vain, or to Purposes of Ruin: and such it must be, if by a mutual Return you make it not the Source of Virtue and Happiness. I shall have Cause either to bless the Time I was acquainted with you, those delightful Moments when I first began to gaze upon your lovely Eyes with more than Pleasure, or else to reckon that the greatest Misfortune of my Life.[43]

Thomson knew that nature was neither benevolent nor just in this direct fashion, not only in his own life, but in his view of the oblivious lover as drowned man. The dream passage is a characteristic expression of the sense of anxiety and uneasiness, of credulousness and the loss of assurance, of the search for and need of love that can only lead to destruction.

> Just as he, credulous, his endless Cares
> Begins to lose in blind oblivious Love,
> Snatch'd from her yielded Hand, he knows not how,
> Thro Forests huge, and long untravel'd Heaths
> With Desolation brown, he wanders waste,
> In Night and Tempest wrapt; or shrinks aghast,
> Back, from the bending Precipice; or wades
> The turbid Stream below, and strives to reach
> The farther Shore; where succourless, and sad,
> She with extended Arms his Aid implores,
> But strives in vain; borne by th' outragious Flood
> To distance down, he rides the ridgy Wave,
> Or whelm'd beneath the boiling Eddy sinks.

> (1061–73)

The narrator who looked on nature and saw its variety and heard the songs of the birds did so willingly; the lover is 'Snatch'd' and sent wandering in space, fearful of the huge, menacing places. He shrinks from the precipice, unlike the shepherd who played upon the grassy brow. Plunged into the stream, he cannot reach his imploring beloved. In his earlier imaginings he was borne in thought to the 'vain Bosom' of his beloved, but now in a dream of heightened sexuality, he cannot reach her arms and sinks beneath the waves. With the submerging, the agony ends. It is an end that repeats the cycle of the deluge, that time when nature was 'deem'd, vindictive, to have chang'd her Course' (308). For now, too, the flood is 'outragious,' outraged at guilty, credulous man or at itself for becoming a river beyond its own control. Forcefully carried by the 'Flood' to distant regions ('down'), he 'rides' the 'ridgy' wave, 'as if controlling,' but is, in fact, controlled by, the flood waters, in a sexual immersion in which he is sacrificed: 'Or whelm'd' (o'erwhelmed) beneath the violently contrary currents, he is engulfed by the futility of his love.

The narrator then turns to the most dreadful abandon of the lover —jealousy. If the preceding description was at least a 'charming' agony of love—this is 'Agony unmix'd' (1078). The organizational procedure is to show increased degrees of abandon, the same situation seen now as total corrosion. It is not developed in terms of wholeness, that is, of necessary climax; rather it is another intensified version of the same situation. This presentation of instances of perspectives differs from the Wordsworthian kind by the narrator's lack of centrality. When the narrator becomes the controlling center of feeling rather than the presenter of versions of experience the discontinuity that is attributed to Thomson is removed. But it must not be seen as discontinuity at all. The poem represents, as I have instanced, a serial way of looking at experience unified lexically and imagistically within completed fragments. Thus when in an exhortation the narrator cries

> Ye fairy Prospects, then,
> Ye Beds of Roses, and ye Bowers of Joy,
> Farewel!
>
> (1080–82)

he refers to the 'gay Visions of unreal Bliss' (988), to the lovers 'Amid the Roses' (999) and 'Bowers' (1059). The gleanings of peace —those moments of identification with the tenderness of nature (1037–40)—disappear. Whereas earlier nature faded 'extinct' (1013) because the beloved seized his mind, now 'the yellow-tinging Plague/ Internal Vision taints' (1083–84).

But the narrator had previously described the lover whose dreams 'o'er the sick Imagination rise,/And in black Colours paint the mimick Scene' (1055–56). The difficulty with the later passage is that it does not arise as a consequence of the previous sickness but as another possibility—the worst—of false love. Yet its viciousness and agony do not possess the terrors sought. What critics have called Thomson's tumidity can here be observed: the use of terms already referred to without differences so that 'Fears' (1092) and 'Views' (1093) 'eat him up' (1095) with 'consuming Rage' (1096). The symptoms of inflation recur; the sudden burst of personified abstractions with formalized adjectives to intensify and summarize 'Jealousy,' to bring to a compass the varieties of behavior; the difficulty is that 'Jealousy' has not yet been conveyed or distinguished from the agonizing charms of love. Thus the climax is truncated and generalizations too hastily imposed as substitutes for detailed responses. When he erupts with two lines that specifically create a storm image (1103–4), their consistency stands out at once, whereas the other images are inconsistent in depicting self-destructive jealousy. For example, the 'poison'd Soul, malignant, sits' (1091) and the absence of 'Charms' is inconsistent with the lover who 'melts in Fondness' (1095). Thus the failure results from inconsistency of imagery, a substituted generality for needed detail, the introduction of a climax which neglects the distinctions it demands so that the method of subtle differentiations collapses into redundancy and rhetoric.

This season concludes, however, not with this evil possibility but with the love that has been evoked in the loveliness of nature, with the 'happiest of their Kind' (1113).

> 'Tis not the coarser Tie of human Laws,
> Unnatural oft, and foreign to the Mind,
> That binds their Peace, but Harmony itself,
> Attuning all their Passions into Love.
>
> (1116–19)

Here recurs the 'blending' of heart and being (1114–15), the 'boundless' (1124) confidence, the idealizing language and clichéd terms of the virtues. The closing section images the human offspring in terms of blossoms as the blossoms had imaged human life.

> Mean-time a smiling Offspring rises round,
> And mingles both their Graces. By degrees,
> The human Blossom blows; and every Day,

Soft as it rolls along, shews some new Charm,
The Father's Lustre, and the Mother's Bloom.

(1145–49)

'Blossom,' 'Bloom,' 'Charm,' 'Spirit,' 'pour,' 'breathe'—the connection of motion with position, of nature with man, of action with
growth—all these are clotted to create the climax of the season which
will conclude the cycle—from descent to ascent. Here the catalog
of joys is enumerated, but only the unagonizing joys. Thus the
listing is part of the ecstatic exclamation of ideal familial love.

The conclusion becomes, therefore, a version of idealized *Spring*:
it is the rhetorical flourish of a world that exists in limited actuality
only for the happy few, who live economically, socially and religiously
self-contained and sheltered from the jarring world. If among the
flowers the narrator spied 'yellow Autumn' (113), here he spies
immortal in mortal bliss. But to present the claims for harmony of
sight, sound, and feeling is not necessarily to make them artistically
convincing. The narrator asserts that varied nature presses on the
heart, but these pressures are not the 'Infinite Numbers, Delicacies,
Smells' (553) of flowers or the harmonies of sound. Such sights of
bliss are not, moreover, available to all men but only to those who
possess an 'elegant Sufficiency' (1161), means ample enough to
afford the ideal:[44]

> An elegant Sufficiency, Content,
> Retirement, rural Quiet, Friendship, Books,
> Ease and alternate Labour, useful Life,
> Progressive Virtue, and approving HEAVEN.
> These are the matchless Joys of virtuous Love.

(1161–65)

The interacting forces among the flowers and animals that made
vigor and growth possible do not, however, exist in this world.
'Friendship,' 'Esteem,' 'Sympathy,' (1120–22) are unlikely ideals
for the harmony that was achieved elsewhere, through moving action.
Here the 'blending' (1115) is not of difference but of sameness, and
the ideal relationship is composed of qualities isolated from rather
than realized in nature. Ideal love may have made Lyttelton a hero,
but the patron, the poet, patriot and lover was a man—in this poem—
untried and untested. This dream of ideal love, therefore, lacks the
excitement, the emotion, the trials of the dream of the fervent lover
who sinks and is overwhelmed by 'the boiling Eddy.' When the

happy lovers, untouched by human suffering, sink (in the 'social Sleep' of death), their 'gentle Spirits' rise (1175) 'To Scenes where Love and Bliss immortal reign' (1176).

The above lines (1161–65) were probably added to the poem in 1744 to flatter Lyttelton, but this was the period of Thomson's intense pursuit of and frustration with Elizabeth Young. And he wrote to her about his revision of *Spring*. Fluctuating in his personal life 'in miserable Uncertainty'[45] he wrote of an ideal that must have appeared to him a vague hope, at best.

> I am going, if I can, to put a finishing Hand to the Description of a Season now in high Song and Beauty, but to which I am dead. You alone I hear, You alone I see: all Harmony and Beauty are comprized in You. Those Parts, however, will be obliged to You which attempt a Picture of virtuous happy Love. O Miss Young! thou loveliest of thy Sex, and the most beloved! as you have taught me the Virtue, so teach me the Happiness of this best Passion! O let the Picture be Ours![46]

Thomson never married Elizabeth Young; the picture of bliss was not his own. Perhaps the divorce from his own feelings is one reason for the artistic barrenness of the idealized passages. Certainly the picture of the distraught lover was much closer to the thinking and feeling of Thomson at this time.

What this quotation implies, is that for Thomson the ideal in the poem was a necessary consequence of the dreadful actuality he was enduring. His wish of virtuous love was based on a hope doomed to be unfulfilled, and unfulfilled at the moment of composition. For the softness, the sexual and social bliss he envisioned were the characteristics of a season 'to which I am dead.' It thus becomes apparent that the ideal can, indeed, be a consequence of Thomson's knowledge of the actual; it can, in other words, function as a dream in which the pain of private experience was concealed behind the praise of a non-existent but wished-for ideal.

In concluding *Spring* the narrator addresses the happy lovers and cries, 'Oh speak the Joy!' (1157), but they remain silent, and the narrator speaks in an elegiac tone for them. He had seen and sung the subtleties, struggles, clashes and blendings of the elements as they led in ways, often not understood, to growth and variety and the lavishness of life. It was perhaps understandable that the ideal should be a retreat, an unattainable hope, a Golden Age vision of happiness, a variety only of bliss—'And nothing strikes your Eye but Sights of Bliss' (1159). In a world of anxiety, movement, frustration and struggle, this ideal is understandable (even though, as in *Spring*, it remains unconvincing), for in such a world to abandon hope is to abandon faith.

The love in *Spring* exists as a blending of nature in space, as a relation between man and woman, as an act of faith in God. As the speaker moves through space he recognizes the beauty that exists in the harmonized colors, sounds, sights. Even within each color or within each view there exists a spatially present variety. The harmony or blending is defined as responsiveness, as reciprocity, as beauty achieved in limited perfection, as the completion of limited action or being in the infinite process and extent of the universe. And love is also love of the ideal, the present and actual approximation of God's perfection attainable only in another world. The need to cling to or possess an ideal stems from secret needs, from a love that comes ultimately from the godliness in man.

Thomson's contribution to the conventional view lies in his experiment with language and syntax in presenting it. The physical presence of nature is expressed in a language that suggests hesitancy, movement or illusion of movement, and uncertainty coupled with beauty. The absence of this uncertainty, the stiffness or destructiveness of forms, convey man's fall and the loss of true love and beauty. Thomson reworked the language of Virgil and converted it into a comment upon the presence of the past—the demonstration that tradition had a place in the continuity of nature and man. The use of science, especially the Newtonian concept of extended space and Boyle's version of the transformation of elements, became a technique for blending the God-given features of the world so that, although man could discern only parts, these had a beauty and a sufficiency, albeit limited.

Thomson did not describe merely the softness of love or the sentimental ideal; even in *Spring* he dealt with men governed by pomp and pride, with the jealous lover and his plagued life. In *Summer* he was to identify the plague with the destruction of social love; in both seasons the natural causes of the destruction of love are inevitable. The individual is driven by secret, uncontrollable inner forces and the plague-poisons cause people to fear for themselves and to forget the love they bear each other. In causing man's personal and social loss of love, nature enacts its possibilities for pain beyond man's knowledge to understand. The very anxieties that lead man to discover the world can, in other contexts, lead him to dread it. Because of this, love of God is man's only salvation.

By the use of inherited and invented comic and ironic techniques, Thomson brought the idea of degree and distinction into his interpretation of nature as love. He conceived of sounds, smells, colors, flowers, trees in forms of God's plenitude and generosity, and in his poem he blended them to indicate God's love and harmony, though he also described objects and actions that did not blend, objects and actions of destruction, of pain, of hardness and death. And, in the rhythmical development of the poem, these move to a prominent place in *Summer*.

NOTES

[1] 'Thomson to David Mallet,' London, August 11, 1726, *James Thomson (1700–1748) Letters and Documents*, ed. Alan Dugald McKillop, Lawrence, 1958, p. 46.

[2] For a record of revisions, see 'Annals of the Seasons,' *Thomson's Seasons, Critical Edition*, ed. Otto Zippel, *Palaestra LXVI*, Berlin, 1908, pp. x–xi. References to editions earlier than 1746 are to texts quoted by Zippel: *Spring* $A = 1728$, $B = 1730$, $C = 1744$; *Summer* $A = 1727$, $B = 1730$, $C = 1744$; *Autumn* $A = 1730$, $B = 1744$; *Winter* $A = 1726$, March, $B = 1726$, June, $C = 1730$, quarto, $D = 1730$, octavo, $E = 1744$; *Hymn* $A = 1730$, $B = 1744$. See below, Chapter IV. For a history of critical attitudes towards Thomson's revisions, see my book, *The Art of Discrimination*, London, 1964, Chap. I.

[3] Patricia M. Spacks, *The Poetry of Vision*, Cambridge, 1967, p. 18, declares: '*Unconfined, unbinding, relenting, loosened, unrefusing:* such modifiers insist on the antithesis, heighten the impression of spring's vitality by reminding one of winter's confinement.'

[4] William Wordsworth, 'Essay Supplementary to Preface' (1815), *Wordsworth's Literary Criticism*, ed. Nowell C. Smith, London, 1905, p. 185.

[5] M. H. Abrams, 'The Correspondent Breeze: A Romantic Metaphor, *English Romantic Poets*, ed. M. H. Abrams, New York, 1960, pp. 37–38.

[6] Geoffrey Tillotson, *Augustan Studies*, London, 1961, pp. 33–39.

[7] Chester Chapin, *Personification in Eighteenth Century Poetry*, New York, 1955; for a listing of other critics who have written on this subject, see *Discrimination*, p. 359, fn. 2.

[8] Spacks, p. 16.

[9] James Thomson, *The Castle of Indolence and Other Poems*, ed. Alan Dugald McKillop, Lawrence, 1961, p. 154.

[10] James Thomson, *Works*, ed. P. Murdoch, 1762, II, 117.

[11] McKillop, *Castle*, p. 20.

For the merging of vernacular syntax and classical terminology, see John Arthos, *The Language of Natural Description*, Ann Arbor, 1949, p. 37.

[12] 'Nutriment' occurs in *Paradise Lost*, VII, 408, and as 'Nutriments' in V, 496. See Tillotson, *Augustan Studies, passim*. D. Nicol Smith, *Some Observations on Eighteenth Century Poetry*, Oxford, pp. 61–65, explains Thomson's Latinate diction by his Scottish background.

[13] C. V. Deane, *Aspects of Eighteenth Century Nature Poetry*, Oxford, 1935, p. 7.

[14] Alan Dugald McKillop, *The Background of Thomson's 'Seasons,'* Minneapolis, 1942, p. 105.

[15] In 'The Argument' to the 1730 *Spring* (and subsequent editions) Thomson declares, 'This Season is described as it affects the various Parts of Nature, ascending from the lower to the higher; and mixed with Digressions arising from the Subject,' Zippel, p. 7.

[16] I owe this expression to John Espey.

[17] Reuben A. Brower, 'Form and Defect of Form in Eighteenth-Century Poetry: A Memorandum,' *CE*, xxix (April 1968), 539; Deane, p. 46.

[18] Thomson, *Castle*, p. 72.

[19] *Ibid.*, p. 82.

[20] See, e.g., *Letters*, pp. 64, 132.

[21] *Letters*, p. 163. Thomson, writing to Lyttelton, July 14, 1743, of his forthcoming visit, includes a line that seems to be the basis for lines 464–66: 'The Mind will not only be soothed into Peace, but enlivened into Harmony.'

[22] After the 'Rill, scarce oozing thro the Grass,/Of Growth luxuriant . . . ' Thomson had written (1728):

> Turgent, in every Pore
> The Gummy Moisture shines, new Lustre lends,
> And feeds the Spirit that diffusive round
> Refreshes all the Dale.

(*A*, 453–56)

Although here the language applies to sexual acts in nature, as a technique it reveals the use of a single particular—a sudden close look at an object—followed by a more general or distant view.

[23] Reuben A. Brower, *The Fields of Light*, New York, 1962, p. 37.

[24] *Ibid.*, p. 41.

[25] Marjorie H. Nicolson, *Newton Demands the Muse*, Princeton, 1946, pp. 22-27, 43 ff. See also McKillop, *Castle*, p. 140: 'In the poet's best and most characteristic work the treatment of special effects and laws is drawn into a larger movement.'

[26] McKillop, *Letters*, p. 103.

[27] Nicolson, p. 114.

[28] *Ibid.*, p. 111.

[29] See 'The Argument' quoted in fn. 15.

[30] *Thomson's Seasons*, ed. E. E. Morris, *British India Classics*, London, 1869, II, fn. 452, 140. Geoffrey Tillotson, *Augustan Studies*, p. 37 writes: '*Smiling*, a common word in eighteenth-century pastoral, may be considered the equivalent of *laetus*, which Virgil constantly applied to crops.'

[31] Tillotson, *Augustan Studies*, p. 37.

[32] McKillop, *Letters*, p. 166.

[33] Albert Gerard writes that in Coleridge's poem 'the relationship between nature and spirit might be one not of similitude but rather of identity, the forms of nature being one with the spiritual energy that gives them life,' 'Counterfeiting Identity: 'The Eolian Harp and the Growth of Coleridge's Mind,' *JEGP*, LX (1961), 417.

[34] By neglecting to examine the procedure of contrary contexts, Josephine Miles does not quite do justice to Thomson's key words. See Josephine Miles, *Eras and Modes in English Poetry*, Berkeley and Los Angeles, 1964, p. 270.

[35] Isabel MacCaffrey, *Paradise Lost as Myth*, Cambridge, 1959, p. 106. For a comment on 'waste' in *The Seasons* see Spacks, *Vision*, p. 42.

[36] For use of Augustan repetition as significant poetic and prose technique, see William Empson, 'Wit in the Essay on Criticism,' *The Structure of Complex Words*, 1951, pp. 84–100, and Martin C. Battestin, 'Fielding's Definition of Wisdom: Some Functions of Ambiguity and Emblem in *Tom Jones*,' *ELH*, 35 (1968), 190.

[37] For 'Voluptas' see B. Farrington, 'Form and Purpose in the *De Return Natura*,' *Lucretius*, ed. D. R. Dudley, London, 1965, pp. 24–5.

[38] Deane, p. 52.

[39] *Works*, II, 43.

[40] *Letters*, p. 148.

[41] *Letters*, pp. 150–51.

[42] Horace E. Hamilton, 'James Thomson Recollects Hagley Park,' *MLN*, LXII (1947), 194–97.

[43] *Letters*, p. 148.

[44] In a letter to his friend, John Sargeant (July 24, 1744), Thomson wrote: 'It pleases me my Friend, to think that you in the Height of Life—and the right Taste is yours—will be able, with an elegant Sufficiency, to enjoy these best Pleasures of the retired philosophical social Life.'

In his later letter to William Paterson (April, 1748), Thomson lowered the ideal of 'elegant Sufficiency' for himself and named as his model the modest Corycius: 'May your Health, which never failed you yet, still continue; till you have scraped together enough to return home, and live in some snug Corner, as happy as the CORYCIUS senex in Virgil's 4th Georgic, whom I recommend both to you and myself as a [*the* deleted] perfect Model of the truest happy Life.'

[45] *Ibid.*, p. 154.

[46] *Ibid.*, pp. 154–55.

II

SUMMER
THE SCORCHING GLORY

i. Unity and Unities

The Seasons when it was published in 1730 had sources in diverse
genres, but it could be fitted to these only by considerable distortion.
Its sources were the *Georgics, Job, De Rerum Natura,* and Milton's
L'Allegro, Il Penseroso and *Paradise Lost.* It was not, however, either
a Georgic or a scientific-didactic poem, and, although it had features
of the epic, it was not an epic in any traditional sense. 'In some re-
spects,' writes T. J. B. Spencer, 'it was a *satura,* a medley of themes:
didactic, narrative, descriptive, satirical, lyrical. But it was certainly
pervaded by the exciting Newtonian science which seemed to be
demonstrating that the physical universe was based on the mathematical laws.'[1]

Mr. Spencer is correct in recognizing that the structure of *The
Seasons* from 1730 to 1746 possessed the fragmentary features of
Augustan satire; the guide to the interpretation of this structure lies
in the conversion that Thomson brings to the form. Many Augustan
satires, such as *Absalom and Achitophel* and Pope's Horatian imitations, take their narrative order from Biblical or classical works,
imposing these upon a contemporary event. Thomson, however, made
the seasonal cycle the basis of his poem. This provided a determined
order of sections with the *Hymn* becoming a song of adoration. The
order of composition associatively related *Winter* with *Summer,* the
extreme seasons, and *Spring* with *Autumn,* the tempered ones. By
placing them chronologically in *The Seasons,* Thomson retained the
similarities and differences but in an alternating and cyclical order
that supported the literary conception; he thus achieved a chronolog-

ical progress that possessed an associative pattern which was achronological.

By working from a literal as well as an associative unity, Thomson freely added Georgic and satiric literary features to this new kind of poem. This he did by evolving a special sensibility that controlled and directed the poem as a whole: the view of man and nature as independent, capable of transformation in time and space but embraced within a larger harmony that God created. Within this unifying stylistic procedure, each season had its own identity and its own kind of unity, because, since the fall, each was a fragment of a once-perfect world, whose total unity was perceivable only by God.

R. S. Crane,[2] in discussing works of discursive or 'philosophical' poetry, such as the *Essay on Man* and *The Seasons*, the forms of which determine the selection and expression of ideas and values, finds in *The Seasons* a predominantly rhetorical end—'that of evoking the sentiments of benevolence and deistic piety in a world which, for all its shortcomings, is yet governed by an Almighty Hand.' But in *The Seasons* benevolence and piety (not 'deistic piety') are merely parts of the 'end' rather than the 'end' itself, though Crane's statement is in the right direction. The 'end' is to persuade man to trust in God's wisdom and love that are only fragmentarily perceptible in the beauty, sublimity, danger and destruction of the known past and present but will be fully perceptible to the good in the future world. Thomson evokes sentiments of beauty, sublimity, benevolence, fear, anxiety and belief in order to urge upon good men that necessary endurance which will enable them to sustain themselves in this world and to lead them to the pleasures of the next. Because Thomson's ends are more broadly conceived than Crane assumes, his 'subsuming form' is governed by concepts of organization that relate actual to metaphoric descriptions, chaos to harmony, change to the ideal. The practical working out of these concepts is to be found in techniques of the completed fragment, description followed by contemplation, the combination of local and prospect views within each season, and with a variety of other techniques among the seasons as a whole.

Spring is the season of love, *Summer* of power, *Autumn* of fulfillment, *Winter* of deformity, but each also contains its own opposite— *Spring* the frustration of love, *Summer* the violence of power, *Autumn* barrenness following fulfillment, *Winter* the preservation of nature despite deformity. This order is, of course, not necessarily related to the actual seasonal order, but in developing his literary idiom Thomson expresses these changes in an artistically ordered fashion: the love of *Spring* is expansive and familial, but in *Summer* the heat of love is transposed into the light of wisdom and beauty as well as into the heat of power and destruction. Such light and heat become in *Autumn* transformed into fulfillment, satisfaction, and subsequent barrenness or desolation. In *Winter* desolation appears, sometimes deceptively, sometimes actually beautiful or destructive, but buried beneath the strange forms there is detectable the renewal of life. It is well-known, of course, that human beings have no special seasons for love-making or killing, and I do not wish to deny that sexual descriptions appear in *Summer* (as they do in *Autumn* and *Winter*) whether of the 'ruddy Maid' (355) or Musidora (1288–1370). But these are subordinated to the emphasis of this season on the power of heat and light rather than, for example, to *Spring*'s emphasis on love dominated by softness or innocence.

This order, then, is a literary one and Thomson describes it by placing his perception against his idealization of reality, always recognizing God's controlling and all-powerful hand and praising Him by meditation and hymns. Thus the ideal and the poet's awe of God's power, wisdom and benevolence are repeated in each season, providing a thematic unity to the poem. The unity of the whole, then, is chronologically progressive, and the recurrence of this progression is cyclical. Only when the poet refers to the immortal world does the movement become infinitely progressive. The function of repetition of storms, sunrises, praises of Britain, of particular words and phrases is to create a unity that operates by degree. The reader is made to perceive that the context of terms and events is sufficient to change their meanings, and in this way each season becomes defined within the whole. This kind of unity, in which the reader examines the same terms in different contexts, can appropriately be conceived as spatial, and the meanings of the terms are altered by the contexts in which they are found.

Thomson's devices for linking the seasons are extensive and deliberate, including images, scenes and the conscious altering of terms to develop the transition. *Summer* is a good instance to use as an example of Thomson's organization because its sun sheds both light and heat, illumination and destruction. The light imagery, the sun's brightness and heat, is connected with *Winter* in terms of the shininess of the snow, which, though bright, is icy-cold. Thus similar appearances within these seasons have contrary effects. So, too, the heat and light of love and harmony of *Spring* become a totally different kind of heat and light in *Summer*. Indeed, 'Spring'—'averts her blushful Face' (7) from masculine 'Summer' whose ardor and heat are exercised not as sexual love but as 'Dominion' (8), as power. The qualities of *Summer* in turn become, paradoxically, connected with light and shadows, the clashing 'Effulgence' and temperateness of *Autumn*. Each season becomes part of the similarity within dissimilarity characteristic of Augustan theories of wit and tradition.

The speaker-commentator, the man of many muses or roles, is another unifying device. For all his changes, his values remain consistent; recognizing the tendencies in man for good and evil, he urges belief in God's wisdom and benevolence, and he advocates the virtues of blending, harmony, peace, commerce and patriotism. As lover of nature, as innocent, as observer of nature and defender of public morality he ridicules or attacks irresponsible, vicious, or falsely proud acts in men, resigns himself to the pain and suffering inflicted by violent nature (whether of elements, beasts or fish) and praises the wonders of the visible and invisible worlds. Socially, the speaker observes the rural workers, the squires and the lords of the manor; moving freely among the different groups, he himself becomes a model of mobility from one class to another. The observer of the poor reapers is also the friend of Lyttelton, so that he is both a defender of class distinctions and a successful social climber. The narrator, by his class anonymity, provides a possibility of moving unnoticed among all classes. Implicitly, the process of nature's changes (the transformation of an element—for example, water becoming clouds) is a model for naturalizing social change. By insisting on careful attention to distinctions, the poet blends with each and demonstrates fitness for the levels to which he attributes the highest virtues.

The establishment of continuity between *Spring* and *Summer* in the 1744 edition based on this double view and on the shift from sexual imagery to that of power and force can be studied in the lexical changes applicable to both seasons. In 1744, Thomson changed 'illustrious' (*Spring*, 190) to 'effulgent' and in the very opening of *Summer*, he changed 'illustrious' (*A*, 2) to 'refulgent' (2), added 'Effulgence of thy Blaze' (103), made it consistent with 'Effulgent' (135) and removed 'the misty Eyes refulge' (*A*, 364) as inconsistent. At the same time, he also added the image 'Bright . . . effulg'd' (1519) to the catalog of heroes.

Thomson changed his initial personification of "Summer" (1727) to effect a clearer distinction between the two seasons:

> FROM Southern Climes, where unremitting Day
> Burns over Head, illustrious Summer comes.
>
> (*A*, 1–2)

> FROM brightening Fields of Ether fair disclos'd,
> Child of the Sun, refulgent SUMMER comes.
>
> (1–2, 1746)

The original had 'illustrious Summer' arriving from the burning daylight of 'Southern Climes'; the revision, correcting the science as well as the poetry, interprets one kind of nature (ether) in terms of another (fields): 'Summer' is a 'Child' of the sun, thus possessing its contradictory qualities of light and heat, and it is 'refulgent' ('burning' and 'shining') rather than 'illustrious,' merely 'shining.' Personified summer is attended 'by the sultry *Hours*' (4) and 'ever-fanning *Breezes*' (5), and 'Spring' in a sexual image turns away from 'Summer's' ardor and leaves to his 'hot Dominion' the 'all-smiling' earth and skies. Though 'all-smiling' also refers to *Spring*, in a typical seasonal epithet, the poem makes clear that the 'smiling' anticipation of earth and skies is a mistake once the heat begins to scorch and dominion becomes tyranny: 'ALL-CONQUERING Heat, oh intermit thy Wrath!' (451).

The major additions to *Summer* (1744), when compared with those of *Spring* (1744), provide a method for studying the unity of the poem. The first of the major additions to *Summer* is the passage about the sun's power in the 'vegetable World' (112–39). Despite the incredible awkwardness of the first sentence (112–16), the insertion connected *Spring* with *Summer* by the rotation of the sun and the seasons. What Thomson did, therefore, was to take lines from the *Spring* shower (143–91) and echo them here:

> 'Tis silence all,
> And pleasing Expectation. Herds and Flocks
> Drop the dry Sprig, and mute-imploring eye
> The falling Verdure. Hush'd in short Suspense,
> The plumy People streak their Wings with Oil,
> To throw the lucid Moisture trickling off;

And wait th' approaching Sign to strike, at once,
Into the general Choir.

(Spring, 161–68)

Mean-time th' expecting Nations, circled gay
With all the various Tribes of foodful Earth,
Implore thy Bounty, or send grateful up
A common Hymn:

(Summer, 117–20)

But who can hold the Shade, while Heaven descends
In Universal Bounty, shedding Herbs,
And Fruits, and Flowers, on Nature's ample Lap?
Swift Fancy fir'd anticipates their Growth;
And, while the milky Nutriment distills,
Beholds the kindling Country colour round.

(Spring, 180–85)

These, in successive Turn, with lavish Hand,
Shower every Beauty, every Fragrance shower,
Herbs, Flowers, and Fruits; till, kindling at thy Touch,
From Land to Land is flush'd the vernal Year.

(Summer, 126–29)

The 'expecting Nations' of *Summer* are the people of various countries and the 'Tribes of foodful Earth' the incipient plants, so that man and plants are here referred to as part of a common image; in *Spring* the 'Herds and Flocks' did the 'imploring' (163) and the birds were the 'plumy People' (165). In *Summer*, the personified sun is seen as moving from 'Land to Land' so that not fertility and mixture are stressed, but 'mighty Power' (134). And the poet descends beneath the earth's surface to the power of light in its bowels.

From the 1730 edition of *Spring*, Thomson transferred lines 136–68 to *Summer*, 1744 (287–317), with minor deletions and revisions. In doing so he achieved a subtle distinction between the animating power of the sun which sets in motion the hum of insects not 'undelightful' (282) and the animating power of God that concealed the stunning sight and sounds of nature's multitudinous life. Here it is followed by a Job-like imperative: 'LET no presuming impious Railer tax/CREATIVE WISDOM' (318–19). In *Spring* it was followed by a change of subject.

97

This transposition results in a unity characteristic of Virgil's *Georgics* which Aubrey Williams describes in his discussion of *Windsor Forest*:

> In the *Georgics* Virgil arranges a number of scenes in vivid counterpoint, concluding Georgic I, for example, with a picture of war and chaos, and Georgic II with an account of the simple, yet profound, pleasures of rural peace. Pope adopts the same procedure [in *Windsor Forest*], and also follows Virgil's art of transferring 'significant details from one context to its opposite for the sake of contrast.'* For the bleak violence of the hunting scenes in the New Forest he therefore fashions a companion piece, the more happy hunting scenes in Windsor Forest which immediately follow. The contexts are different, but the activities—those of the hunt and the chase—are the same, and the similarities are as important as the differences.[3]

Thomson's purpose in transposing passages, however, is not for contrast but to show their relevance to the particular season and the surrounding passages.

Of the parallel passages added to the two seasons, there are the games (fishing in *Spring*, sheep-shearing and swimming in *Summer*) and the personal allusions (descriptions of Amanda, of Lyttelton and Hagley Park in *Spring*, of Elizabeth Stanley, of Richmond in *Summer*). Games can convey the attitudes of the ritualistic character of the society; they can conceal in play what might be censored in reality, and they can be used to give contrasting tones. In their playful way, the games counterpoint the stuffiness of the voice of public morality. Thomson gives himself a greater range of interpretation and incident, an indirect way of commenting upon his own moral declamation, just as Pope in the game of ombre in *The Rape of the Lock* makes an ironic commentary upon social attitudes.

The games of *Spring* and *Summer* are mock-heroic, idyllic, playfully ironic, or, as in the hunting scenes, vicious and destructive. The fisherman at his sport in *Spring* is treated with playful irony. And *Summer*'s fire is expressed in the paradoxical impurity of Musidora's invitation to love. The ritual of sheep-shearing idealizes the relation of man to animal by the benevolent use of power, although misunderstood by the sheep. The flies sail happily down the stream to be snatched suddenly by the trout or salmon, and the nightingale is caged or killed for sport.

* E. K. Rand, *The Magical Art of Virgil*, 1931, p. 218.

Thomson added to the personal elements of the poem in 1744: he had written some heroic couplets, 'Epitaph on Miss Elizabeth Stanley' (whom he knew), probably soon after she died in 1738, praising the young woman on her escape from physical pain but not quite bringing off the ironic condition of her 'hapless mother':

> To join thee there, here with thy dust repose,
> Is all the hope thy hapless mother knows.
>
> ('Epitaph on Miss Elizabeth Stanley')

The inclusion of Elizabeth Stanley in the revised *Summer* probably represents an attempt to improve upon an inadequate poem by weaving a revision into his most successful work. This compositional practice Thomson followed throughout *The Seasons*, making the poem an artistic as well as personal history. But the organizing principle governing the placement of the passage at this point is again to relate the actual to the ideal and to connect this elegy with a contrasting one in *Winter* (see Hammond). Elizabeth Stanley is now 'Beneath the heavenly Beam of brighter Suns,/Thro endless Ages, into higher Powers' (583–84). The poet hears the voice of 'holy Calm' (550) explain the toil necessary to achieve calmness. The immortalized ideal is placed against the naturalistic or observational view that describes the suffering involved in its achievement. Organizationally the passage is made part of a cycle of suffering and redemption by placing Elizabeth Stanley within the context of turbulent life that subsides into calmness.

The idealizing of his friends and their estates explains, too, the 1744 additions of Lord Lyttelton and Hagley Park to *Spring* (904–62) and the sight from Richmond to *Summer* (1406–16). Hagley Park is described in detail and it is placed in *Spring* because its gardens are the embodiment of rural peace, social and personal love. From it, the fertility of villages ('embosomed soft in Trees') and the smoking ascension of the towns and the whole landscape appear as part of heaven. The view from Richmond sweeps the 'boundless Landskip' (1409) and turns 'To where the silver Thames first rural grows' (1416); both are sights of 'radiant Summer' (1407), the sublime 'glorious View' (1414), the peaceful embowering 'Shades' (1421) that gradually lead the poet to Clermont's 'Height' (1429) and Esher's 'Groves' (1430).

It is worth noting, too, the way in which Thomson added to *Spring* (950–62) (see above, Chap. I, pp. 68, 71–2) and revised in *Summer* the concluding prospect views.

HEAVENS! what a goodly Prospect spreads around,
Of Hills, and Dales, and Woods, and Lawns, and Spires,
And glittering Towns, and gilded Streams, till all
The stretching Landskip into Smoke decays!
Happy BRITTANIA! where the QUEEN OF ARTS,
Inspiring Vigor, LIBERTY abroad
Walks, unconfin'd, even to thy farthest Cotts,
And scatters Plenty with unsparing Hand.

(*Summer*, 1438–45)

Both these views are 'prospects'[4] and so identified by the poet;
that is, they are extensive views of a series of objects, from a height, that
fan out from the object immediately in front of the viewer to infinity.
In *Spring* the narrator is describing Lord Lyttelton's walk; in *Summer*
the narrator himself bursts into an exclamation. In *Spring* the prospect
leads from the hospitable Hagley Hall to the gentle past and peaceful
heaven; in *Summer* the prospect moves from the hills and dales, to
the 'glittering' effects of the sun upon town and stream, to the effects
of burning ('Smoke') and this 'Smoke' is advantageous because it
is indicative of England's power.

The similar passages, therefore, are made organizationally relevant
to each of the seasons. In *Spring* the view stresses extent, simultaneity,
plenitude, features that signify love by blending and expansiveness.
In *Summer* the natural view is interpreted in terms of light (glitter,
gild) that transforms the streams (water) and the 'Landskip' (earth)
connecting these with British power, with economic and political
plenty, with productivity. *Spring* stresses the harmony of family
and nature, of past and present. *Summer* stresses the patriotism
and power stemming from this view. Thus the two instances, while
differently applied, become part of the general method used by
Thomson to connect the bounded with the unbounded, to relate
the literal to the ideal, to associate the naturalistic view with its
transformation to a political, economic and religious conception.

The political implications in Thomson's spatial views are connected also with the method of describing the view. To rise and
see the country and city becomes a method for blending nature
with patriotism and the heavens. By mounting a high place[5] the speaker
sees comprehensively, and since such height is on the aristocratic
estate, the view is related to the true aristocratic ideal of embracing all
of Britain. The linguistic technique is to select single nouns of height

and depth and connect these with large wholes ('Towns' and 'Streams') by images of motion—spreading and stretching. This describes a merging of the particular into the infinite or into non-static forms ('Smoke' or 'Clouds') that enact the transformation seen from the estate. The view sees all as a harmony and becomes the ideal perspective.

Thomson's method for relating prospects to other aspects of life than the merely visual reveals what has already been made clear in *Spring*: his poetry is not a poetry of sight but of space in which sight is only one of the means of perception, a poetry that sings of the sounds, the touch, smell, taste of nature. He describes the unseen and indicates an awareness of the unheard, and he agrees with Dodington, to whom he writes from Paris in 1730 that

> there are scarce any travellers to be met with, who have given a *landscape* of the countries through which they have travelled; that have seen (as you express it) with the *Muse*'s eye; though that is the first thing that strikes me, and what all readers and travellers in the first place demand.[6]

Seeing through any eye, let alone the '*Muse*'s eye,' was one of the most perplexing problems for eighteenth-century philosophers. Although Locke accepted sight as the primary sense, he was unsure about how it operated. The issue, formulated in Locke's *Essay*, has come to be known as Molyneux's problem. Molyneux wrote to Locke asking whether a blind man who recognized a cube by feeling it, would, if given his sight, recognize it merely by looking at it. Locke did not think so, and this enquiry implied that sight, in certain instances, was no sufficient substitute for touch, was not primary in the experience of a man who learned of objects by feeling them. This problem formed the basis for Berkeley's claim that only color was given in sight—all other aspects of sight had to be corrected by the judgment as a result of touch, smell and the other sense experiences.[7] Moreover, in sight, the experience of the viewer corrected what impressions he had of seeing merely one side of an object. The relations between judgment and sight, between other senses and sight, between actually experiencing distance and sight—all these formed a basis for the perception of the visible.

Thomson sees nature as blending or clashing, but in both instances he seeks to describe nature's transformation in space. This awareness of matter in motion made it possible for him to appeal to a variety of the senses and to see this movement within a larger fixed harmony, while recognizing that in the observable world fixity can become rigidity, stiffness and death. But the spatial world of *The Seasons* is not one-sided; the observer sees, feels and hears, but he is also seen, felt and heard. The speaker sees nature at times precisely, at times generally, but he is also snatched up by nature, his 'eye' wandering and compelled by the environment. This concept of perception involves not merely a speaker who sees and is compelled to see, but an omniscient and omnipresent poet who can describe this reciprocal relation. In *Spring* I noted the reciprocity of nature in affecting man, and I have pointed out that in *Summer* God's secret-working hand penetrates to nature and thus causes it to grow and flourish or to disrupt into chaos.

One of the ways to approach the poet's perception in this poem, and that of his numerous speakers, is to examine the metonymical and other uses of the term 'Eye' which occurs 103 times in the poem ('eye'—81; 'Eyes'—19; 'eyed'—3). The seasonal breakdown is *Spring*—25, *Summer*—41, *Autumn*—23, *Winter*—14. These computations refer to 'Eye' as substantive and to 'eye' and 'eyes' as verbs and to 'eyed' as an adjective. The term 'eye' as a metonym for man's emotional response can be 'the cherish'd Eye' (*Spring*, 89) or the 'raptur'd Eye' (*Spring*, 111), the 'fix'd serious Eye' (*Summer*, 17), the 'fresh-expanded Eye' (*Summer*, 477); the mariner can look at the setting sun with a 'mournful Eye' (*Summer*, 948) or the plague-stricken sailor has a 'beamless Eye' (*Summer*, 1045). There can be 'Imagination's vivid Eye' (*Spring*, 459), 'Fancy's Eye' (*Summer*, 1155), the 'Mind's creative Eye' (*Autumn*, 1016), the man 'of philosophic Eye' (*Autumn*, 1133). Providence is called 'that ever-waking Eye' (*Winter*, 1020) and there is 'Reason's Eye' (*Winter*, 1049). Thomson, writes Martin Price, 'creates phrases to distinguish the eye that can look at eternity from the merely sensual eye.'[8] The eye of man is used to embrace the imagination, the reason, the sight and feelings, so that in the Thomsonian sensibility the primary sense becomes transformed into an imaginative power, a reasoning power, and is used to describe Providence as well as man and animals. This 'Eye' examination supports the assumption that Thomson is not writing descriptive verse, but dealing with the meaning of experience, touching upon its different aspects in the different seasons in order to reveal the beauty and power of God. Thus the incorporation of personal detail, of fragments from his life, can become absorbed into what appears, but only appears, to be 'objective' description.

Thomson added to *Spring* and to *Summer* passages that referred to his beloved Amanda. In *Spring* the inclusion was understandably related to sexual elements, but in *Summer* it reveals the powerlessness of the speaker to interest Amanda:

> And thou, AMANDA, come, Pride of my Song!
> Form'd by the Graces, Loveliness itself!
> Come with those downcast Eyes, sedate and sweet,
> Those Looks demure, that deeply pierce the Soul;
>
> (*Spring*, 483–86)

And to *Summer* he added:

> Which Way, AMANDA, shall we bend our Course?
> The Choice perplexes. Wherefore should we chuse?
> All is the same with Thee. Say, shall we wind
> Along the Streams? or walk the smiling Mead?
> Or court the Forest-Glades? or wander wild
> Among the waving Harvests? or ascend,
> While radiant Summer opens all its Pride,
> Thy Hill, delightful *Shene*?
>
> (*Summer*, 1401–8)

The recurrence is, perhaps, an example of Thomson's ambiguity, for it was at this time that he was pursuing Amanda without much success, indeed, without any reply: 'Which Way, AMANDA, shall we bend our Course?' 'All is the same with Thee' is a statement of the poet's pleasure in her company, since she makes every way equally pleasant. In his poem to Amanda (1744–5) Thomson uses a phrase similar to 'All is the same with Thee' in a context of admiration without any hint of playfulness.

> It matters not, my Dearest! where we be,
> In Town or Country; 'tis the same with thee:
> Thy powerful Presence Time and Place beguiles,
> And everlasting Eden round thee smiles.[9]

It is a clue, perhaps, that Thomson chooses to describe Amanda's environment in the language he used for Amelia's: 'creative Love/ Still bade eternal Eden smile around' (*Summer*, 1193–94), since Amelia was struck by lightning, and Celadon was left with the ashes of his beloved. The passage immediately preceding begins, 'Now from the

World,/Sacred to sweet Retirement, Lovers steal' (1397–98). At any rate, it seems that this passage is placed in *Summer* because it shows the absence of heat. When lovers steal away and Thomson calls to his love to go with him and hear a lover's transport (1399), he sings not of personal love, but of love for nature and state.

Within each season are to be found clusters of consistent imagery, such as the rose-bosom-earth imagery of *Spring*, the heat-shade imagery of *Summer*, the water imagery of *Autumn*. These help control the quality and wholeness of each season and reveal its complex individuality. In addition, the imagery is usually combined with one of the elements that in turn undergoes numerous transformations. Thomson seems to support Boyle's theory of the transmutability of the four elements,[10] and in the view of changing nature, it is not surprising to discover that this aspect of contemporary science was, very likely, used to give coherence to the poem.

Thomson declared in his 'Argument' to *Summer* (1746) that '*As the Face of Nature in this Season is almost uniform, the Progress of the Poem is a Description of a Summer's Day.*' This 'Progress' involved three separate divisions, each with a retouching of the emotional tone which unifies *Summer*: the double function of fire, of the sun, to illuminate with its light and burn with its heat. Thomson's statement about chronological organization shows his own loose sense of the structure of *Summer*, but his exposition of this season's unity does it less than justice. *Summer* is divided into three parts (1746 ed.) that are confirmed by the revisions. The first part (1–634) begins and concludes with the hastening into the shade, and with an address to the 'Fancy'—the narrator's imagination:

> Now, while I taste the Sweetness of the Shade,
> While Nature lies around deep-lull'd in Noon,
> Now come, bold *Fancy*, spread a daring Flight,
> And view the Wonders of the *torrid Zone*:
> Climes unrelenting! with those Rage compar'd,
> Yon Blaze is feeble, and yon Skies are cool.
>
> (629–34)

The second part (635–1102) begins with a description of the equatorial sun and concludes with the violence of suffocating winds, hurricanes and plague.

> But 'tis enough; return, my vagrant Muse:
> A nearer Scene of Horror calls thee home.
>
> (1101–2)

The third part (1103–1805) begins with a 'Scene of Horror' in the temperate zone and concludes with a belief that if the sun sets it will rise, and if this dark state is hidden from man, the other boundless world will illuminate it.

These divisions, dominated by the light-heat implications of fire (the sun), move in Part I from the early light and enlightenment to growing heat and finally the refreshing shade; in Part II from the refreshing shade of the torrid zone to the fires of the torrid zone; in Part III from the continuing fires (lightning, storms) of the temperate zone to the night shade, the evening lights and enlightenment (limited though it is). The organization of *Summer*, therefore, controlled by the dual implications of the sun, moves through space of the temperate and torrid zones implying in each part the possibilities for good and evil, the whole season operating cyclically to reaffirm the spatial and ideological opposites that illustrate God's power through nature and man.

The unity within each season is, despite the well-defined large-scale divisions, deliberately loose; it is composed of eulogies, elegies, hymns, prospect views, narratives, historical catalogs, and descriptive scenes. Some of these, like eulogies, elegies, hymns, narratives, are genres and are complete in themselves with their own conventions. Others, like prospect views, historical catalogs, descriptions, are conventions, usually forming part of some larger unit in the poem. These larger units of organization I have called 'completed fragments,' and in Thomson's version of the Georgic poem, a season is a 'whole' in the sense that it is composed of a cluster of completed fragments joined by various devices of transition and internally joined by imagery, repetition, thematic and stylistic interplay.

The completed fragments themselves can be organic and closed (the narratives) or organic and open-ended (scenes of 'sad Presage'); they can be associative, i.e. inorganic, in numerous ways: they can develop by contrasts, by chronological succession, by related themes, by spatial succession, etc. Since I use the term 'completed fragment' to refer to widely varied units, I try to define the fragment in each instance by noting the context. Some examples of such fragments, in addition to the narratives, include the 'infusive Force of Spring in Man' in *Spring* (867–1176), the patriotic panegyric in *Summer* (1438–46) (this includes smaller fragments, such as the catalog of British heroes and the praise of British manhood and womanhood), and the discourse on 'Industry' in *Autumn* (43–150).

Since both the progressions within cycles and the seasonal cycles themselves are in constant movement or change, Thomson uses the range of events to indicate simultaneity, exactly as the prospect views, spectrum views, and his imagery indicate simultaneity by focussing upon the particular followed by the general. In this kind of cyclical unity he emphasizes the change and the simultaneity of response rather than the necessity of organic progression, though this exists within a narrative or within any other completed fragment. The enquiry whether any particular line or event is necessary to the place in which it is put is answerable in *The Seasons* by reference to its being an uncompleted or completed fragment or by relating the completed fragment to a particular season, or to the poem as a whole.

In dealing with the unity of the poem, Jean Hagstrum suggests that Thomson is making use of the picture-gallery method of 'see and respond':

> Thomson's total form had to take account of what Dr. Johnson called 'appearance subsisting all at once,' and the only manner of proceeding he could use to express such appearances was the picture-gallery method of 'see and respond.' This, as we have seen, was a form common in neoclassical England; Thomson in *The Seasons* has given this form of alternating description and reflection one of its most notable uses.[11]

I think this is a possibility, though I find the evidence for literary explanations more persuasive. This loose unity (it can also be called varied kinds of unity) is indigenous to the sensibility of the poem. In so far as *The Seasons* is a poem about nature and the nature of the world, urging the need for endurance and faith, Thomson as speaker derives his knowledge from observation, but since his observation is, by definition, limited, he must make himself accessible to new knowledge, to the reduction of his limitations. Thomson is an orthodox believer, although, as I shall point out, it is his version of orthodoxy, and he realizes that certain kinds of knowledge are inaccessible and must be taken on faith. But man's increase in available knowledge requires an organization that permits constant expansion based on new information. The dominant revisionist procedure, as critics have noted, is additive, and, indeed, the changes in the poem itself enact this conception of variation and extension.

In this respect, the poem as a whole is like a palimpsest, the depth implications supporting those of extension, for it combines Thomson's early with his late poetry. The edition of 1746 contains poetry that dates from 1726 and makes the poem a model of the conception of history it advocates, for it illustrates the artistic absorption of natural change, creating, for example, a simultaneous awareness of the joy and elegiac quality of the *Winter* season; the children at play have their life before them, whereas Hammond's life has been completed. Critics have remarked upon Pope's change from *Windsor Forest* to the conclusion of *The Dunciad*, from his stress on formal control to his mid-century bitterness, defeat and resignation. But *The Seasons* is the most extensive Augustan poem in which a method has been developed for giving substance to this phenomenon. This palimpsest quality provides a temporal or chronological depth that does not, however, lead to a symbolic view of language. The simultaneity of past and present, the poet's creation of an associative ease of transition—these provide a linguistic surface of perspectival usages. Just as the sun warms the surface of the earth and penetrates beneath the surface to impregnate gems to create a harmony, so the style of the poem is a consequence of beliefs, thoughts and feelings that control the appearance of the surface.

The palimpsest method of composition must not be confused with the practice of rewriting the same passage again and again. I use the term to imply that portions of the poem are erased or removed and others added to it so that some portions are separated in time of publication by eighteen years. And yet, this procedure does not emphasize temporal differences within the poem. These are illustrated by having the speaker refer to events of the past as well as events of the present. Thus the revisions can be interpreted as an unconscious reflection of the conscious temporal distinctions the poet makes. Moving back and forth in time to emphasize the continuity of tradition, reasserting the values of Job and Virgil in the present, the poet develops even in his method of composition a procedure that expresses his deepest beliefs.

ii. Paradoxes of Pleasure and Pain (1–634)

In *Spring* the first-person narrator is a wanderer amidst the flowers and birds. He appeals to the birds to help him participate in their 'Symphony', and he joins with the elements in singing 'th' infusive Force of Spring on Man' (868). But the singer of *Summer* does not, at first, appreciate the doubleness of this season: the illumination and parching due to the sun's power. If *Summer* is the celebration of this double power of nature, the narrator, a singer of light, does not, at first, celebrate the suffering caused by heat. He flees to the shade and depths of nature; there he finds in the midnight darkness (during the height of the day) the great sources of inspiration and the basis for accepting the heat. He accepts the unexplained sources of creative inspiration and power. And at the very beginning of *Summer* are heard two voices of this narrator: the voice of pleasant observation and the voice invoking inspiration and the sublime.

> HENCE, let me haste into the mid-wood Shade,
> Where scarce a Sun-beam wanders thro' the Gloom;
> And on the dark-green Grass, beside the Brink
> Of haunted Stream, that by the Roots of Oak
> Rolls o'er the rocky Channel, lie at large,
> And sing the Glories of the circling Year.
>   Come, *Inspiration*! from thy Hermit-Seat,
> By Mortal seldom found: may Fancy dare,
> From thy fix'd serious Eye, and raptur'd Glance
> Shot on surrounding Heaven, to steal one Look
> Creative of the Poet, every Power
> Exalting to an Ecstasy of Soul.
>
> (9–20)

The grammatical moods of the two paragraphs in this passage differ: the first is imperative, with descriptive vocabulary of nature; the second is an invocation with the sublime vocabulary of 'dare,' 'fix'd,' 'serious,' 'raptur'd,' 'Ecstasy,' concluding with a rhapsodic cry, 'every Power/Exalting to an Ecstasy of Soul' (19–20).

After a hymn to the 'ALL-PERFECT HAND' (41) in bunching the plants, the narrator of *Summer* turns to specific moments in time when 'meek-ey'd Morn' (47) rises, and is followed by 'Young Day' (52), who is then supplanted by the 'powerful King of Day' (81). The 'Young Day' passage is a valuable example of a prospect that illustrates Thomson's imagistic techniques that allude to the previous season.

> Young Day pours in apace,
> And opens all the lawny Prospect wide.
> The dripping Rock, the Mountain's misty Top
> Swell on the Sight, and brighten with the Dawn.

Blue, thro the Dusk, the smoaking Currents shine;
And from the bladed Field the fearful Hare
Limps, aukward: while along the Forest-glade
The wild Deer trip, and often turning gaze
At early Passenger. Musick awakes,
The native Voice of undissembled Joy;
And thick around the woodland Hymns arise.

(52–62)

'Young Day' is both a personification and a natural description, because it 'pours in' and 'opens' the prospect. Since the imagery is that of light, the inanimate objects—'dripping Rock' and 'misty Top'—swell (grow larger and larger) and brighten. The 'smoaking Currents'— the lakes or perhaps mist that looks like 'Currents' —shine 'Blue' (either the color of the waters or the growing light of the morning, a color that will be death-like in *Autumn*). In the subsequent waterfall (585–606) the blue water turns white as it moves from the sky-height to earth, and it sends up from the rocks on which it falls a misty cloud of foam that 'forms a ceaseless Shower' (598). These moments are characteristic Thomsonian touches, the sensitive transformations of nature. By shifting from passive to active and completing the action, the passages indicate the limited nature of completion, for the action is merely part of an infinite cycle. The shifts in color belong to the transformational techniques of active-passive, metaphoric-literal, personifications and natural description, metonymic images and metaphors that describe one natural feature in terms of another, personified periphrasis, and the organization techniques of sudden and deliberate shifts of time and place.

Spring described the union of sight and sound in the invocation where birth of beauty and of fruition blended with music:

While Music wakes around, veil'd in a Shower
Of shadowing Roses, on our Plains descend.

(3–4)

So, too, the sound of music blended with the loves of the birds:

But no sooner grows
The soft Infusion prevalent, and wide,
Than, all alive, at once their Joy o'erflows
In Musick unconfin'd.

(587–90)

109

The *Summer* day begins with the joyous sounds blending with the innocent sights, but *Summer* does not dwell on the sexual or love implications of this harmony. The sounds of *Summer* continue to resemble those of *Spring* in the sense that they are all hymns to God, songs of thankfulness—"'Tis Beauty all, and grateful Song around' (*Summer*, 1233)—but the power of God in *Summer* creates sounds of awe and terror, sights of blinding beauty of light and fear of heat and destruction. The dreadful heat imposes a silence, an awareness that music can turn into noise, into the voice of the thunder.

The powerful sunrise 'King of Day' (81–90) passage belongs with unifying and repetitive nature governing all seasons.

> BUT yonder comes the powerful King of Day,
> Rejoicing in the East. The lessening Cloud,
> The kindling Azure, and the Mountain's Brow
> Illum'd with fluid Gold, his near Approach
> Betoken glad. Lo! now apparent all,
> Aslant the dew-bright Earth, and colour'd Air,
> He looks in boundless Majesty abroad;
> And sheds the shining Day, that burnish'd plays
> On Rocks, and Hills, and Towers, and wandering Streams,
> High-gleaming from afar.

Spring (189–97) describes the sunset:

> Till, in the western Sky, the downward Sun
> Looks out, effulgent, from amid the Flush
> Of broken Clouds, gay shifting to his Beam.
> The rapid Radiance instantaneous strikes
> Th' illumin'd Mountain, thro the Forest streams,
> Shakes on the Floods, and in a yellow Mist,
> Far smoking o'er th' interminable Plain,
> In twinkling Myriads lights the dewy Gems,
> Moist, bright, and green, the Landskip laughs around.

The *Spring* passage deals with the setting of the sun; the *Summer* passage with its rising. The difference in emphasis—aside from the greater density and detail of the first—is the 'power' of the summer sun. The majestic light becomes the expression of God's authority and the sun one aspect of this authority. With this in view, the introduction of 'awful world-revolving Power' (32) that launched the planets is understandable; it is the 'Power' of God setting the world in motion.

110

The distinction between *Spring*'s expansiveness and sexuality and *Summer*'s ambiguous power of light and heat underlies the revisions, providing differences of tone despite the similarity of the descriptions. *Spring* dealt with the soft surface scenes of nature; *Summer* not only treats these as parts of a continuing change, but also deals with the 'mighty Power' of light below the surface:

> NOR to the Surface of enliven'd Earth,
> Graceful with Hills and Dales, and leafy Woods,
> Her liberal Tresses, is thy Force confin'd:
> But, to the bowel'd Cavern darting deep,
> The mineral Kinds confess thy mighty Power.

> (130–34)

The powerful force of the sun in the dark leads to a series of paradoxes that characterize this season. The 'UNFRUITFUL ROCK' (140) is 'impregn'd' (140), in 'dark Retirement' (141), and the sun forms the 'lucid' stone (141). These lead to an instance of the completed fragment, a form of the spectrum in the varied jewels, 'Collected Light, compact' (143). And this spectrum is followed by further paradoxes—the desert joys through his 'melancholy Bounds' (166), 'Rude Ruins glitter' (167)—concluding with a hymn to God, who is paradoxically, 'LIGHT HIMSELF, in uncreated Light/Invested deep' (176–77); thus the section moves from light in darkness to darkened ('uncreated') light.

Kester Svendson notes that even in *Paradise Lost* the 'sun as life-giver is a stock image of creativity' and he quotes two passages that may have served as sources for Thomson:

> [What wonder then if fields and regions here
> Breathe forth *Elixir* pure, and Rivers run
> Potable Gold, when with one virtuous touch]
> The Arch-chemic Sun is far from us remote
> Produces with Terrestrial Humor mixt
> Here in the dark so many precious things
> Of colour glorious and effect so rare [?]
> > *Paradise Lost*, III, 606–612

This is 'the mounted Sun' that

> Shot down direct his fervid Raies to warme
> Earth's inmost womb.
> > V, 301–3[12] [my additions are in parentheses]

111

Thomson uses the sun's power as an example of unexplainable but ongoing harmony in a post-Lapsarian world, whereas Milton describes the 'Sun' in a pre-Lapsarian world in which such powers are neither paradoxical nor inexplicable.

Organizationally, Thomson's passage moves from cyclical generalization to dispersed and fragmented illustrations of power, to invocation or hymn, all of which make it a completed fragment. The paradoxes here indicate the unexpected range of the sun's power, although the narrator can only do reverence to God when he has to explain the nature and origin of this power. There are paradoxes throughout the poem but they are no more than confirming instances of the different types of fragmented responses or perceptions— 'sweet Pain' (*Spring*, 253); 'cruel Care' (*Spring*, 1110); 'charming Agonies' (*Spring*, 1074); 'kind contending' (*Spring*, 599); 'savage Kind' (*Spring*, 826); 'kind Oppression' (*Summer*, 360); 'Joy-mixt Anguish' (*Summer*, 1668); 'solid Torrents' (*Summer*, 802); 'dreadful Beauty' (*Summer*, 643); 'Securely stray' (*Summer*, 772); 'discordant Joy' (*Autumn*, 425); 'gay Care' (*Autumn*, 1251); 'sordid Pleasure' (*Summer*, 1637); 'loose-revolving Fields' (*Winter* 278); 'pleasing Dread' (*Winter*, 109). The paradoxes stress the puzzling quality of the world of man and nature. In *Summer* the additional basis is the ambiguity, the unexpectedness of power. All man sees are fragmented views and isolated moments, some of which are completed and blended, others of which—like the 'sad Presage' episodes—remain open-ended, comprehensible only in terms of faith or in some sudden and overarching harmony view that expresses God's oneness.

Although Thomson's paradoxes apply to more than mere social behavior, they are confined, overwhelmingly, to the range of the beautiful, of the social world. They deal with pathetic or comic situations and illustrate the pull of Augustan conventions upon the poet, for Popean paradoxes operate overwhelmingly within this range. These clear paradoxes support the more common Thomsonian technique of using terms in a variety of contexts, including those which contradict his normal usage (oxymoron). Some are formalized conventions, but 'Securely stray' is a Miltonic allusion, and 'cruel Care' matched by 'gay Care,' 'dreadful Beauty' matched by 'pleasing Dread' and 'kind contending' and 'loose-revolving Fields' are artistically successful in communicating Thomson's vision.

The paradoxes of *Summer*'s power draw attention to a procedure extending beyond that used in *Spring*; in this sense the season may, organizationally, be seen as varying within the cycle. *Spring*'s expansiveness was everywhere present as a surface element in sight and sound, and when the sun penetrated the earth it was to release growth that became visible just as the silence preceding the storm was merely a suspension of sound and motion. In *Summer* the idea of process or transformation is based on power that is visible, but also on power beneath the surface (out of sight) and in silence (beyond sound). God is 'Invested' in 'uncreated Light' concealed from mortal or angelic eye, yet the very fact that light exists is proof of God's blessedness. And in a revision made in 1744, the poet adds unhearable sounds to the unseeable light of God. For if man grew silent in God's praise, the living objects of nature would continue to praise him.

> And yet, was every faltering Tongue of Man,
> Almighty Poet! silent in thy Praise,
> Thy matchless Works, in each exalted Line,
> And all the full, harmonic Universe,
> Would tuneful, or expressive, Thee attest,
> The Cause, the Glory, and the End of All!
>
> (*A*, 170–75)

This was revised to read:

> AND yet was every faultering Tongue of Man,
> ALMIGHTY FATHER! silent in thy Praise;
> Thy Works themselves would raise a general Voice,
> Even in the Depth of solitary Woods,
> By human Foot untrod, proclaim thy Power
> And to the Quire celestial THEE resound,
> Th' eternal Cause, Support, and End of all!
>
> (185–91)

The major difference between these two passages is the deliberately altered and elliptical sentence structure to stress power and inwardness rather than harmony, and to insist on the paradox of silent songs. It is, however, the paradox of the insect world that Thomson describes. Compare, for example, the passage about God hiding his face and the stars and planets reeling into chaos (175–84) with the passage in which man fortunately does not hear (his eyes and ears are closed by nature) the noisy multitude of insects:

> These, conceal'd
> By the kind Art of forming HEAVEN, escape
> The grosser Eye of Man: for, if the Worlds

In Worlds inclos'd should on his Senses burst,
From Cates ambrosial, and the nectar'd Bowl,
He would abhorrent turn; and in dead Night,
When Silence sleeps o'er all, be stun'd with Noise.

(311–17)

Silence becomes part of the power of God; in this silence are the immensity of noises that cannot be heard and questions that cannot be asked. It is not the silence of death, but the silence that man does not and cannot understand—in the same sense that Job had to be made to accept what he did not understand. If in *Spring* the music that is heard is the song of living love, in *Summer* the music that is unheard is the silence of God's love.

For Wordsworth, sudden silence—the cessation of noise and the sudden unaware insight—becomes an illumination of the unknown. For Thomson silence—the not hearing—is a blessing when one realizes that multitudinous sounds exist but are fortunately unheard. These silences operate not as insight but as awe. Before God's power one must remain silent in admiration and ignorance. The silences between passages, the implicit silences, suggest ironies or paradoxes beyond man's capacity to understand, but they are instances of what appear to be anxious, even agonizing moments of experience.

The paradox of a 'dead' night that can turn into a cacophony is based on the assumption that man would be unable to endure existence if he were responsive to all its variety. The 'Silence' of the night, therefore, is a form of limitation that benefits man while it subdues his pride. This interpretation reinforces the point made in *Spring* that Thomson's absolute terms, like 'Silence' or 'dead Night,' are implicitly limited generalizations. The silence that precedes the shower in *Spring* creates also a sense of admiration for and expectation of God's goodness: "Tis Silence all,/And pleasing Expectation' (161–62). The invocation to silence that concludes the poem reveals again that man cannot, in words, do justice to the power and glory of God: 'Come then, expressive Silence, muse HIS Praise' (*Hymn*, 118).

The conscious statements about or the conscious lapses into silence occur at highly emotional moments in which talk cannot express the feelings of the speaker; they are a kind of 'sacred Terror, a severe Delight' (*Summer*, 541), an admission of the poet's humility. In

Coriolanus (II, 1) Thomson named such a moment an 'emphatic silence that makes words/ Void and insipid.' In the last line of the *Hymn* he calls the moment of religious exaltation in which the poet loses himself in God, 'expressive Silence.' In contrast to these silences are the poet's efforts to capture the violences, the sounds, the feelings and the sights of the universe as in *Spring* where 'Every Copse' and 'Bush' 'are prodigal of Harmony' (598). As the poet welcomes the shades in *Summer*, 'the fresh-expanded Eye/And Ear resume their watch' (477–78). The *Summer* passage that deals with the controlled '*Breath*' (291) of heaven, leads into an imperative injunction against disbelievers. In this transition, there is a shift in mood from the conditional, a shift usually implying that it is preceded by a pregnant pause or 'emphatic silence.'

Throughout the poem one of Thomson's techniques for controlling transitions is to imply a pause or silence, resignedly or ironically accepting the puzzling changes in the world. In *Spring*, for example, the deluded lover finds his brightest aims extinguished (1111) and all 'His lively Moments running down to waste' (1112). The next stanza begins, 'BUT happy they! the happiest of their Kind!' (1113)— a transition from those governed by 'cruel Care' (1110) to those in whom hearts and fortunes 'blend' (1115). Here, the change in mood is from indicative to vocative.

In the *Summer* narrative of Celadon and Amelia the change is not of mood but of subject—from the death of a human being to a view of nature. In *Autumn* such a silence is implied in the shift from praise of industry with its enthusiastic and hortatory tone to the colloquial tone of the reapers in the field. In *Winter*, the narration of winter sports is changed in tone and person when the poet begins his description of 'infant Winter' (794). Some of the more evident of these transpositions occur when the poet describes in the third person and then speaks in his own person (as in *Summer*, 451). All of these shifts imply pauses or silences; they establish an implicit relationship with the reader based on the concept of resignation, humility, man's limitations and the irony of human existence.

The emphatic silences are implicit directions by the narrator to attend to the puzzles and paradoxes of nature. The silences make demands upon the reader to accept the apparent discontinuity or incompleteness of a finite world, to accept by an act of faith the oneness governing all fragmentation. The silences, therefore, are implicit commentaries. But there are also explicit commentaries throughout the poem, urging man to behave with benevolence and charity in all matters under his control and hymning God's praise for His power and beauty.

The narrator who asks for 'Some easy Passage, raptur'd, to translate' (195) turns to a description of the tired, sluggish and sleepy domestic animals, moving from the inactive cows and dogs to the noisy, buzzing insects. This song which is 'Not mean tho simple' (239) does not exclude organizing terms like the 'noisy Summer-race' (237), used to define the life-span of the insects, nor does it exclude such a construction as 'Ten thousand different Tribes!/People the Blaze' (249–50). The style is the illusive allusion found in *Spring*, here expressing comic and slightly ironic attitudes. The density of nature is depicted in playful personifications, and the poet interprets the snatching of the flies by the fish as the consequence of the insects' 'fatal Instinct'.

> To sunny Waters some
> By fatal Instinct fly; where on the Pool
> They, sportive, wheel; or, sailing down the Stream,
> Are snatch'd immediate by the quick-eyed Trout,
> Or darting Salmon.
>
> (250–54)

This playful style in *Summer* recalls the earlier fishing and comic barnyard scenes of *Spring*. It describes the insects waked by the 'warmer Ray' (241), the 'animating Fire' (240) that paradoxically leads some to their death, some to propagate in the summer heat, and some to 'meet their Fate' (265) inadvertently and mock-heroically in the life-giving 'milky Stream' (264) or bowl.

The 'gloomily retir'd' spider (268–80) is not very successfully burlesqued with heavily exaggerated evil terms like 'villain,' 'cunning, and fierce,' and the fly becomes a 'dreadless Wanderer' (273) ensnared in the spider's web, crying for the 'helping hospitable Hand' (280) that does not come. This cry is but one of the sounds of *Summer*; others, not undelightful, please the noon walker, or shepherd, apparently aware only of the 'ceaseless Hours' (282). In a typical conjunction, Thomson joins a Job-like attack upon the doubters of God's goodness with a statement about man's ignorance of divine power:

> And lives the Man, whose universal Eye
> Has swept at once th' unbounded Scheme of Things;

116

Mark'd their Dependance so, and firm Accord,
As with unfaultering Accent to conclude
That *This* availeth nought?

(329–33)

The passage concludes with a deliberate challenge, for the insects
are swept away in winter; and those men, who are like insects in their
aimlessness and unbelief, can also be swept away. But it is not the
practice of swarming or 'sporting' (344) that is wicked, but rather
the empty motion, the false moral 'Shine' (347), the 'Season's
Glitter' (348). For there can be a proper 'swarming,' and Chesterfield's virtues make him 'shine/At once the Guardian, Ornament,
and Joy,/Of polish'd Life' (*Winter*, 661–63). The insects swarming
over the leaves and pools and rocks, the villagers swarming over the
mead—'Now swarms the Village o'er the jovial Mead' (352)—the
flocks swarming in the brooks (371–392), all represent the consequences of *Summer*'s warmth and light, joyful activity in which
'resounds the blended Voice/Of happy Labour, Love, and social
Glee' (369–70), a parallel with the description of the insect hum:
'Resounds the living Surface of the Ground' (282).

The hay-making, sheep-shearing and the concluding praise of
Britain all belong together as a completed fragment of harmonious
exposure to the heat and light of *Summer*. For the 'ruddy Maid' (355),
the hay cut by her and all the 'rustic' folk, the sheep's wool and
Britain's 'Treasures' are happy instances of the transformation from
one kind of summer motion to another. The maid, 'Half naked,
swelling on the Sight, and all/Her kindled Graces burning o'er her
Cheek' (356–57) is not seen in the sexual softness of *Spring* but
rather in the ripeness of *Summer* that brings out her graces and her
mature sensuality. Even the infants are seen in terms that, with
playful paradox, imply pleasure in work—loaded with hay, they
'amid the kind Oppression roll' (360).

The haymakers 'spread the breathing Harvest to the Sun' (363)
just as, after the sheep are washed, these 'spread/Their swelling
Treasures to the sunny Ray' (388–89) and Britain

commands
Th' exalted Stores of every brighter Clime,
The Treasures of the Sun without his Rage.

(424–26)

Recurring to the same words in different contexts—'swelling,' 'spreading,' 'Treasures'—Thomson moves from the harmony of man, animal and harvest to that of the nation in which political behavior becomes an analogue to forms of natural behavior, and the transformation becomes the equivalent of a naturalistic blessing.

This procedure was discussed in *Spring* with reference to the contrary contexts of 'waste,' but throughout the poem there is a wide range of intervening applications of the same term, illustrating the variations between extremes, not unlike that demonstrated by Empson in Pope's use of 'wit.' Thomson had earlier in *Summer* applied the same terms to the sun and the 'mineral Kinds' (134), indicating that the force of nature invested what it touched with some of its own characteristics. Like the personifying procedure, this technique serves to reveal the presence of God's shared power in different features of the universe. Thus marble 'shines' (135) and 'burnish'd War/Gleams on the Day' (136–37). The political and military actions become part of God's blessing, and this permits Thomson patriotically and propagandistically to threaten France (428–30) in the terms that bless mankind.

But in a typical manner that causes even the patriotic praise to be qualified, the view of *Summer* as tyrannical is introduced. In *Spring* the penetrative sun caused growth and expansion:

> the penetrative Sun,
> His Force deep-darting to the dark Retreat
> Of Vegetation, sets the steaming Power
> At large,
>
> (79–82)

In *Summer*, the penetrative sun caused the gems to glow:

> to the bowel'd Cavern darting deep,
> The mineral Kinds confess thy mighty Power
>
> (133–34)

But now the sun, in its raging heat, parches the vegetation, subdues the sounds and distresses, not enlivens, nature:

> Deep to the Root
> Of Vegetation parch'd, the cleaving Fields
> And slippery Lawn an arid Hue disclose,
> Blast Fancy's Blooms, and wither even the Soul.
> Echo no more returns the cheerful Sound

Of sharpening Scythe; the Mower sinking heaps
O'er the humid Hay, with Flowers perfum'd;
And scarce a chirping Grass-hopper is heard
Thro the dumb Mead. Distressful Nature pants.

(439–47)

Thomson had earlier referred to the effect of 'tyrant Heat' (209) upon insect life that thrived on heat—'to the Sun ally'd,/From him they draw their animating Fire' (239–40)—in contrast to the domestic animals who sought the shade. In this sublime description of tyrannical power the raging noon is described as 'a dazzling Deluge' (435) and an 'undistinguish'd Blaze' (436), awesome and dangerous and uncontrolled. The allusive quality of the language can be observed in the submerged ambiguity of 'dazzling' and 'undistinguished,' the words playing against each other—showy and unshowy—and in the violence of conflicting elements used to describe the sun—a 'deluge' and a 'Blaze.' These two elements, embodied in the sun, act against the earth while stilling the motion and resounding of air. The pun on 'reigns' is again typical of Thomson's illusive allusion.

The narrator, crying out against this suffering and wrath, flees to the shades and their shelter (469–79). Just as the brook shelters the flock, the shade shelters the narrator; and at the height of noon, suffering from the heat, he plunges 'into the midnight Depth' (516) and finds himself in the haunts of meditation: 'The Scenes where antient Bards th' inspiring Breath,/Extatic, felt' (523–24).

Suffering is not in itself a basis for inspiration, but suffering that is not merely accepted, can lead, as it does in *Job*, to a sudden confrontation with nature's forces. These forces are, in a sense, sought for, because they are inquired after; they come from exploring one's limits, from acting out of curiosity and inquiry. Such action is motivated by psychological forces which are not always understood or controllable. The poet finally achieves the peace and shade he has sought; he can, then, with assurance and comfort fly in '*Fancy*' to the hottest region of the earth, because in so doing, he can securely stray, search for the source of inspiration and power in *Summer*. After he has explored the new responses, it becomes clear that the same forces operate in one zone as in another.

There is, in the temperate zone, a 'holy Calm' (550) that can be attained even while the sun scorches. The visions, the midnight haunt, the seraphic strain, these form for the narrator a search for

119

calmness and self-control, discovered by relating himself to the prophetic vision. He thus calls upon Elizabeth Stanley. And rapt in this
vision he continues to ascend the mountain—'Thus up the Mount,
in airy Vision rapt,/I stray, regardless whither' (585–86)—until the
physical scene breaks the vision and leads into the analogy with
nature's violence and consequent subsidence.

As the narrator tastes the 'Sweetness' of the shade, with the knowledge of pain and inspiration, he can confidently call upon 'bold
Fancy' (631) with a disdainful comment upon the terrors of the heat:

> Now come, bold *Fancy*, spread a daring Flight,
> And view the Wonders of the *torrid Zone*:
> Climes unrelenting! with whose Rage compar'd,
> Yon Blaze is feeble, and yon Skies are cool.
>
> (631–34)

The daring imaginative flight is an action derived from curiosity and
desire, but its point is that in the temperate zone there are, once the
imaginative dangers and pleasures are over, real dangers as well as
real pleasures. The organizing procedure, the mixture of imagination
and literal description, reflects the imagistic procedure that mingles
these on a lexical level. The narrator as singer and poet, one of 'the
tuneful Race' (611), rests like them subdued by the heat, but in a
parallel between man and nature, his 'bold *Fancy*' (632) is like the
'steep-ascending Eagle' (608) that soars

> With upward Pinions thro the Flood of Day;
> And, giving full his Bosom to the Blaze,
> Gains on the Sun.
>
> (609–11)

When he returns to the temperate zone ('return, my vagrant Muse:/
A nearer Scene of Horror calls thee Home' (1101–2)), he finds that
its horror and delight match that of the torrid zone.

In the 1727 edition, the 'vagrant' muse had been referred to as
'digressive':

> Thus far, transported by my Country's Love,
> Nobly digressive from my Theme, I've aim'd
> To sing her Praises in ambitious Verse;
> While, slightly to recount, I simply meant,
> The various Summer-Horrors, which infest
> Kingdoms that scorch below severer Suns.
>
> (*Summer*, *A*, 601–15)

But the digressions are not the 'various Summer-Horrors.' These, in 1746, are 'vagrant' only because they are not in the temperate zone, but they are not digressive, irrelevant to the theme. The praises of fervid Britain in *Summer* and again in *Autumn*, where they occur with praises of 'Industry,' are considered parts of a 'wandering Song' (*Autumn*, 150). Nevertheless, these are retained, exactly as is the explanation of the origin of springs in 1746, despite the poet's acknowledgment of its inaccuracy. Patriotism, as the poet declares, is a form of transport, of excited and noble love of country; it has, therefore, a place in *Summer* where Britain is an 'ISLAND of Bliss' (1595), the model of public power, 'the Wonder, Terror, and Delight,/ Of distant Nations' (1597–98). The praise of industry and Britain in *Autumn* explains the origins of urban as well as rural rewards, and thus has a tangential relation to the season. Nor does the poet digress when he turns to the frigid zone in *Winter* (795–96). He is moving from the pleasures and pains of the temperate zone to those more intense, to a sense of desperation, of inhuman anxiety: 'Can human Force endure/Th' assembled Mischiefs that besiege them round?' (1008–9). This intensity leads to the necessity of faith, to the belief in another and better world.

iii. Repetitions and Reversals (635–1102)

Lines 629–897 form the largest single addition to *Summer* and they counterbalance the original torrid zone section which dealt with nature's horrors. In providing, therefore, a view consistent with the first part of *Summer* and with his general view of nature, Thomson created a series of devices connecting the addition to *Summer*, and to the other three seasons. The passage begins with the rising of the sun in the royal (power) imagery of *Summer* (81–90). The temperate sun is seen in terms of gilded light and its powers—but after the obvious and hasty connection the point of view is awkwardly changed from that of the sun to that of the scenes of nature which see the sun, a characteristic but not a successful reversal:

> Great are the Scenes, with dreadful Beauty crown'd
> And barbarous Wealth, that see, each circling Year,
> *Returning Suns* and *double Seasons* pass.

> (643–45)

The scenes are 'crown'd,' though it appears that the scenes were themselves the objects of ambiguous wonder ('dreadful Beauty') and savage power ('barbarous Wealth'); it is the scenes that 'see' the sun and the *double Seasons.*' In the whole passage, this dreadful beauty moves from the earth, the waters, the winds—the elements leading back ultimately to the sun as raging fire. The retreat in the temperate zone had been an escape from heat to inspiration. The descent into the torrid zone, the ready plunge into horror, paradoxically provides cooling and refreshing relief from the heat. The speaker discovers the pleasures before he discovers the horrors of the torrid zone.

> Here, in eternal Prime,
> Unnumber'd Fruits, of keen delicious Taste
> And vital Spirit, drink amid the Cliffs,
> And burning Sands that bank the shrubby Vales,
> Redoubled Day, yet in their rugged Coats
> A friendly Juice to cool its Rage contain.
>
> (657–62)

The fruits drink 'Redoubled Day,' yet in their rugged 'Coats' they contain a juice to cool the sun's heat. This complicated image of counteraction is contrasted with the succeeding Pomona passage (663–98), a series of invocations to Pomona in which the poet asks the goddess to bear him to one or another of the huge shading fruit trees. And as he begs in the posture of the recipient, of the follower ('lead me,' 670), he finally recognizes in the 'creeping' imagery of the berries that the immensity of trees is no necessary sign of superior shade: 'Oft in humble Station dwells/Unboastful Worth, above fastidious Pomp' (683–84). And from being the recipient of the action the poet is suddenly moved to become the actor, and addressing the pineapple, he cries: 'Quick, let me strip thee of thy tufty Coat,/ Spread thy ambrosial Stores, and feast with *Jove!*' (688–89). This return to the 'rugged Coats' (661), is a counteraction image in which participation in internal pleasures becomes more rewarding than external ease. The containment image is bound together in this artistic construction with depth, distance, and immediate pleasures of taste.

The complicated view of nature's goodness in this passage includes the realization that the trees are nourished by the sun at the same time that they create a shade from the sun; the 'Cocoa's milky Bowl'

(677) is drunk by man who benefits from the Sun at the same time that he protects himself from it. Drinking from the coconut or feasting upon the pineapple, the narrator closes the distance between himself and the nature which merely shades him. He participates in its values instead of merely profiting by removing himself.

The passage (663–89) can be studied as an example of Thomson's method of incorporating extension as a process of change into the very syntax of his sentences. The address to the goddess of fruit trees begins with the speaker asking to be borne to the groves, and while the entire passage continues in this imperative the speaker wishes to be passive, to have things done to him. He signals his removal from the passive state by addressing himself to the 'Anana' (685) as witness of the conventional view that 'Oft in humble Station dwells/ Unboastful Worth, above fastidious Pomp.' In stripping the fruit and spreading out the feast, the poet moves from low station to high, from humility to power. He recognizes the nourishing value of humility and the spiritual consequences that permit him to become like a god. In *Spring* he had referred to the food grown during the Golden Age as containing 'secret Stores/Of Health, and Life, and Joy' (235–36). The sense of harmony under the tree recreates for a moment some of the pleasures of that sacred period.

The physical relationship becomes, at this point, indicative of the moral relationship, and not by a ladder of degree, but by spreading the 'ambrosial Stores' (689). The verbs that control the passage all imply physical space, and in the relation among the objects this becomes apparent. The poet notes the groves containing 'the Lemon and the piercing Lime/With the deep Orange, glowing thro the Green' (664–65). In addition to their blended colors is the complementary idea of their kind (citrus) harmonizing through extent. The orange peeps through the green to suggest a spatial depth and harmony. So, too, the poet wishes to lie reclined 'Beneath the spreading Tamarind' (667), and the tamarind 'spreads' because it is fanned by the breeze, an action of motion, width, extent. In asking that his hot limbs be 'quenched' (670)—extinguished—he refers to immersion 'Deep in the Night.' Implicit in the term of extent—physical and temporal. 'Deep'—is the idea that the black extent will extinguish the red-hot flame and that the night is not only color but atmosphere —cool—and that the coolness will subdue the heat. Here the maze, 'Embowering endless' (671) is a reference to the dense intertwining branches of the fig tree in their broad extent and density (as in

Autumn, for example, where Lavinia's 'close-embowering Woods' (208) create a sheltered and isolated and protective environment). Extent is defined in depth and height, in the very movement and sounds of the air, 'by breezy Murmurs cool'd' (673), and by the high palmettos that 'lift their graceful Shade' (675).

The idea of motion, of extent and the density of extent, is present even in the supine position of the poet:

> O stretch'd amid these Orchards of the Sun,
> Give me to drain the Cocoa's milky Bowl,
> And from the Palm to draw its freshening Wine!
> More bounteous far than all the frantic Juice
> Which *Bacchus* pours.
>
> (676–80)

Lying in leisure and indolent care, even the process of drinking is that of 'draining'—drawing off by degrees—then drawing the 'Wine' from the palm which is considered 'far' more bounteous than what Bacchus 'pours.' The antithesis between 'draining' and 'pouring' is emphasized by the 'frantic' juice which demands wild action in the heat, removal of ease and the sense of gradual extent. There are additional antitheses at work here between 'freshening' and 'frantic'—that which refreshes and that which creates frenzy—and between 'Wine' that is renewing and 'Juice' that is maddening. And the 'Low-bending' (681) twigs of the pomegranate followed by the 'creeping' (682) berries describe the fruit as actually moving through space. The 'draining' image resembles the 'trickling,' 'distilling' image of *Spring*. Both are examples of the water or liquid that refreshes and both lead to renewed life. In *Spring* the flowers are born; in *Summer* the narrator becomes active and suddenly gains new strength.

The purpose of this analysis is to contrast the function of spatial density and extent in *Spring*, where these operate sexually, with that in *Summer*, where they are connected with heat and power. In *Spring*, too, I indicated that extent could be understood in terms of developing movement from finite space to infinity, from mortality to immortality, from local views to prospect views. To convey a world in fragmented transformation, but still capable of positing the ideal, demands movement through space by the narrator, demands different views of the same space to illustrate the kinds and degrees of plenitude and density. The phenomena are pleasurable, cooling, refreshing, but they can also be harmful, unbearable, destructive. Thomson's universe is thus a 'maze'; some of its embowered places are cooling and protective, but others, like that of the maze in which Celadon and Amelia walk, look like Eden but do not protect the innocent.

Thus although the passage is followed by a prospect scene and the narrator actually moves on, the continuity is maintained by position terms, for the plains 'Lie stretch'd' as the narrator lay 'stretch'd:'

> Plains immense
> Lie stretch'd below, interminable Meads,
> And vast Savannahs.
>
> (690–92)

The narrator had just described himself as 'stretch'd amid these Orchards of the Sun' (676), and whereas at first he was himself the object shaded by nature, he reverses the position and now the fields are seen below him, suggesting the perplexing goodness of the area. This unifying device is supported by the analogical image of the plains as a 'verdant Ocean' (693) and the metonymy by which flora 'showers with sudden Hand/Exuberant Spring' (696–97). So, too, the crocodile is described in natural terms—'Like a fallen Cedar' (707).

The varying of the prospect is a method of observing the diversity of nature, and in *Summer*, the density and extent and power of nature. The technique used here for indicating extent has been mentioned in *Spring*: one aspect of nature is seen in terms of another; it belongs to the procedure of different contextual uses of the same term discussed above. If the plains are the 'verdant Ocean,' the ocean becomes a 'green Domain' (*Summer*, 859). And the 'verdant Cedar' (674), 'verdant Ocean' and 'fallen Cedar' suggest within this passage the transformatory interaction among tree, ocean and crocodile. This interrelation points to the similarity of natural features, to the idea of an exchange in nature where one object can be seen in terms of another. But it also suggests, by relating plain to ocean, how one element has features (greenness and extent) of another and that these make possible the blending of elements in the universe because these elements are capable of transformation. Thus a 'Tide' which is vanquished (857) can become a tide of beauty. The 'green Serpent' (898) can become an object of power, beauty and terror, while the valleys change their greens to browns and become green again, indicative of their shifting response to sun or rain. The 'Deluge' of *Spring* (309) can become the beautiful 'deluge' of silver moonlight in *Autumn* (1098). In *Spring* (31) 'fleecy' refers to gossamer-like clouds, in *Summer* (398) 'fleecy Stores' refers to the wool shorn from the sheep, and in *Winter* (227) 'fleecy World' refers to snow-laden clouds; so, too, the stag, the 'branching monarch of the Shades' (*Autumn*, 427) is metaphorically related to the 'branching Alps' (*Autumn*, 781), the 'branching Oronoque' (*Summer*, 834) and quite literally to the 'branching Elk' (*Winter*, 818). 'Gems' can refer to precious stones in 'Rocks rich in Gems' (*Summer*, 646), to dew-drops 'In twinkling Myriads lights the dewy Gems' (*Spring*, 196) and to the light of the glow-worm, 'the Glow-Worm lights his Gem' (*Summer*, 1683); 'ether' can refer to the upper air in 'light o'er Ether bear the shadowing Clouds' (*Spring*, 398); it can be a field in 'brightening Fields of Ether fair disclos'd' (*Summer*, 1), or the airy lightness can become 'solid Ether' in reference to the sapphire (*Summer*, 149). 'Flame' can refer to a blaze of lightning (*Summer*, 1138), to a liquid that shines, as the October ale 'Flames in the Light refulgent' (*Autumn*, 522), to a solid mineral that glows, the ruby 'with a waving Radiance inward flames' (*Summer*, 148). And, playing upon the drinking of a blaze and the 'burning' of grapes, Thomson writes that the vineyard

> drinks amid the sunny Rocks,
> From Cliff to Cliff increas'd, the heighten'd Blaze.
> Low bend the weighty Boughs. The Clusters clear,
> Half thro the Foliage run, or ardent Flame,
> Or shine transparent.
>
> (*Autumn*, 688–92)

The 'Flaming' here is distinguished from, not identical with 'shining transparent.' All these transformations create a sense of nature in process of change, with unexpected beauties even in its awesome and dreadful moments, and this procedure reflects and interacts with two other techniques of Thomson: the shift between the literal and the metaphoric in an image and the use of periphrasis dependent upon personification.

Thomson's repetitions of words like 'deluge,' 'blaze,' 'solid,' 'pour,' etc., shuttle between metaphoric and literal uses, blending the actual with the imaginary. The words shift not only from one use to another but also from one tone to another, at one time appearing serious, at another comic. Thomson usually gives such words precision of meaning, not an uncommon Augustan procedure. It is inevitable, however, for frequent repetitions to dull the freshness of words, especially if some of the repetitions are ineffective.[13] Thus, Thomson's usages that actively advance his thought and feelings have to be discriminated from those that are imprecise or neutral.

In the broadest sense, these procedures indicate the commitment to degree, to differences within similarities, to the Augustan view of a world in which knowledge is achieved by recognizing degrees of sameness and difference. They are stylistic consequences of Thomson's beliefs, thoughts and feelings. Thomson's use of periphrasis, dependent upon personification, reflects the interrelatedness of man and nature; naturalization in imagery draws together animate with inanimate nature. 'Verdant Ocean' is not merely poetic diction; it gives the plains the extent, the rolling quality, the sublimity of the ocean in order to imply transformational capabilities, the infinite potentialities of nature beyond even the poet's comprehension. The mountains can be seen as airy clouds and the waters as billowy masses. Rainy torrents can be solid, and solid masses can become fluid. If, in other words, the transformatory process can be potentially beautiful, it can also be potentially destructive.

The interrelatedness of nature is present even in these areas, where the strangeness, differentness, powerfulness, even unexpected beauty, is indicated by the language—'vast Savannahs,' 'Crocodile,' 'Behemoth'—and by allusion to earlier passages. Allusion operates, for example, in the hippopotamus eating among the hills:

> Where, as he crops his vary'd Fare, the Herds,
> In widening Circle round, forget their Food,
> And at the harmless Stranger wondering gaze.

(713–15)

For in the *Summer* dawn

>   along the Forest-glade
> The wild Deer trip, and often turning gaze
> At early Passenger.

(58–60)

The deer, curious and in the dawning light, shared the morning with early wanderers. Here the 'Behemoth'—the powerful animal who resists 'darted Steel'—is the harmless stranger gazed upon (not intending harm as the slaughtered *Autumn* birds are 'harmless, unsuspecting Harm' (985), or as the 'dreadless wanderer,' the fly that is caught in the spider's net.)

127

The passage continues, although in a new verse paragraph, with the transition 'beneath primeval Trees, that cast/Their ample Shade o'er *Niger*'s yellow Stream' (716–17). Here it is the 'primeval' nature that antedates man, that shades the elephant, 'wisest of Brutes' (721). And in an ironic commentary upon man's misuse of nature's possibilities, the elephant becomes the object of man's pride, avarice and brutality. Thus man may be seen here exploiting nature's resources by perverting them, by making the wise and gentle elephant a weapon in man's destruction of man.

And the final scene of the transformational possibilities of the torrid zone is the flight of birds over tree-covered rivers.

> Like vivid Blossoms glowing from afar,
> Thick-swarm the brighter Birds. For nature's Hand,
> That with a sportive Vanity has deck'd
> The plumy Nations, there her gayest Hues
> Profusely pours.
>
> (734–38)

The birds are imaged as 'Blossoms,' but they are also the 'plumy Nations.' That the poet uses 'Birds' as well as the periphrasis and simile indicates that at least for him there was a distinction. And one can notice this same distinction in 'gelid Race/Of Berries' (682–83) and the 'never-resting Race of Men' (726). Implied in the 'Birds' —'plumy Nations'—distinction is the belief that birds, bees and men form part of a common nature. The distinction between 'Birds' and 'plumy Nations' is governed by the blossom image and the more general distinction of all birds as 'plumy.' For the flowers apply only to the 'brighter Birds,' whereas nature 'with a sportive Vanity' has decked all birds everywhere—'plumy Nations'—but, in the torrid zone, 'there her gayest Hues/Profusely pours.' So, too, 'Philomel' is part of the blended operation of nature, for she humbles these torrid birds in song even if she does not equal them in color. This entire passage is an example of the narrator's subtlety in suggesting the interrelations between the ornithological and human world as instances of the participating involvement in the sun and shade.

> Nor envy we the gaudy Robes they lent
> Proud *Montezuma*'s Realm, whose Legions cast
> A boundless Radiance waving on the Sun,
> While Philomel is ours, while in our Shades,

Thro the soft Silence of the listening Night,
The sober-suited Songstress trills her Lay.

(741–46)

The feathers, used by Montezuma's soldiers, compete with the
light of the sun in a gaudy exercise of pride, but the nightingale
provides a peace and gentleness for the 'Shades.' The single sentence
contains the clash between 'gaudy,' 'Proud,' 'Radiance' and the
'soft Silence,' 'Shades,' 'Night' and 'sober-suited' songstress.
There is, too, the distinction between the gentleness of the speaker
and the military gaudiness of the Mexicans. But the narrator has
separated himself from the cruel acts of avarice of those who pursue
the elephant by aligning himself with the serious and mournful song
of the nightingale. The 'boundless Radiance waving on the Sun'
becomes a gaudy falsification of proper procedure, contrasting with
Autumn, for example, when the despondent flock is truly without
brightness—'With not a Brightness waving o'er their Plumes' (981)—
or with the *Spring* nightingales that are caged, their plumage dull and
'all its brightening Lustre lost' (706).

That there is to be such a distinction is seen at once in the comparison of the poet's harmless, free-ranging muse (759) and the
mocking Christians, who deck themselves in 'social Commerce'
(754) but come to rob the Africans. The poet's muse functions here as
commentator, for it is compared with the free-ranging bee, that
Augustan model of true social commerce moving without attempts at
power—a gay, useful yet 'harmless Bee' (759). And 'harmless'
recalls the powerful yet gentle behemoth and the allegedly gentle but
vicious and powerful Christian exploiters. In the temperate zone the
bee had been earlier described as the diligent carrier of fragrant balm
(*Summer*, 626–28), and in *Spring* the bees had been described as
harmonious voyagers pollinating the flowers (508–15). It is, therefore,
characteristic of Thomson's interpretation that the harmless bee (or
bee-hive) also becomes the object of destruction by vicious forces,
and this is what he describes in *Autumn* (1172–1200), comparing the
'murder' of the hive with the cities destroyed by earthquakes.

The poet's muse boldly pierces the secret bounds of 'jealous
Abyssinia' (752) and, in doing so, seems to act like the Jesuit exploiters.
But the latter come to seize wealth and kill peace, whereas the muse,
like the bee, moving through the prospect from the summit, gives
spirit and joy to the poet.

129

There on the breezy Summit, spreading fair,
For many a League; or on stupendous Rocks,
That from the Sun-redoubling Valley lift,
Cool to the middle Air, their lawny Tops;
Where Palaces, and Fanes, and Villas rise;
And Gardens smile around, and cultur'd Fields;
And Fountains gush; and careless Herds and Flocks
Securely stray; a World within itself,
Disdaining all Assault: there let me draw
Etherial Soul, there drink reviving Gales,
Profusely breathing from the spicy Groves,
And Vales of Fragrance; there at distance hear
The roaring Floods, and Cataracts ,that sweep
From disembowel'd Earth the virgin Gold;
And o'er the vary'd Landskip, restless, rove,
Fervent with Life of every fairer kind:
A Land of Wonders! which the Sun still eyes
With Ray direct, as of the lovely Realm
Inamour'd, and delighting there to dwell.

(765–83)

The conclusion returns to the sun which, like the muse, delights to dwell upon this beautiful prospect—'Fervent with hope of every fairer kind.' The direct rays of the sun become a form of love, a correspondence momentarily established among the view, the poet-viewer, and the sun as viewer—'the Sun still eyes/With Ray direct.' A. D. McKillop remarks that 'the Abyssinian landscape is to *Summer* what the description of Lapland is to *Winter*; both passages idealize the scene, contrast it with surrounding horrors, and omit unfavorable details prominent in travelers' accounts.'[14] Although the scene is selective, its purpose seems to be to show the possibility of harmony and the manner in which similar features of nature or man can be converted into forms of disharmony. It is significant, in other words, that the muse should, like the missionaries, 'boldly pierce' secret bounds and that the sun's rays should strike nature lovingly or dangerously. Such procedures in Thomson define the characteristic sensibility of his poetry.

The next scene, although it, too, takes place at noon with the sun's rays shining direct, establishes no such blending; the sun is oppressed by other aspects of nature—clouds and winds. It begins:

130

How chang'ed the Scene! In blazing Height of Noon,
The Sun, oppress'd, is plung'd in thickest Gloom.

(784–85)

Earlier in *Summer*, Thomson had described 'raging Noon' (431) in the temperate zone, which parched the vegetation and caused 'distressful Nature' (447) to pant. In the torrid zone, at blaze of noon, the sun is itself oppressed, and 'Still/Horror reigns' (786), and elements are at war in a furious tropical storm. Thus even the great powers of nature are seen in contrary roles of oppressors and oppressed, as subjecting elemental features and being subjected by them, both instances having their source in a higher power that can create sublime contradictions. For within the torrid zone the sun becomes an oppressor, having been 'oppress'd':

> The Parent-Sun himself
> Seems o'er this World of Slaves to tyrannize;
> And, with oppressive Ray, the roseat Bloom
> Of Beauty blasting.

(884–87)

The verse paragraph immediately following the Abyssinian prospect shifts the scene in a typical Thomsonian technique for establishing transition. Some of the first lines of verse paragraphs that introduce such transitions follow:

> BEAR me, *Pomona*! to thy Citron-Groves; (663)
> FROM These the Prospect varies. (690)
> PEACEFUL, beneath primeval Trees, (716)
> WIDE o'er the winding Umbrage of the Floods, (733)
> BUT come, my *Muse*, the Desert-Barrier burst, (747)
> How chang'd the Scene! In blazing Height of Noon. (784)

The paragraphs suggest abrupt changes of scene and the narrator seems to move rapidly from place to place. But the unifying devices of theme and imagery create emotive qualities that hold the passages together regardless of the changes. Thus the first four transitions deal with the distance between man and nature, suggesting the goodness and refreshment of harmonious participation, the hostility of disharmony and exploitation.

The arbitrary power of nature in *Summer*, conveyed by sudden shifts, also implies a disdain for normal order in its preference for fragmentation. The abrupt transitions, however, do not mean that the thematic material has undergone a change. The poem exploits similar emotive responses in different situations and places, and the critic needs to discover how large these operative units are.

The sudden shifts of scene, especially prominent in *Summer*, reflect the intensity and power of underlying forces in this season. Such wrenching of transition remains relevant here because the sun appears in contradictory situations. Sudden collocation is a form of inharmonious mixture; breaking the 'Desart Barrier' (747) leads to an Edenic scene followed by a 'malignant' storm. The sudden transition implies a hidden force which operates unexpectedly; it is one of the means used to express intensity in this and other seasons. The storm illustrates several of these techniques, some of which are especially related to the experiments of *The Seasons*.

Intensity is normally expressed in the poem by a vocabulary of highly charged words, such as 'malignant,' 'tempestuous,' 'tremendous'; words implying immense size or extent or violence ('burning,' 'raging,' etc.). But Thomson adds to these uses the repetition of a word usually with an intervening preposition or conjunction, the formal term for which is 'epizeuxis,' to suggest extension in space or time: 'Clouds on Clouds continual heap'd' (791), 'Hues on Hues Expression cannot paint' (*Spring*, 554), 'Farther and farther on, the lengthening Flight' (*Spring*, 750), 'Where Rapture burns on Rapture' (*Spring*, 1046), 'In Circle following Circle' (*Summer*, 1653), 'And Woes on Woes, a still-revolving Train!' (*Summer*, 1772), 'From thundering Steep to Steep, he pours his Urn' (*Summer*, 820), 'you heard the Groans/Of agonizing Ships, from Shore to Shore' (*Summer*, 1046–47), 'Enlarging, deepening, mingling, Peal on Peal' (*Summer*, 1142), 'From Field to Field the feather'd Seeds she wings' (*Summer*, 1163), 'Spike after Spike, their sparing Harvest pick' (*Autumn*, 166), 'Reels fast from Theme to Theme' (*Autumn*, 540), 'Snows swell on Snows amazing to the Sky;/And icy Mountains high on Mountains pil'd' (*Winter*, 905–6). In these instances repetition implies a cyclical pattern of time or extension in space, linear or blended ('Far-distant Flood to Flood in social join'd' (*Winter*, 975); references to passions imply increased states of feeling, the references to nature imply endless extension as do those to time. In a clause such as 'and Horror looks/More horrible' (*Winter*, 1007–8), the method of using the comparative with an absolute term to suggest the ever-extending bounds of dreadfulness is consistent with Thomson's view that human suffering in this world can know only the bounds of death, and with his technique exemplifying this—the use of the limited to suggest the unlimited.

This procedure is a companion to that described in *Spring* in which the poet uses unlimited terms in specifically limited ways. The intensity that is created can be dreadful as well as delightful. The basis for distinction is blending or harmony as contrasted with chaos or shapelessness. Thus in *Spring* the mountain-cloud imagery is seen as a form of blending: the landscape

> roughens into rigid Hills;
> O'er which the *Cambrian* Mountains, like far Clouds
> That skirt the blue Horizon, dusky, rise.
>
> (960–62)

But in *Winter* the snow-mountains that appear like clouds are examples of shapelessness and dislocation due to the new snows:

> And icy Mountains high on Mountains pil'd,
> Seem to the shivering Sailor from afar,
> Shapeless and white, an Atmosphere of Clouds.
>
> (906–8)

The figure of epizeuxis as used by Thomson usually includes a prepositional phrase that forms the basis for intensity as spatial extension. As a technique of sentence structure it is related to the prepositional phrases modifying nouns, adjectives or adverbs to give precision. Even in 'icy Mountains high on Mountains pil'd' the 'icy Mountains' refer to the illusionary mountains and the second 'Mountains' to the actual. The frequent absence of identical repetition is a characteristic device of Thomson's to indicate extension of meaning, here corresponding to spatial expanse. Epizeuxis isolates an object, action or idea by repetition attributing to them a self-expanding quality that can, as 'icy Mountain,' delude, or, as 'Steep to Steep,' be accurate.

Other forms of repetition have been discussed as unifying devices or forms of subtle differentiations and of contrary contexts. There are, of course, the usual types of repetition for emphasis in verse structure—as 'Rich in Content, in Nature's Bounty rich' (*Autumn*, 1259), though even here the first 'Rich' refers to moral behavior and the second to natural products. The attempt within very limited scope to use repetition as cyclical, to effect a constant sense of change within apparently unchanged words, can be observed in the following:

> These, in successive Turn, with lavish Hand,
> Shower every Beauty, every Fragrance shower,
> Herbs, Flowers, and Fruits; till kindling at thy Touch,
> From Land to Land is flush'd the vernal Year.
>
> (*Summer*, 126–29)

Above, I suggested some of the repetitive techniques by which the poet organizes sections of the poem as he does with dawn in the torrid zone (635), or with 'blazing Height of Noon' of the torrid zone (784) that is like "Tis raging Noon' (432) of the temperate. These are attempts to set up parallel passages from different points of view. Another procedure is to conclude or begin a section with a change of the speaker's tone in contrast to the prevailing tone of the section.

When the narrator urges his muse to depart from the beauty and variety of Montezuma's realm to observe the African desert—'But come, my *Muse*, the Desart-Barrier burst' (747)—he is, within the torrid zone, re-establishing the contrasts that caused him initially to depart from the temperate zone. But if the temperate zone is to be the appropriate zone for man, then the journey to the torrid zone is an attempt to establish an empirical basis for this realization. The inquiry for knowledge must be pursued although it will become apparent that the temperate zone can be as intemperate as hottest 'Climes': 'return, my vagrant Muse:/A nearer Scene of Horror calls thee home' (1101–2).

In the torrid zone, there are, despite the ferocity of heat, majestic woods that provide 'A boundless deep Immensity of Shade' (652). The gaudy feathered robes of Montezuma's soldiers cast 'A boundless Radiance waving on the Sun' (743). The immensity of shade and the immensity of light form two contrary instances of the torrid zone's comfort and beauty. These positive values lead the muse to probe further into the secret areas of the hot countries, and the scene changes to the powerfully war-like *Summer* storm where the 'furious elemental War' (800) dissolves the conflicting force and pours 'solid Torrents' (802). The paradox, 'solid Torrents,' in which the water is described as firm, implies a chaotic transformation, though in *Winter* the waters do become frozen and solidified, and it is the 'Torrents' (*Winter*, 749) that are metaphoric, only seeming to move and roar, representing a congealed and falsely fanciful nature.

The storm does not, however, bring destruction; on the contrary, the 'Unbroken Floods and solid Torrents' are 'Treasures' because they lead to the overflow of the Nile. There follows a description of the Nile and the African and South American rivers that overflow and bring wealth to the inhabitants of their shores. This procedure is, of course, Thomson's technique of perspectivism, for the deluge in *Spring* and the overflow in *Autumn* (330–50) wreak havoc, as do the *Summer* 'Equinoctial Rains' (1026) that bring pestilence. It should be noted that 'torrid' and 'Torrents' have the same Latin derivation— *torrere*, to burn, to parch and to flow impetuously. Thus *Summer*'s waters are related to fire and can become raging or pestilential as well as benevolent.

The rivers are described as wandering through space—African and South American; the Nile is personified and this personification is mixed with natural description. It grows in time (age) as it wanders in space; so, too, the Niger and the other Eastern rivers reveal their bounty, and just as the Nile 'pours his Urn' (820), these rivers 'ope their Urns,/And pour untoiling Harvest o'er the Land' (830–31), and the South American rivers flow 'pouring on' (856), seeking the ocean. The overflow of nature possesses a varied intensity and these move-ments of the rivers reflect the ranging power of nature and its con-sistency. The beauty and nourishment given by these rivers imply extension as a value even in the overflow. They spread beyond their borders bringing joy and harvest, so that there is a continuity between *Spring*'s 'Shower/Of shadowing Roses' (3–4) and *Summer*'s Aurora that 'sheds/On *Indus*' smiling Banks the rosy Shower' (828–29).

The Oronoque, the Orellana, and the Rio Rivers are instances of power:

> With unabated Force,
> In silent Dignity they sweep along,
> And traverse Realms unknown, and blooming Wilds,
> And fruitful Desarts, Worlds of Solitude,
> Where the Sun smiles and Seasons teem in vain,
> Unseen, and unenjoy'd. Forsaking These,
> O'er peopled Plains they fair-diffusive flow,
> And many a Nation feed, and circle safe,
> In their soft Bosom, many a happy Isle;
> The Seat of blameless *Pan*, yet undisturb'd
> By christian Crimes and *Europe's* cruel Sons.
>
> (845–55)

135

These rivers, described in terms of power and order, reflect the maze quality of the universe precisely because they traverse realms unknown and paradoxically create 'fruitful Desarts' and pass through countries where 'Seasons teem in vain.' The order is beyond the capacity of man to grasp, for the rivers also 'many a Nation feed.' And in these happy isles the people live without the corruptions brought by Christianity and inhabitants of the temperate zone. Thomson had a few lines earlier (758) attacked the 'purple Tyranny of *Rome*,' and he implies the possibility of a primitive society without the cruelties of Jesuitical civilization. He had written that the elephant was wise and gentle, 'Tho powerful, not destructive' (723), and that the rivers showed a plenitude not governed by mere human needs.

But the repetition of range, of intensity, of plenitude, expressed in the overflow with its mixed imagery and paradoxical order in disorder is suddenly confronted by the narrator with another series, another and different instance of intensity. For the spreading rivers are followed by a series of rhetorical, elliptical questions so that the declarative mood is contrasted with the interrogative. And the interrogations are so intense that the narrator truncates the grammatical order to call into question the plenitude, wonder and power of these rivers:

> BUT what avails this wondrous Waste of Wealth?
> This gay Profusion of luxurious Bliss?
> This Pomp of Nature? what their balmy Meads,
> Their powerful Herbs, and *Ceres* void of Pain?
>
> (860–63)

These Job-like questions, answered elsewhere in *The Seasons* by submission to mystery and faith, are answered here with the exclamation 'Ill-fated Race' (875). For the primitive peoples are without the virtues of the temperate zone: humanizing muses, godlike wisdom, progressive truth, investigation calm, and equal rule. But there was 'many a happy Isle' and these virtues were countered in the preceding passages by European cruelties. This, therefore, if Thomson is not to contradict himself within ten lines, must refer to tribes other than the happy ones. Since 'their balmy Meads' seem to refer to all the peoples in the preceding, the 'their' remains ambiguous.

The inflated moral catalog asserts qualities that do not, however, grow out of the observed experiences, and are not related even to their examples in the temperate zone. When, for instance, the poet writes, 'Love dwells not there,/The soft Regards' (890–91), the assumption is that love is reciprocated by God in ready ways. But the narrative of Celadon and Amelia—'They lov'd' (1177)—makes precisely the opposite point that love and innocence do not prevent the 'fated Flash.' The catalog conceals the moral complexity of the universe. There is no basis for 'Ill-fated' in the torrid zone thus described, and the passage deliberately overlooks its wisdom and peace. I do not think the passage can be taken ironically, but it is inept and this leads to difficulties of tone and thought. It substitutes for the virtues of the torrid zone a catalog of those of the temperate. In this zone, the behemoth was referred to as a 'harmless Stranger' (715) and the elephant as 'wisest of Brutes' (721); it is, therefore, likely that the statement, 'The very Brute-Creation there/This Rage partakes, and burns with horrid Fire' (896–97), belongs with a dialectical shift badly managed. For just as the penetrative sun affects minerals and flowers, it also affects man. That such a shift was intended seems likely by reference to the oppressive sun. But the transition from the pleasure to the terrors of the tropics is achieved by a series of moral assertions. These cannot function contrastingly to the described nature since they seem in no way a contradiction of or alternative to it. They, therefore, name virtues and values that have, in this context, no available reference, and the catalog becomes an inflation.

The series of terrors continues the enumerative method, beginning with animals of contrasting size, the 'green Serpent' (898) and the 'small close-lurking Minister of Fate' (908), followed by the roving beast of prey. And there is a contrast between the herds looking at the peaceful behemoth (709–15) and the herds, frightened by the lion that 'with Horror hear/The coming Rage' (931–32).

The heard 'Horror' causes the flocks to gather around their guardian; the mother, guarding her child, behaves in the same way as the swain. Even the escaped man hearing the 'Uproar' wishes for the security he left. Man and animals are described in the same terms, and the threat of unleashed violence holds the passage together. But the lonely man who sits on the 'jutting Eminence' is an affecting figure not because of the threat of violence but because of the threat of loneliness. He has to create images of his own, waiting for the reality, observing the rhythmic rise and fall of the waves and the mirages of clouds that appear as ships. As his heart sinks 'down,' the 'Roar' of the waves rises. Although he is safe from the dangers of the sea, he is lost, for tedium is itself a terror. But even this lonely world of imagined terror is preferable to the loss of liberty, as witness Cato, who returned to this land of monsters in preference to living among the Roman tyrants (monsters). This passage (951–58) comments upon the 'sweet Humanity' of the temperate climate, distinguishing between tyranny and liberty, the tyranny of the sun being preferred, apparently, to the tyranny of man. The failure of these lines is a lack of connection not with the preceding ideas, but with the mood and rhythm of the preceding lines, playing with 'these *black* Abodes' and '*unappal'd*' (my italics) in contrasts that clash with the despairing melancholy.

The roar of the beasts and the sea is followed by that of fire, for the earth itself is burning. The element transformed becomes a fiery though eerily beautiful ('glittering Waste') expanse, and the air becomes a deadly weapon.

> Breath'd hot,
> From all the boundless Furnace of the Sky,
> And the wide glittering Waste of burning Sand,
> A suffocating Wind the Pilgrim smites
> With instant Death.
>
> (961–65)

Here the unity is only trivially held by the sounds of the storm; rather the transformational qualities of nature are exploited. Thus the sands in 'gathering Eddies play' as though they were unthreatening waters or birds, for, in *Autumn*, the birds are the 'feather'd Eddy' (840), and the sand dunes arise 'whole continuous Wilds' (973) when the absence of vegetation is itself the menace. Finally, 'Beneath descending Hills, the Caravan/Is buried deep' (976–77). The caravan itself becomes part of the overwhelming sandstorm, and what was seen as 'Wilds' now includes man and animals as well.

Thomson moves from one element to another, from the earth to water, from fire to wind, from the sandstorm to the typhoon to illustrate the transformation of power. The furious heat and power of the torrid zone (786–802) was described in terms of elemental conflicts, but the typhoon is seen as deceptive:

> Amid the Heavens,
> Falsely serene, deep in a cloudy Speck
>
> (986–87)

....
A faint deceitful Calm,

(992)

And when the ship is engulfed, it is 'Hid in the Bosom of the black Abyss' (1000).

The peaceful rivers had been described with the bosom image suggesting enclosure, safety and nourishment. They circled safe 'In their soft Bosom, many a happy Isle' (*Summer*, 853), their 'unabated Force' (845) being completely consistent with their protective value in this season. But the dual nature of *Summer*'s power is revealed in the sinking ship, unsheltered, though 'hid' in the bosom of the tempestuous waters. And the vessel that 'drinks the whelming Tide' (909) is not nourished but overwhelmed. I have traced the duality of the 'Bosom' ('Gulph,' 'Abyss,' 'Breast,' 'embowering') image in *Spring* and in *Summer*; the possibilities of nature's embrace recur in *Autumn* where the hills shelter Lavinia (210) and the earthquake 'engulphs' (1207) Palermo. In *Autumn*, too, the safety of the image is burlesqued as the pastor, whose paunch is 'a black Abyss of Drink' (566), but who nevertheless survives all his flock. In *Winter* the elks sleep 'in the white Abyss,' an abyss that is home, an appearance ('Abyss') of dislocation that is its opposite.

Here again the narrator moves from a terror passage to political implications. For Vasco da Gama, led by ambition and avarice to dare these mad seas, brought the development ('rising') of trade, 'For then from antient Gloom emerg'd/The rising World of Trade' (1005–6). And it was left for Don Henry, Prince of Portugal, to rouse mankind 'To love of useful Glory' (1011) and to 'mix' the world in 'unbounded Commerce' (1012). In this, the prince functions like the bee (759) and unlike the Christians with their mask of 'social Commerce' (754). One can understand the role of the moral commentator here and above to suggest that there are political terrors worse than loneliness, and that mad storms need not necessarily lead to death and destruction, but this interference disorders the continuity. Especially so in the sea storm which continues, after the Da Gama interlude, to detail how sharks add to the terrors of sinking slaveships:

one Death involves
Tyrants and Slaves; when strait, their mangled Limbs

139

Crashing at once, he [the shark] dyes the purple Seas
With Gore, and riots in the vengeful Meal.

(1022–25)

Just as the brute creation 'burned' (897), and the earth burned so
now the water is dyed red, the color of the burning sun. And, by
allusion, the action of the shark in demanding his share of prey
('dyes the purple Seas') is related to the 'purple Tyranny' of the
Jesuit missionaries who sought

> With consecrated Steel to stab their [African] Peace,
> And thro the Land, yet red from Civil Wounds,
> To spread the purple Tyranny of *Rome*.
>
> (*Summer*, 756–58)

The concluding section on the torrid zone contains a series of plague
passages (related to heat) from the historical narration of Admiral
Vernon, whose men were struck down by plague at Carthagena, to
the scene of the slaying of the plague-stricken 'Wretch' (1091).
Thomson describes the natural causes of the plague, but he also
moralizes about man whose 'guilty Domes' (1060) become the
'Prey' of the plague as do the drowning men of the sharks. He writes
of the plague:

> Her awful Rage
> The Brutes escape. Man is her destin'd Prey,
> Intemperate Man! and, o'er his guilty Domes,
> She draws a close incumbent Cloud of Death.
>
> (1058–61)

But the patriotic sailors of 'gallant VERNON' (1041) were also attacked,
and they were neither 'guilty' nor 'intemperate.'

The section of the terrors is climaxed in the plague passage. It is
not a satisfactorily achieved passage, but it connects the mother and
child, the flocks and swain, and the mariner who began the section,
with the plague-stricken village. The contrast is between a society
that clings together for protection and social union, a society that
is the 'first of Joys,' and a sick society in which such ties are abhorred.

> Dependants, Friends, Relations, Love himself,
> Savag'd by Woe, forget the tender Tie,
> The sweet Engagement of the feeling Heart.
>
> (1080–82)

The two plagues follow one another—the isolated ship and the sickening city—and allude to the two references to plagues in *Spring*, the first of which refers to the insects, carried by the poisoned air, a plague that the farmer fights. The *Summer* plague has man as its 'destin'd Prey' (1059) so that the plague which destroys the field is conquered by man, and then there is the plague that destroys the conqueror. But the other plague reference in *Spring* is to the jealous lover, for jealousy is a 'yellow-tinging Plague' (1083). The imagery of the plague leads to the destruction of the lover on whose cheeks the 'poison'd Soul, malignant, sits,/And frightens Love away' (1091–92). Love is destroyed by poisoned feelings exactly as the plague destroys the social feelings of the city. Feelings of tenderness are conditioned by the environment in which the individual finds himself.

The relation of the plague metaphor of *Spring* to the plague actualities of *Spring* and *Summer* is typical of Thomson's technique in moving from the literal to the metaphoric. The actual destructive powers of nature (or the reverse) can be matched by man's capacity to wound himself, for the most benevolent relationships can be destroyed by one's own powers or those of violent (poisoned) nature. In *Summer*, Vernon's men meet the plague with controlled fear, whereas the city's wretches act with wild frenzy. Thus the jealous lover belongs with the frenzied wretches, and the point is that even love can be a plague when its agonies move beyond control. The metaphor is related to the literal plague passages although it deals with private rather than natural consequences. It permits the poet to contrast the idea of heat referring to love with the actual, destructive, fetid climate to suggest that, indeed, in each season as in human action, what can be glorious can also be base.

If one compares the stricken wretch of the plagued city with the stag who flees to his friends only to be selfishly rejected ('the watchful Herd, alarm'd,/With selfish Care avoid a Brother's Woe,' *Autumn*, 447–48), then it will be apparent that Thomson has described an unresolvable dilemma of social love. For the wretch loving his friends can only infect them; yet, at the same time, the cause of his infection is the poisoned air—'delightful' nature itself.

This duality is developed in the plague scene by a technique that recurs throughout the poem and that I have named, applying a term from Thomson to my own purposes, scenes of 'sad Presage' (1050). They deal with the relation of the living to the dead, indicating the anxiety and puzzlement of the unexplainable violence and destruction of nature upon harmless and innocent creatures. Such episodes imply anxiety, terror, and puzzlement: the mother clutching the child, the impatient merchant, the sailor fixed in amazement, the British sailors burying the corpses, the guards firing at the infected wretches. Each is a unified episode, and as a group they exemplify attitudes that recur in other passages of *The Seasons*: the mother and her 'thoughtless Infant,' guiltless Amelia struck down by lightning in *Summer*, the lonely mariner of *Summer*, the Russian exile in *Winter*, the caravan buried in the sands (*Summer*), the shepherd buried in the *Winter* snow, the drowned traveller in *Autumn*, the shark (*Summer*), the Leviathan in *Winter*, the death of Vernon's men, Sir Hugh Willoughby's men frozen to death in *Winter*, the terror of the plague and the terrors of *Autumn* meteors.

The grim gestures that conclude the episodes become silences invoking the mystery of apparent evil. They move from an isolated scene to a kind of infinite questioning:

> In *Cairo*'s crouded Streets,
> Th' impatient Merchant, wondering, waits in vain,
> And *Mecca* saddens at the long Delay.
>
> (977–79)

The density of the streets suggests the irrelevant human plenitude available to, but not exploited by, the merchant. The 'wondering' separates 'impatience' and 'in vain,' for there will be no answer to his impatience. The 'sadness' of the long delay is no longer business-like, but rather the resignation to an inevitable misfortune. So, too, the moral implications of the corpses buried in the sea:

> you heard the Groans
> Of agonizing Ships, from Shore to Shore;
> Heard, nightly plung'd amid the sullen Waves,
> The frequent Corse; while on each other fix'd,
> In sad Presage, the blank Assistants seem'd,
> Silent, to ask, whom Fate would next demand.
>
> (1046–51)

The 'wondering' of the merchant, the 'sad Presage' of the 'blank Assistants'—these bring to the reader's attention the contemplative puzzle at the same time that these scenes are 'fix'd.' They contrast with the motions and movements immediately preceding them. The 'heard' groans of the ships and the plunging of the corpses leads to unspoken questions; the merchant's unfulfilled expectations and the 'sad Presage' at the unpredictability of death.

The action can be told from the point of view of the omniscient observer who sees the traveller buried by a sandstorm and who completes the narrative by turning to the expectant merchant waiting and wondering. This point of view applies to the man in *Autumn* misled into the marshes and to the shepherd in *Winter* disastered in the snow. All are examples of shifts in point of view, contrasting the dead with the incompleted actions of the anxious living.

Not only do these gestures present living, anxious contrasts with the dead, but they represent permanent and unending moments of wonder and perturbation. They are human responses to the maze-like quality of nature, and they represent fragmented moments that will have no completion. In the poem they are moments when men have not yet come to realize the immensity of the suffering in store for them, and, in contrast to those hushed moments in nature when the benevolent showers fall, these resemble moments of calm before the violent storms. Yet the dreadful storms must be accepted on faith, for the incompleted gesture arises after nature's destruction of man. In this respect the incompleted scene of 'sad Presage' is a disruption of harmony and it contrasts with the prospect or spectrum view that provides a sense of completion.

The classical source of this procedure is *De Rerum Natura*, III, 894 ff., in which men bemoan the fact that a dead man shall no longer be welcomed by wife and children; Lucretius comments saying that the dead man no longer has such feelings and is at peace in death. Thomson places these scenes within the Augustan context of nature's power that stresses the pitiful condition of the living who do not comprehend man's fate. Within Thomson's particular version there is the gulf imagery, in which sands, water, air or snow become destructive elements and bury or rigidify the victim. The living family are seen as immobilized by anxiety in contrast to the buried dead and in terms of the effects of one member of the family upon another, the stiffness of the victims is transferred, in part, to the anxious living. G. Wilson Knight has identified such gestures as 'action-poses,' the attempt to merge space and time in poetry through reference to sculpture[15] and Rachel Trickett has written that 'those Augustan poets who wished to claim for their own art all the advantages of painting, were particularly attracted by images of a statuesque effect.[16] These writers point to an aspect of Thomson's poetry that is surely present, though it is an extension of the 'emphatic silence' techniques discussed above.

Because the scene of 'sad Presage' is an incompleted gesture, it becomes an aspect of the fragmented appearance of the world, an unanswered puzzle. The handling of these scenes forms a unity in *The Seasons*, though within each season, an individual scene of "sad Presage" can prove more impressive than its relation to the immediately preceding or subsequent passages.

iv. Thomson on Poetry

Since the scenes of "sad Presage" are connected with statuesque effects, they raise the question of Thomson's view of imagination in art. Thomson has no single systematic view of the imagination, but he does propose several conventional views: the Platonic view of imitation in which art is only a shadow of actuality, and the prophetic version of this—that art is a visionary communication from God and the angels. The first view is expressed in *Spring*:

> But who can paint
> Like Nature? Can Imagination boast,
> Amid its gay Creation, Hues like hers?
>
> (468–70)

> If Fancy then
> Unequal fails beneath the pleasing Task;
> Ah what shall Language do? Ah where find Words
> Ting'd with so many Colours; and whose Power,
> To Life approaching, may perfume my Lays
> With that fine Oil, those aromatic Gales,
> That inexhaustive flow continual round?
> YET the successless, will the Toil delight.
>
> (473–80)

This interpretation of the poet's competition with nature presupposes that such effort enhances his creative ability, for even though he is unable to match nature, yet 'will the Toil delight.' The poet can never achieve the harmony of nature, but by seeking to approximate its actuality, he is challenged to a 'pleasing Task.' Thus this interchange forms the basis for the poet's own limited harmony or accomplishment. And this applies not only to the poet but to the landscape gardener. In *Autumn* Thomson writes,

Not *Persian Cyrus* on *Ionia*'s Shore
E'er saw such silvan Scenes, such various Art
By Genius fir'd, such ardent Genius tam'd
By cool judicious Art; that, in the strife,
All-beauteous Nature fears to be outdone.

(1043–47)

This view of poetic creation seems to apply to the beautiful, for in Thomson's reference to the angels in *Summer* the competition involves suffering and sacrifice on the part of the poet before calm can be reached. Thomson does not slight inspiration, for even in the *Spring* passage the poet is stimulated by the sensuous life of nature.

In this passage, 'Imagination' and 'Fancy' are used interchangeably, as they are throughout *The Seasons*, and they are separated from the language which expresses their 'gay Creations.' Since the passage is part of *Spring*, Thomson is here concerned with the joyful rather than the solemn associational power of the imagination. This healthy imagination is, in conventional Renaissance manner, distinguished from the unhealthy or sick imagination which mimics the world in black rather than natural views:

Exhausted Nature sinks a while to Rest,
Still interrupted by distracted Dreams,
That o'er the sick Imagination rise,
And in black Colours paint the mimick Scene.

(*Spring*, 1053–56)

These references to imagination and to the 'gay' (*Autumn*, 1055) or the 'bold' (*Summer*, 631) ranging fancy imply that the poet does not consider imagination a controlling concept but merely one aspect of artistic imitation, others being techniques of verse (song) and diction, imitations of human experiences, descriptions of nature. This imitative view is attributed to Pope by Maynard Mack, who quotes Pope's couplet in *Windsor Forest*, 'See Pan with flocks, with fruits Pomona crowned/Here blushing Flora paints the enamelled ground,' and declares that Flora is 'blushing'

because she is young, a symbol of the warm life flowing in the earth at that season [spring] as it does in the veins of a young girl. She is *painting* something, the colors coming to life and disposing themselves under her brush as the flowers do upon the earth. There is an interanimation between 'blushing' and 'paints,' so that we are

145

forced to recognize in the blushing artist something richer than the picture she is making, in the creative force itself something more mysterious than any of its expressions.[17]

This Popean version of imitation is shared by Thomson, who finds that nature enhances nature, but art inevitably lags behind; the poet urges Amanda to gather 'Fresh-blooming Flowers, to grace thy braided Hair/And thy lov'd Bosom that improves their Sweets' (*Spring*, 492–93). And he writes of Lavinia, 'Her Form was fresher than the Morning-Rose,/When the Dew wets its Leaves' (*Autumn*, 192–93) contrasting and complementing the human form with nature's. But if this applies to descriptive poetry, there is a genuinely inspired poetry that properly competes with nature.

In his 'Preface' to the second edition of *Winter*, Thomson distinguishes between the abuses of poetry, features in which it lags behind life, and 'her ancient Truth, and Purity.'[18] The abuses refer to 'low, venal, trifling, Subjects' in contrast to the true and pure poetry inspired by heaven that is 'fair, useful, and magnificent,' executed 'so as, at once, to please, instruct, surprize, and astonish.'[19] But Thomson is aware that true poetry in England no longer matches that of the inspired poets up to Milton's time. There is needed, he declares, a single heroic figure to restore poetry to its ancient state:

> But this happy Period is not to be expected, till some long-wished, illustrious Man, of equal Power, and Beneficence, rise on the wintry World of Letters: One of a genuine, and unbounded, Greatness, and Generosity, of Mind; who, far, above all the Pomp, and Pride, of Fortune, scorns the little addressful, Flatterer; pierces thro' the disguised, designing, Villain; discountenances all the reigning Fopperies of a tastless Age: and who, stretching his Views into late Futurity, has the true Interest of Virtue, Learning, and Mankind, intirely, at Heart—A Character so nobly desirable! that to an honest Heart, it is, almost, incredible so few should have the Ambition to deserve it.[20]

Thomson's hero is an inspired prophet who scorns flatterers, pierces disguises of villains, disregards foppery, is governed by religious views of a better world, knows and advocates 'the true interest of Virtue, Learning, and Mankind.' These views of the Preface were incorporated into later revisions of the poem, and they were combined with an attack on bad poetry resembling that of the satirists. But in contrast to these, Thomson felt that the best method for reviving poetry was to choose 'great and serious Subjects, such as at once amuse the Fancy, enlighten the Head, and warm the Heart.'[21] For Thomson, thought or enlightenment is mixed with feeling and imagination to define 'Inspiration' and 'Rapture.' Such subjects cause rapture in the writer and reader, though Thomson is aware that subjects to be properly effective must have geniuses to express them. He distinguishes artificial expressions or poetic skill expended on trivial subjects from skill expended on sublime ones. And his point is that 'Genius' is necessarily attuned to great subjects:

> And what are we commonly entertain'd with, on these Occasions, save forced, unaffecting, Fancies; little glittering Prettinesses; mixed Turns of Wit, and Expression; which are as widely different from Native Poetry, as Buffoonery is from the Perfection of human Thinking? A Genius fired with the Charms of Truth, and Nature is tuned to a sublimer Pitch, and scorns to associate with such Subjects.[22]

Although Thomson makes reference to subject and expression, and believes that great subjects can inspire the poet, he does see the need for 'genius,' which, in the context, refers not only to the inspired poet but also to his skilful and attuned expression. Of the subjects that call forth a response in the poet and reader, Thomson writes,

> I know no Subject more elevating, more amusing; more ready to awake the poetical Enthusiasm, the philosophical Reflection, and the moral Sentiment, than the Works of Nature. Where can we meet with such Variety, such Beauty, such Magnificence? All that enlarges, and transports, the Soul! What more inspiring than a calm, wide, Survey of Them? In every Dress Nature is greatly charming! whether she puts on the crimson Robes of the Morning! the strong Effulgence of Noon! the sober Suit of the Evening! or the deep Sables of Blackness and Tempest! How gay looks the Spring! how glorious the Summer! how pleasing the Autumn! and how venerable the Winter!—But there is no thinking of these Things without breaking out into Poetry; which is, by the bye, a plain, and undeniable, Argument of their superior Excellence.[23]

In this 'Preface', Thomson does not make a very clear distinction between responding to nature and responding to nature in poetry. It seems that the subjects themselves call forth poetry, but what Thomson means is that such subjects stimulate the intellectual, emotional and artistic powers of men of genius. And for this reason 'the best, both Ancient, and Modern, Poets have been passionately fond of Retirement, and Solitude. The wild romantic Country was their Delight. And they seem never to have been more happy, than when lost in unfrequented Fields, far from the little, busy, Worlds they were at Leisure to meditate, and sing the Works of Nature.'[24]

Although the 'Preface' provided a rationale for *Winter, The Seasons* came to include city scenes, and comic and burlesque voices. The ancient and modern poets that were Thomson's guide were gradually absorbed into his sensibility. The distinction which he made here between genius and nature was superseded by the more common one between art and genius, and the very 'Preface' itself that scorned flattery included flattering mentions of Aaron Hill and David Malloch, a procedure that Thomson did not eschew in *The Seasons*.

But Thomson's attempt to write 'poetry that seems to be the peculiar Language of Heaven,'[25] to address an audience in whom he wishes to restore, by means of this art 'the most charming Power of Imagination, the most exalting Force of Thought, the most affecting Touch of Sentiment,'[26] persisted throughout the revisions of *The Seasons*. It explains the tradition in which he saw himself and the rural subjects that he treated. It explains, too, the frequent personal note that moves through the poem: 'I only wish my Description of the various Appearance of Nature in Winter and, as I purpose, in the other Seasons may have the good Fortune to give the Reader some of the true Pleasure which they, in their agreeable Succession, are, always, sure to inspire into my Heart.'[27]

The role of the poet as maker whose informing wisdom comes from philosophy (see *Spring*, 859–60: 'But, though concealed, to every purer Eye/The informing Author in his Works appears') is dependent upon the development of cultured society (though obviously the inspired prophets of the Bible are an exception). The movements, breathing and softening, that create the illusion of life are a refining of wisdom by artistry.

> the Canvas smooth,
> With glowing Life protuberant, to the View
> Embodied rose; the Statue seemed to breathe,
> And soften into Flesh, beneath the Touch
> Of forming Art, Imagination flushed.
>
> (*Autumn*, 136–140)

148

In this respect 'All is the Gift of Industry' (*Autumn*, 141), and skill requires inspired genius to give it force and genius requires skill to make its poetry effective. This skill Thomson also finds in the masters of poetic art—the inspired prophets, Homer, Virgil, Spenser, Shakespeare and Milton.

But if the art of imitating involves wisdom, diligence, sacred knowledge, skill and gentle competition, the love of and awe for this world spring unpremeditated from love of God. This feeling may be the sublime voice of angels for the 'sudden-starting Tear' at the approach of melancholy (*Autumn*, 1006). The strains of angels and birds are 'artless' (*Autumn*, 977) and the poet is compared to the bird-muse even to the extent of Lyttelton[28] referring to Thomson in *The Castle of Indolence* as one who 'Poured forth his unpremeditated Strain' (I, LXVIII; see also *Autumn*, 1054–65). This praise was probably a reference to Milton's 'unpremeditated verse' and was not a denial of artistry, but a recognition of the genuineness of feeling that governed Thomson's verse. Lyttelton was in fact saying no more than Thomson in his 'Preface,' who, referred to an outburst of poetry following upon contemplation, upon 'thinking' of God's works: 'But there is no thinking of these Things without breaking out into Poetry.'[29] The quality of the poetry, however, depended upon the poet's artistry. In *Summer* Thomson uses 'Inspiration' as an insight into nature which he then 'translates' into poetry:

> To me be Nature's Volume broad-display'd;
> And to peruse its all-instructive Page,
> Or, haply catching Inspiration thence,
> Some easy Passage, raptur'd, to translate,
> My sole Delight.
>
> (192–96)

Thomson uses 'Inspiration' to mean an awareness, an energy, a force that has a supernatural origin but can be apprehended and 'caught'. In *Spring* (853) he calls God 'Inspiring God'. Thus the relation of inspiration to imitation is that of energy to art. When Thomson 'translates' his inspiration, he insists on his own manner of writing,[30] but admits the limitation of poetry in matching nature. Nevertheless, as poet, he tries to imitate the power and beauty of his inspiration. In bringing his talents to trial, he applies his challenging, competitive spirit to his own work, altering and revising it to improve the imitation.

In Thomson's version of this doctrine there is always a distinction between 'mimic *Art*' (*Spring*, 506) and the truth of actual and 'Unbounded Beauty' (*Spring*, 507). Although art cannot have the same force as life, its greatest success is to appear life-like and full of energy. In *The Seasons* this approximation to life is locatable in the human and natural variations. When Thomson asks for the 'mazyrunning Soul of Melody' to be poured 'Into my Varied Verse!' he wishes the poetry to reflect the variations of life that exist around him.

In *Spring*, Thomson writes:

> Nor is the Mead unworthy of thy Foot,
> Full of fresh Verdure, and unnumber'd Flowers,
> The Negligence of *Nature*, wide, and wild;
> Where, undisguis'd by mimic *Art*, she spreads
> Unbounded Beauty to the roving Eye.
>
> (503–7)

In *Summer*, he writes of the sun as light:

> THE very dead Creation, from thy Touch,
> Assumes a mimic Life. By thee refin'd,
> In brighter Mazes, the relucent Stream
> Plays o'er the Mead. The Precipice abrupt,
> Projecting Horror on the blacken'd Flood,
> Softens at thy return. The Desart joys
> Wildly, thro all his melancholy Bounds.
> Rude Ruins glitter; and the briny Deep,
> Seen from some pointed Promontory's Top,
> Far to the blue Horizon's utmost Verge,
> Restless, reflects a floating Gleam. But This,
> And all the much-transported Muse can sing,
> Are to thy Beauty, Dignity, and Use,
> Unequal far, great delegated Source,
> Of Light, and Life, and Grace, and Joy below!
>
> (160–74)

In these quotations there appear two complementary aspects of nature as artist. In the first '*Nature*' refers to the expression of God's bounty in the animated world of flowers and greenery. In this respect, nature needs no human artistry to reveal its beauty, and God, acting through 'nature' in secret ways, is the consummate artist; indeed, in the 1727 edition of *Summer* Thomson called God the 'Almighty Poet'

(171). There is a second aspect of nature, however, in which God causes one force, such as the sun, to give 'mimic life' to inanimate or 'dead' creation, making it appear livelier and human. The view of art here is that one aspect of nature can reflect some of its beautiful features upon others, and thus nature is the model even for the human artist. The difference is that the sun does not possess the consciousness of the artist, though as a delegate of God's power, it does have a purposive end. At the conclusion of *Summer* the poet compares philosophy to light and declares:

> TUTOR'D by thee, hence POETRY exalts
> Her Voice to Ages; and informs the Page
> With Music, Image, Sentiment, and Thought,
> Never to die! the Treasure of Mankind!
> Their highest Honour, and their truest Joy!
>
> (1753–57)

The 'philosophy' that tutors some poetry (not all, as Thomson explains in his 'Preface') is scientific truth that, in conjunction with religious truth, makes possible all advances in learning. Thomson calls it 'Effusive Source of Evidence, and Truth' (*Summer*, 1732). Thus the poet, when he is tutored by faith and knowledge, conveys such truths as never die. He is always subordinate as maker to God, but he is immensely superior to those poets who do not reveal God's power, beauty and presence.

Addison pointed out (*Spectator* 416) that 'Among the different kinds of Representation, Statuary is the most natural, and shews us something likest the Object that is represented.'[31] Statuary is, in Augustan poetry, a basis for comparison with the softness of life or the stiffness of death, continuing the Renaissance nature-art relationship, occurring, for example, in *The Winter's Tale*. In *The Seasons*, the statue in *Autumn* is praised as lifelike because it appears 'soft.' Figures in life, moreover, are compared with sculpture when they lose their life-giving energy: as the *Spring* lover's spirit flies to his beloved, it

> leaves the Semblance of a Lover, fix'd
> In melancholy Site, with Head declin'd,
> And love-dejected Eyes.
>
> (*Spring*, 1022–24)

The *Summer* cattle lie 'a lifeless Groupe' (1152) and the sheep have the harmless look 'They wore alive' (1154). The lover, Celadon, 'Pierc'd by severe Amazement, hating Life,/Speechless, and fix'd in all the Death of Woe' (*Summer*, 1218–19) is compared with the marble mourner who only appears to have lost his love for life:

> So, faint Resemblance, on the Marble-Tomb,
> The well-dissembled Mourner stooping stands,
> For ever silent, and for ever sad.
>
> (1220–22)

So, too, Willoughby and his men frozen to death are compared to statues:

> he with his hapless Crew,
> Each full exerted at his several Task,
> Froze into Statues; to the Cordage glued
> The Sailor, and the Pilot to the Helm.
>
> (*Winter*, 932–35)

The world is a maze, but the power that can make even frozen death artistic demands allegiance and faith. Thomson places this theory within his spatial context of literal and metaphoric nature, of man's limited capacity to approximate God's plenitude and subtlety. In a world in which God creates life and permits death, the statuesque figures even in death illustrate God's artistic handiwork.

One disagrees with Alan D. McKillop on Thomson only with the greatest hesitancy, but I believe his interpretation of Thomson's theory of art incorrectly explains Thomson's use of statuesque comparisons. It is Thomson's position that sculpture becomes valuable only as it appears lifelike, since life and force are the criteria of art. In this he shares Pope's view that 'marble soften'd into life grew warm.'[32] The expression of true human feeling does not require sculpture; at best sculpture can only approximate human warmth. Cold sculpture is a form of death, bare fragmentary remains, appearing to have beauty without actually possessing it. McKillop writes that 'A complete or ideal expression of human feeling was taken to point to a reconciliation of the dynamic particular and the static universal,'[33] but, for Thomson, sculpture was not the ideal expression; rather it was a form that most approximated life without possessing it, a fixed object that lacked life though appearing beautiful. Language, however, though lacking color and substance, did possess the capacity for change.

In accordance with the different roles of the poet as observer and seer, Thomson illustrates different versions of the mimetic imagination; the poet who is interested in creating a semblance of life is also the one who is granted visions of what life can be. As the prophet-poet, he wishes to become part of the source of poetry in God, imitating a 'higher' truth than the observer-poet. In this aspect, he uses the imperative of prayer, he flees from the observation of nature into its recesses, and there he hears the heavenly voices and feels 'A sacred Terror, a severe Delight' (*Summer*, 541). In these scenes the poet describes the source of prophetic imagination, springing from contemplation and meditation, from a religious awareness of God's power. Thomson's theory does not disengage sight from feeling and thought; his very terms of imagination involve extent feelingly combined with beauty or power. Through communion with the angels, the poet understands his mission; through deep contemplation he reaches an exalted state of poetic expression: the angels invite the poet to sing with them

'A Privilege bestow'd by us, alone,
On Contemplation, or the hallow'd Ear
Of Poet, swelling to seraphic Strain.'
(*Summer*, 561–63)

These two mimetic versions of imagination do not provide the reasons for goodness or badness in *The Seasons*. But they do explain the experimentalism in language, the attempt to create words that establish a contrast between life and lifelessness, motion and motionlessness, softness and stiffness. They explain the poem's associative unity, its flights of fancy, its use of burlesque, comic, colloquial, beautiful and sublime diction. The prophetic, sublime imagination provided a vision of religious truth; the observational, beautiful imagination described the world of man. These two 'imaginations' correlate the broad spatial view and the limited private one; the broad view extends to infinity in terms of variety, a spatial mixture of all elements and the private view leads to privileged visions.

These two views have corresponding figures in the conception of the muse as birds; in the address to Lord Wilmington in *Winter*, Thomson reviews this conception with reference to each of the seasons. The muse can be a singing bird or a soaring eagle, it can sing beautiful songs or see sublime visions. In *Spring*, when he turns to describe the singing birds, he writes:

153

My Theme ascends, with equal Wing ascend,
My panting Muse.

(573–74)

And addressing the nightingales, he begs, 'Lend me your Song, ye
Nightingales!' (576), and in the same season he refers to the muse's
'Brothers of the Grove' (703). In *Summer*, it is the imaginative soaring
of the eagle that is identified with the poet's muse, and the *Winter* lines
correctly describe it: 'on Eagle-Pinions borne,/Attempted thro the
Summer-Blaze to rise' (20–21). Early in *Summer* the poet identifies his
fancy as soaring eagle-like:

as thro the falling Glooms
Pensive I stray, or with the rising Dawn
On Fancy's Eagle-wing excursive soar.

(196–98)

And deliberately disengaging the soaring eagle from the 'tuneful
Race' (611), overcome by the heat, Thomson writes:

the steep-ascending Eagle soars,
With upward Pinions thro the Flood of Day;
And, giving full his Bosom to the Blaze,
Gains on the Sun; while all the tuneful Race,
Smit by afflictive Noon, disorder'd droop,
Deep in the Thicket; or, from Bower to Bower
Responsive, force an interrupted Strain.

(608–14)

And the poet, rejecting the sweetness of the shade, addresses his
fancy in terms that describe the eagle,

Now come, bold *Fancy*, spread a daring Flight,
And view the Wonders of the *torrid Zone*.

(631–32)

The predominant muse of *Summer* is daring and sublime, but in
Autumn the song of the tuneful, beautiful birds is no longer heard.
The concept of mimesis, therefore, extends to the poet as singer, to
his correspondence to the bird realm. Consistent with the organizational rhythm of the seasons, *Autumn* is related to the tuneful muse
of *Spring* because it is the beautiful songs that have been stilled,
whereas *Winter* is related to the eagle-imagery of *Summer* because,
again, it is the soaring and wide-ranging fancy of the sublime
imagination that is described:

154

And now among the Wintry Clouds again,
Roll'd in the doubling Storm, she tries to soar;
To swell her Note with all the rushing Winds;
To suit her sounding Cadence to the Floods;
As is her Theme, her Numbers wildly great.

(23–27)

If these two muses can be interpreted as exemplifying two general views of the imagination, then the specific muses, the comic muse, the tragic muse, the historic muse must be interpreted as specific representatives of particular poetic styles. The two types of muse, therefore, relate particular human experience to the general, and the personified allusions to Clio (history), Thalia (comedy), Melpomene (tragedy) form part of the heavenly family of muses that can be understood, metaphorically, to include birds and humans. The muses, like Thomson's other allegorical personifications, hover between natural description and classical allusion.

v. The Interpolated Narratives (1103–1805)

The narrator calls upon his 'vagrant Muse' (1101) to return to the temperate zone, and this connecting device, clearly suggesting a new division in the poem, leads paradoxically to a unifying climactic storm that creates a consistency between the zones which the narrator had previously denied: 'Climes unrelenting! with whose Rage compar'd,/Yon Blaze is feeble, and yon Skies are cool' (633–34). 'Rage,' 'Blaze,' terms of *Summer*'s heat and anger, now present a new interpretation of the season, for the rage of the temperate storm exceeds in force, violence and doom the powers of the 'unrelenting' climes. Horror and violence exist wherever nature does, and man, animals, and inanimate nature are common parts of a world, the meanings of which are to be taken on faith.

The torrid storm (788–802) was an elemental struggle in which the 'Vapours' made the air yield to the clouds, laden with ocean moisture. The 'conflicting Winds' (797) clashed together, and fiery thunder was king (798). The storm of conflict ended in the victory of the deluge, but the temperate storm turns on inverse light imagery with its developing, progressive beginning in the darkness over the 'lurid Grove' (1103–7), gradually mounting to the heavens—darkness being drawn from 'the secret Beds,/ Where sleep the mineral Generations.' Yet it was the minerals that confirmed by their light the sun's mighty power (*Summer*, 134), so that the minerals are both the expressions of light and of darkness, just as there are two kinds of overflow, two effects of sun—heat and light—both of which can be either good or bad. Here it should be noted that the scientific terms give a mystery and para-doxical allusion to the peaceful sources of the storm, since the trans-formed 'wrathful Vapour' is drawn from 'Beds' in which the minerals 'sleep,'

> Thence Niter, Sulphur, and the fiery Spume
> Of fat Bitumen, steaming on the Day,
> With various-tinctur'd Trains of latent Flame,
> Pollute the Sky.
>
> (1108-11)

This contrast develops in terms of sight (darkness and flame) and then of sound, including the 'Dash of Clouds, or irritating War/Of fighting Winds' (1114-15) of the first storm and the dreadful antici-patory silence of the second: 'A boding Silence reigns' (1116). The silence, the reference to the forest leaf 'without a Breath' (1120), the cattle who cast a 'deploring Eye' (1125), these are connecting links with the *Spring* storm:

> Gradual, sinks the Breeze,
> Into a perfect Calm; that not a Breath
> Is heard to quiver thro the closing Woods,
> Or rustling turn the many-twinkling Leaves
> Of Aspin tall.
>
> (*Spring*, 155-59)

The remarkable quality of the storm passage is based on the combina-tion of internal allusions, of sound and sight, of the mingling of the elements in the eruption of the storm, shuttling between personi-fication and natural description.

The consequences of the storm include the shattering of the pine (1150), the blasted cattle (1152), dead flocks (1153-55), the struck tower (1156-8), the mountain's avalanche (1161-68) and the death of Amelia (1169-1222). The powerful destruction carries with it as a primary allusion the reference to escape to the shade in *Summer* through the address to Stanley (564-84). The address to the shade and the refreshing trees was a refuge from the heat: 'Welcome, ye Shades! ye bowery Thickets, hail!/Ye lofty Pines! ye venerable oaks!'

(469–70). But the storm gives no welcome to the pines, nor to the cattle. There was the brook containing the herds and flocks and the 'strong laborious Ox' (490) providing refreshment and ease. Herds, flocks, cattle—all are now dead. The earlier passage read, 'A various Groupe the Herds and Flocks compose' (485); the later reads, 'stretch'd below,/A lifeless Groupe the blasted Cattle lie' (1151–52). The raging power of the storm defies explanation as it disorders the seasons (by an avalanche in *Summer*) and strikes down the harmless flocks (1153). For these, with the looks 'They wore alive' (1154), are another example of imitated life without life and without the vigor, warmth and movement of life.

The 'midnight Depth/Of yonder Grove' (516–17) with its 'listening Gloom' (521) was a haunt of meditation, but the storm enters the recess of the woods and creates terror there. The angels and inspiring bards had spoken to the narrator in the meditative haunts, and only at this point in the poem does the meaning of one part of their message become clear: if some have to toil through tempestuous lives to attain calm (*Summer*, 548–50), others live lives of 'holy Calm' (550), only to be killed by tempests. The episode of Celadon and Amelia, a narrative told in the idealized language of the moral commentator, is an ironic commentary upon 'stormy Life' and 'Tempest-beaten.'

> Alone, amid the Shades,
> Still in harmonious Intercourse they liv'd
> The rural Day, and talk'd the flowing Heart,
> Or sigh'd, and look'd unutterable things.
>
> (1185–88)

Caught in the storm as they walk in the woods, innocent Amelia is terrified, and Celadon, echoing the reference to the earlier seraphic strain (563) declares:

> 'that very Voice,
> Which thunders Terror thro the guilty Heart,
> With Tongues of Seraphs whispers Peace to thine.
> 'Tis Safety to be near thee sure, and thus
> To clasp Perfection!'
>
> (1210–14)

The implicit commentary upon such naïve belief is the conclusion:

> From his void Embrace,
> (Mysterious Heaven!) that moment, to the Ground,
> A blacken'd Corse, was struck the beauteous Maid.

But who can paint the Lover, as he stood,
Pierc'd by severe Amazement, hating Life,
Speechless, and fix'd in all the Death of Woe!
So, faint Resemblance, on the Marble-Tomb,
The well-dissembled Mourner stooping stands,
For ever silent, and for ever sad.

(1214–22)

John Scott (1788), who was an intelligent and careful critic of *The Seasons*, missed the point of Celadon's speech and the function of the idealized language here, finding the innocent speech 'tedious.'[34] Scott is right about its tedium though it is supposed to be a series of false claims. For the point is that the idealized clichés can provide no proper interpretation of the moral control of the universe. The seraphs and angels warn the poet that the innocent do not necessarily avoid the sacrifices which may be demanded of the guilty.

Thomson's narratives belong to a typical eighteenth-century procedure—the interpolated story. In my analysis of Thomson's unity these belong with the spectrum descriptions, the actions of 'sad Presage' and the prospect views as instances of 'completed fragments,' the organizational units in the poem. Here it is proper to distinguish between the type of completion in the scenes of 'sad Presage' and those of the narratives. The former are open-ended, the conclusion leaving an anxious and worried figure waiting for a clue to the action that seems endlessly puzzling. The narratives, however, are complete, providing clear solutions to the episodes. Structurally, the narratives are organic units in an inorganic poem. They are highly-knit units told in a style that contrasts with the preceding or following fragments that are associatively developed. The narratives stand out, together with the scenes of 'sad Presage,' because in them humans move to the forefront, become the subject of the episodes.

The organic wholeness of the human narratives reveals an important feature of the poem's organization. Interrelatedness within these fragments creates momentarily a world that appears complete and self-explanatory, but the point that should be made is that such organicism is an illusion the narratives do not convey the total vision of the poem, they merely provide an aspect of human experience. For Thomson the organic is part of the incomplete, the fragmented conception of experience. To have it otherwise is to create a world that does not resemble the world man feels and knows. The difference between Thomson's organization and Coleridge's, for example, is that what is an incidental kind of unity for the first is the essential unifying procedure of the second. And this applies to the concept of opposites, too. For Thomson, these are another form of blending because no complete unity is possible; for Coleridge, they fuse into a unity.

There are three interpolated stories; Celadon and Amelia, Damon and Musidora, Palemon and Lavinia. There are other narratives, though not stories, which need to be mentioned in a study of the technique: the fishing scene in *Spring*, the dying shepherd in *Winter*. The primary difference between these is that the stories deal with the relations between human beings, the others describe an individual in his relation to nature. The first group are all love stories; the second describe, and I use 'describe' deliberately, actions depicting man's and nature's power. These descriptions are merely more detailed, more extensive than other scenes in *The Seasons*, and they occupy an intermediate position between descriptions of places and the stories about people.

The narratives offer perspectives on human love, keeping before the reader the vision of a lost Eden or a Golden Age. Celadon and Amelia live in the bosom of nature, 'with each other blest' (1193), and their 'creative Love/Still bade eternal *Eden* smile around' (1193–94). But no Eden can be created by man himself, and in the storm innocent Amelia is struck dead by lightning. In the *Autumn* story, Palemon is described as living the life of the Golden Age, and he accidentally finds Lavinia and wins even greater happiness:

> The Pride of Swains
> Palemon was, the Generous, and the Rich,
> Who led the rural Life in all its Joy,
> And Elegance, such as *Arcadian* Song
> Transmits from antient uncorrupted Times;
> When tyrant Custom had not shackled Man,
> But free to follow Nature was the Mode.
>
> (*Autumn*, 217–23)

In the narratives Thomson presents characters of innocence, purity, and prurience, and then demonstrates that success or failure is unrelated to an innocent life. The success or failure of love is accidental; only in heaven is there true reward for virtue. On earth, therefore, the fragments of human experience are often determined by secret-working and accidental and unknown causes. Although human beings may be happy, may indeed find personal harmony, this harmony is not necessarily the reward of God. The uncertainty and anxiety which overtake the individual are the result of God's ways unknown to man. Thomson suggests this uncertainty by hinting at an allegorical interpretation of Amelia and Celadon; they are personified *Spring* and *Summer* appropriately related, yet the relation is destroyed. ('Hers the mild Lustre of the blooming Morn,/And his the Radiance of the risen Day' (1175–76) and 'each was to each a dearer Self' (1183).

They are the allegorical couple of a prelapsarian world or garden, and they function in Thomson's vocabulary as 'Emblems' (*Summer*, 465) of virtue:

> such their guileless Passion was,
> As in the Dawn of Time inform'd the Heart
> Of Innocence, and undissembling Truth.
>
> (1177–79)

So, too, are Palemon and Lavinia. What the poet does to enforce this is to enclose his characters in the hiding-place of nature, and then create an ironic situation of actuality. Straying in the far 'Mazes' (1192), Amelia is killed; moving into the fields, 'compell'd/By strong Necessity's supreme Command' (*Autumn*, 214–15), Lavinia meets Palemon and her fortune is made. Both are turn-of-fortune stories resting on broad ironies. Celadon's assurances of the correspondence between virtue and happiness are exaggerated and overly obvious; Palemon's accidental good fortune at least is treated with possible skepticism since, when love and desire spring up in his bosom 'to himself unknown' (*Autumn*, 232), he succumbs not to his feelings but to his sense of social appropriateness:

> For still the World prevail'd, and its dread Laugh,
> Which scarce the firm Philosopher can scorn,
> Should his Heart own a Gleaner in the Field.
>
> (*Autumn*, 233–35)

Structurally speaking, the narratives make overt the relation of God's power to man, presenting man as the pawn and pride of creation.

The 'emblematic' stories illustrate particular qualities of the season; thus Celadon and Amelia in the storm illustrate the ironic unenlightenment of lightning; Musidora illustrates the heat of cooling water. The three stories are love stories: love that is struck down, love that is discovered, and love that is uncovered.

160

The Musidora narrative is mock heroic, alluding to the legends of Paris, of Venus's birth. The connection between Celadon and Amelia and that of Musidora is made by the tempering of nature's power, but the narrator rebukes man for forgetting the faith which the storm taught, 'That Sense of Powers exceeding far his own' (1242). There is no necessary reason why swimming should follow at this point: it might perhaps be governed by the associative principle of contiguity: water passages flow together; or it might be seen as the principle of resemblance, for the clouds pour 'prone-descending' 'a whole Flood' (1146) and the youth plunges 'headlong down the circling Flood' (1249). But there is no doubt about the ironic contrast which connects Musidora's swimming with the boy's. The narrator remarks, 'Even, from the Body's Purity, the Mind/Receives a secret sympathetic Aid.' (1267–68). Musidora's swimming leads her to welcome a sexual surrender.

The mock-idyllic style of the Musidora episode is a deliberate contrast to, even while echoing, the idyllic narrative of Palemon and Lavinia in *Autumn*. It was revised in 1744, the same time Thomson added some lines to the *Autumn* narrative, and the poetic procedure here is governed by the same illusive allusion as that in the eagle-barnyard comparison of *Spring*. Thomson wrote of Musidora,

> She felt his [Damon's] Flame; but deep within her Breast,
> In bashful Coyness, or in maiden Pride,
> The soft Return conceal'd; save when . . .
>
> (*Summer*, 1277–79)

He composed the following lines about Lavinia:

> By Solitude and deep surrounding Shades,
> But more by bashful Modesty, conceal'd.
>
> (*Autumn*, 184–85)

The tender idyllic life of Lavinia had not the special 'purity' of Musidora's. When Musidora rushes naked into the water, while spied upon by Damon, the narrator compares her to the lily and rose (retained from the 1730 edition):

> As shines the Lily thro the Crystal mild;
> Or as the Rose amid the Morning Dew,
> Fresh from *Aurora*'s Hand, more sweetly glows.
>
> (1325–27)

161

Lavinia's external appearance is described as follows:

> Her Form was fresher than the Morning-Rose,
> When the Dew wets its Leaves; unstain'd, and pure,
> As is the Lily, or the Mountain Snow.
>
> (*Autumn*, 192–94)

There is an ironic distinction between the clothed innocence of Lavinia and the naked Musidora in the brook. One is untouched and unstained, the other more 'sweetly glows' through the water. So, too, Lavinia is veiled in a simple robe, but Musidora's simple robe permits Damon's gaze a more intimate view with the illusive pun on 'rose':

> thro the parting Robe, th' alternate Breast,
> With Youth wild-throbbing, on thy lawless Gaze
> In full Luxuriance rose.
>
> (1311–13)

The design of the episode is to illustrate how Musidora's concealed feelings become exposed when her body is exposed. The attitude of the poet to Damon, who observes Musidora undressing, is mock-heroic.

> Thrice happy Swain!
> A lucky Chance, that oft decides the Fate
> Of mighty Monarchs, then decided thine.
> For lo! conducted by the laughing Loves,
> This cool Retreat his MUSIDORA sought.
>
> (*Summer*, 1285–89)

The 'dubious Flutterings' of Damon's soul are stilled after no serious conflict and he resigns himself to watching his beloved disrobe. The description of Musidora proceeds with extravagant sexual imagery, and Damon is compared to Paris:

> when aside
> The Rival-Goddesses the Veil divine
> Cast unconfin'd, and gave him all their Charms.
>
> (*Summer*, 1305–7)

The comparison of peeping Damon with heroic Paris, and the rather dissimilar situations involved, plays with the tradition of immortal sexuality; and Damon is near madness from this 'Soul-distracting View.' Thomson creates an analogy between Damon's sensuousness and that of nature: 'Then to the Flood she rush'd; the parted Flood/ Its lovely Guest with closing Waves receiv'd' (1321–22).

The departure of Damon ('Check'd, at last,/By Love's respectful Modesty') is a burlesque of the distraught lover, for he 'struggling from the Shade,/With headlong Hurry fled: but first these Lines,/Trac'd by his ready Pencil' (1337–39). The return of Musidora to the shore continues the mock-heroic comparison only to conclude with an invitation to love. The next line of the poem begins a description of the sun: 'THE Sun has lost his Rage . . .' (1371). The revisions of the original passage, which was a maturation sequence rather than a mock-heroic sexual one, suggests the irony. Thus there were added the 'dubious Flutterings,' and the lines, while gazing on naked Musidora, 'But, desperate Youth,/How durst thou risque the Soul-distracting View.' The exchange of notes, together with its sensual, teasing implications, was also added. In *Liberty*, IV, 175–84, Thomson described the Venus di Medici in the sensuous and playful tone he had used earlier in the Musidora episode, indicating that he identified her with a "dissembled sense/Of modest shame':

> The queen of love arose, as from the deep
> She sprung in all the melting pomp of charms.
> Bashful she bends, her well-taught look aside
> Turns in enchanting guise, where dubious mix
> Vain conscious beauty, a dissembled sense
> Of modest shame, and slippery looks of love.
>
> (*Liberty*, IV, 175–80)

The revised Musidora passage was followed by a passage on manners, added in 1744, to parallel the Lyttelton addition to *Spring*:

> THE Sun has lost his Rage: his downward Orb
> Shoots nothing now but animating Warmth,
> And vital Lustre.
>
> (1371–73)

It has become customary to treat *The Seasons* as though Thomson's diction is solemnly inflated or enthusiastically sentimental, except for his openly acknowledged burlesque in *Autumn*. But this is to misunderstand Thomson's language as well as his attitude to sex. Not only do the sexual references in *Spring* provide a sensual attitude to human behavior, but the reference to Musidora and some of those to the lower classes, whether to the ruddy maid, 'half-naked' (*Summer*, 356) or the *Autumn* 'Village Toast' (1225) with her 'not-unmeaning Looks' (1227) present characteristic Thomsonian attitudes. In the colloquial language of his letters, Thomson expresses himself with robust frankness. He writes to William Paterson, April 1748, referring to his friends as 'Brother-Gardeners': 'They happily for themselves, have no other Idea, but to dig on her, eat, drink, sleep and mow their wives.'[35] And in the same letter: 'Peter Murdoch is in Town, Tutor to Admiral Vernon's Son, and is in good Hopes of another Living in Suffolk, that Country of Tranquillity, where he will then burrow himself in a Wife and be happy.'[36] Thomson's comic blasphemy shocked William Shenstone, who in reporting Thomson's visit to Leasowes in 1746, made the following comment: 'Hearing the Dam there was made by the Monks, O! says he [Thomson] that is God-dam, the wit of which I could not see.' Shenstone was referring to a comic, blasphemous remark, but there have been very few critics who have recognized unblasphemous wit or comedy in *The Seasons*.

The laxness of 'Shoots nothing now' and the shift from light as 'Nature's resplendent Robe' (92) to the clouds as 'those beauteous Robes of Heaven (1374) signal the movement from the fiery sun to its gentle influence, to the 'pathetic Song' (1383), to the ebbing of power. When the speaker isolates himself by a retreat to the 'fairer World' of the ideal, he becomes, like the poet in *Spring*, lost in a 'Dream' in which the 'Swellings of the soften'd Heart,/ . . . waken, not disturb the tranquil Mind' (*Spring*, 465–66).

Here loneliness permits harmony and social visions (dreams) of 'a fairer World,' and the lonely mariner is not present to question the idyllic image of which the 'Vulgar never had a Glimpse' (1387). As in his other efforts at idealized language, Thomson offers formal repetition as an organizational procedure to substitute for harmonic interchange, and he moves from this passage into the upper-class catalog discussed earlier, beginning, 'Heavens! what a goodly Prospect spreads around' (1438), a passage that had, in 1727, been placed at the conclusion of what I have called Part I. In that edition, the first part of *Summer* ended with a highly nationalistic praise of Britannia, which Thomson considerably extended and reordered in 1744. The shift possesses an organizational significance for two reasons: in the 1744 edition the praise follows the inserted passage of Thomson's friends and their stately homes, relating national attachment to love of landscape, and in the concluding evening passage, the rhetoric of glory serves as a contrast to nature's changing forms.

When Thomson was composing *Summer* in August, 1726, he wrote Mallet that his verses 'contain a Panegyric on Brittain, which may perhaps contribute to make my Poem popular. The English People are not a little vain of Themselves, and their Country. Brittania too includes our native Country Scotland.'[37] Although Thomson was not unwilling to win readers by flattery, his removal of the passage from its original place in the design served to support the conception of organization, even though the entire fragment is far from being an artistic success.

The relation between local attachment (love of place) and love of country is self-evident from the original passage, only slightly revised in 1744:

> Happy Britannia! where the Queen of Arts,
> Inspiring Vigour, Liberty, abroad,
> Walks thro' the Land of Heroes, unconfin'd
> And scatters Plenty with unsparing Hand.
>
> (*Summer, A*, 498–501)

The image of the 'Queen of Arts' scattering plenty redundantly 'with unsparing Hand' has its complement in the *Autumn* squire who permits his husbandmen to fling 'From the full Sheaf, with charitable Stealth,/The liberal Handful' (168–69). The rewards of industry are spread at home and abroad by benevolent powers.

The tribute to Britain's glory concludes with the exclamation 'Island of Bliss!' (1595) and an invocation to God to 'Send forth the saving Virtues round the Land,/In bright patrol' (1604–5). Some of these virtues are personifications—'tender-looking *Charity*' (1606), '*Courage* compos'd, and keen' (1609), 'That first paternal Virtue, *public Zeal*' (1616)—but others are too faint to be so considered, functioning without any relational force in the passage: 'white *Peace*, and social *Love*' (1605), 'Undaunted *Truth*, and Dignity of Mind' (1608). These virtues constitute a static painting of a scene of allegorical patriotism with paternal zeal in the forefront:

> While in the radiant Front, superior shines
> That first paternal Virtue, *public Zeal*,
> Who throws o'er all an equal wide Survey,
> And, ever musing on the common Weal,
> Still labours glorious with some great Design.
>
> (1615–19)

The static use of transformatory terms of movement like 'shares,' 'throws,' 'labours' reduces the vigor of the language and thought. In terms of Thomson's sensibility this kind of impoverishment results from a movement that becomes internalized without providing any corresponding action to illustrate the transformation. Thus 'public Zeal,' although surveying the virtues and musing on the commonweal, 'labours glorious,' but only in the sense of contemplating some great design. In 1727 the joining passage following this reads:

> To sing her Praises, in ambitious Verse;
> While, slightly to recount, I simply meant,
> The various Summer-Horrors, which infest
> Kingdoms that scorch below severer Suns.
>
> (*Summer*, *A*, 612–15)

But the dreary catalog of nationalism is followed in the 1744 version by a description of the setting sun that contrasts sharply with the didactic tone of the attendant virtues.

Thomson's nationalism mixed with a defense of property has been called 'Whig panegyric,' and A. D. McKillop, quoting *Winter*, 973–75, and *The Castle of Indolence*, II, xxvii, refers to this as the 'Augustan compromise': 'This is the Augustan compromise we may say, reconciling pleasure and social purpose, with landscape gardening as the representative art.'[38] He finds that Addison in *Spectator* 414 'lays down the program clearly.' This program may represent Thomson's version of the ideal, as it does in the above praise of Britain and in his admiration of Hagley Hall and Stowe, for he sees these as reflecting man's version of natural harmony, a blending of different elements. But it must not be assumed that for Thomson they were anything other than an ideal.

There is a direct relation between Thomson's conception of the family of nature and his patriotism. In his imaginative flights to the torrid and frigid zones and in his awareness of the simultaneous existence of an ideal historic past, he assumed that harmony among groups involves a commerce that can be financed only by wealth and carried out only by authority. There are in *The Seasons* numerous ideal look-out points, and these can exist even in the frigid home of the Laplanders, but the functioning of this ideal as responsible social and economic commerce, the sharing of Britain's granary with less fortunate countries, requires ships, merchants, labourers, and the resources of many enterprises. Thomson praises Britain and takes pride in his country because it creates international harmony and commerce among the family of states. The dangers that men face in nature make it necessary for them to have faith in God's wisdom, but simultaneously they must have faith and pride in a secular authority that acts to maintain the known and observed harmony. And Britain is such a state.

Thomson recognized in *The Seasons* that squires often neglected to honor their responsibilities and he saw that nature often did not correspond to man's desires. He did not overlook man's inhumanity to man, nor did he find that pleasure was always reconciled with social purpose. Although such reconcilement was desirable, he found it necessary to stress retreat as an aspect of the ideal, such withdrawal being sometimes made necessary by the untrustworthy nature of political behavior. In holding to an ideal that was difficult of achievement, he necessarily felt the anxiety that surrounded its fulfillment. He urged benevolence upon man, but he knew that pride interfered with its practice and that landscape, for all its art, was inferior to the sublimity of 'Nature, wide and wild.'

Summer is the season of light and heat, of power, of spatial extent, of brilliance and destruction accompanied by abrupt changes of place. The power and intensity of summer led the narrator to explore the torrid zone with its fierce changes from the temperate. The anxiety as well as the pleasure which he finds there, he ultimately discovers again in the temperate zone. But he also finds, despite the contradictory powers of love and destruction, the possibilities for boundless love and wisdom in religious faith.

Thus as the sun sets and darkness descends, man's mind rises to the possibilities for escape from his bounded and often painful existence. And just as the sun can descend in his power and glory, man can rise by giving himself up to love of God. But the ironic, vain behavior of man does not permit him always to accept this choice, and as the preceding sections have developed a realization of nature's contrary powers, so at the conclusion of *Summer* man and nature are correspondingly developed with regard to the ensuing darkness. For if the sun sets, it will rise, and if this dark state is hidden from man, the other boundless world will illumine it.

The pomp and glory of the setting sun is concluded with the line 'Gives one bright Glance, then total disappears' (1629), which is immediately followed by a comment on man's vanity, for if the sun has to set, who is man to believe he is greater than nature. Nature, the sun, willingly accepts its cyclical descent, but man persists in his sordid vanity as though he is no slave to any descent but his own.

FOR ever running an enchanted Round,
Passes the Day, deceitful, vain, and void;
As fleets the Vision o'er the formful Brain,
This Moment hurrying wild th' impassion'd Soul,
The next in nothing lost.

(1630–34)

The 'cruel Wretch' (1636) who has spent himself in pleasure, disregarding the needy, is then contrasted with the man of 'generous still-improving Mind' (1641): 'To him the long Review of order'd Life/Is inward Rapture, only to be felt' (1645–46).

The personified sun and personified evening are both mixed with natural description conveying the quiet order of descending nature, and making it possible for the good man to be seen in these terms. Thus he diffuses his beneficence in silence, 'Boastless, as now descends the silent Dew' (1644), exactly as the sun sets in silence, and evening sends its soft shadows to earth. By this naturalizing metaphor the good man's silences are not even 'emphatic'; their modesty is so great that they compare with the cyclical changes in gentle nature. But the attempt to identify the pleasure-seeking man with wild motion, with abnormality rather than with the normal and expected part of nature, falsifies his meanness. Viciousness can wear the disguise of beauty, just as beneficence can appear destructive; to identify beneficence in men and nature with idealized gentleness is to describe a pastoral Eden, not actual behavior. Indeed, this description of the cycle of nature soon turns to the actual in the game of the shepherd and the ruddy milkmaid.

Summer dealt with the beautiful, the enlightening, the violent and destructive aspects of nature, and the innocent Amelia was a victim, just as the innocent animals were victims. To assume a necessary harmony between man and nature is to idealize a moment, to suggest that in the cycle of nature, seeds are sown and food always springs up. Thus even paradoxes can be idealized, for as darkness closes 'the Face of Things' (1654), a white shower descends, and the 'Shower' of 'vegetable Down' is not merely a transformation, but a foreshadowing of food:

Wide o'er the thistly Lawn, as swells the Breeze,
A whitening Shower of vegetable Down
Amusive floats. The kind impartial Care
Of Nature nought disdains: thoughtful to feed
Her lowest Sons, and clothe the coming Year,

168

From Field to Field the feather'd Seeds she wings.

(1658–63)

In *Winter*, Thomson describes the falling snow as 'the whitening Shower descends' (229), and this snowfall covers 'Earth's universal Face' (238). The 'Face of Things' and 'Earth's universal Face' refer, of course, only to those portions of the earth's surface that are dark in the first instance and snow-covered in the second. In the personification of both instances the poet uses one aspect of nature to influence and alter another. If in *Summer* it creates a metaphoric harmony, in *Winter* it creates an apparent consistency that belies the burial of normal forms. That the poet in *Summer* exploits the parental metaphor to sentimentalize nature reveals that he is converting poetical description into ideal movement. For nature here is not wildly hurrying but winging purposefully and reasonably.

Yet Thomson specifies the degree of available understanding of nature, for the poet's commentary—that nature 'nought disdains'—turns on the shepherd who loves 'Unknowing what the Joy-mixt Anguish means' (1668). The *Spring* lover knew, but the *Summer* shepherd is unenlightened. Not only does the shepherd not understand the paradoxical feelings of love, but as the lovers stroll home, they do not even seek to understand those signs of puzzling and mysterious behavior, the grave of the suicide, the lovely and ghost-claimed towers. There exist in nature scenes and feelings not understood, but which can be understood, and those which, like the storms and destruction, cannot be understood and must be taken on faith. The joyous, gentle, idealized moment of sunset is replaced by the actualities of evening. The twinkling glow-worm gives to the beauty of the night an autumnal uncertainty and anxiety:

A faint erroneous Ray,
Glanc'd from th' imperfect Surfaces of Things,
Flings half an Image on the straining Eye.

(1687–89)

Then, with sudden brilliance, Venus appears. Certainty replaces uncertainty. And star Venus is compared allusively to the impure Venus di Medici described earlier. The poet breaks out in his own person. The descent of the night leads to the ascent of the poet—'th' Effulgence tremulous I drink' (1699)—and imbibing truly and purely the beauty of Venus, he both joys in and enjoys the heavens.

Since *Summer* was the season of the power of heat and light, of wandering despite sacrifice, the climax of *Summer* is the participation in God's power, the 'dread Immensity of Space' (1706). For the poet's drinking of *Summer*'s 'Effulgence' is interrupted by the shooting comet. And the 'rushing Comet to the Sun descends' (1708) as the sun descended below the horizon, as the shadows of evening descended upon earth, as man let his beneficence descend. The blazing comet is seen rushing through space, frightening guilty nations and the 'fond sequacious Herd' (1713) enslaved by superstitious terrors. But the poet in his hunger for movement and in his curiousity belongs with the enlightened few—those who love light and do not fear its power:

> th' enlighten'd Few,
> Whose Godlike Minds Philosophy exalts,
> The glorious Stranger hail.
>
> (1714–16)

Just as the herds gazed at the hippopotamus—'the harmless Stranger' (*Summer*, 715)—who possessed strange form and power, so the few hail the flying comet, and their courage and godlike quality is exalted by natural science, 'Philosophy,' 'That wondrous Force of Thought, which mounting spurns/This dusky Spot, and measures all the Sky' (1718–19). The enlightened are those who do not fear the fires in space, despite the seeming terror, but know that comets 'work the Will of all-sustaining Love' (1724). For even if they know the scientific justification for comets, there is also an act of faith which extends beyond this knowledge.

The enlightened few possess a 'wondrous Force of Thought' (1718) that mounts to the skies, and the technique of moving from the passive observers to active doers illustrates the transformatory power of science. The enlightened are analogically 'blazing wonders' of the skies. When the poet, therefore, hails 'philosophy' in a concluding invocation, he does so in the imagery of space, light and power, the characteristics of *Summer*. But the invocation to philosophy, scientific knowledge, because it 'crowns' (1731) the season, is puffed out of proportion to its place in the poem.

At the outset of *Summer* 'Inspiration' was invoked, so that the narrator might

> steal one Look
> Creative of the Poet, every Power
> Exalting to an Ecstasy of Soul.   (18–20)

Thus the powers stolen from inspiration are as necessary as the powers of philosophy. Philosophy sheds a lustre 'o'er th' ennobled Mind' (1733) that soothes with 'nourish'd Powers, enlarg'd by thee' (1737). But neither the 'ennobled Mind' nor the 'nourish'd Powers' have any very clear definitions, and the idealized claim that philosophy leads reason and fancy to true and clear views of God and the world is not meant to justify either deism or rationalism. Philosophy is and remains dependent upon the secret workings of God in nature, in society or in man.

Summer concludes with a statement of the limits of philosophy. At the opening of Part II, the scenes in the torrid zone were paradoxically described 'with dreadful Beauty crown'd/And barbarous Wealth' (633–34); although philosophy is a crown of light, its halo shines only in this world. Ultimately it leaves man in 'this dark State'— for all the flight and light of philosophy, it is, in explaining final causes, a cloud of unknowing. It answers neither the initial question of why man and nature are what they are, nor the final question of how God's perfection works. Knowledge without inspiration or industry or the secret-working hand of God is insufficient, just as each of these without knowledge is insufficient for enlightenment. But Thomson fails to indicate this blending; here he substitutes for the actual the idealized view of what might be:

> taught by Thee,
> Ours are the Plans of Policy, and Peace;
> To live like Brothers, and conjunctive all
> Embelish [*sic*] Life.

(1774–77)

The life of man, however, is not the life of brotherhood in *The Seasons*, even though there are some men who represent justice and some who act as brothers; for Christians exploit the savages and pleasure-seeking men disregard the needs of the poor. Even in Britain, most political heroes are those who have died or been martyred as a result of their heroism, for it was Raleigh who

> found no Times, in all the long Research,
> So glorious, or so base, as Those he prov'd,
> In which he conquer'd, and in which he bled.

(1508–10)

The glorious and the base are at the heart of *Summer*, and the conclusion is that philosophy cannot penetrate 'this dark State,' that only in the immortal state can the rising mind 'prove' God's love and wisdom, until then to be taken on faith. Man cannot answer the questions about God's perfection, and it is ironically appropriate for *Summer* that, despite the high-flying mind, it should in the season of fire, light and power conclude with man's mortal darkness, his ultimate powerlessness:

> But here the Cloud,
> So wills ETERNAL PROVIDENCE, sits deep.
> Enough for us to know that this dark State,
> In wayward Passions lost, and vain Pursuits,
> This Infancy of Being, cannot prove
> The final Issue of the Works of GOD,
> By boundless LOVE and perfect WISDOM form'd,
> And ever rising with the rising Mind.

(1798–1805)

NOTES

[1] T. J. B. Spencer, 'Lucretius and the Scientific Poem in English,' *Lucretius*, ed. D. R. Dudley, London, 1965, p. 137.

[2] R. S. Crane, 'Notes toward a Genealogy of the Man of Feeling', *The Idea of the Humanities*, 1967, Chicago, I, 183–84.

[3] Aubrey Williams and E. Audra, ed., *Pastoral Poetry and the Essay in Criticism*, the Twickenham edition of the Poems of Alexander Pope, London, 1961, I, 138-39.

[4] Deane has a discussion of 'The Prospect Poem,' pp. 100–9. Thomson distinguishes among 'landscape (*Spring* (3), *Summer* (4)) as an inclusive term for a rural scene observed from ground level; 'prospect' (*Spring* (3), *Summer* (4), *Autumn* (3), *Winter* (3)), an extended view from a height; 'vista' (*Spring* (2)), a view between rows of trees, and 'view'. (*Spring* (4), *Summer* (3), *Autumn* (9), *Winter* (3)), a general term for that which is observed by the eye or mind.

[5] John More, *Strictures Critical and Sentimental on Thomson's 'Seasons'*, London, 1785, was the first critic to notice this procedure. See p. 54.

[6] *Letters*, p. 78.

[7] George Berkeley, *Works on Vision*, ed. Colin Murray Turbayne, Indianapolis, 1963, p. xxx.

[8] Martin Price, *To the Palace of Wisdom*, New York, 1964, p. 353.

[9] Quoted by Douglas Grant, *James Thomson*, London 1951, p. 233.

[10] Marie Boas, *Robert Boyle and Seventeenth-century Chemistry*, Cambridge, 1958, pp. 96-98.

[11] Jean Hagstrum, *The Sister Arts*, Chicago, 1958, p. 256.

[12] Kester Svendson, *Milton and Science*, Cambridge, 1956, pp. 66-67.

[13] Tillotson, *Augustan Studies*, p. 96, points out that the mixing of the formal genres in a single poem may have caused the diction of the different kinds to be confounded.

[14] McKillop, *Background*, p. 155.

[15] G. Wilson Knight, *The Poetry of Pope*, New York, 1965, pp. 83, 86, 94.

[16] Rachel Trickett, 'The Augustan Pantheon,' *Essays and Studies*, London, 1953, p. 82.

[17] Maynard Mack, 'On Reading Pope,' *CE*, VII (1946), 264-65.

[18] Quoted by Zippel, p. 240.

[19] *Ibid.*, p. 240.

[20] *Ibid.*, p. 240.

[21] *Ibid.*, p. 240.

[22] *Ibid.*, p. 241.

[23] *Ibid.*, p. 241. Eighteen years later, in a letter to Lyttelton (14 July 1743) Thomson found that the spring and summer seasons no longer had quite the attraction they originally possessed for him. He now preferred autumn to them, a season which he called 'serious and tempered joy'— though *Autumn* with its burlesque episode and constant changes seems only in part to resemble the actual season to which Thomson refers:

As this will fall in Autumn, I shall like it the better, for I think that season of the year the most pleasing and the most poetical. The spirits are not then dissipated with the gaiety of Spring and the glaring light of Summer, but composed into a serious and tempered joy—The Year is perfect. (*Letters*, p. 163).

[24] *Ibid.*, pp. 241-2.

[25] *Ibid.*, p. 239.

[26] *Ibid.*, p. 239.

[27] *Ibid.*, p. 243.

[28] McKillop, *Castle*, p. 195.

[29] Zippel, p. 241.

[30] *Letters*, p. 46.

[31] *The Spectator*, ed. Donald F. Bond, Oxford, 1965, III, 540–41.

[32] 'Imitations of Horace,' Epistle II, *The Poems of Alexander Pope*, ed. John Butt, New Haven, 1963, p. 641.

[33] McKillop, *Background*, p. 71, declares that Thomson's statues 'are both realistic and sentimental; they often represent natural catastrophes that are bizarre rather than sublime and are used as decorations that surprise and shock by an odd lifelikeness. They are, in fact, poetical wax-works.'

[34] John Scott, 'On Thomson's *Seasons*,' *Critical Essays on Some of the Poems of Several English Poets*, London, 1785, p. 306.

[35] *Letters*, p. 196.

[36] *Ibid.*, p. 197.

[37] *Ibid.*, p. 48.

[38] McKillop, *Castle*, p. 51.

III

AUTUMN
SUBSTANCE AND SHADOW

i. The Secret Forces of Change (1–150)

Autumn begins by struggling to release itself from the power and effulgence of *Summer*. As the season unfolds it describes the maturity of nature and its subsequent decline. It is, therefore, the season of radical changes tempered by the poet's view of melancholy, though pleasing, resignation. In *Spring* (49–52), the poet addressed the breezes, dews, showers and sun to lead to 'the perfect Year' (52), and the invocation treats *Autumn* as the achievement of this change:

> Whate'er the Wintry Frost
> Nitrous prepar'd; the various-blossom'd Spring
> Put in white Promise forth; and Summer-Suns
> Concocted strong, rush boundless now to View,
> Full, perfect all, and swell my glorious Theme.

(4–8)

Winter's frosty burial of nature, *Spring*'s multitudinous unfolding, *Summer*'s strength lead to *Autumn*'s completion, which will, before the end of the season, subside into bare boughs and melancholy gentleness.

The allegorical personification of the poet in *Autumn* is the conventional figure 'Crown'd with the Sickle and the wheaten Sheaf.'[1] But the recurrent image is the 'Flood of Corn' (42), the showers of fruit (630) and leaves (895). The references to water and its various conversions or to liquids as substitutes for water become organizing aspects of this season: the vulgar and generous pleasures of wine, the conversion of mists to rain, of moonlight to tides. Although the

174

poet expresses attitudes toward change in the other seasons, in this he urges the acceptance of those changes, expected or unexpected, in nature and man. When Thomson concludes the season with a Virgilian paraphrase, he acknowledges the changes but finds an understanding of them beyond his powers. He refers to the 'sluggish' (1368) blood streams around his heart and begs God to place him near the pacifying, harmonious brook and to 'whisper to my Dreams' in a direct vision that will soothe and comfort him.

> But if to that unequal; if the Blood,
> In sluggish Streams about my Heart, forbid
> That *best* Ambition; under closing Shades,
> Inglorious, lay me by the lowly Brook,
> And whisper to my Dreams.
>
> (1367–71)

I defined the various changes in *Spring* and *Summer* by treating Thomson's techniques of rhetoric and organization as they reflect his attitude to the elemental changes that objects and living things undergo. These techniques capture nature and man in transformation from one state to another, from one kind of beauty to another, from the beautiful to the sublime, from rapturous to awesome sublimity, from harmony to disharmony. The scientific basis for this change is the belief that elements are not stable but infinitely transmutable, and meteorologically that the seasons are capable of immense changes within prescribed naturalistic limits, underlying which there is a unity and harmony, even though not always observable by man. But even changes that can occur in the known world are often beyond man to detect or explain except by faith. For example, the sun darts deep to the roots of flowers, its light and heat giving them life and color. But heaven's lightning can strike and kill innocent Amelia. The elements can create reciprocal responses, but they can also create disharmony and cause dissimilarities. Light can create infinite colors but it can also extinguish colors, just as clouds (water) can send a shower of roses or a drowning torrential downpour. The reasons that determine such decisions are beyond human understanding.

In depicting a natural and human world in change Thomson captures the similarity of actions and the fragmentariness of perception. A storm in one place, shade in another, primitive man and civilized states, these are depicted as simultaneous occurrences, and they sometimes become part of a harmony image that implies a greater harmony than is immediately visible. The effects of harmony can appear in the birth and growth of flowers as well as in the continuity of virtue in the heroic representatives of past society and the idealized figures of the present. But fragmentation, man's partial perception of the present, also includes scenes of human and natural destruction that the speaker witnesses but cannot explain. The deaths of the distressed good and the plagues that separate loved ones and lead man to abnegate his social sympathies imply powers beyond man's understanding.

The concept of God's secret-working hand permits Thomson to avoid deism, the belief that God's views can be read in his works, that God operates by second causes rather than direct intervention. God operates directly by means of his secret-working powers, by commanding nature, and the poet, in turn, addresses him directly. In *Winter* it is God who walks amid the storm:

> Till Nature's KING, who oft
> Amid tempestuous Darkness dwells alone,
> And on the Wings of the careening Wind
> Walks dreadfully serene, commands a Calm;
> Then straight Air Sea and Earth are hush'd at once.
>
> (197–201)

In *Summer* God is directly present in the creation and continuity of light (175–84) and acknowledged by all nature:

> AND yet was every faultering Tongue of Man,
> ALMIGHTY FATHER! silent in thy Praise;
> Thy Works themselves would raise a general Voice,
> Even in the Depth of solitary Woods,
> By human Foot untrod, proclaim thy Power,
> And to the Quire celestial THEE resound.
> Th' eternal Cause, Support, and End of All!
>
> (185–91)

In a passage that echoes *Job*, Thomson asserts the need for belief, ridiculing man's attempt to understand God's wisdom and perfection:

> And lives the Man, whose universal Eye
> Has swept at once th' unbounded Scheme of Things;
> Mark'd their Dependance so, and firm Accord,
> As with unfaultering Accent to conclude
> That *This* availeth nought? Has any seen

176

The mighty Chain of Beings, lessening down
From INFINITE PERFECTION to the Brink
Of dreary *Nothing*, desolate Abyss!
From which astonish'd Thought, recoiling, turns?
Till then alone let zealous Praise ascend,
And Hymns of holy Wonder, to that POWER,
Whose Wisdom shines as lovely on our Minds,
As on our smiling Eyes his Servant-Sun.

(*Summer*, 329–41)

The need for faith, for hymns of 'holy Wonder,' result from man's necessary belief in God's wisdom, not from his knowledge of it. The narrative of Celadon and Amelia, or the destroyed harvest of the good husbandman, or the death of the shepherd in *Winter*, or the destruction of Palermo by earthquake and other passages argue for Thomson's implicit view that there is no necessary relation between human goodness and mortal reward. Thus the operation of God's hand can create nourishment, can cause health, can lead to man's acts of recognition of God's goodness. But the belief that man can understand the operation of God's power in the world or that there exists an exact correspondence between natural forces and temporal moral rewards is not supported by the evidence.

William Thompson, who in 1726 wrote *A Poetical Paraphrase on Part of the Book of Job*, argues that in *Job* man is seen as immediately under God's direction and care, and James Thomson's view seems to support this interpretation. William Thompson wrote:

Nothing could therefore be more becoming or worthy of God than the following Speech, which contains such evident Signs of his Wisdom and Power in the Formation of his Creatures, and the Disposal of natural Things. The greatest Instance, which the Greek or Latin Poets give of the Power and Might of their Gods, is Thunder and Lightning, or perhaps, on some extraordinary Occasion, an Earthquake; whereas the true God is here represented as wielding all the Elements of Nature and commanding each Part thereof, Light and Darkness, Snow and Vapour, Wind and Storm fulfilling his Word. To consider God in the Manner he is here represented, as immediately producing all the Appearances in Nature, without the Interposition or Concurrence of second Causes, brings him home to the Minds of Men, which was particularly the Method that was to be taken with Job, who imagined that God had

177

forgot him in his Misfortunes, and stood far off from him. This Conception of God must convince us, that we are immediately under his Direction and Care, and that we need only open our Eyes to behold him in every thing about us. This Reflection also must humble and subdue the Pride of Philosophers, who will for ever be unable to account for any of his Works, without having Recourse to his immediate Power.[2]

James Thomson was aware that nature could, in part, be understood by scientific explanations, but these never explain origins and final causes.

Thomson did not believe in the sufficiency of reason, even if he believed that 'reason'[3] is an emanation of the divine mind, because man only too often does not understand the messages he receives. The guilty, the proud, and the luxurious can live without necessarily being punished in this world. In heaven, knowledge leads to greater and greater wisdom and virtue in contrast to life here in which knowledge is fragmentary and human nature often fails to progress. Thus here the conception is that of a family with some members refusing to learn or obey whereas in the future world, only the good ascend and they will then know the reasons that now remain hidden.

The anxiety to which *Autumn* can lead is stressed when, after the effusive eulogy to Onslow, with its distending, spreading, glowing, the mildness of the season is suddenly interrupted by the returning 'Effulgence' of the *Summer* sun. The initial description of natural change—what might be called the tension between departing *Summer* and arriving *Autumn*—displays stylistic traits of imbalance and sudden extension. But the resolution of this change leads immediately into another, for *Autumn* proceeds by tracing man's change from primitivism to patriotism.

This change results from the awakening of unconscious forces and secret powers. The *Autumn* passage is, as I shall point out in *Winter*, only one of several perspectives on primitivism and progress; what I wish to pursue is the idea of the secret forces of change both as they appear here and as they are present throughout the poem. Thomson writes, 'In the unconscious Breast/Slept the lethargic Powers' (53–54), 'powers' that, when awakened, led to advances in civilization. But the secret forces are not merely forces for good; they caused man to decline from the Golden Age, released the chaotic storms, misguided the shepherd in his revolving fields. These contrary possibilities lurk in man and nature, and Thomson is not clear how they operate, but he is clear that they exist. 'Power(s),' 'force,' 'forceful,' 'powerful,' 'potent,' 'secret,' 'concealed'—these words as a group and in combinations occur more than one hundred times in *The Seasons*, and they characterize not merely the external energy of man and nature, but the secret-working power of God and His forces. God can intervene directly or can leave to man and nature the possibilities for growth or havoc. Thus man and nature are endowed with powers by God that they can use but not understand.

In *Spring* the poet, speaking of the forest, declares,

> At once, array'd
> In all the Colours of the flushing Year,
> By Nature's swift and secret-working Hand,
>
> (95–97)

In *Summer*, hailing the launching of the planets and the rotation of the seasons, he exclaims,

> 'TIS by thy secret, strong, attractive Force,
> As with a Chain indissoluble bound,
> Thy System rolls entire.
>
> (97–99)

And in *Autumn*, tracing the origin of waters, he asks,

> SAY then, where lurk the vast eternal Springs,
> That, like CREATING NATURE, lie conceal'd
> From mortal Eye, yet with their lavish Stores
> Refresh the Globe, and all its joyous Tribes?
>
> (773–76)

In *Summer* he writes that the 'Angels of Wrath,/Let loose, the raging Elements' (960–61), and in *Winter* he refers to the 'Demon of the Night' (193). Both these agents are personified forces that cause destructive changes and imply secret powers that govern the contrast between motion and motionlessness, between apparent stillness and actual stiffness. Although man spies the visual aspect of nature, there is God's power lurking within. Newton discovers what is discoverable, not what man cannot and ought not to know. For Wordsworth the secret powers become overt and part of an 'active universe.'[4] The mountains, lakes, winds and clouds in *The Prelude* are, writes Danby, '*powers*, agents in an active universe.'[4] But for Thomson their activity is secret, hidden from man's knowledge.

The poet tries to convey God's secret operations by inventing the technique of conversion that I discussed in *Summer*. In *Spring* the river appears immobile before a storm, but in *Winter* the river becomes motionless. In *Summer* Celadon appears like a statue, but in *Winter* Willoughby's men are actually frozen rigid into statues of ice. The conception serves to illustrate that God can actualize any metaphoric situation imagined by the poet. It also illustrates God's secret-working power in making appearances beautiful and the actuality painful, or the actuality beautiful and appearances painful. Such a view underlies the inevitable anxieties man feels in this world, for he cannot be sure of his capacity to interpret God's ways. This technique shares with personification and periphrasis a blend of the metaphoric with the literal. Although it has no necessary relation to irony, it bears a considerable similarity to Swift's procedure of 'literalization' as described by Maurice Quinlan: 'Basically it is a type of ambivalence achieved by contrasting the metaphorical and the literal significance of a term, in order to reveal an ironic disparity between the two meanings.'[5]

The unconscious forces stress the underlying anxieties man feels about nature and himself. For nature's powers are elusive and nature is paradoxical. Rivers appear motionless but they are full of motion and, in *Winter*, they are literally motionless but they are also full of motive power. In *Winter* when men become frozen as statues, they become part of the false shapes of the universe. They appear to have form or specific shape, but they become, as the disastered swain or Willoughby's men, part of the destructive and chaotic drifts. This would apply to the caravan in *Summer* and to all aspects of lifelessness which are destructive of the possibilities of order. If God is the 'informing Author' (*Spring*, 860), His 'form' here is surely concealed from mortal eyes.

The secret powers go beyond God's presence in nature; they are used to explain man's failure to recognize God:

> But wandering oft, with brute unconscious Gaze,
> Man marks not THEE, marks not the mighty Hand,
>
> (*Hymn*, 28–29)

But they can also be the source of moments of unexplainable delight. In *Summer*, praising the exercise of swimming, Thomson writes:

> Even, from the Body's Purity, the Mind
> Receives a secret sympathetic Aid.   (1267–68)

In *Autumn*, Palemon's love springs 'to himself unknown':

> That very Moment Love and chaste Desire
> Sprung in his Bosom, to himself unknown.
>
> (231–32)

Man cannot fathom God's reasons for acting, and when he presumes to do so, he is, like Celadon, subject to shock and disaster.

The secret forces can now be seen as related in part to the emphatic silences discussed in *Summer*, for these moments of pause are also moments of man's awareness of God's power. The secret powers are also applicable to an interpretation of Thomson's statements about poetry. Expression cannot paint the 'Hues on Hues' (*Spring*, 554), because the secret of variety is beyond man to conceive. Man's imitation of nature cannot possess its vividness because the sources by which vividness is created are hidden from him. Even God's goodness often comes as a surprise for it is a 'silent-working Heaven, surprising oft/The lonely Heart with unexpected Good' (*Spring*, 885–86).

ii. Stylistic Devices illustrating Change (151–706)

At the opening of *Autumn*, there is a breaking of the poise, and the sentence structure shows a marked alteration by shifting the phrasal modifier 'by Fits' that first follows then precedes the word it modifies:

> Rent is the fleecy Mantle of the Sky;
> The Clouds fly different; and the sudden Sun
> By Fits effulgent gilds th' illumin'd Field,
> And black by Fits the Shadows sweep along.
> A gayly-checker'd Heart-expanding View,
> Far as the circling Eye can shoot around,
> Unbounded tossing in a Flood of Corn.
>
> (36–42)

The short main clause is unbalanced by a co-ordinate clause composed of a series of abrupt terms that appear synonymous, followed by a series of appositives and phrases that contrast with it. The 'sudden' sun, with the strange use of an adjective of violent motion to modify 'Sun' that rotates in order, is just the kind of surprising change that characterizes the sun's *Summer*, not *Autumn*, behavior. For the sun is described 'by Fits effulgent' which alludes to the ferocity of 'fierce Effulgence' (25); but the 'Fit' is golden and it thus brings back the quality of parting *Summer* which has been replaced by the 'serener Blue' (26) of *Autumn*.[6] The 'illumin'd Field' refers again to *Summer*'s sudden return because *Autumn* suns send their rays 'thro lucid Clouds,' but the clouds have been 'Rent' (36) and the fields normally 'illumin'd' are now 'gilded.' The sun also hides as suddenly as it appears—'black by Fits the Shadows sweep along' (39)—with the large shadows of the clouds floating over the grain.

The concluding appositive refers to the entire shifting action of the sun and the effect it creates: 'A gayly-checker'd Heart-expanding View' (40) in which 'Heart-expanding' is the result of the sweeping motion and the light and shadow; it conveys a sense of extent, of the human expansion to match nature's surprising changefulness, and the eye 'shoots around' at the scene, looking directly at each change while seeing them all. 'Unbounded tossing' can modify 'View' with 'tossing' describing the view (in a 'tossing' flood of corn) or the 'circling Eye' can toss unbounded (in a circle) in the flood while 'shooting' looks all round. The image of the eye shooting in the flood depends upon getting the viewer to sympathize with nature; it also resolves the clash of suns by turning to a water image that converts the fields into tossing rivers. The stylistic devices—repetition for alteration, changed word order to convey unexpected effects, resolution of spatial distinctions by converting them to another element, and reconciling momentary and fragmented actions by conceiving of them as heart-expanding yet circular—support the view that fragments can be understood as parts of a larger harmony.

Adjective inversion, indeed inversion in general, is, of course, a characteristic device of poetry; in eighteenth-century nature poetry, in the tradition of Milton, it is often used to give impressiveness to the language, but there are varieties of inversion among Augustan poets; Alexander Pope's inversions, for example, can connect subject with object to create the import of an appositive or to hold together parts of speech that are opposed in meaning, by giving them the same modifiers or constructing apparently balanced lines. Thomson's sentence structure tends often to keep such grammatical entities deliberately discrete. Thus in Pope's 'checquer'd Scene' of *Windsor Forest* there is inversion of object and verb, but it functions, as do the sentences, differently from Thomson's 'Heart-expanding View.'

Here waving Graves a checquer'd Scene display,
And part admit and part exclude the Day;
As some coy Nymph her Lover's warm Address
Nor quite indulges, nor can quite repress.
There, interspers'd in Lawns and opening Glades,
Thin Trees arise that shun each others Shades.[7]

(17–22)

In Pope's lines, the opposites 'admit' and 'exclude' are preceded by the adverb 'part' just as 'indulges' and 'repress' are preceded by 'quite.' The groves are personified and interpreted as functioning normally by presenting alternate and contradictory responses, very much as a coquette neither quite welcomes nor rejects advances. Pope's lines indicate man's awareness of the partial, successive functioning of nature, while drawing attention to diverse, simultaneous actions of nature with the 'Here' and 'There.' Pope's interpretation is governed by a nature with formal likes and dislikes; it admits, excludes, shuns. Thomson's nature is spatially expansive, sweeping erratically along, rather than moving with Pope's ordered contraries. Whereas Pope looks to man for his model, Thomson looks to the transformation of elements, the gilded light now seen as yellow corn while the light from the fiery sun is transformed into a 'flood.'

As the *Autumn* morning begins—trembling 'o'er the Sky'—the poem continues the transition from the 'Stores' of *Autumn* (149) to the collection of these stores by the reaper. The personified morning 'trembling' (151) and unfolding 'the spreading Day' (152) continues the theme of *Autumn* with its uncertain changes. At the opening of *Spring* (11–47) an anxiety regarding change seems a necessary part of the cycle of imperfect nature and man. Ravaging and deforming Winter departs and the mountain-forests resume their *Spring* forms, but such resumption is interrupted and occasionally deformed again. Thus uncertainty is here identified with the difficulty of the season to release the latent possibilities of the previous one. Thus *Autumn* resembles *Spring* in its difficulty in removing itself from the domination of the previous season, but when it succeeds in doing so, the inevitability of change gradually leads to an acceptance of the vagaries of time and fortune, to the unexpected good fortune of Lavinia and the bad fortune of the husbandman. As the season begins to unfold, these two episodes imply the basis for exercising charity to others. For only as one exercises charity when he has wealth, does he set an

example of the possibility for charity when he loses it. The turns of
fortune are not, however, contingent upon man's giving or not
giving. The loss of fortune, like its renewal, is in God's power to
determine.

The dependent gleaners, in contrast to the husbandmen, have but a
'sparing Harvest' (166); their 'sparing Harvest' though matched by
the sparing of the winds is contrasted with the storm that drowns the
harvest of the husbandmen:

> all that the Winds had spar'd,
> In one wild Moment ruin'd, the big Hopes,
> And well-earn'd Treasures of the painful Year.
>
> (341-43)

In the sense of the transitoriness of fortune, the term 'sparing' (giving
frugally, not freely), 'spar'd' (341) (leaving free or untouched),
'sparing' (355) (giving freely, but retaining frugally)—suggests another
type of reciprocal relation between man and nature. It is desirable for
a man to give freely because in doing so he sets a model for others
to do likewise to him, should he some day be in need. Man must be
generous because he never knows when fortune will make him dependent upon others. Man's relation to man can and should be charitable
to anticipate this change of fortune. The speaker concludes by
admonishing the husbandman not to be too 'narrow.'

> The various Turns
> Of Fortune ponder; that your Sons may want
> What now, with hard Reluctance, faint, ye give.
>
> (174-76)

The implied cyclical pattern between master and gleaner explains
one aspect of Thomson's sympathy for the poor. The turns of fortune
can reverse human positions and wealth, and kindness, therefore, is in
a sense a preparation for the future and one's own possible fate.
Reversals must be understood as part of the pattern of the universe,
just as the *Summer* sun can be oppressor or oppressed, as man can
be hunter or hunted. Lavinia's fortune changes from poverty to
wealth, but that of the husbandman whose herds, flocks and harvests
are drowned changes from wealth to poverty.

The ideal or idyllic language of the Palemon and Lavinia episode
comparing the characters to nature in terms of concealment is similar
to that used in the presentation of Lyttelton and his wife in *Spring*.

Here the purpose is to illustrate Lavinia's resignation and the turn of fortune that befalls her. The poet stresses the need, because of such turns, to exercise charity to the less fortunate. He urges the husbandman to consider the gleaners and be generous to them, and he describes them as 'these unhappy Partners of your Kind' who 'Wide-hover round you, like the Fowls of Heaven,/And ask the humble Dole' (*Autumn*, 172–74). This is the language he uses in describing the fowls in *Winter*:

> The Fowls of Heaven,
> Tamed by the cruel Season, croud around
> The winnowing Store, and claim the little Boon
> Which PROVIDENCE assigns them.
>
> (242–45)

The gleaners and the fowls are thus interpreted as parallel in depending upon the charity of man or God. The husbandman is God-like in his exercise of charity, though the poet is aware that not all husbandmen choose to exercise this possibility.

The Lavinia episode is an idyllic pastoral narrative in imitation of the story of Ruth, but it is fitted into the structure of this season as a contrast to the praise of industry and effort. Lavinia and her mother are 'Almost on Nature's common Bounty fed' (189) and they live retired in a 'woody Vale' (183). When Lavinia ventures forth for the first time, a complete change of fortune occurs. 'All,' writes the poet, 'is the Gift of Industry' (*Autumn*, 141), but for Lavinia 'all' is the gift of love, gratitude and pity (260). Palemon says: 'The Fields, the Master, all, my Fair, are thine' (290). The generosity of the father returns to the daughter.

This idyllic *Autumn* passage achieves its effectiveness by imagery conveying the privileged sense of nature's protection:

> As in the hollow Breast of *Appenine*,
> Beneath the Shelter of encircling Hills,
> A Myrtle rises, far from human Eye,
> And breathes its balmy Fragrance o'er the Wild;
> So flourish'd blooming, and unseen by all,
> The sweet LAVINIA.
>
> (209–14)

Thus the phrases 'in the hollow Breast,' 'of *Appenine*,' the enclosure within the mountain chain, still further enclosed by 'Beneath the

Shelter of encircling Hills,' is followed, finally, by the subject and verb of the clause, 'A Myrtle rises,' yet separated by another phrase, 'far from human Eye,' before the compound verb and object, 'breathes its balmy Fragrance,' is concluded with a final phrase, 'o'er the Wild.' That the myrtle is a flower sacred to Venus, with leaves in a circular order, indicates the intensity of implications of the passage. Here again, as in the *Spring* flower passage and the *Summer* spectrum passage, the principle of illusive allusion functions to give added spatial dimension to an image falling within the range of the beautiful. The co-ordinate clause, with its present participle and past participle, 'blooming, and unseen by all,' indicates the difference between the possession of powers and the non-recognition of them. For the line does not read 'seen by none' but 'unseen,' that is, all are not *able* to see it. Although the concluding clause has, too, a predominantly phrasal construction, it expresses the abandonment of place by inflating the compulsion for leaving. Lavinia is involved in the shift from retirement to exposure and the tone stresses the compulsion that would cause exposure as well as the equanimity that would accept it. Unfortunately, both of these are achieved by redundance: 'strong Necessity's supreme Command' (215) and 'With smiling Patience in her Looks, she went' (216).

The defects of sentence structure in the language of moral discourse or in that of the idyllic speaker can be observed in the speech of Palemon to Lavinia. The exclamations, supposedly simple emotive expressions, become ludicrous because they are sandwiched between clichés of nature imagery.

> 'AND art thou then ACASTO's dear Remains?'
>
> (265)

> 'Oh yes! the very same,
> The soften'd Image of my noble Friend.'
>
> (267–68)

Robert Shiels records an anecdote of Thomson's response, in the last year of his life, to a situation not unlike that of Palemon: 'He did not at first recognize the man and said: "Troth, sir, I cannot say I ken your countenance well. Let me therefore crave your name?" When he heard the reply, he could not restrain his emotion, and exclaiming "Good God! are you the son of my old benefactor?" he embraced him with the greatest tenderness, overjoyed at the unexpected meeting.'[8] The diction here, if it is a verbatim report, is

without the sentimentalizing of 'dear Remains' and 'soften'd Image.'
It seems reasonable to speculate that the simple diction here, or the
mixture of simple and scientific diction served to control some of
Thomson's lexical extravagance.

> 'say, ah where,
> In what sequester'd Desart . . . '
>
> (272–73)

> 'It ill befits thee, oh it ill befits
> ACASTO'S Daughter . . . '
>
> (282–83)

When these exclamations are compared with the narrator's subtlety
it can be seen how much more effective than the overt moral discourse
for conveying change of fortune is the illusive allusion:

> Won by the Charm
> Of Goodness irresistible, and all
> In sweet Disorder lost, she blush'd Consent.
>
> (298–300)

Here the antithesis of 'Won' and 'lost' is played upon; the disorder is
'sweet' as the charm, and the 'all' refers to her composure as well as
to the poverty and isolation that are now well lost.

The passage which follows is one of loss, of defeat. And here the
unity operates by paradox, for industry—'the Labours of the Year'
(311)—is overturned by the *Autumn* storm. The storm recalls the
'Attemper'd Suns' passage, in which suns shed

> A pleasing Calm; while broad, and brown, below
> Extensive Harvests hang the heavy Head.
>
> (30–31)

So at the beginning of the storm, a calm reigns:

> At first, the Groves are scarcely seen to stir
> Their trembling Tops; and a still Murmur runs
> Along the soft-inclining Fields of Corn:
>
> (313–15)

The *Autumn* storm converts all the elements to water imagery connecting them with the earlier unifying image of 'flood of corn': the
forest pours 'A rustling Shower of yet untimely Leaves' (321); the

187

harvest becomes a 'billowy Plain' (327). The poet addresses Palemon, urging him to be kind to his gleaners:

> Think, oh grateful think!
> How good the GOD of HARVEST is to you,
> Who pours Abundance o'er your flowing Fields.
>
> (169–71)

But in what is an ironic interchange of water imagery, the husbandman's fields have abundance poured on them in a literal sense, and the fields are drowned:

> Exposed, and naked to its utmost Rage,
> Thro all the Sea of Harvest rolling round,
> The billowy Plain floats wide.
>
> (325–27)

With characteristic irony Thomson concludes this storm passage by remarking on what the 'deep Rains,/And all-involving Winds have swept away' (358–59), and begins the next paragraph with the windy clamor of the murdering sportsman: 'the rude Clamour of the Sportsman's Joy' (360), a change in organization to establish a parallel between nature and man. The hunt passage is a description of what the squire, not nature, destroys; it is destruction for private pleasure, a transformation wholly to be deplored. Thus in the first passage, the request is for charity and kindness; in the second, for submerging one's pride by not assuming the authority of nature or God in joyfully destroying living creatures.

The *Autumn* game is the hunt, and it follows the destruction of the harvest, becoming a commentary upon man's destructive tendencies, and, by implication, a commentary upon God's mysterious ways. The hunt—although Thomson apparently meant only the pursuit of the fox—is the only scene which he overtly claimed as a burlesque. In the earlier sections of this passage he distinguishes between the instinctive killing by animals and the wanton killing by man, called, in this behavior, a 'steady Tyrant,' just as the sun in his heat was called 'tyrant Heat' (*Summer*, 209):

> Not so the steady Tyrant Man,
> Who with the thoughtless Insolence of Power
> Inflam'd, beyond the most infuriate Wrath
> Of the worst Monster that e'er roam'd the Waste,

188

> For Sport alone pursues the cruel Chace,
> Amid the Beamings of the gentle Days.
>
> (390–95)

The hunter's brutality appears in every season: in *Spring* there are references to the 'tyrant Man' who cages birds (704), to those who rob nests (718–20), and to the unfeeling schoolboy (690–701). In *Summer* there is the stock-dove's mate, 'Struck from his Side by savage Fowler's Guile' (619). In *Winter* there are hunters who 'Worse than the Season, desolate the Fields' (791) and the ruthless hunter who, with clubs, beats the elks to death (820–26). Human cruelty exists in all seasons, and in *Autumn*, man, as hunter, appears twice (see lines 983–87). (Sharks and leviathans are hunters who sport with men, and they, too, have a place in *The Seasons*.)

The descriptions of the hunt are among the finest passages of this season. There is the controlled physical movement of the spaniel stalking his prey:

> How, in his Mid-career, the Spaniel struck,
> Stiff, by the tainted Gale, with open Nose,
> Outstretch'd, and finely sensible, *draws* full,
> Fearful, and cautious, on the latent Prey.
>
> (363–66)

These are a reworking of Pope's lines in *Windsor Forest* (99–102) effecting contrasts between action and cessation of action, between the effectively dangerous immobility of the pointer and the ineffective flight of the birds, killed or wounded in motion. Thomson gives his inimitable stamp to the passage by describing the animal 'out-stretch'd'—'stiff' in the sense of being tense and completely alive (in contrast to dead stiffness) and he sees him in motion. Pope places the spaniel in his properly ordered place, sees him moving within furrows, and when the dog smells the prey, he is made motionless and ironically formalized: he 'meditates':

> Before his Lord the ready Spaniel bounds
> Panting with Hope, he tries the forrow'd Grounds,
> But when the tainted Gales the Game betray
> Couch'd close he lyes, and meditates the prey.[9]

In *The Seasons* there is the contrast between the surging flight of the birds and the sudden death.

189

Nor on the Surges of the boundless Air,
Tho borne triumphant, are they safe; the Gun,
Glanc'd just, and sudden, from the Fowler's Eye
O'ertakes their sounding Pinions; and again,
Immediate, brings them from the towering Wing,
Dead to the Ground.

(372-77)

When Thomson wishes to suggest the brutality, the inhumanity and, therefore, the disorderliness of such killing, he alters his word order and music to create awkward inversions and antithetical, oxymoronic juxtapositions:

O let not, aim'd from some inhuman Eye,
The Gun the Music of the coming Year
Destroy; and harmless, unsuspecting Harm,
Lay the weak Tribes, a miserable Prey,
In mingled Murder, fluttering on the Ground!

(983-87)

'The Gun the Music' and 'harmless, unsuspecting Harm' are juxtapositions that suggest two contrary views. The gun and the music are paradoxically equated as well as obviously opposed, and the contrasting attitudes of the birds who are seen to be harmless themselves and who, with regard to the hunters, do not suspect any harm, reveal the typical Thomsonian shift from one perspective to another. And this word order is deliberate in its economy.

The hare that retires 'to some lone Seat' is not like Queensbury who in Ham's embowering walks lives 'in spotless Peace retir'd' (*Summer*, 1421). For the frightened animal has no bower and he has no peace. The description of his retirement is a catalog of unbecoming, precautionary hiding-places, the names of which are indicative of uncomfortable security, 'the rushy Fen; the ragged Furze,/Stretch'd o'er the stony Heath; the stubble chapt;/The thistly Lawn' (403-5). But security is non-existent. And the pack, described in storm imagery, overwhelm the small animal—the protective places overrun by shouting, savage forces—an episode in which the hare 'to some lone Seat/Retir'd' (401-2) finds neither the safety nor the bounty that protects Lavinia, 'far retir'd/Among the Windings of a woody Vale' (182-83).

Although Thomson, with a rhetorical flourish, declares, 'THESE are not Subjects for the peaceful Muse' (379), he does proceed, contrary to his practice in *Spring*. The difference, of course, is that grossness and vulgarity were inconsistent with his version of love, although the lover's pain and suffering were not. But grossness and vulgarity are, after all, as characteristic of man as love and gentleness, and in *Autumn* all have their place, whether within scenes or between scenes. Palemon feels love but he is ashamed to acknowledge such a passion for a gleaner. When he discovers Lavinia is Acasto's daughter, she becomes socially acceptable and he feels gratitude as well as love. This love for another is contrasted with the hunter's viciousness to the hare and the stag. The husbandman sees a prospect of destruction, and he feels a sense of dread for the future. The hunter is comfortable in his future but, for his own pleasure, ruthlessly wreaks destruction among the animals. Thomson's implication here is that in hunting man loses his charity and humanity and leaves himself open to meaner passions. In the post-hunting scenes man himself becomes hunted by his meaner passions, an object of ridicule and disgust.

In the comic ('ludicrous') fox-hunt Thomson admonishes the hunters:

> give, ye BRITONS, then
> Your sportive Fury, pityless, to pour
> Loose on the nightly Robber of the Fold.
>
> (470–72)

The hunt of the hare and the stag is told by a narrator sympathetic to the hunted. But the fox-hunt is addressed with broad irony and hyperbole to the hunters (452–501). The rapid change from broad ditch to high hedge to deep morass conveys extremes of motion and idea— and as the riders head through 'the perilous Flood' (a recurrent image in this season) not sympathy, not understandable excitement, but comic exaggeration is sought, a burlesque of Pope's lines in *Windsor Forest*:

> See! the bold Youth strain up the threatening Steep,
> Rush thro' the thickets, down the Vallies sweep,
> Hang o'er their Coursers' Heads, with eager Speed,
> And Earth rolls back beneath the flying Steed.[10]
>
> (155–58)

Thus riding the torrent, the riders themselves become noisy and wild like the raging waters:

Then scale the Mountains to their woody Tops;
Rush down the dangerous Steep; and o'er the Lawn,
In Fancy swallowing up the Space between,
Pour all your Speed into the rapid Game.

(483–86)

The imperatives lack the degrees of difference characteristic of the didactic instruction in 'INDUSTRY' (*Autumn*, 72–95); they are wild extremes. The pun on 'Game' and below on 'grace' and '*Whist*' indicates the poet's burlesque at work. The happy leader of the chase is treated ironically: 'O glorious he' (492). The hunters assemble in ancient halls 'with woodland Honours grac'd' (495)—and 'grac'd' is an especially ironic term since the hunters here and throughout the poem lose their 'grace,' which exhibits the trophy of God's gentle stag equally with the fur of the vicious fox, and the family figures, 'antick Figures fierce,' becoming part of the grotesque inhumanity of the hunt. The satire consists in combining the trophies of hunter and hunted, the mingling of a human past with an animal-like present. This is what I have identified as a typical Thomsonian procedure, here ridiculed because revealing not man's humanity and brotherhood with nature but his unwitting self-identification with brutish behavior. Thomson then contrasts the 'decent' dead with the inappropriate living:

he then is loudest heard,
When the Night staggers with severer Toils,
With Feats *Thessalian* Centaurs never knew,
And their repeated Wonders shake the Dome.

(498–501)

For the noise of the revelers, and their drunkenness—the 'severer Toils'—make the very night stagger, and the narration of the swine-like feats are shouted so that 'their repeated Wonders shake the Dome' (501).

Thomson's burlesque moves with ironic analogy from the extreme activities of the hunter to the activation of the inanimate objects, a transformation of objects and actions: the chimney blazes, the tankards foam, the table groans so that the entire scene begins to move with action and the external glory is matched by the 'internal' glory. The fur hangs and the sirloin is 'stretch'd immense'; England's 'Glory' is connected with the grossness of gluttony. Plunging into the 'Pasty' coincides with the 'Glories of the Chace.' The personified desires of '*Hunger*,' of '*Thirst*' for 'brown October' ale, deliberately abstract the actions making them things—mingled with the needs that convey the sense of varied and uncentered activities, the comic qualities of which rest on exaggeration and allusion. Thus the strong smell of the 'mighty Bowl' is compared to the delicious breath of '*Maia*, to the lovesick Shepherdess./On Violets diffus'd' (516–17), and the ale is referred to as drawn from his 'dark Retreat' (520), the term used to describe man's ideal retirement or the bitter irony of the hunted hare. And comic touches appear even in the versification:

> To cheat the thirsty Moments, *Whist* a while
> Walks his grave Round.
>
> (524–25)

Here '*Whist* a while' suggests, in the procedure of illusive allusion, a personification that is playful without violence, though he cannot long cheat the moments from their noisy descent to debauchery.

The final step in the caricature of the glorious hunt is the drinking bout which closes the evening:

> At last these puling Idlenesses laid
> Aside, frequent and full, the dry Divan
> Close in firm Circle; and set, ardent, in
> For serious Drinking.
>
> (530–33)

The looseness of the previous activities is supplanted by the position of and attitude toward inebriation. Debauchery now becomes a serious activity. The bowls which earlier sent off a powerful odor now are poured over, as well as into, each drinker:

> earnest, brimming Bowls
> Lave every Soul, the Table floating round,
> And Pavement, faithless to the fuddled Foot.
>
> (535–37)

The element of water is burlesqued, and wine sets the scene afloat. Thomson's ironic water imagery with its burlesqued deluge is a variant of a similar passage in Dryden's translation of Juvenal's sixth satire in which the movements of 'thrust,' 'advance' and 'dance' become lustful actions. Thomson writes:

> Before their maudlin Eyes,
> Seen dim and blue, the double Tapers dance,
> Like the Sun wading thro the misty Sky.
> Then, sliding soft, they drop.   (554–57)

193

Dryden translates:

> Full Brimmers to their Fuddled Noses thrust;
> Brimmers the last Provocatives of Lust.
> When Vapours to their swimming Brains advance,
> And double Tapers on the Table dance.[11]

Thomson captures the violence, wildness, and vulgarity of the hunt in the drunkenness of the hunters. The ironic, rapid changes, shifts in attitude control the scene. The catalog adds to the perplexing mixture of a drunken gathering. The hunters slip beneath the table from their chairs and the objects remain rattling above them—indicators of the confused drunken scene. The image of *'Lubber Power,'* the drunken vulgar power that commands the 'ghostly Halls of grey Renown' (494), the personification of country vulgarity—the ironic king of the hunting revelry to match the ideal rural queen of the *Summer* sheep-shearing—this visualized picture is the concluding hunt image. *'Lubber Power'* sits astride the fallen hunters in 'filthy Triumph': the hunter hunted—the conqueror conquered.

Immediately following the personification is the description (added in 1744) of the pastor ('doctor') 'of tremendous Paunch' (565), an actual version of *'Lubber Power.'* For the pastor whose function is spiritually to heal others 'Outlives them all' (567). Retirement and rumination suggest once again the perplexing quality of the world, not in the puzzlement of the clergyman, but in the ironic mocking comment of the narrator, who recognizes that the 'doctor,' whose paunch is 'a black Abyss of Drink' (566), nevertheless retires 'from his bury'd Flock' (567), a shepherd who knew how to look after himself. The poet in *Winter* utters an injunction against just such shepherds: 'Now, Shepherds, to your helpless Charge be kind' (265). The mocking quality alludes to the dreadful moment in *Summer* in which the mariner's vessel 'drinks the whelming Tide,/Hid in the Bosom of the black Abyss '(999–1000) and sinks; the parson drinks the tide of liquor and survives not only the tide but all others of his congregation who drink, and his black coat is not only his garb but his mourning suit for those who are drowned in, rather than producers of, the abyss.

As the pastor leaves his somnolent flock who have been ridden down and killed by *'Lubber Power'* in the typical transformation of hunters to hunted, he, too, undergoes a transformation, taking on the ruminative character of the 'flock' he is supposed to lead. All other uses of 'ruminate' (*Winter*, 86) or 'ruminating' (*Summer*, 478, 931, 1154) refer to herds and flocks.

In the injunction to women not to participate in the hunt, the narrator speaks in his idealizing and moralizing voice. The lines suddenly become excessively end-stopped and the catalog of female activities deliberately closes off the difficulties involved in attaining the ideal. This section is transitional between the vulgar drunkenness and the grape-crushing and wine-drinking of the joyous, not vulgar, world (570–706). The intertwining images of man and nature, the frequency of repetition of terms, the equanimity and balanced fulfillment which these *Autumn* scenes represent, are a version of fulfillment without satiety, of conversion from solid to liquid nature.

Even the reference to women's clothing contains a water image: 'May their tender Limbs/Float in the loose Simplicity of Dress!' (589–90)—a harmony image to which Thomson had referred in *Summer*: 'The *Zephyrs* floating loose' (123). The lover 'crushes' down the tree for the nuts, or shakes them down in a 'glossy Shower' (620) and they turn out to be 'an ardent Brown,/As are the Ringlets of MELINDA's Hair' (620–1). The 'Breeze' and the 'beating Ray' 'melt' a 'mellow Shower' (630) from the fruit-laden orchard and in doing so they, too, perform the lover's function. The water imagery recurs, converting nuts and fruit to 'showers,' so that the harvest that poured abundance (171) is translated into specific kinds of showers:

> Obedient to the Breeze and beating Ray,
> From the deep-loaded Bough a mellow Shower,
> Incessant melts away. The juicy Pear
> Lies, in a soft Profusion, scatter'd round.
> A various Sweetness swells the gentle Race;
> By Nature's all-refining Hand prepar'd,
> Of temper'd Sun, and Water, Earth, and Air,
> In ever-changing Composition mixt
> Such, falling frequent thro' the chiller Night,
> The fragrant Stores, the wide-projected Heaps
> Of Apples, which the lusty-handed Year,
> Innumerous, o'er the blushing Orchard shakes.
>
> (629–40)

Nature's attention to the juicy pears is described in terms similar to those of the mother and her offspring (600–1); Nature's 'Sweetness' that swells the fruit 'the gentle Race' (633) is similar to the woman's duty to 'sweeten all the Toils of human Life' (608). The apples fall through the night, shook down by the 'lusty-handed Year' (639–40), just as the nuts fall in a shower shaken from the tree by the lover. Structurally, the associative asides to Melinda and Phillips are analogical, for just as Melinda transcends her graces by not priding herself on them, so Phillips, although inspired by nature to poetry, rose above imitative limitation by simple 'Rhyme-unfettered' verse (646).

This passage, full of hyphenated words, seems to use them to support *Autumn* transformations. The poet refers to 'the . . . Joy-resounding Fields' (625) 'the deep-loaded Bough' (630), 'Nature's all-refining Hand' (634), 'ever-changing Composition' (636), 'the wide-projected Heaps' (638), 'the lusty-handed Year' (639). The term 'Joy-resounding' belongs with the noun-participle combinations, but when contrasted with 'far-resounding Waste' (*Spring*, 829) or 'loud-resounding Rocks' (*Summer*, 596) it lacks the relation between space and sound, paradoxical sounds in empty space, or the enactment of echoing sound. The combinations which Thomson develops do not always function well, and, sometimes, the hyphen is merely a printing convention, such as 'Hay-cock' (*Summer*, 367), or 'Hazel-Bank' (*Autumn*, 610) or 'Summer-Blaze' (*Winter*, 21). These should be distinguished from ineffective hyphenated uses or from distinctions which have the same structure but not the hyphen; for example, 'ever musing' (*Summer*, 1618) is not hyphenated whereas 'ever-changing' (*Spring*, 298) is. This inconsistency should not be confused with the apparent inconsistency in hyphenating periphrastic terms like 'Tulip-Race' (*Spring*, 539) and 'Swallow-People' (*Autumn*, 838) and not hyphenating 'finny Race' (*Spring*, 395), 'plumy Race' (*Winter*, 137) or 'feather'd Youth' (*Spring*, 729). Here the basis for hyphenation is the conjunction of two nouns, and normal modifiers of nouns are not hyphenated. The purpose of noun hyphenation in periphrasis is to connect part with whole, a species within a 'Race' or the totality of species in order to convey parallels with man. With a single item of a class the hyphenation signifies different aspects: there is 'Mountain-brow,' 'Mountain-Snow,' 'Mountain-tops,' etc.

Granted, therefore, certain perplexities and shortcomings in these hyphenated words, it would seem that altered word order contains certain artistic implications, for which the *Autumn* passage can serve as a representative example. The adjective 'deep-loaded' suggests weight and extent, and Thomson wishes to use this term to characterize the paradoxical quality of *Autumn* in which the bough that is 'deep-loaded' 'melts away,' the solid matter dissolving from the branch and falling to the ground. Thus what is firm and solid gradually becomes unfirm and dissolving. A similar synaesthetic image was mentioned in *Spring* where the poet could 'taste the Smell of Dairy' (107), and it recurs in the present context (also of a traversed 'Maze') in which he wishes to 'taste, reviv'd,/The Breath of Orchard big with bending Fruit' (627–28). This paradoxical quality of physical change and extent is further explored by the turning to the 'juicy Pear' (631) created by 'Nature's all-refining Hand.' In the poem, 'refining' normally refers to the finishing or smoothing procedure, but here the term refers to the 'swelling' of the fruit with sweetness.

The combining modifiers, 'deep,' 'all,' 'ever,' 'wide,' are among the most frequently used terms to form adjectival combinations, 'deep,' 'all' and 'wide' being combined seventeen times and 'ever' twelve times. These terms are unbounded in contrast to a term like 'dark-brown' (*Spring*, 383) or 'hollow-sounding' (*Winter*, 737) that is precise in its reference. Yet these absolute terms are forms of intensity, not to be taken as everywhere applicable. Thus nature's 'all-refining' hand refers to the capacity of nature to refine all, not to the fact that it always does, for in the *Autumn* storm as well as in acts of violence and disorder nature does not 'refine' the environment. So, too, 'ever-changing' composition does not mean that nature is never the same but that the elements can be changed. In contrast to combining words with 'all' or 'ever,' Thomson combines six words with 'never' and seven with 'half,' but one must also add terms combined with 'many' (3) and all others which are bounded terms. The purpose in creating such terms is to suggest plenitude and blending. Plenitude is implied by the combination, blending by the paradox of word order; for example, 'ever-changing Composition' refers to the changeability of the elements of the mixture, 'temper'd Sun, and Water, Earth, and Air.'

The relation of 'deep' to 'wide' indicates another aspect of the hyphenated words: two different views of space. The passage deals with the loaded tree, and then the loaded earth. The first is the fruit seen as 'deep-loaded' (630) concentrated in masses on the branches; the other sees it as 'wide-projected,' existing in a series of extended heaps or piles. If the pears are seen as 'melted' from the bough (Thomson's allusion to a Biblical usage), the chiller autumn temperature congeals the apples into heaps. The gentleness which causes them to 'melt' to the ground is an 'all-refining Hand,' but the apples are seen as 'fresh' and 'keen,' and they have to be shaken by the 'lusty-handed' year. The two processes of 'refining' and lustily shaking the fruit are metonymous expressions for what appears to be feminine 'Nature' and masculine 'Year.' The hyphenated terms draw together the two-handed process of nature which inflates ('swells') with one hand and condenses or draws down with the other.

In the passage under discussion hyphenated terms happen to serve as adjectives, yet most of them form parts of phrases, 'from the busy Joy-resounding Fields,' 'From the deep-loaded Bough,' 'By Nature's all-refining Hand prepar'd,' 'In ever-changing Composition mixt,' the exception being 'the wide-projected Heaps.' One of the adjectival functions, therefore, is to provide one type of qualification (a phrase) with still another. The phrase achieves extent and the hyphenated term emphasizes precision and complication of action or space. It prevents the looseness of a highly phrasal and clausal structure from being uncontrolled, and thus serves in its way to provide precision, as does repetition by significant alteration and subtle change.

Hyphenated words frequently occur within a short compass (see *Summer*, 900–11, 1042–46; *Spring*, 582–603) as they do here to suggest a fusion of contrasting procedures, of space or time or sound. In *Spring*, 'faint-warbled' (587) is contrasted with 'Shrill-voic'd' (591), but 'faint-warbled' is related to 'long-forgotten,' two efforts to suggest time and sound; the artistry of the second is to enact the shrillness of the lark: 'Up-springs the Lark/Shrill-voic'd, and loud, the Messenger of Morn' (590-91). Here the passage deals with change and fusion, but it is typically *Spring*'s spatial expansiveness. The initial quality is transformed. Normally the bird would be 'shrilly voiced' but the alteration of the adverb to an adjective connects quality with action to imply to single total response. The functional use of hyphenation can be detected in 'close-lurking' (*Summer*, 908) in which the adjective 'close' replaces 'closely.'

Thomson's present participles enhance his view of changing nature and these particles are most frequently single and unhyphenated. Their use is, in some of the most memorable lines, expressive of uncertainty and incompletion. According to John Arthos, the present participle was 'used distinctively in scientific prose as an epithet to point out some quality native to the thing described. Very often, more than indicating the appearance of a thing, it defines the nature of a thing.'[12] Thomson, however, converted the participle to his own poetic purposes. In *Spring*, he writes of the rays of the moon, 'the trembling Languish of her Beam' (1038), and in *Summer*, the beams from the whitening opal 'form/A trembling Variance of revolving Hues' (158), and in *Autumn*, describing the moonlight, 'The whole Air whitens with a boundless Tide/Of silver Radiance, trembling round the World' (1101–2). Thomson's use of 'trembling,' a typical Augustan term,[13] contrasts with Pope's. Pope ridicules Budgel's heroic style in 'angels trembling round his *falling Horse*'[14] (*Imit. of Horace*, Sat. II, ii, 1. 28); the uncertainty of physical nature demands a sense of decorum from the unknowing participant. The uncertainty 'principle' also appears in the language of *The Seasons*. The uncertainty with which the first three seasons begin, fluctuating between present and past, stresses the perturbation felt by God's creatures. The first *Autumn* description flits between black shadows and bright sunlight. The contrary scenes of the poem, the depiction of innocents killed and guilty unpunished, the processes of change that are the result of secret and unknown forces—these provide the basis for anxiety.

The language of opposites (cf. 'smile,' 'rage,' 'soft,' 'hard,' 'frozen'), of alternating views, was mentioned in *Spring*. I list the frequencies of contrasting verbs to illustrate the omnipresence of the active, shifting, transforming emphasis in the language of the poem. Terms like 'ascend' (15), 'raise' (27), 'rise' (56) are counterbalanced by the opposites, 'descend' (32), 'fall' (38), 'sink' (17). And these are connected by terms implying transformation of elements and feelings: 'gleam' (15), 'glitter' (13), 'melt' (15), 'mingle' (24), 'pour' (44), 'refine' (14), 'scatter' (20), 'swell' (60), 'stretch' (19), 'spread' (41), 'shine' (39), 'turn' (37).[15] This list is by no means exhaustive, but it reveals that the spatial terms are also fluctuating terms, that movements can be either positive or negative depending on the context. The ultimate context is the 'secret-working' power of God.

For Thomson, the world can possess a 'radiant' (19) beauty as well as a 'trembling' (19) delicacy and motion. But to tremble is also to be fearful and nature in its 'gleaming' and 'swelling' suggests an amplification of the movements of light or air. The intangible world is full of anxiety, just as the 'trembling Steed' (*Spring*, 808) and the 'trembling Wretches' (*Winter*, 1004) are unnerved. The participles illustrate the characteristic movement from the literal to the metaphoric and back that is identified with Thomson's actuality of suffering, with his idea of the analogical relation between man and nature, with his awareness that the same qualities in nature can be both beautiful and dangerous.

Thomson gives to the present participles an uncertainty, a spatial and expansive quality, a cyclical motion, a visual and auditory mingling. The mystery of the cycles of nature pervades the processes Thomson describes. Seymour Chatman, in a study of Milton's participles, remarks that 'it is Thomson's style that is more heavily participial than any other. Indeed it is a most pronounced mannerism. Unlike Milton and Dryden, and like Pope, Thomson introduced as many present as past participles.'[16] Chatman finds that the Miltonic participles 'compact time distinctions,' contribute to the sense of halt at line endings, assist the exposition and fit the argumentative design. But Thomson's uses fit his own transformational interests, and although the compacting of time and exposition resemble Milton's, the uncertainty procedures, the constant mixture of present and past, the need for qualification and simultaneity of past and present, all represent his own use, indeed his 'mannerism.'

Thomson's past and present participles are syntactically related to phrases, and this procedure achieves a considerable degree of specificity by having the participle modified by a phrase or, if the participle precedes a noun, having a phrase modify the same noun. The purpose is to move from a cyclical and continuing action to a stable and precise limit. The procedure corresponds to the prospect view; the purpose of both is to suggest a world in which the specific object, while complete or beautiful or precise in itself, is nevertheless part of a larger and mysterious whole hinted at by distance that extends beyond sight.

Examples of the Latinate construction in which a participle (or an adjective) is preceded or followed by an object or a modifier include: 'Wide-shading All'—(Winter, 51); 'Defeating oft the Labours of the Year'—(Autumn, 315); 'Dew-dropping Coolness'—(Summer, 216); 'wondering what this wild/Outrageous Tumult means'—(Summer, 390–91); 'Resounding long in listening Fancy's Ear'—(Winter, 71); 'Wrapt in black Glooms'—(Winter, 73); 'Deep in the Night'—(Summer, 669); 'deceitful o'er the Moss'—(Autumn, 1153); 'By Fits effulgent'—(Autumn, 38); 'Unbounded o'er the World'—(Autumn, 730); 'display'd,/In full Luxuriance'—(Spring, 92–93); 'From Clear to Cloudy tost'—(Spring, 332).

In *The Seasons*, adjectives or participles, such as 'deep' or 'wrapt,' that begin a blank verse line create trochaic feet and thus vary the meter. By leading into a modifying phrase they create two modifiers: the adjective and the phrase that modifies the adjective. Since the adjective and phrase are both modifiers they imply the importance of this limiting process as compared with the lack of weight given to the words modified. Thus the word order becomes a form of extension and supports the poem's view of a world of changing objects and places, creating a variety of distinctions.

The poem contrasts the shifting, changing forms with the chaotic destruction of these forms. Thus participles in *Spring* describing the flood—'disparting' (310), 'fractur'd' (313), 'streaming' (315)—create not anxiety but terror, not blending but confusion. There are fewer fluctuating terms in *Winter* than in any other season, since *Winter* presents stiff, frozen, congealed forms. *Winter* demands an act of faith more imperatively than any other season precisely because it is dominated by seemingly fixed and changeless shapes. *Autumn* and *Winter* are thus associatively connected by the extensiveness of change in the former and its apparent congealing or suppression in the latter.

In *Spring* the speaker strayed through Hagley Park, in *Summer* through Richmond and the Thames valley, and in *Autumn* he finds himself in the 'green delightful Walks' (654) of Dodington's estate in Dorset.

> In this glad Season, while his sweetest Beams
> The Sun sheds equal o'er the meeken'd Day;
> Oh lose me in the green delightful Walks
> Of Dodington! thy Seat, serene and plain;
> Where simple Nature reigns.
>
> (652–56)

The 'simple Nature' that should be a version of the ideal presented in *Spring* and *Summer* eludes the narrator, who, while turning to a prospect view without the sharp contrasts of the earlier seasons, still claims a 'boundless Prospect' (658) 'yonder,' 'Here' and 'there' (658–59). The violence of the language remains—the 'Grandeur,' 'thy lofty Dome,' 'seizes on the ravish'd Eye' (660-61)—but the images of 'rising,' 'swelling' and the temporary return of *Spring* express gradual change.

New Beauties rise with each revolving Day;
New Columns swell; and still the fresh Spring finds
New Plants to quicken, and new Groves to green.

(662-64)

If the voice of the personal narrator is compared with that in *Summer*, the artistry of Thomson becomes pointed. The *Summer* narrator says:

To me be Nature's Volume broad-display'd;
And to peruse its all-instructing Page,
Or, haply catching Inspiration thence,
Some easy Passage, raptur'd, to translate,
My sole Delight; as thro the falling Glooms
Pensive I stray, or with the rising Dawn
On Fancy's Eagle-wing excursive soar.

(192-98)

In *Autumn*, the narrator declares:

Here wandering oft, fir'd with the restless Thirst
Of thy Applause, I solitary court
Th' inspiring Breeze; and meditate the Book
Of Nature, ever open, aiming thence,
Warm from the Heart, to learn the moral Song.

(668-72)

In both passages, the narrator seeks inspiration from the 'Book/ Of Nature.' *Summer* expresses this at first in the appeal to nature, and the imagery of reading is consistent with the grammatical mood. The subordinate clause separating 'Gloom' from 'Delight' conveys the kinds of incomplete wandering—through 'falling' dusk at evening, 'soaring' through the early dawn. The *Autumn* passage begins with 'wandering,' but its imagery of the elements never unites the wandering image that is implicit. The speaker is synaesthetically 'fir'd' with 'Thirst' of applause, but the implication of pride and the reduced importance of the excursion expose these as clichéd conventions. Thus the 'courting' of inspiration ('The inspiring Breeze') seems ineffective in satisfying 'Thirst,' and meditating upon the book of nature, the poet concludes simply that he learns 'the moral Song' as it comes 'warm from the Heart.' The violence of the elemental image far exceeds the emotional content of the passage, and only as he describes his wandering among *Autumn* fruits does it become clear that the 'pleasing Theme' of *Autumn* (675) is the moral song arising upon the sight of nature's bounty.

Reuben A. Brower, who is one of the few critics to have recognized the 'illusive allusion' in Thomson's style, does not find in *The Seasons* any organizing vision. He comments upon the lines immediately following those above:

> And, as I steal along the sunny Wall,
> Where Autumn basks, with Fruit empurpled deep,
> My pleasing Theme continual prompts my Thought:
> Presents the downy Peach; the shining Plumb,
> With a fine blueish Mist of Animals
> Clouded; the ruddy Nectarine; and dark,
> Beneath his ample Leaf, the luscious Fig.
> The Vine too here her curling Tendrils shoots;
> Hangs out her Clusters, glowing to the South;
> And scarcely wishes for a warmer Sky.
>
> (673–82)

The subtle harmony of coloring, the blending of subdued shades of similar value is admirable; the rhythmic progress and emphasis suit the slightly dreamy succession of images, accenting just enough their visual and tactile appeals. The sensuous haze dulls us, conveniently, to some curious grammar: 'Presents the downy peach' has for subject, 'Theme,' a very odd thing for a 'theme' to be doing. Or do we unconsciously take the subject as 'Autumn'? ('Autumn basks' and 'Presents'?) Thomson's form in this and similar passages may be fairly called impressionistic, since attention to particular points of sensation is lost in the total though qualitatively distinct response. There is also the faintest sense of a presiding genius of the scene, the half-sleeping spirit of Autumn, though the exact connection between the spirit and the scene is as uncertain as the grammar.

Whether we feel in the attained and actual form of the passage any further relationship unifying the poem is the next question. We do feel some qualitative likeness between this and similar descriptions, in the melting impressionism of image and rhythm. The rare reader of the whole of *The Seasons* may also argue that the descriptions are connected by the *Deus ex machina* of modern criticism of seventeenth- and eighteenth-century literature, the

'Great Order of Nature,' a resource so convenient as to be almost useless.

Thomson's failure to achieve vital poetic connection between his faintly imagined beings and the scenes they introduce is paralleled by his unsuccessful attempt to see the whole of nature in the 'light' or 'teaching' of 'severe Philosophy.' By Reason's power—and up-to-date scientific evidence—the poet traces in Nature

> The chain of causes and effects to Him
> The world-producing Essence, who alone
> Possesses being . . .

In numerous other passages, where the relation between Nature and Nature's God is much more vague than here, Thomson hails a dimly personified nature as teacher and 'power.' The addresses and exclamations, the bald lack of transitions to these insights, are signs that Thomson is trying to substitute a willed and imposed order for the lack of a unifying vision active in the separate descriptions.[17]

The grammar, however, is neither curious nor odd, since a book does have a 'theme,' and the speaker, in meditating the 'Book/Of Nature' (670–71), derives his 'theme' from the bountifulness of the book. If nature is a book (Thomson used this conventional metaphor in *Summer*, 192–96), the subject or theme is the blessed variety of objects—fruits, trees, etc.—in it. Thus the theme is constantly reflected in the particulars; the theme presents peaches, plums for the speaker's and reader's consideration and contemplation. The 'theme,' the expression of praise and awe of God, the 'moral' song, is based on objects which call forth these thoughts and warm feelings. Not only is the grammar active, but the sentence order, too, is pertinent. To assume that 'particular points of sensation' are lost in the total though quantitatively different response is, unfortunately, to miss the response. For the moral song that arises 'warm from the Heart' upon the meditation of nature is paralleled by the vine that matures from the warm sun. All the globular varieties of fruit, reddening ('empurpled') under the rays of the sun, become individually different in color or texture of skin ('downy,' 'shining,' 'ruddy,' 'dark,' glowing,') and size, each syntactically pertinent, responding in its own way as does the poet to the forces of warmth. The passage is held together by the comparison of the poet stealing 'along the sunny Wall' and the personified vine extending her tendrils and hanging out her clusters 'glowing to the South.' As the theme of nature leads the poet to present the fruits to his sight and mind, so the vine in its desire for growth presents its fruit to the warm sky. The moral of God's power and blessedness is what the poet celebrates.

The poet writes, 'as I steal along the sunny Wall./Where Autumn basks,' and he identifies himself in Dodington's seat at Eastbury as merging with the wealth and harvest of the estate. In stealing along, his thoughts and his walk imperceptibly merge with the rewards of the *Autumn* sun, just as, in *Spring*, he described Lyttelton courting the muse by stealing along the dale of his estate:

> There along the Dale,
> With Woods o'erhung, and shag'd with mossy Rocks,
> Whence on each Hand the gushing Waters play,
> And down the rough Cascade white-dashing fall,
> Or gleam in lengthen'd Vista thro the Trees,
> You silent steal.
>
> (909–14)

At the beginning of *Summer*, Thomson referred to the constant changes of the seasons in terms of gentle and imperceptible 'stealing': 'the Seasons ever stealing round' (40). In the declining day of *Summer*, the walker 'converses' with nature, feels its harmony and communicates it to others.

> Now the soft Hour
> Of Walking comes: for him who lonely loves
> To seek the distant Hills, and there converse
> With Nature; there to harmonize his Heart,
> And in pathetic Song to breathe around
> The Harmony to others.
>
> (1379–84)

It is at this time that lovers 'steal' from the world and 'pour their Souls in Transport' (1399). Thus 'stealing' is a form of interchange between man and nature, in which the harmony of one succeeds in infusing harmony in the other. There are repetitive moments of retreat appropriate to the season. In *Spring*, the rough cascade leads associatively to soft and peaceful thoughts; in *Summer*, harmonious transport in the shade follows upon the not yet fulfilled transports of Damon and Musidora; and in *Autumn*, the harmony proceeds between man and harvest.

Whatever may be the faults of Thomson, and I have not sought to excuse them or explain them away, they are not 'the lack of a unifying vision active in the separate descriptions.' This 'vision' is not merely a matter of visual and tactile appearance, but the results of a version of Augustan harmony and disharmony. The poet's perspectives provide varied and distinguished felt responses. He observes the peach at a distance and then observes the 'shining' yet 'cloudy' plum very closely. The exposed nectarine is followed by the concealed fig, and the whole is concluded with the close observation and extended view of the vine and its grapes. Not only are these characteristic of Thomson's harmonious prospect and spectrum procedures, but his vision is to be found in the paradoxical details of a 'shining' plum that is 'clouded,' set off by the consistency of 'ample' and 'luscious.'

The associative 'turning' (683) to the vineyards (of other countries, perhaps France) reasserts the interrelation among the kinds of nature suggested in the preceding passage so that this represents an amplification of as well as a climax to the wine section. The potent sun 'elates'—raises and causes rejoicing—so that the vineyard 'swells' and reacts upon the day, flashing light and fruitfulness: it 'Spreads' (687), 'climbs' (687), and in a concluding synaesthetic image it 'drinks' (688) the blaze of the sun. The passage descends to increasing particularity: the vineyard, the boughs (690), the clusters (690-92), the dew on the clusters (692-93), and finally the crushing of the grapes (699). This inverted view moves from a distant sight to a deliberate and precise examination to an actual participation in converting grapes to wine. Thus in typical procedure the vineyard and the clusters do act with respect to nature and then are acted upon, and acted upon 'by degrees' (701).

The concluding lines are generalized:

> Then comes the crushing Swain; the Country floats,
> And foams unbounded with the mashy Flood;
> That by degrees fermented, and refin'd,
> Round the rais'd Nations pours the Cup of Joy:
> The Claret smooth, red as the Lip we press,
> In sparkling Fancy, while we drain the Bowl;
> The mellow-tasted Burgundy; and quick,
> As is the Wit it gives, the gay Champaign.

(699–706)

Thomson alludes to the flood—'The billowy Plain floats wide' (327), to the rain that descends 'In one continuous Flood' (332) and to the drunken scene with 'the Table floating round' (536)—but here, the flood and foam, although 'unbounded,' are obviously controlled. For wine, like man, can be the consequence of refinement and the forces of love and industry. Modern man had, by degrees, achieved civilization and

> pour'd
> The generous Glass around, inspir'd to wake
> The Life-refining Soul of decent Wit.
>
> (87–89)

So, too, Phillips had told how 'high-sparkling Wines/Foam in transparent Floods' (648-49); thus the wine is for 'rais'd Nations,' the drink of enlightenment. In the sensuous taste and smell, 'we' drink in and consume the joy which nature gave to the wine and the smooth, mellow, gay wines are the consequence of man's and nature's fulfillment.

I have pointed out above that one of the methods of unifying *The Seasons* was the use of a sentence with alteration of the modifiers to create a distinct shift. Such a method applies also to shifts in place, for in the temperate climes the vineyard is 'elated high' (685), 'swells refulgent' (686), 'spreads,' 'climbs' and 'drinks' the 'heighten'd Blaze.' The speaker was 'fir'd' with 'Thirst' (668), and here the vineyard 'drinks' the 'Blaze' of the sun, pouring the sun into the ripening grapes, causing the grapes to 'shine' or 'flame.' (In *Summer*, the diamond 'drinks' the sun's 'purest Rays' (142). This reciprocal action from passive to active agent occurred in *Summer* when the poet drank the 'Effulgence tremulous' of Venus (1699) and looked with love on the evening star and the subsequent lightning.) The grapes glow like the flame of the sun; then as the swains crush the grapes, the grapes float the swains and the reaction follows. The ripe juice of the grapes provides a joyous, floating, foaming 'Flood' (700).

The relations between 'drinking' and 'blazing,' between water and fire, exist throughout the poem, and these form an image cluster not unlike the enclosure group ('abyss,' 'breast,' 'bosom,' 'gulph') discussed in *Summer*. The terms for 'fire'—'blaze,' 'burn,' 'flame,' 'kindle,' 'rage'—and for water—'drink,' 'flood,' float,' 'pour,' 'shed,' 'quench,' 'thirst'—can be blended to bring nourishment, as in

Spring (180–85), or elation and harmony and growth as above. In such water-fire images, the blending of the elements suggests the secret-working powers in nature and man. Since imagination can only approximate the actuality, synaesthesia and other forms of blended imagery suggest the process of change taking place in nature.

When the poet wishes to describe the tyrannical aspects of the world, he does so by insisting on the disjunction of elements. In the image of the green serpent, before whose 'flaming Crest, all other Thirst, appall'd,/Or shivering flies' (*Summer*, 905–6), there is clear opposition between the serpent's flame and others' thirst. And the *Winter* prison image, 'Thirst and Hunger burn' (363) refers to disorder (painful sensations), not to the pleasures of harmony. The water-fire cluster, therefore, illustrates the procedure of varied contexts, the blending or conflict of elements. Water and fire are not opposites reconciled, because they need not be opposites at all, since thirst can burn and fire can drink. They are elements whose spatial blending implies how heaven and earth, man and nature can combine for God's benevolent purposes. And, of course, these same elements can be seen in opposition tyrannically creating fear and disorder—the reasons for which remain, as before, hidden.

iii. The Implications of Water Imagery (707–949)

After the narrator burlesques the flood of wine in *Autumn*, and after he suggests the possibilities of vinous wit and pleasure, he moves to a different kind of befuddlement: the natural befuddlement due to fog, nature's correspondence to the drunken burlesque scene. The mountain ceases to be mighty and varied but rather 'from the baffled Sense,/Sinks dark and dreary' (716–17). The fogs give a mistiness and bluntedness to the river as well as to the mountains and sun. The illusionary spatial quality of the fog creates a fear (724) resulting from the deception. Although *Autumn* is dominated by water, this element can, in the shape of storm, wine and fog, deceive and transform, and at its worst the fog becomes the basis for con-fusion:

> Till at last
> Wreath'd dun around, in deeper Circles still
> Successive closing, sits the general Fog
> Unbounded o'er the World; and, mingling thick,

> A formless grey Confusion covers all.
> As when of old (so sung the HEBREW BARD)
> Light, uncollected, thro the Chaos urg'd
> Its Infant Way; nor Order yet had drawn
> His lovely Train from out the dubious Gloom.
>
> (727–35)

The fog that 'sits . . ./Unbounded o'er the World' becomes an image of chaotic powers in its formless 'Confusion.' Just as there is a harmony of thought which arises from the mind of the pensively tranquil poet, and a harmony enacted by the active forces of the elements so there is a disharmony that can arise from apparent motionlessness, from 'sitting,' or a disharmony resulting from the clash of elements. The passage reworks several references from *Summer*, giving them the implication of controlled confusion. 'Sober Evening,' described in *Summer* as a commanding figure sending shadows on earth, is a personified figure ordering the gentle, normal and slow extinction of light.

> First *This*
> She sends on Earth; then *That* of deeper Dye
> Steals soft behind, and then a *Deeper* still,
> In Circle following Circle, gathers round,
> To close the Face of Things.
>
> (1650–54)

This passage, with its repetitions of depth and extent and its descriptions of stealth and softness, exemplifies the beauty of evening. The fog sits 'unbounded,' that is, without controlled order or form, and its mingling does not lead to harmony, to the normal cyclical ending, but to confusion. This confusion is identified as the period before creation with 'Light, uncollected,' whereas in *Summer* even the diamond is described as a form of 'collected Light':

> The lively Diamond drinks Thy purest Rays,
> Collected Light, compact.
>
> (142–43)

Thus 'unbounded' and 'uncollected' become terms of negative value, of wrong extension.

The implications of the use of generalized language here ought not to be overlooked, for it appears that the poet is writing about a fog that suffuses the world and a confusion that 'covers all.' It is apparent that Thomson is not describing the fall of man or even the period before creation; it is rather a specific moment in historic time. But he wishes the reader to follow his allusion 'so sung the HEBREW BARD' to the Biblical theme, the purpose being to recognize in the historic present the similarities governing all men. Thus the generalizing terms here and elsewhere attempt to describe the observational world as though it is capable of infinite extension and composed of moments into which can be read the personified (or allegorical) purposefulness of God's will.

Thomson compares the fog to chaos, but, contrastingly, the passage which follows describes the advantages of the fog—the filling of the mountain cisterns which provide water for the rivers:

> those ample Stores
> Of Water, scoop'd among the hollow Rocks;
> Whence gush the Streams, the ceaseless Fountains play,
> And their unfailing Wealth the Rivers draw.
>
> (739–42)

At this point Thomson removed some lines in 1744 (omitted 833–44, condensed 750–52, omitted 764–74) and added many more, now numbered 756–835. The alteration gives a different tone to the passage: it omits a series of questions about the effects of the mists of 'weighty Rains, and melted Alpine Snows' (738), insisting on the incongruity between the unknown cause of the massive waters and the stated explanation.

> But sure 'tis no weak, variable cause,
> That heaps at once ten thousand thousand floods,
> Wide-wandering o'er the world, so fresh, and clear,
> For ever flowing, and for ever full.
>
> (A, 746–49)

The second omitted passage dealt with the restorative powers of streams, irrelevantly and fatuously referring to Amelia, 'the royal maid,' daughter of Caroline and George II, as a benefactress, matchless in virtue and given new graces by the water.

In cementing the passage after these omissions, Thomson clarified the unity by making the two parts correspond to the double view of man and nature, of the chaos and disorder after the fall and the prophetic or Godly order before. It was the contrast between the actual fog and the vision of ordered effusions. Thus the allusion to Milton, *Paradise Lost*, X, 223–301, regarding the origin of rivers and fountains, which was retained, now becomes part of the paradisial view of ordered nature, and the additions contrast the immediacy and menace of fogs with the prophetic sight into them as part of an overwhelming order. The tone of the revised passage, too, is established by the rejection of false science:

> But hence this vain
> Amusive Dream!
>
> (756–57)

Thomson did not discard the passage of false science (743–56); he merely changed the tone of the speaker. For the history of the hoarse wave that is sucked into the stratum and that rises, strained by flowing in mazy ridges until thoroughly purified, is the story of the redemption of nature, to which is added the new, more adequate version of nature transformed:

> SAY then, where lurk the vast eternal Springs,
> That, like CREATING NATURE, lie conceal'd
> From mortal Eye, yet with their lavish Stores
> Refresh the Globe, and all its joyous Tribes?
> O thou pervading *Genius*, given to Man,
> To trace the Secrets of the dark Abyss,
> O lay the Mountains bare! and wide display
> Their hidden Structure to th' astonish'd View!
>
> (773–80)

The prophetic, sublime tone in which the speaker wishes to lay bare the mountains, strip the Alps, uncover the watery secrets of the great and distant places—this long view contrasts with the close and particularized description of the sitting fog. The awesome mountains and caverns are asked to disclose their secrets. It is at this point that the speaker becomes the poet-prophet:

> I see the Rivers in their infant Beds!
> Deep deep I hear them, lab'ring to get free!
> I see ...
>
> (808–10)

As he sees into the nature of the hidden rivers, he begins to understand the interrelatedness of the elements necessary to produce the waters of the earth: in this sense nature operates in 'social Commerce'

(834), 'The full-adjusted Harmony of Things' (835), and the poet, like Newton, sees connections previously undiscovered.

The idea of things to be discovered, of things 'stored,' is appropriate to *Autumn*, in which fulfillment and harvest play so large a part. The term 'Stores' which occurs in two of the above quotations reappears eight times in *Autumn* (*Spring* (5), *Summer* (6), *Winter* (4) [twice as 'Store']) in contrasts of plenitude and tradition. In the address to 'Industry,' Thomson referred to churches whose 'Luxury within/ Pour'd out her glittering Stores' (135–36), in which the 'Stores' were paintings and sculptures, external signs of wealth and inner resources. At the conclusion of this address, he writes of personified 'Industry's' rewards in each of the seasons:

> Without him Summer were an arid Waste;
> Nor to the autumnal Months could thus transmit
> Those full, mature, immeasurable Stores,
>
> (147–49)

In the harvest of the 'immeasurable Stores' art and nature complement each other.

In the origin of water passage, the term occurs in the literal sense of stock or accumulation—'those ample Stores/Of Water' in the mountain-cisterns that serve the streams, fountains and rivers. The second use, however, refers to concealed springs, and these 'lavish Stores' lave and refresh nature, though they cannot, as the cisterns can, be seen. The third use of watery 'Stores'—'O'erflowing thence, the congregated Stores,/The crystal Treasures of the liquid World' (823–24)—implies a unifying function. The waters are congregated (massed as crystals), become clear as crystals and by flowing out become precious as crystals ('Treasures'). They nourish the earth and by their own interchange (commerce) make social commerce possible.

In *The Seasons* water has a public as well as private significance. It is the element that permits Britain to be the granary of the world; the ships that sail the Thames and the ocean in social commerce are the patriot-pride of the poem. In *Summer* the seas surrounding Britain are called the 'subject Seas' (1595), and the poet's public voice praises the island's powerful 'Naval Arm' (1599). Politically the seas are seen as subjects comparable to the other political subjects of the kingdom. But, privately, when the poet speaks as observer, the waters become the womb and the tomb of mankind, capable of benevolence or destruction.

212

The explanation of the origin of springs, by which the subterranean waters rise through the earth led by the sand 'in faithful Maze' (753) contrasts with the description of *Spring* showers falling from the clouds. The 'spouting Rills' (756) become as the flowers and they sprout from the watery womb. But this false explanation is supplanted by that of rivers in their 'infant Beds' (808) laboring to get free (to be born?). When the rivers burst through sands, they are then, in cyclical fashion, drawn up into the atmosphere and again released as rain, in a harmony image that concludes the prospect view in depth: 'As the geographical panorama insisted that the farthest corners of the earth contribute to gather the waters, so this geological one reveals how many kinds of matter help to purify and transmit "the crystal treasures of the liquid world." '[18]

The double quality of the rivers operates in each season so that the birth becomes comic or mocking when, in *Spring*, physical objects are newly christened in fluid terms or when, in *Summer*, sheep are renewed (whitened) and shorn. The sexual implications of the watery womb apply not only to the flouncing monsters of *Spring*, but also to the personified water that embraces Musidora representing the wish-fulfillment of Damon. The waters are also a tomb, a grave, an abyss in which the *Spring* lover drowns, in which the shark 'riots' (*Summer*, 1025) and the leviathan sports (*Winter*, 1014–15).

The fogs belong to the 'declining Year' and the subsequent passage analogically relates the birds to the fogs, indicating their gathering and flight at the same time:

> WHEN Autumn scatters his departing Gleams,
> Warn'd of approaching Winter, gather'd, play
> The Swallow-People; and toss'd wide around,
> O'er the calm Sky, in Convolution swift,
> The feather'd Eddy floats.
>
> (836–40)

Just as the fogs are governed by imagery of position—forced down as they steal up—so the sense of disorder is characterized by the paradoxes of 'scattering' gleams while the swallows 'gather' and the 'calm' sky is filled with eddies 'toss'd wide around.' The inversion of the sentence structure and the imagery of waves in which the birds joyfully toss and turn continue the transformation imagery of fogs into clouds—here birds into clouds. The initial meeting is full of movement and suggested disorder: 'for, thronging, now/Innumerous

Wings are in commotion all' (847–48). The multitudinous flow and
overflow in *Autumn* suggests the fruition of nature and the consequent nudity of the season. For the difference between 'Innumerous'
and 'numerous' is that the one refers to what is uncountable and
unrhythmic, whereas 'numerous' refers to what is rhythmic—as in
'numerous verse' and 'numerous Wave.' The harvest and the hunt,
traditional autumn scenes, are indicative of the possibilities of pleasure
and grossness, just as the waters indicate the possibility of growth
and destruction, and the rollings of fogs and birds are examples of the
paradoxical possibilities of dread and joy, the unsought natural
advantages and departures whether in 'copious Exhalations,' in
'roving Mists' or in 'Tribes.'

Thomson's world is full of objects and of contrary aspects of the
same object. 'Innumerous,'[19] therefore, suggests the variety of value
in the universe; it can suggest wildness and chaos as in the glaring
eyes of the vicious animals in *Summer* (925); it can suggest the harmony
of the birds in *Spring* or the playfulness reduced to order in *Autumn*.
Thus the birds become part of the heavens in the prospect of infinity,
just as the mountains merge with the clouds in a spatial view, implying
the concept of a spatial continuum in which objects, as they become
distant, mix and merge with cyclical nature. The sentence describing
the storks' departure becomes an example of ordered structure of
'Congregation' in contrast to the 'Convolution swift' of the swallows'
gathering.

> And now their Rout design'd, their Leaders chose,
> Their Tribes adjusted, clean'd their vigorous Wings;
> And many a Circle, many a short Essay,
> Wheel'd round and round, in Congregation full,
> The figur'd Flight ascends; and, riding high
> Th' aërial Billows, mixes with the Clouds.
>
> (856–61)

The initial balance between adjectives and nouns, the use of repetition
to suggest motion—'many a . . . many a . . .'—'round and round'—
lead finally to the mingling of the circling waves, 'Billows,' with the
'Clouds.'

The organization of this passage is built on a conjunction of time
and place that ends in the merging of sound and sight. It begins
with a 'when' clause (836), and leads to a series of 'where' clauses,

214

indicating the different needs of different birds—the cheerful twittering birds go south in winter, but the numberless bolder birds fly to 'farthest *Thule*'; and the passage concludes with an ambiguous harmony image—'one wild Cry.'

> OR where the *Northern* Ocean, in vast Whirls,
> Boils round the naked melancholy Isles
> Of farthest *Thule*, and th' *Atlantic* Surge
> Pours in among the stormy *Hebrides*;
> Who can recount what Transmigrations there
> Are annual made? What Nations come and go?
> And how the living Clouds on Clouds arise?
> Infinite Wings! till all the Plume-dark Air,
> And rude resounding Shore are one wild Cry.
>
> (862–70)

This remarkable passage typically interrelates natural description with metaphor by means of allusive water imagery. The concluding line of the preceding verse paragraph interprets the stork flight as 'aërial Billows,' followed by the whirling waves of the ocean lashing the 'naked' isles and the Atlantic 'pouring' in among the Hebrides. The freezing ocean 'Boils' around the isles and the Atlantic invades the 'stormy' Hebrides. As the waves invade the islands from the ocean, the birds invade it from the air, 'living Clouds on Clouds arise,' and air and ocean become 'one wild Cry.' The birds that retreated to the warmer climes—the storks—moved in gentle and more orderly groups; the bolder birds that reach the Hebrides are part of wild and raging nature, the 'Nations' like the 'vast Whirls' of the ocean that 'come and go.'

'Here' in the Hebrides (871), then, it is the native, the local shepherd, who is mild, surrounded by raging nature. In his 'sea-girt Reign' (874) he lives a difficult life—'to the Rocks/ Dire-clinging, gathers his ovarious Food' (874–75)—and gathers feathers (plumage) for the quilts of those who live in luxury; he

> treasures up
> The Plumage, rising full, to form the Bed
> Of Luxury.
>
> (876–78)

At this point Thomson flies with his muse to a height sufficiently high to see 'CALEDONIA, in romantic View' (880)[20], a prospect view of

215

his homeland (inserted here in 1730 from its original place in *Summer*). But this overt praise of Scotland does not show Thomson at his best. The characteristic formal devices are present: repetition, diverse elements, catalogs of orderly differences descending in degree— 'Her airy Mountains,' 'her Forests huge,' 'her azure Lakes,' 'her fertile Vales'—views of nature which ought to suggest 'romantic' fulfillment. But except for the momentary reference to himself, the poet lacks the sense of flowing and moving order that his devices are formally constructed to attain. The appeal to some patriot 'To chear dejected Industry' (914) in Scotland concedes the dreariness of home, since *Autumn* opened with praise of industry: 'ALL is the Gift of INDUSTRY' (141). And joined to 'love' of country and call to patronage is the appeal to nationalism directed against the Dutch fishing fleets. I have suggested that blending is a demonstration of God's harmony and blessedness and 'commerce' the economic term for such a relation. The poet identifies his patriotic defense of commerce with God's benevolence and thus creates an analogy between the natural and the national, although Scotland seems not to be a recipient of this benevolence.

In observing Caledonia 'in romantic View' the poet engages in a technique that is characteristic of this poem and of other Augustan works—the series or catalog, consisting of more than three parallel items. The procedure in general serves to provide a way for dealing with variety, for establishing an order that is indicative of the great chain of being, for indicating the common basis, by means of parallelism, of a wide variety of items or actions. Thomson's specialized use of this technique, in contrast to his occasional conventional one, is to join items in such a way as to suggest simultaneity of views while implying change, either by allusion or by collecting the items into a harmony figure.

The Caledonian catalog is narrated by the poet in his sublime position with the muse, 'High-hovering o'er the broad cerulean Scene' (879):

> Her airy Mountains, from the waving Main,
> Invested with a keen diffusive Sky,
> Breathing the Soul acute; her Forests huge,
> Incult, robust, and tall, by Nature's Hand
> Planted of old; her azure Lakes between,
> Pour'd out extensive, and of wat'ry Wealth

Full; winding deep, and green, her fertile Vales;
With many a cool translucent brimming Flood
Wash'd lovely, from the *Tweed* (pure *Parent-Stream*,
Whose pastoral Banks first heard my *Doric* Reed,
With, silvan *Jed*, thy tributary Brook)
To where the North-inflated Tempest foams
O'er *Orca*'s or *Betubium*'s [Berubium's] highest Peak.

(881–93)

This view, which begins and ends with the mountains, uses the catalog to indicate Scotland's extensive possibilities; the order proceeds in geographical descent: mountains, forests, lakes, vales. The descriptions are unified by the fertilizing waters which flow over the valleys and create the clouds that 'invest' the mountains.

There are, however, numerous other uses of the catalog, even in *Autumn*, for catalogs can be used in burlesque or sublime passages, in those of historical narration—in fact, in any context of the poem. For Thomson, this prevalence acts as a unifying device, a cyclical procedure and a method of relating the particular to the general. A burlesque catalog can be noted in the scene of the drunken hunters:

Confus'd above,
Glasses and Bottles, Pipes and Gazetteers,
As if the Table even itself was drunk,
Lie a wet broken Scene.

(557–560)

And in the use of infinitives there is:

May their tender Limbs
Float in the loose Simplicity of Dress!
And, fashion'd all to Harmony, alone
Know they to seize the captivated Soul,
In Rapture warbled from Love breathing Lips;
To teach the Lute to languish; with smooth Step,
Disclosing Motion in every Charm,
To swim along, and swell the mazy Dance;
To train the Foliage o'er the snowy Lawn;
To guide the Pencil, turn the tuneful Page;
To lend new Flavour to the fruitful Year,
And heighten Nature's Dainties; in their Race

217

To rear their Graces into second Life;
To give Society its highest Taste;
Well-order'd Home Man's best Delight to make;
And by submissive Wisdom, modest Skill,
With every gentle Care-eluding Art,
To raise the Virtues, animate the Bliss,
Even charm the Pains to something more than Joy,
And sweeten all the Toils of human Life;
This be the female Dignity, and Praise.

(589–609)

The first series, connecting objects of drinking, smoking and reading by making them parts of a 'wet broken Scene,' illustrates the use of the series as disharmony. And the second, with its series of infinitives, creates a 'Harmony' of female grace: 'May their tender Limbs/ Float in the loose Simplicity of Dress!' The qualities blend in a sentimentalized version of womanhood. The catalog of virtues is quite undistinguished as compared with the allusive catalog of the flowers in *Spring* with its particularity changing simultaneously into a general view.

There is, however, another Thomsonian series that occurs in the poem—the historical catalogs in *Summer* and *Winter*. Just as Thomson's Latinate and Biblical terms apply past meanings to present purpose, so the historical catalogs place eminent figures from the past in a simultaneous relation with living ones, sharing virtues and aims.

When Thomson declares that the coming of melancholy is betokened by a series of physical symptoms, he falls into a catalog:

His near Approach the sudden-starting Tear,
The glowing Cheek, the mild-dejected Air,
The soften'd Feature, and the beating Heart,
Pierc'd deep with many a virtuous Pang, declare.

(1006–9)

This use of the series, by its parallelism, creates simultaneous behavior which suggests, imagistically, the blended elements—'Tear', 'glowing Cheek,' 'mild-dejected Air'—that four lines later lead man's thoughts far 'Beyond dim Earth' (1013). Here the physical symptoms and elements are contrasted with the series resulting from the actual presence of melancholy. And the catalog consists of passions generalized replacing symptoms particularized.

iv. *Autumn* and Melancholy (950–1082)

As Thomson pursues the decline of the season, he moves from the mists to the birds to the trees, and in the descent he relates each to the heavens. As he looks at the woods he sees the fading colors transform the country into shadows that become analogous to the clouds that soften the light of the sun:

> BUT see the fading many-colour'd Woods,
> Shade deepening over Shade, the Country round
> Imbrown; a crouded Umbrage, dusk, and dun,
> Of every Hue, from wan declining Green
> To sooty Dark. These now the lonesome Muse,
> Low-whispering, lead into their leaf-strewn Walks,
> And give the Season in its latest View.
>
> (950–56)

The imperative 'see' (950), that has been interpreted as a command for visualization, because of early eighteenth-century assumptions about sight, functions in a far more extensive way in this and other passages. The imperative, in contrast to the indicative, is a method for involving the reader and the poet in the view of nature as conjoined with and equal to the world of man. Thus 'see' leads the reader into the melancholy of the season and 'bear me' leads him, through this melancholy, to a vision of an angelic world existing in the dusk. The imperative is, in *The Seasons*, the mood of involvement of man's world with nature's, whereas the indicative is the mood of involvement within one of these worlds. The imperative, then, urges and sometimes even commands such involvement, and in this respect, it becomes, also, a unifying device.

The injunction to 'see' the fading colors is expressed by spatial epizeuxis and the subtleties of sound. The density of 'Shade deepening over Shade' (951) is supported by the shading of sound in 'Country,' 'round,' 'Imbrown,' 'crowded' and in 'Umbrage,' 'dusk,' 'dun.' The *Summer* evening (1647 ff.), for example, indicated not a density of varied colors but a massive intensity of growing darkness. *Autumn* is seen as 'fading,' 'declining,' exemplifying the melancholy harmony by the variety of sombre hues in contrast to *Spring*'s bright harmony.

In the water imagery of 'Wine' (958), 'Current' (960), 'imbibe' (961), 'shed' (963), Thomson describes the calm that settles upon the 'peaceful World' (963). And, touched by the inevitable decline of the

season and the subsiding of activity, the poet responds and accepts
the sadness and loss of power, growth and movement.

> Then is the Time,
> For those whom Wisdom and whom Nature charm,
> To steal themselves from the degenerate Croud,
> And soar above this little Scene of Things;
> To tread low-thoughted Vice beneath their Feet;
> To soothe the throbbing Passions into Peace;
> And woo lone *Quiet* in her silent Walks.
>
> (963–69)

In *Spring* and *Summer* the reader was urged to seek the shade when
the sun caused langour or suffering, but in *Autumn* the poet responds
in conformity to the gentle sun. In *Spring* the poet is lulled by the woods
and waters, and as he rests, disengaging himself from the season,
his musing associations 'Soothe every Gust of Passion into Peace'
463); in *Autumn* the poet does not disengage himself from, but aligns
himself with, the gentle season and is urged 'to soothe the throbbing
Passions into Peace.'

It is the speaker, then, who prays to wander over the 'russet
Mead' (971) and who is identified with the muse and with the ideal
wise man. Thus the poet through sympathy becomes part of the
solitariness of the saddened grove, and in reflecting on the relation
between sadness and pleasure, he touches on the ambiguous feature
of the season in which a 'dying' (diminishing and expiring) strain
is thought to 'chear the Woodman's Toil.'

> THUS solitary, and in pensive Guise,
> Oft let me wander o'er the russet Mead,
> And thro the sadden'd Grove, where scarce is heard
> One dying Strain, to chear the Woodman's Toil.
> Haply some widow'd Songster pours his Plaint,
> Far, in faint Warblings, thro the tawny Copse.
> While congregated Thrushes, Linnets, Larks,
> And each wild Throat, whose artless Strains so late
> Swell'd all the Music of the swarming Shades,
> Robb'd of their tuneful Souls, now shivering sit
> On the dead Tree, a dull despondent Flock!
> With not a Brightness waving o'er their Plumes,
> And nought save chattering Discord in their Note.
>
> (970–82)

The birds robbed of their 'tuneful Souls' are dull and despondent, a contrast to the poet who is pleased by and can accept the changes and to the ruthless and unsympathetic hunter who, in his own way, is a representative of discord.

The moving description of the solitary birds compared with the pleasure of the solitary narrator who is singing of the absence of the birds' songs stresses the desolation to which human cruelty adds gratuitous murder. There is a distinction drawn between the sympathetic narrator and the murderous bird-hunter. In an irony that is typical, the line 'In mingled Murder, fluttering on the Ground!' (987), is followed by 'THE pale descending Year, yet pleasing still.' In proceeding with the gentle and pleasing mood of declining autumn, the narrator sees the leaf as it 'slowly circles thro the waving Air' (992) in contrast to the murdered birds 'fluttering on the Ground' (987).

The leaf circling through the air, the leafy deluge, the choking showers of 'wither'd Waste' (997)—the withdrawal of the 'flowery Race'—each is an instance of an *Autumn* storm or shower of desolation, and yet 'The desolated Prospect thrills the Soul' (1003). This passage represents an experiment in language and tone that depends upon knowledge of earlier passages in *Autumn* for its allusive effect, upon the difference between a 'timely' and an untimely shower. The early *Autumn* storm also dealt with a deluge of leaves:

> But as th' aërial Tempest fuller swells,
> And in one mighty Stream, invisible,
> Immense, the whole excited Atmosphere,
> Impetuous rushes o'er the sounding World;
> Strain'd to the Root, the stooping Forest pours
> A rustling Shower of yet untimely Leaves.
> High-beat, the circling Mountains eddy in,
> From the bare Wild, the dissipated Storm,
> And send it in a Torrent down the Vale.
>
> (316–24)

The leaf storm, described as 'pleasing still,/A gentler Mood inspires' (988–89), reads as follows:

> for now the Leaf
> Incessant rustles from the mournful Grove.
> Oft startling such as, studious, walk below,
> And slowly circles thro the waving Air.

221

But should a quicker Breeze amid the Boughs
Sob, o'er the Sky the leafy Deluge streams;
Till choak'd, and matted with the dreary Shower,
The Forest-Walks, at every rising Gale,
Roll wide the wither'd Waste, and whistle bleak.
Fled is the blasted Verdure of the Fields;
And, shrunk into their Beds, the flowery Race
Their sunny Robes resign. Even what remain'd
Of bolder Fruits falls from the naked Tree;
And Woods, Fields, Gardens, Orchards, all around
The desolated Prospect thrills the Soul.

(989–1003)

The sailing leaf which slowly descends through the 'waving Air' is like one of the departing birds described earlier in *Autumn*. The involved imagery of the sobbing breeze that results in a streaming leafy deluge is a fine example of the intertwining of personified and natural traits to create a metaphorical storm of the movement of withered nature. Despite nature's sobbing, fleeing and shrinking, the poet responds to the scene with sensuous awareness. The description gains in intensity by the sound images as well as the image of physical movement. The breeze is transformed to a water (stream, deluge) image, and the 'Verdure' (the greenness of the earth) flees; in another image resulting from the stream, the 'flowery Race' shrink into their earthy beds and give up to the stream their (fire-like) 'sunny' robes. And as the birds submit to the season, so too must the flowers; the transformation of the elements creates a naked 'desolated Prospect.' But for man there is a 'thrill,' a tremor of excitement in the inevitable transformation of nature. Its pleasure comes from the acceptance of the transformation, the fleeing, shrinking, resigning, falling—the resignation to the very process of natural change.

In a letter to his sister on October 4, 1747, Thomson made some comments that help explain his conjunction of melancholy with 'not unpleasing' feelings:

Would to God poor Lizy had lived longer, to have been a father [*sic*] Witness of the Truth of what I say, and that I might have had the Pleasure of seeing once more a Sister who so truly deserved my Esteem and Love! But she is happy, while we must toil on a little longer here below. Let us however do it cheerfully and gratefully, supported by the pleasing Hope of meeting you again on a safer

Shore, where to recollect the Storms and Difficulties of Life will not perhaps be inconsistent with blissful State. You did right to call your Daughter by her Name: for you must needs have had a particularly tender Friendship for one another; endeared as you were by Nature, by having past the affectionate Years of Youth together, and by that great Softener and Engager of Hearts, mutual Hardship That it was in my Power to ease it a little I account one of the most exquisite Pleasures of my Life—But enough of this melancholy tho not unpleasing Strain.[21]

Thomson interprets the period of decline and death as a not unpleasing recollection because there looms before the individual the prospect of an eternal life of love. He does not deny actual hardship; in an earlier letter (January 21, 1743/44) he declares, 'true Happiness is not the Growth of this mortal Soil.'[22] But the prospect that life's fever is coming to an end is a not uncheerful thought. The anxiety, the hardships of life form a bond among men, and those occasional moments when nature declines seem to offer the possibility of a not too distant renewal. Thus there appears an understandable paradox between the decline of nature and man's thrill of peaceful anticipation. The bird's 'dying' strain can cheer the woodsman's toil because it eases the loneliness, provides a sense of nature's cycle, reminds him of a time when toil will be no more.

Thomson distinguishes between this natural or gradual decline and that of man suddenly struck down by earthquakes, sandstorms, ice and frost. These create terror and awe. But as he declares in *Winter*, referring to '*Vapours*, and *Clouds*, and *Storms*' (3):

> Be these my Theme,
> These, that exalt the Soul to solemn Thought,
> And heavenly Musing.

(3–5)

The exaltation results from man's contemplation of his own hardship and of God's power to move nature. He turns to moments of winter joy in childhood, because even winter is not without its pleasures. But the 'solemn Thoughts' that dominate that season derive from a contemplation of the hardships and a determination to rise above these by the anticipation of a blessed futurity.

If this is the *Autumn* version of the 'pleasing Dread' ('Or is this Gloom too much?' 1037), there is also in *Winter* a welcome to horrors: 'Welcome, kindred Glooms!/Cogenial Horrors, hail!'

(5–6). The pleasure in contemplating desolation and gloom has a considerable past in Burton, Milton and other seventeenth-century writers. In *The Seasons* the pleasure in desolated nature derives from the altered character of reality: just as flowering nature is thrilling, so, too, deflowered nature is thrilling. The thrill of one is in the wealth, variety and excitement of the vividness of nature. The thrill of the other is in the sorrow at the loss of this glory, while anticipating the excitement of its renewal. Thus contemplation of desolation associatively recalls lost glory and the values it represented.

The reference to the 'desolated Prospect' can be compared with the 'bursting Prospect' (951) of *Spring* and the 'goodly Prospect' (1438) of *Summer* where the catalog of nature moves from space nearby to the distant mountains and clouds on to infinity. In *Autumn*, the prospect moves not to infinite space but to empty space, to the naked tree.

The 'pleasing Dread' (*Winter*, 109) of the desolate prospect creates a sense of pleasurable anxiety that has its sources in the strange, uncertain possibilities of the world; it was this curiosity that drove the poet, to venture imaginatively into the torrid zone. The anxiety is also pleasurable; it creates a tingling sense of aliveness, of newness and wonder at the surrounding world. The process of gentle change is a form of 'progress' by degree, and any moment can become the basis for a 'thrill.' It can perhaps be seen that such a 'thrill,' divorced from the view of which it is a part, can become sought for its own sake. When this occurs, extravagant Gothic behavior results.

In *Spring*, the poet identified 'sweet Pain' with the act of love, referring to its 'charming Agonies' (1074). Even in the Golden Age such 'thrills' were essential:

> in the rosy Vale
> Love breath'd his infant Sighs, from Anguish free,
> And full replete with Bliss; save the sweet Pain,
> That, inly thrilling, but exalts it more.

(251–54)

The nerve-like responsiveness enhanced love by creating a shiver, tremor, vibration. Such emotional and physical vibrations were characteristic of pleasure because the feelings 'moved,' and by moving heightened but did not destroy bliss. Both 'pleasing Dread' and 'sweet Pain' assume a world that can create dread without 'pleasing' or anguish without sweetness.

The speaker observes by imaginative exercise or contemplation induced by the 'POWER/Of PHILOSOPHIC MELANCHOLY' (1004–5), and invoking this power, the poet asks to be borne to 'vast embowering Shades' (1030) to hear the prophetic voices of angels that will give him inspiration. The *Autumn* lines recall the prophetic haunts of *Summer* (516 ff.), where the message of suffering was given, and relate the retirement scene to the sweeping, transforming shadows (1033) and the mysterious, deep-sounding angelic voices that remind the poet of future worlds: 'And Voices more than human, thro the Void/Deep-sounding, seize th' enthusiastic Ear' (1035–36).

The entire passage on Stowe beginning, 'OR is this Gloom too much?' (1037) was introduced in the 1744 edition, obviously to flatter Pitt, the elder, and Lord Cobham, proprietor of Stowe and Lyttelton's cousin. In terms of instruction it provides the smiling pleasures of the 'fair Majestic Paradise of STOWE!' (1042) as an alternative to gloomy melancholy. It presents, again, the public voice of the poet and contains, as do similar passages in other seasons, a direct address: 'And there, o PITT, thy Country's early Boast' (1048) and 'What pity, COBHAM' (1072).

The artistic difficulty with the Stowe passage is that it treats the actual in terms of sublime exaggeration, yet often disregards the paradisial ideal merely to flatter the person addressed. Thus Cobham is pitied because he is not engaged in war, though the ideal world of Stowe would seem to be ample reward for any man.

> What pity, COBHAM, thou thy verdant Files
> Of order'd Trees shouldst here inglorious range,
> Instead of Squadrons flaming o'er the Field.
>
> (1072–74)

The nationalistic and warlike passage sharply contrasts the *Autumn* idea of retreat in paradise with the supposed need to become a military leader to suppress the French, 'Those polish'd Robbers, those ambitious Slaves' (1079). This patriotism fits strangely into the two surrounding passages about withdrawing autumn. Originally the two nature passages appeared in *Winter* (1726): the first dealt with the withdrawal from outward peace to shades creating inward visions; the second with the movement of the fogs and moon to mingle in social commerce with other elements. The shifting of the *Winter* passages to *Autumn* emphasizes nature's desolation, followed by the social and philosophic thoughts it aroused and the narrator's with-drawal. At this point, in 1744, Thomson added the Stowe passage as an example of a model of earthly paradise, except that, instead of describing a retreat and withdrawal, he describes the political action that will give fame to Pitt and the loss of military action that with-holds fame from Cobham. This inevitably suggests that if the poet found retreat a value, the paradise was merely a waiting station for the great public figures to whom the poet looked as the standard of the 'purest faith' of nature. But observed nature presents no such simple-minded world.

The Stowe passage, despite its clichés, occupies an ambiguous place in the structure of *Autumn* because it falls into the pattern of the illusion of withdrawal without actual withdrawal, of seeming paradise without the love or actual life of paradise. In *Autumn*, therefore, it would appear that to include this section in this place is to call into question the very public values it offers. I do not find evidence to support Thomson's conscious questioning of these values, but artistically this is precisely what seems to be taking place.

v. Knowledge and Change (1083–1373)

Thomson's scientific subject matter provides a precise justification of God's wisdom and variety and mystery, for the knowledge is transformed into images and sentences that support the fictive struc-tural elements of the poem. The scientific passages convey the extent and limits of knowledge, the variety of the world that is scientifically valid and the unexplained and perhaps unexplainable mysteries. Thus although in *Spring* the 'sage-instructed Eye' (210) taught by Newton can unfold 'The various Twine of Light' (211), the ignorant swain

> wondering views the bright Enchantment bend,
> Delightful, o'er the radiant Fields, and runs
> To catch the falling Glory;

(213–15)

to the 'sage-instructed Eye,' the universe has a limited, recognizable order, but a few lines below this passage, at the upspringing of the living herbs, God's creativeness is 'beyond the Power/Of Botanist to number' (223–24).

In the conclusion to *Summer*, as the comet flies through the sky, the wisdom of the 'enlighten'd Few' (1714) is distinguished from the superstitious 'fond sequacious Herd' (1713) who respond only to their fear of the comet. The enlightened see it as part of 'all the Sky':

> they in their Powers exult,
> That wondrous Force of Thought, which mounting spurns
> This dusky Spot, and measures all the Sky.
>
> (1717–19)

But, while distinguishing between the scientifically informed and the scientifically ignorant, the poet realizes the limitations of all knowledge. Although the scientist can discover order and beauty where the uninformed find only chaos and terror, he nevertheless accepts—indeed, welcomes—an act of faith in God's goodness realizing his knowledge is limited. He cannot see into origins and causes, into life 'Unfetter'd, and unmix'd' (1798).

> Enough for us to know that this dark State,
> In wayward Passions lost, and vain Pursuits,
> This Infancy of Being, cannot prove
> The final Issue of the Works of GOD,
> By boundless LOVE and perfect WISDOM form'd,
> And ever rising with the rising Mind.
>
> (Summer, 1800–5)

It is apparent that these concluding lines troubled Thomson, for the last verse paragraph of Summer underwent several revisions from 1727 to 1746. Even as revised they reflect the poem's ambiguity regarding man's knowledge of God's goodness. For it is possible to interpret 'cannot prove' as meaning that the present 'dark State' cannot lead one to 'know' but merely to believe that the final issue of God's work is indeed love and wisdom. If love and wisdom, the characteristics of God's works, are dependent upon the 'rising Mind,' how can one escape from the cloud of unknowing which 'sits deep' upon it? The answer to this is, I believe, to be found in Thomson's letter to William Cranstoun, October 20, 1735:

Death is a Limit which Human Passions ought not, but with great Caution and Reverence, to pass. Nor indeed can they easily pass that Limit; since beyond it things are not clearly and distinctly enough perceived formally to excite them. This, I think, we may be sure of: that a future State must be better than this; and so-on thro the never-ceasing Succession of future States; every one rising upon the last, an everlasting new Display of Infinite Goodness![23]

God is no dim, personified nature; the conclusion to *Winter* is an invocation to man to endure the hardships of life and trust in God, a view expressed in other passages and letters. In consoling Elizabeth Young on the death of her sister, Thomson writes (January 21, 1743/44):

> Consider, she is escaped (as Shakespear calls it) from Life's fitful Fever, now warmed with Hope, now chilled with Disappointment, while we are still toiling here below, deluded Day after Day with false Views and vain Appearances of Things; for true Happiness is not the Growth of the mortal Soil, but of those blessed Regions where she now is. Sometimes indeed a few Seeds of that heavenly Plant fall below, and flourish in Love and Virtue. But what ought to settle our Hearts into perfect Peace, and joyful Serenity, is, the Consideration that infinite Wisdom and Goodness, who make and rules all, does [*and* deleted] cannot but do every Thing for the best. His Works are continually going on from Excellence to Excellence, from Bliss to Bliss, and will thro' eternal Ages ever be disclosing new Sources of inexhaustible Wisdom and Goodness. There is no real Evil in the whole general System of Things; it is only our Ignorance that makes it appear so, and Pain and Death but serve to unfold his gracious Purposes of Love.[24]

Even in the year of his death, his letter to William Paterson in the middle of April, 1748, reaffirms this need to trust in God's wisdom: 'Let us have a little more Patience, Paterson: nay, let us be cheerful. At last, all will be well; at least, all will be over—Here I mean: God forbid! it should be hereafter. But as sure as there is a God, that will not be so.'[25]

In the earlier passage of the mists in *Autumn*, Thomson introduced the rejected scientific theory of the origin of rivers by the clause 'Some Sages say' (743), impugning the reliability of some scientific sages. But even when he does not doubt their knowledge, he doubts its extent. In *Autumn*, the meteor panics the crowd, but the 'Sage' is unpanicked:

> Not so the Man of philosophic Eye,
> And Inspect sage; the waving Brightness he
> Curious surveys, inquisitive to know
> The Causes, and Materials, yet unfix'd,
> Of this Appearance beautiful, and new.

(1133–37)

Even though the sage sees beauty, not chaotic war in the heavens, and is inquisitive to know 'The Causes, and Materials,' he can be sure only of God's wisdom. And this is why, at the conclusion of *Autumn*, in his prayer to God as nature, the poet writes that the search for meaning is a 'Search, the Flight of Time can ne'er exhaust' (1366), a search that necessarily eludes man except in parts, and these parts are, after all, signs of his limitations as well as of his knowledge.

One of the scientific descriptions that the poet makes is found in his passage about the moon as it sails through the evening clouds:

> Mean-while the Moon
> Full-orb'd, and breaking thro the scatter'd Clouds,
> Shews her broad Visage in the crimson'd East.
> Turn'd to the Sun direct, her spotted Disk,
> Where Mountains rise, umbrageous Dales descend,
> And Caverns deep, as optic Tube descries,
> A smaller Earth, gives all his Blaze again,
> Void of its Flame, and sheds a softer Day.
> Now thro the passing Cloud she seems to stoop,
> Now up the pure Cerulean rides sublime.
> Wide the pale Deluge floats, and streaming mild
> O'er the sky'd Mountain to the shadowy Vale
> While Rocks and Floods reflect the quivering Gleam,
> The whole Air whitens with a boundless Tide
> Of silver Radiance, trembling round the World.
>
> (1088–1102)

This passage and the two following verse paragraphs are typical examples of the subtlety and power of Thomson's observational speaker. The image of the moon 'stooping' and rising through the heavens creates a motion analogical to the rolling fogs. Since *Autumn* is a poem dealing with the appearance of nature after its substantial harvest, the moon becomes a natural symbol of reflected, not actual, light, implying, in this water image, the beauty of illusion.

The passage fulfills multiple possibilities for expressing Thomson's meaning. It combines the other elements with the dominant *Autumn* waters of the sky, with the stream of light, the 'Tide/Of silver radiance.' In Wordsworth's organic universe objects interact with and reflect each other. Here, one object dominates and colors the others in the way in which light is untwined, in the characteristic Thomsonian procedure of moving from the moon to the mountain, vale, rocks,

and floods that merely reflect to the 'whole Air' the boundless and infinite space which becomes like a prospect view, an instant of infinity.

The dominant image is that of the moon as a 'pale Deluge' (1098)
—an image which is one of the four interpretations given to 'Deluge';
in *Summer* the sun is described as a 'dazzling Deluge' (435) that blazes;
the 'branching' 'Oronoque' overflows in a 'brown Deluge' (835);
in *Autumn* 'Deluge' refers not only to the overflowing rivers, but to
the tumbling leaves: 'o'er the Sky the leafy Deluge streams' (994);
and in *Winter*, the 'Plain/Lies a brown Deluge' (76-77). The deluge
is seen as fire, air ('vapory Deluge,' *Winter*, 226), water and earth,
and its function is dictated by the dominant concept of the season.
In contrast to the blazing and brown deluge, here the moon's light
is a 'pale Deluge,' and the allusions to the other uses are implicit.
The combination of literal, scientific, personified and natural description builds to the passage by beginning with 'Moon,' followed by
'broad Visage,' 'spotted Disk,' 'smaller Earth' and 'pale Deluge.'
This procedure is, as I have pointed out above, characteristic of the
natural objects that have a scientific order in which they resemble
the human order, with characteristic implications of social man—
'stoop,' 'rides sublime.' But in respect to its own mobile power, nature
becomes part of infinity and gives the appearance of its own uncertain
dominance. The movement of a world being circled with silver
radiance, is conveyed by the intermingling of 'shadowy' with
'quivering,' 'whitens,' 'trembling,' of activity of light with momentary
changes of time reasserted in 'Now' (1096), 'Now' (1097).

The light of the moon is described in intensifying order, beginning
with the overflowing of light, rolling over the mountains and dales and
finally conveying a sense of the whole world as deluged by silver light.
The movement through space is here not a matter of heavy physical
detail, as it was in the early deluge of *Autumn*. The storm destroys
the substantial harvest, but the insubstantial light of the moon creates
a beauty which is also part of God's power. There are deluges of
beauty as there are of terror, and in such transformational passages
some of the finest poetry is to be found—and the reason is that this
view exposes Thomson's deepest sense of God's place in the universe.
One need only point to the fact that in *Spring* a similar passage
conveys this poetic as well as natural power in terms of chaos
('from the Center to the streaming Clouds/A shoreless Ocean
tumbled round the Globe' (315-16)), as does the fine passage of the
deadly beauty of the snowfall in *Winter*:

Earth's universal Face, deep-hid, and chill,
Is one wild dazzling Waste, that buries wide
The Works of Man.

(238–40)

There is a sense of anxiety and wonder that results from disengaging an element and turning it into its opposite. The 'rays' become a 'Deluge,' that moves through space with a joyful lightness it never possessed when it functioned literally to bring terror and destruction. In contrast to the extension from the particular to the heavenly, from the immediate scene to the eternal, this procedure suggests a dialectical relation by which the actual can become the infinite, the cyclical pattern by which the material becomes the immaterial. The 'Deluge' of light suggests both beauty and danger—of being drowned even in light—and it becomes part of the paradoxical beauty of the environment. Christopher Ricks, in discussing Milton's transposition of senses in *Paradise Lost*, attributes the procedure to the suggestiveness of his language in creating the harmony of Paradise.[26] Thomson, too, manages harmony in this way, but he also manages disharmony, and the technique is tied, in *The Seasons*, to the extensive interplay of science, natural description and imagination.

In typical organization, the following verse paragraph (1103 ff.) begins with an adversative conjunction of time, leading to a contrary condition of the moon, when, indeed, its 'paleness' is not of radiant beauty, but of sickness and death:

Or quite extinct her deaden'd Orb appears,
And scarce appears, of sickly beamless White;
Oft in this Season, silent from the North
A Blaze of Meteors shoots.

(1106–9)

Since the moon is merely an orb without its own life, it reflects that of the bright sun at one moment and appears sickly pale at another. At such times the shooting meteors give to the sky not a sense of peace, calm and beauty, but of puzzling, thwarting disharmony— a 'Maze' (1114) of light. To the unenlightened the meteors appear like 'Armies in meet Array' (1117) and the sight of war in heaven creates panic. The enlightened man, however, finds no reason for panic; he finds the meteors a 'waving Brightness,' not a superstitious war among the heavenly stars—although he, too, does not know the causes.

Then, in an ironic juxtaposition, the poet describes the fate of a a 'benighted Wretch' (1145) riding through the dark night. The passage begins with a reference to the immense shade, but the shade is a 'quenching Gloom.'

> Now black, and deep, the Night begins to fall,
> A Shade immense. Sunk in the quenching Gloom,
> Magnificent and vast, are Heaven and Earth.
>
> (1138-40)

The description of the shade contrasts with the similar description in torrid *Summer*:

> Majestic Woods, of every vigorous Green,
> Stage above Stage, high-waving o'er the Hills;
> Or to the far Horizon wide diffus'd,
> A boundless deep Immensity of Shade.
>
> (*Summer*, 649-52)

This *Summer* shade is a rising prospect scene, leading to infinity; the sublimity of extent and height is achieved by reference to the 'Stage above Stage' of the woods as they stretch in height and width. The 'boundless deep Immensity of Shade' becomes in the *Summer* context a scene of majestic, powerful and 'dreadful Beauty,' meaning beauty causing awe and providing safety and refreshment. The *Autumn* image is related to falling and sinking as a drowning image— 'Sunk in the quenching Gloom'—and thus it becomes, in the conception of the poet, indicative of chaos and destruction by water. The shade is not refreshing but dangerous, and the black and deep night is like a huge tide of 'Gloom' which sinks the (lighted) earth.

Not only does night overtake the rider, but he is also overcome by his own fancies. He cannot see his way; the false light of the 'Wild-fire' (1152) decoys him into the marsh, and he sinks, in an image paralleling that of the heaven and earth above, into a dreadful 'Gulph' continuing the water imagery of the season.

> Whither decoy'd by the fantastick Blaze,
> Now lost and now renew'd, he sinks absorpt,
> Rider and Horse, amid the miry Gulph.
>
> (1154-56)

Yet the rider's failure of perception is assisted by the unfathomable darkness of the night. Sometimes men are led safely 'by the *better*

232

Genius of the Night' (1160), but at other times they are misled by
their own limitations and nature's false appearances.

> Now black, and deep, the Night begins to fall,
> A Shade immense. Sunk in the quenching Gloom,
> Magnificent and vast, are Heaven and Earth.
> Order confounded lies; all Beauty void;
> Distinction lost; and gay Variety
> One universal Blot: such the fair Power
> Of Light, to kindle and create the Whole.
> Drear is the State of the benighted Wretch,
> Who then, bewilder'd, wanders thro the Dark,
> Full of pale Fancies, and Chimeras huge;
> Nor visited by one directive Ray,
> From Cottage streaming, or from airy Hall.
> Perhaps impatient as he stumbles on,
> Struck from the Root of slimy Rushes, blue,
> The Wild-Fire scatters round, or gather'd trails
> A Length of Flame deceitful o'er the Moss;
> Whither decoy'd by the fantastick Blaze,
> Now lost and now renew'd, he sinks absorpt,
> Rider and Horse, amid the miry Gulph:
> While still, from Day to Day, his pining Wife,
> And plaintive Children his Return await,
> In wild Conjecture lost.
>
> (1138–59)

This scene of 'sad Presage' with the pining wife and plaintive
children began with a reference to the *Autumn* fog and to the 'formless
grey Confusion' that covers all. That was the confusion caused by
Autumn transformational fogs, but this is the dark evening, a normal
event that creates danger and destruction. In the quenching gloom
of night order lies confounded and gay variety is 'One universal
Blot.' The typical Thomsonian feature of illusive allusion governs
the relation between the black 'Night' and the 'benighted Wretch,'
between the 'bewilder'd' man, the 'wild Fire' and the wife and children
'In wild Conjecture lost.' The puns on 'Night' and 'benighted' and on
'wild' and 'bewilder'd' indicate the selected correspondence between
man and nature. The fire wanders and the man wanders. Thus the
poor wanderer assumes some features of the night—its gloom and
loss of order—for as heaven and earth are sunk in the gloom so the

rider sinks into the gulph. As he sinks, he is lost, becoming one with the gulph, exemplifying the 'Distinction lost.' The passage, describing spatial movement through the dark, distinguishes between the 'fair Power/Of Light,' and the 'pale Fancies' and 'Flame deceitful.' The elements can be deceptive as well as directive, and the wild fire is struck from the 'Root of the slimy Rushes.'

If one compares this scene with a similar passage in *Paradise Lost*, some of the similarities and differences between Thomson and Milton can be pointed out. Satan leads Eve to the forbidden tree:

> He leading swiftly rowl'd
> In tangles, and made intricate from straight,
> To mischief swift, Hope elevates, and joy
> Bright'ns his lust, as when a wand'ring Fire,
> Compact of unctuous vapour, which the Night
> Condenses, and the cold invirons round,
> Kindl'd through agitation to a Flame,
> Which oft, they say, some evil Spirit attends
> Hovering and blazing with delusive Light,
> Misleads th' amaz'd Night-wanderer from his way
> To Boggs and Mires, and oft through Pond or Pool,
> There swallow'd up and lost, from Succour far:
> So glisten'd the dire Snake, and into fraud
> Led *Eve* our credulous Mother, to the Tree
> Of prohibition, root of all our woe;
> Which when she saw, thus to her Guide she spake.
>
> (631–46)

Although both poets are describing the 'will-o'-the-wisp,' their contexts are, of course, different. Yet both give accurate scientific descriptions of the phenomenon to illustrate the dangers of a God-created environment. But Thomson establishes the secret influence of nature upon man so that his vocabulary illustrates an illusive interrelation between them, and he also conceives of this relation in spatial and social terms so that the wanderer is not 'visited' by any directive light; he 'stumbles,' the wild fire 'scatters round' or 'trails.' This procedure differs from that of Milton, who compares Satan's movements to the 'wand'ring Fire.' Milton avoids the social implications (he does not bring in the cottage or the hall) and separates Satan's movement from that in the epic simile. Although Milton refers to the 'wand'ring Fire' and to the 'Night-wanderer' misled, relating

234

man's behaviour to nature's, Thomson's version of this differs from
Milton's consistency in which the fire is the subject of the action and
the sentence. In his typical procedure Thomson shifts from the
wandering benighted wretch to the wandering fire and concludes
with the man as he sinks. The interrelation and the procedure of
being submerged embody Thomson's sense of a nature that man
cannot predict.[27] In *The Seasons* it is possible for beauty to destroy
and for terror to be identified with beauty or the sublime ('Gloom/
Magnificent and Vast'), for industry and goodness to be destroyed
by wicked men.

The last serene autumnal morning shines, and the

> myriad Dew-Drops twinkle round.
> AH see where robb'd, and murder'd, in that Pit,
> Lies the still heaving Hive!
>
> (1171–73)

Mansions are cast into the gulf, bees into the pit. The bees are destroyed in the midst of tending public cares; the moral narrator
addresses man as 'tyrannic Lord!': 'how long, how long/Shall
prostrate Nature groan beneath your Rage' (1189–90). But the destruction of the city of bees becomes a metaphor for the destruction
of human cities by equally arbitrary powers, just as Palermo was
destroyed by an earthquake and the rider misled by betraying lights
of nature.

> Thus a proud City, populous and rich,
> Full of the Works of Peace, and high in Joy,
> At Theater or Feast, or sunk in Sleep,
> (As late, *Palermo*, was thy Fate) is seiz'd
> By some dread Earthquake, and convulsive hurl'd,
> Sheer from the black Foundation, stench-involv'd,
> Into a Gulph of blue sulphureous Flame.
>
> (1201–7)

Heaven and earth 'sink' into gloom, the rider 'sinks' into the gulf,
the proud and peaceful city is 'sunk in Sleep'; 'oppressive Steam
ascends' (1180) and the bees are poisoned; Palermo is hurled 'Into
a Gulph of blue sulphureous Flame' (1207). These are held together
by the water imagery of destruction, converting 'Flame' to a 'Gulph'
and indicating that 'sinking' and 'ascending' can both be fatal.
Although *Spring* and *Autumn* show many features of gentleness,
the later season modifies the earlier by returning to some of its phases

and altering the context. In *Spring* the idealized couple finally leave their model earthly life:

> Together down they sink in social Sleep;
> Together freed, their gentle Spirits fly
> To Scenes where Love and Bliss immortal reign.
>
> (1174–76)

But the *Autumn* bees, 'tending public Cares, and planning Schemes/ Of Temperance, for Winter poor' (1177–78), are murdered in the hive and Palermo 'sunk in Sleep' is hurled into the abyss.

At the beginning of this chapter I identified the pattern of *Autumn* as pre-eminently displaying changes in man and nature. The rapidity with which this season undergoes contrary alterations can be traced from the fading season when

> The dewy-skirted Clouds imbibe the Sun,
> And through their lucid Veil his soften'd Force
> Shed o'er the peaceful World.
>
> (961–63)

> How clear the cloudless Sky! how deeply ting'd
> With a peculiar Blue! th' ethereal Arch
> How swell'd immense! amid whose Azure thron'd
> The radiant Sun how gay! how calm below
> The gilded Earth!
>
> (1213–17)

The poem moves from the solitariness encouraged by the season to the cruel, murdering hunter untouched by this encouragement. From the desolation of nature to the tender love of mankind, from prophetic glooms to wide-extended walls, from the moon that sheds a softer ray to the moon as deaden'd orb, from rising and falling meteors, from deceiving lights at night to the serene light of morning, from nature dispelling fogs and man creating steam to destroy the bees and then nature convulsively engulfing man—all these rapid transformations (and within them there are many others that I have not cataloged) conclude with *Autumn* growing calm and appearing secure. Such security results in festive joy, in heightened movement and play, and the poet comments:

> Thus they rejoice; nor think
> That, with to-morrow's Sun, their annual Toil
> Begins again the never-ceasing Round.
>
> (1233–35)

The harvest games of the rural youths and maids convey the total absence of cares by the illusive allusion of the 'Toil-strung' youth (1223) whose strings are played upon by music and who leaps 'wildly graceful' (1225) in the dance, an action in which violent uncontrol is joined with natural grace. Implicit in this view of the lower classes is the colloquial tone of sympathetic and playful irony—'Her every Charm abroad' (1226) and 'Age too shines out; and, garrulous...' (1231). For these classes are seen as rejoicing in the immediacy and sensuousness of their own over-confident security.

The conclusion to *Autumn* beginning with 'O! knew he but his Happiness' (1235) is a rewriting of passages from Virgil's *Georgics*, II, 458 ff. It can serve as a representative example of how Thomson absorbs literary allusion into his conception of human experience governed by the needs of the particular season.[28]

The Virgilian lines read as follows:

> *O fortunatos nimium, sua si bona norint,*
> *agricolas! quibus ipsa, procul discordibus armis,*
> *fundit humo facilem victum iustissima tellus.*
>
> (458–60)

Thomson's paraphrase reads:

> OH knew he but his Happiness, of Men
> The happiest he! who far from public Rage,
> Deep in the Vale, with a *choice Few* retir'd,
> Drinks the pure Pleasures of the RURAL LIFE.
>
> (1235—1238)

This passage Thomson connects with and distinguishes from that in *Spring*:

> But happy they! the happiest of their Kind!
> Whom gentler Stars unite, and in our Fate
> Their Hearts, their Fortunes, and their Beings blend.
>
> (1113–15)

The passage makes clear that the poet is writing in the idealized voice and that he wishes to connect two similar situations involving the select few. In *Autumn* it is the swain removed from public life, whereas in *Spring* it is the loving husband and wife. But the *Autumn* retirement not only has the unfortunate drinking image which substitutes for Virgil's more appropriate one, but it deliberately contrasts the 'pure Pleasures of the Rural Life' with a whole series, extending far beyond

237

Virgil's listing, of impure courtly pleasures. Those are developed in the liquescent imagery—'vomits out' (1240), 'floating loose' (1244), 'tributary Life/Bleeds not' (1247–48), 'costly Juice' (1250), 'sunk in Beds' (1250), 'melts' (1252)—that in illusive allusion to earlier uses of theme terms suggests the false transformations.

When Thomson returns to the swain, he does so by creating a contrast between 'hollow' and 'solid':

> Their hollow Moments undelighted all?
> Sure Peace is his; a solid Life, estrang'd
> To Disappointment, and fallacious Hope.
>
> (1256–58)

Thomson sharpens these opposites and interprets human conduct as a constant tossing and turmoil, with which he contrasts the ideal of a blended harmony image. The seasons rotate in joy and harmony though *Autumn*'s storms leave no joy in the heart of the husbandman. Thomson alludes to Virgil and uses the pagan poet to support his ideal version of harmony through movement:

> whatever greens the Spring,
> When Heaven descends in Showers; or bends the Bough,
> When Summer reddens, and when Autumn beams;
> Or in the Wintry Glebe whatever lies
> Conceal'd, and fattens with the richest Sap:
> These are not wanting.
>
> (1260–65)

The underlying concept of movement appears even in the plants concealed but growing and fattening in the wintry earth, a movement which is a natural harmony in repose, like the movements of the human heart that 'waken, not disturb the tranquil Mind' (*Spring*, 466).

The wild movements of wicked men can become, contrastingly, grotesque actions, verging close to the burlesque hunt at the beginning of the season. The descriptions of wicked actions not only lack Virgil's control; they lack that sense of normal disregard of hunters or the exploitative desires of Jesuit missionaries:

> Let such as deem it Glory to destroy
> Rush into Blood, the Sack of Cities seek;
> Unpierc'd, exulting in the Widow's Wail,
> The Virgin's Shriek, and Infant's trembling Cry.
>
> (1280–83)

But Virgil can sometimes help control Thomson's tendency for exaggerated contrast:

> Let some, far-distant from their native Soil,
> Urg'd or by Want or harden'd Avarice,
> Find other Lands beneath another Sun.
> Let This thro Cities work his eager Way,
> By legal Outrage, and establish'd Guile,
> The social Sense extinct.

(1284–89)

In the lives men lead, base motives often govern human behavior; if for some, glory governs, for others, want, avarice, and the absence of social sympathy. Thomson sees as the ideal the paradisial life in which love of God speaks for love of man, and this voice can be heard directly or through nature. In this, of course, he departs from Virgil, but only if one does not recognize the secret-working hand of God in nature can he assume that the following passage is deistic:

> The Fall of Kings,
> The Rage of Nations, and the Crush of States,
> Move not the Man, who, from the World escap'd,
> In still Retreats, and flowery Solitudes,
> To Nature's Voice attends, from Month to Month,
> And Day to Day, through the revolving Year;
> Admiring, sees Her in her every Shape;
> Feels all her sweet Emotions at his Heart;
> Takes what she liberal gives, nor thinks of more.

(1302–10)

This ideal solitary begins to be above the battle, yet able to describe it, and he is brought back to the actuality of the poem by being converted into the poet:

> In Summer he, beneath the living Shade,
> Such as o'er frigid *Tempè* wont to wave,
> Or *Hemus* cool, reads what the Muse, of These
> Perhaps, has in immortal Numbers sung;
> Or what she dictates writes.

(1316–20)

And again, in *Autumn*,

> thro the tepid Gleams
> Deep-musing, then he *best* exerts his Song.

(1325–26)

The retired solitary in 'Summer' (1316), protected from the heat by the 'living Shade,' such as, according to Virgil (*Georgics*, II, 769, and II, 488), waved over 'frigid *Tempè*' or '*Hemus* cool,' reads what the great poet has said of nature or is inspired by nature itself to express his own thoughts in poetry. This view is completely consistent with what Thomson wrote in his 1726 'Preface' regarding the tradition and composition of poetry. As *Autumn* falls the solitary joins in the general joy, but it is the mixed joy described earlier in the season, for 'his Heart distends/With gentle Throws' (1324–25). The idea of composition proceeding best in this condition of gentle uneasiness supports the views, expressed in *Spring* and *Autumn*, that gentle strife with nature or poetic tradition is essential for some kinds of creativity. Thus the 'tepid' (faint and lukewarm) gleams lead the poet to 'deep' musing and his best exertions.

The concluding verse paragraph is an invocation to 'Nature,' and although it begins with a reference to Virgil's line '*Felix, qui potuit rerum cognoscere causas*' (490), it reworks a passage that Thomson quoted in his 'Preface' to the second edition of *Winter*, 1726.

It was this Devotion to the Works of Nature that, in his Georgicks, inspired the rural Virgil to write so inimitably; and who can forbear joining him in this Declaration of his, which has been the Rapture of Ages.

> Me vero primum dulces ante omnia Musae,
> Quarum Sacra fero ingenti perculsus Amore,
> Accipiant; Coelique Vias et Sidera monstrent,
> Defectus solis varios, Lunaeque labores;
> Unde tremor Terris: qua vi Maria alta tumescant
> Obicibus ruptis, rursusque in seipsa residant:
> Quid tantum Oceano properent se tingere soles
> Hyberni: vel quae tardis Mora Noctibus obstat.
> Sin, has ne possim Naturae accedere Partes,
> Frigidus obstiterit circum Praecordia sanguis;
> Rura mihi et rigui placeant in vallibus amnes,
> Flumina amem silvasque inglorius.

Which may be Englished thus:

> Me may the Muses, my supreme Delight!
> Whose Priest I am, smit with immense Desire,
> Snatch to their Care; the Starry Tracts disclose,
> The Sun's Distress, the Labours of the Moon:

Whence the Earth quakes: and by what Force the Deeps
Heave at the Rocks, then on Themselves reflow:
Why Winter-Suns to plunge in Ocean speed:
And what retards the lazy Summer-Night.
But, least I should these mystic-Truths attain,
If the cold Current freezes round my Heart,
The Country Me, the brooky Vales may please
Mid Woods, and Streams, unknown.[29]

In placing a paraphrase of Virgil at the end of *Autumn* it became
an allusion, an invocation and a prayer. The invocation, 'OH NATURE!
all-sufficient' (1352), sounds like a deist manifesto, but although
the use of the term 'nature' reflects Thomson's practice of multiple
meanings, here 'nature' means the effect of God's power and variety.
This 'nature' includes future worlds, the present world, and man's
human nature or passions; it signifies something different from
'Nature's Bounty' (*Autumn*, 1259) in which 'nature' clearly refers to
herbs and fruits. It is the same use of 'Nature' that occurs in the
invocation in *Winter* (106–9):

> NATURE! great Parent! whose unceasing Hand
> Rolls round the Seasons of the changeful Year,
> How mighty, how majestic, are thy Works!

Asking God for the capacity to see and scan the sublimity of the
moving heavens and of the varied earth—

> The vary'd Scene of quick-compounded Thought,
> And where the mixing Passions endless shift—
>
> (1363–64)

the poet is aware that he will be unable to exhaust his search for this
sublime wisdom. He concludes, therefore, in a manner thoroughly
consistent with *Autumn*, by acknowledging the endless changes in the
universe, yet finding within these the all-sufficient power of God.
Thus while singing of these changes he nevertheless dwells on them,
and he hymns his overwhelming love of God who, in His wisdom,
power and omnipresence is the source and end of poetry and life.

> From THEE begin,
> Dwell all in THEE, with THEE conclude my Song;
> And let me never never stray from THEE.
>
> (1371–73)

Thomson thus adds to Virgil the voice of the poet-prophet, who while 'inglorious,' without renown under the rural shades, is nevertheless a singer aware of God's harmony in the varied world. And in beginning with nature as God's creation, dwelling on it and ending with it, he provides a unity of feeling and thought. This was the Biblical reference in Thomson's early 'Paraphrase of Psalm CIV':

> I'll to God's honour consecrate my lays,
> And when I cease to be I'll cease to praise.

(111–12)

And in the *Hymn* it is the poet as psalmist sheltered by nature's beauty who sees in nature's changing movements the one God of the seasons:

> Or if you rather chuse the rural Shade,
> And find a Fane in every sacred Grove;
> There let the Shepherd's Flute, the Virgin's Lay,
> The prompting Seraph, and the Poet's Lyre,
> Still sing the GOD OF SEASONS, as they roll.

(89–93)

Throughout Chapter II I indicated how allusions *within the poem*—allusions by words, passages, themes—identify seasonal differences, help unify the poem, and illustrate tradition and development. But allusion implies, normally, reference to works other than the one under discussion: I wish to conclude by relating the passages from Virgil and Milton to Thomson's sensibility, his ways of thinking and feeling.

Thomson translates Virgil directly in the second edition of *Winter*, and then paraphrases the same passage in *Autumn*. This is an important distinction in Thomson's use of sources; although there may be occasional words or phrases that Thomson incorporates into his poem, there are no extended quotations from Virgil or Milton; rather there are paraphrases or adaptations; and numerous instances of Thomson's handling of his other sources can be found in A. D. McKillop's study, *The Background of Thomson's Seasons*.

The purpose of allusion can be to refer to the presence of the past, to display the knowledge of the past or to contrast the poet's skill with that of his chosen adversary or model. But in *The Seasons*, allusion to Biblical, scientific or classical passages provides a sense of the sources' values and significance for the present. Thomson, in reworking a text, incorporates it into the imagery appropriate to the season, making it part of the transformation of nature and knowledge. Such instances exemplify the inevitable changes in man and nature without minimizing the continuity of literary tradition. In this respect it seems unlikely that in paraphrasing Virgil, Milton or Job, Thomson thought he was improving upon them. He cannot here be considered demonstrating superiority to his models. Rather, he was trying to illustrate how these fitted his personal conception of nature, man, and God. This is apparent in the conversion of the story of Ruth to a change-of-fortune narrative, relating it to the poem as a whole and connecting the themes of concealment, idyllic love, and the secret forces of God with the particular season and the imagery of retirement and naturalization.

Although *Paradise Lost* and the *Georgics* are reworked in various ways, Thomson does not find in each the same resources. In a fashionable sense, both provide set subjects for imitation; in a more profound sense, *Paradise Lost*, with its Son of God and the fallen angel, becomes the model for Thomson's religious view whereas the *Georgics* is his authority for combining various genres and fragments into a unity. Thomson's innovations within these traditions consist of the following features. First, he combines the religious tradition with an interpretation of man and nature in transformation. These become part of the continuing cycle of the seasons and of fluctuating human life since the fall. Within this view, man and nature are imperfect; occasionally man perceives and even achieves harmony or its ideal, but it cannot endure and necessarily leads to an act of faith. Thomson experiments with the organizational procedures so that they become a palimpsest of public and personal history, tied by scientific conceptions and by varied repetitions that impose a literary order upon natural change. Since the poets he admires are part of his tradition, he makes room for them in his style through allusive illusion and other poetic procedures that join the past to the present in comic and serious ways. He converts received views of harmony into gentle concord or competition as illustrated by the family, though competition all too frequently becomes chaos or destruction. Finally, by placing nature in the forefront of his poem, Thomson stresses the sensuous awareness of man's environment, in which joyous pleasures and unexpected hardships must be experienced before even deserving men are redeemed.

NOTES

[1] Thomson's conscious unifying procedure in 'The Argument' is his narration of events that are related to the season in chronological order:

The Subject propos'd. Address'd to Mr. ONSLOW. *A Prospect of the Fields ready for Harvest. Reflections in praise of Industry rais'd by that View. Reaping. A Tale relative to it. A Harvest Storm. Shooting and Hunting, their Barbarity. A ludicrous Account of Fox-hunting. A View of an Orchard. Wall-Fruit. A Vineyard. A Description of Fogs, frequent in the latter part of* AUTUMN: *whence a Digression, enquiring into the Rise of Fountains and Rivers. Birds of Season considered, that now shift their Habitation. The prodigious Number of them that cover the northern and western Isles of* SCOTLAND. *Hence a View of the Country. A Prospect of the discoloured, fading Woods. After a gentle dusky Day, Moon-light. Autumnal meteors. Morning: to which succeeds a calm, pure, Sun-shiny Day, such as usually shuts up the Season. The Harvest being gathered in, the Country dissolv'd in Joy. The whole concludes with a Panegyric on a Philosophical Country Life.*

[2] William Thompson, *A Poetical Paraphrase on Part of the Book of Job,* 1726, 'Preface.'

[3] 'Reason' occurs ten times in the poem: *Spring* (5), *Summer* (2), *Winter* (3). Thomson prefers 'thought' and its derivatives—'thought(s) (5) 'thoughtful' (3) and 'low-thoughted' (1): *Spring* (16), *Summer* (11), *Autumn* (10), *Winter* (12). Thomson applies 'thought' to birds (*Spring,* 585, 602) as well as men, and, in his usage, feelings can corrode thought (*Spring,* 585, 602, 1074), just as the 'patient Fires of Thought' (*Summer,* 878) can help to humanize feelings. The proper relation between thought and feeling resides in their harmonious blending. For a discussion of the social passions and their place in Thomson's thought see Chapter IV.

[4] John F. Danby, ed. *The Prelude,* New York, 1963, p. 3.

[5] Maurice J. Quinlan, 'Swift's Use of Literalization as a Rhetorical Device,' *PMLA,* 82 (1967), 516.

[6] For a discussion of this passage that misconstrues the relation of *Summer* to *Autumn,* see Bernard Fehr, 'The Antagonism of Forms in the Eighteenth Century,' *English Studies,* XVIII (1936), 201, 202.

[7] Pope, *Windsor Forest,* I, 150.

[8] Quoted in George C. Macaulay, *James Thomson,* London, 1908, pp. 78-79.

[9] Pope, *Windsor Forest,* 99-102.

[10] *Ibid.,* 155-158.

[11] John Dryden, *Poems,* ed. James Kinsley, Oxford, 1958, II, 420-23.

[12] John Arthos, *The Language of Natural Description in Eighteenth-Century Poetry,* Ann Arbor, 1949, p. 35.

[13] Geoffrey Tillotson, *Augustan Poetic Diction*, London, 1964, p. 49.

[14] Pope, Epistle II, I, 28.

[15] See Josephine Miles, *Eras and Modes in English Poetry*, Berkeley, 1957, p. 270.

[16] Seymour Chatman, 'Participles in *Paradise Lost*', *PMLA* (1968), 1393 ff.

[17] Reuben A. Brower, 'Form and Defect of Form in Eighteenth Century Poetry: A Memorandum,' *CE*, (1968). 538-39.

[18] Spacks, *The Language of Vision*, p. 34.

[19] 'Innumerous' occurs seven times in *The Seasons*: *Spring* (3), *Summer* (2), *Autumn* (2). 'Numerous' has eight occurrences: *Spring* (1), *Summer* (4), *Autumn* (3); *Winter*, for obvious reasons, avoids statements about seasonal plenitude. It should be noted, however, that the impression of plenitude is conveyed by serial and repetitive procedures, by diverse perspectives rather than by single terms.

[20] 'Romantic' occurs once in the 'Preface' (1726) and five times in the poem. Thomson refers to 'romantic' mountains, shapes, views (*Spring*, 1028; *Summer*, 459, 1375; *Autumn*, 252, 880).

[21] *Letters*, pp. 190-91.

[22] *Letters*, p. 170. For the entire quotation, fn. 24.

[23] *Letters*, p. 100.

[24] *Letters*, p. 170.

[25] *Letters*, p. 197.

[26] Christopher Ricks, *Milton's Grand Style*, Oxford, 1963, pp. 100–2.

[27] Thomson's debts to Milton are traced in Macaulay, pp. 141–45, 157–58, 160, 166–70.

[28] Thomson's allusions to Virgil are discussed in Dwight L. Durling, *Georgic Tradition in English Poetry*, New York, 1935, pp. 43–44. For extensive references to Virgil and other sources, see McKillop, *Background*, *passim*, and *Discrimination*, pp. 19–21. I regret that the most recent book on this subject, John Chalker, *The English Georgic*, London, 1969, was published too late for my consideration here.

[29] Zippel, p. 242.

IV

WINTER

DISLOCATION, DEFORMITY
AND RENEWAL

i. Revisions—*Winter*, 1726, 1730, 1744, 1746

Winter began the poem that—in 1730—became *The Seasons*; as first published in 1726, it contained only a few of the stylistic or organizational characteristics that Thomson developed in the final poem. It was an early work and shared with 'Of a Country Life' (1720) and 'Hymn on Solitude' (1725, 1729) the varied perspectives of a single physical and emotional condition (solitude) or the varied aspects of a rural life. The original *Winter* presented the change in season from autumn to winter, and was, indeed, addressed to both, with the conclusion hinting at the rebirth of spring. The changes in *Winter* from 1726 to 1746 can be considered representative of changes in the other seasons.[1]

Revisions in *The Seasons* are of three kinds: transpositions, changes in diction and sentence structure for stylistic purposes (these are often made with the transpositions), and additions. The transpositions can perhaps best be noted by first describing the plan of the original poem. The 1726 *Winter* begins with an address to the reader to observe the coming of the personified season, and is followed by an invocation to 'kindred Gloom' (*A*, 5). And just as the glooms 'exalt the Soul to solemn Thought' (*A*, 4), so, too, 'Autumn,' in the second stanza, is seen as 'Inspirer of the toiling Swain' (*A*, 17). The poet depicts the 'temper'd' (*A*, 19, 33) season, and it is not until the line, 'For see! where Winter comes, himself, confest' (*A*, 112), that the wintry season is announced.

The change from autumn to winter when the 'golden Hours are on

246

the Wing' (*A*, 20) is controlled by the image of aerial motion—the flying hornet (*A*, 23–29), the wise who 'soar' (*A*, 36), the strain of the nightingale (*A*, 44–45), the leaves wavering in the air (*A*, 48), the rustling woods, the fluctuating main, the wheeling woodcocks, the falling fruit. The encompassing image of flight, of aerial motion which includes 'soaring,' 'rustling,' 'breathing,' and 'falling,' is continued throughout the autumn references, distinguishing the natural phenomena which are declining, from the human thoughts which seek separation and isolation. The contrasts that become characteristic of the later poetry are here merely touched on in the melancholy that 'bears' the 'swelling Thought aloft to Heaven' (*A*, 67), and, in the poet's request: 'bear me then to high, embowering, Shades' (*A*, 74). The evening glides, the fogs swim, and, in the distance, the stars shine and the moon glows and rides. This imagery of autumn is then discontinued, and the stormy motion begins. No longer is the gentle, golden image of the fleeing hours dominant, but winter brings violent, destructive movement introduced without irony by the 'giddy Youth' (*A*, 104) who stains 'the guiltless Grove' (*A*, 105).

When *The Seasons* was published in 1730, this entire passage was transposed, in part revised and altered, to the end of *Autumn*—the season first issued in this edition. The conscious plan of the poem confined autumnal events to *Autumn*; events paralleling those in other seasons were to suggest a world in which physical changes do not necessarily lead to moral changes; in fact, despite differences in time of year, it is still possible for man to respond in an unchanged manner. Thus the original 'Philosophic Melancholly' (*A*, 66) connected with midnight 'Contemplation' (*A*, 199) in *Winter* (1726), was transferred to *Autumn*, and in that season the 'POWER/OF PHILO-SOPHIC MELANCHOLY' (1014–15) was associated not merely with the inherited golden light imagery, but with the relation between the gentleness of this golden or pale light and its opposite—the violence and dreadfulness of the imagined flickering light (*Autumn*, 1145 ff.). The shift in organization absorbed the passage into the general conception of *The Seasons*—each season containing within it a dominant element modified by the range of transformation with the other elements, illustrating man's fragmentary perception of the beauty and sublimity of the world and leading to an act of faith in God's love and wisdom.

Thomson also introduces into the revisions the simultaneity of events that lead to reciprocal responses composing a harmony. Thus a passage containing instances of natural description in which the shadowing clouds temper the rays of the sun becomes, when revised, an instance of the ambiguous, simultaneous actions in nature. Continuing the idea of 'tempering,' Thomson now suggests the complicated interrelation involved in this action.

The original read:

> Sometimes, a Fleece
> Of clouds, wide-scattering, with a lucid Veil,
> Soft, shadow o'er th' unruffled Face of Heaven;
> And, thro' their dewy Sluices, shed the Sun,
> With temper'd Influence down.

(A, 29–33)

The revised version reads:

> MEAN-TIME, light-shadowing all, a sober Calm
> Fleeces unbounded Ether; whose least Wave
> Stands tremulous, uncertain where to turn
> The gentle Current: while illumin'd wide,
> The dewy-skirted Clouds imbibe the Sun,
> And thro their lucid Veil his soften'd Force
> Shed o'er the peaceful World.

(Autumn, 957–63)

This revision also produces changes in diction and sentence structure. The simple sentence with the compound verb is made complex by introducing two subordinate clauses, several phrases and replacing the three participial adjectives by five new ones. The consequence of this is that the idea of evanescence, of shadow and substance, becomes imaged in the paradox of 'light-shadowing all,' in the sober calm in which each wave stands 'tremulous,' and in the awkward personification of 'dewy-skirted Clouds' that drink the sun. The complication is not a matter of inflation or a failure to grasp simple sentences, but a deliberate mixing of natural description with personification: sober calm 'Fleeces' unbounded ether—a description in which calmness gives the upper air, which is motionless, the appearance of white, soft fleece. The unbounded ether is composed of waves of air, each of which seems to know how to turn within the undirected boundlessness. And the clouds 'imbibe the Sun,' seem to absorb the sun's rays and then gently shed them. In the original the clouds shadowed heaven and tempered the rays, but the revision creates a deliberate, reciprocal action. The revision distinguishes between the ether and the clouds; the latter are 'illumin'd,' yet at the same time they 'imbibe' the illumination, in an example of the fire-water imagery of *Autumn*.

It is noteworthy that the same procedures regarding alterations in parts of speech within each season are evident in this act of revision. The noun 'Fleece' becomes a verb, 'Fleeces'; 'wide-scattering' is reduced to 'wide,' and 'dewy' becomes hyphenated as 'dewy-skirted'; the verb 'shadow' becomes the (gerundive) participle 'shadowing.' In both original and revision the active verb forms are prominent, giving movement to objects in the poem, conveying a sense of penetrable and dense space in which simultaneous actions are occurring. This simultaneity adds a new procedure to the original *Winter*, in which terms like 'now' indicated successive time.

In distinguishing 'Ether' from 'Clouds,' Thomson introduces a more accurate scientific description, but, more than this, he joins natural science to personification, a type of revision that artistically reinterprets the moon-visage passage originally in *Winter* (*A*, 88–96) (discussed above in Chapter III). This passage revised in 1730 and again in 1744 exemplifies the mixing of personification and natural description to show the blending of elements, the metaphoric relation by which the actual can become infinite, the cyclical pattern by which the material becomes immaterial.

The transpositions are organizing strategies, and though not always successful, they propose aesthetic changes that reveal Thomson's awareness of his scientific and spatial innovations. This is especially pertinent to such additions as those in *Summer* and *Winter* that give a broad scope and paradoxical interpretation to spatial change. The speaker returns from the torrid, but not from the frigid zone, where dislocation leads to an invocation of faith. He is no longer the joyful singer of *Spring* showers:

> Not such as wintry Storms on Mortals shed,
> Oppressing Life, but lovely, gentle, kind,
> And full of every Hope and every Joy,
> The wish of Nature.

> (152–55)

He is not even the early singer of *Winter* who looks to pleasurable 'kindred Glooms' (5); rather he is aware that life can be painful and oppressive, and although the 'unbounded SPRING' (1069) will come in heaven to good men, *Winter* on earth is no 'unceasing Joy' (9).

Thus Winter falls,
A heavy Gloom oppressive o'er the World,
Thro Nature shedding Influence malign,
And rouses up the Seeds of dark Disease.

(57–60)

In seeking to understand the changes, one must, of course, note the significance of the continuous or unchanged passages. And the first of these is the invocation to personified *Winter*. Thomson made only one change in 1730: he altered 'Wish'd, wintry, Horrors, hail!' (*A*, 6) to 'Cogenial Horrors, hail!' He substituted a further stress on the fact of kinship or cogeniality for the idea of the desired or wished-for horrors. This cogeniality made the horrors of *Winter* cousin to those undergone by man, for man and nature had one common parent. And continuing the idea of the acknowledged but not particularly desired horrors, Thomson changed, in 1744, 'the red, evening, Sky' (*A*, 14) to 'the grim Evening-sky.' The poet welcomes the 'kindred Glooms' (5) because '*Vapours* and *Clouds*, and Storms' (3) exalt 'the Soul to solemn Thoughts/And heavenly Musing' (4–5). Such thoughts lead, in the invocation, to momentary recall of the poet's childhood, his 'cheerful Morn of Life,' when the vapours and storms formed an environment of pleasure and expectation of *Spring*.

The Poet's recollected childhood—'Trod the pure Virgin-Snows, myself as pure' (11)—identified as it is with the purity of the snow may seem to some readers to foreshadow Wordsworthian nature. But this Thomsonian child is recollected in a season of stress to provide a memory of cheerfulness, an ideal fiction, in a sullen and sad time.

The *Summer* sun was described as spreading a glow over 'Ether' (49), giving a brilliance to the season; the *Autumn* sun began with fits and starts, but the *Winter* sun 'Scarce spreads o'er Ether the dejected Day' (45). The beginning of *Winter* is thus seen in terms of difficulty of achieving the normal order, of space not being extended but narrowed, of darkness falling not in order, but in disorder. The *Summer* sunset, for example, sees the shadows falling in order:

First *This*
She [Evening] sends on Earth; then *That* of deeper Dye
Steals soft behind; and then a *Deeper* still,
In Circle following Circle, gathers round,
To close the Face of Things.

(1650–54)

250

But, in *Winter*, night shows no such orderly darkness. Shadows, clouds and turbulence envelop the world:

> Mean-time, in sable Cincture, Shadows vast,
> Deep-ting'd and damp, and congregated Clouds,
> And all the vapoury Turbulence of Heaven
> Involve the Face of Things.

(54–57)

Winter 'involves'—conceals, obscures, incloses—nature. The description of the flocks as 'Untended spreading' (65) suggests that 'spreading' is here a term of disorder ('Untended'), characteristic of *Winter*'s deceptive control or absence of control. Neither of these views is appropriate to all of *Winter*, but they form the basis for the dominant character of the season, the disorder, especially dislocation as disorder, the spatial chaos and temporal violence.

The revisions from the 1726 *Winter* to the 1746 *The Seasons* contribute to the unity of the poem, add to its aesthetic subtlety, extend its social and scientific scope.[2] I think it should be clear from my analysis of the previous seasons that I wish this generalization to apply to the overall intelligent purposiveness and coherent artistry of the revisions, even though there are instances when the artistry fails of its end. In the 1746 version of *Winter* the most important lexical and syntactical change is the proportion of verbs to adverbs, as words, phrases, and clauses. The number of inflected verbs decreases substantially and that of adverbs increases. To readers unaware of the implications, such increase in adverbial phrases and decline in verbs implies a decrease in action and increase in wordiness. But such readers misunderstand the revisory procedure. Thomson reduces the actions of men and nature and increases the specificity of such action. The later work, therefore, shows a high increase in phrases of place and manner—modification of general adjectives, such as 'deep' or 'far,' that limit their generality. But, in addition to limiting the generality of adjectives or adverbs, these adverbial phrases alter sentences to stress the idea of the world as maze. Implicit in the shift from verb to adverb is the idea of degree, of the making of distinctions to present a world puzzlingly detailed. The phrases also present distinctions in space, using sentences to imitate the intertwined and knotty quality of the physical world itself.

The double view that becomes prominent in *The Seasons* of 1730 was developed and expanded in subsequent revisions by giving prominence to participles and their modifiers, and thus attributing actions to places and things. But the action was, as I have indicated, anxious and uncertain. This feeling of uncertainty and its consequent anxiety was enforced through diminishing the verbs and increasing the adverbial modifiers. At the same time Thomson developed a group of attitudes that consistently urged the need for faith and trust in God.

Thus one can understand the claim that Thomson inflated the poem as he revised it, since the evidence seems to confirm the reduction of verbs and the increase in phrases.[3] But to assume that this is inflation rather than a consequence of a poetic vision is either to assume that such shifts are always poetically bad or that this particular one is. Neither position seems to me tenable because the first implies an absolute standard of judgment and the second implies that the shift is inconsistent with the values of the poem. But the poem relates the fragmentarily known to the imagined; it describes a world in change with its momentary beauty, awe and uncertainty urging upon the reader an act of faith. Phrases and other adverbial modifiers point to moments of time and place undergoing change; the danger, anxiety and beauty of the world become revealed by those parts of speech which function to evoke the very process they describe.

ii. The Social Implications of Thomson's World (1–690)

In *Spring* the jealous lover is plague-ridden, in *Summer* the desert winds and the intemperate storms destroy the living, in *Autumn* the plentiful, long-awaited harvest is flooded—in each season man is not without the suffering inflicted by natural forces just as the birds and beasts are the victims of the brutality of the hunter. The partial order that the enlightened man detects by knowledge and thought is but a part of what is to be apprehended; the other must be grasped by the prophetic imagination or a simple act of faith. It is the enlightened man who has to 'bear up' because the disorder of the world is beyond reason to comprehend. The description of the submergence of the 'disparting Orb' (*Spring*, 310) is the archetype of disorder, one element overwhelming all the others, the earth exploding and sinking. *Winter* deals with the fall of man in the sense that the limited, post-lapsarian coherence and uniformity of earth is replaced by deceiving forms: the fields become dislocated, Alps collapse, wolves become an avalanche. The order of the world is dislocated by tempests, and the literal objects—valleys, hills, rivers, trees, people—that underwent changes consistent with their nature in the other seasons become rigidified, buried, concealed or deformed in *Winter*. *Winter* has as its recurrent image the loss of form, shape, mould, order, just as in *Spring* it is expansive love, converted in *Summer* to the power of heat and light, quenched and tempered by *Autumn*'s transformational mists which are rigidified and thus fixed and falsified in *Winter*. At the beginning of *Spring*, when personified *Winter* temporarily returns, he bids his 'driving Sleets/Deform the Day delightless' (20–21). No reason can explain the secret force causing this false form; it is the result of those secret powers in nature that only God can understand. Such powers create the beauty of the destructive snow and the illusionary beauty of the stiff and congealed river as well as the spatial chaos and the temporal violence.

In the address to Wilmington, Thomson indicates that his style will be the sublime; as his muse sought to rise in the *Summer* blaze so she will try to soar among the wintry clouds.

> Since has she rounded the revolving Year:
> Skim'd the gay Spring; on Eagle-Pinions borne,
> Attempted thro the Summer-Blaze to rise;
> Then swept o'er Autumn with the shadowy Gale;
> And now among the Wintry Clouds again,
> Roll'd in the doubling Storm, she tries to soar;
> To swell her Note with all the rushing Winds;
> To suit her sounding Cadence to the Floods;
> As is her Theme, her Numbers wildly great.
>
> (19–27)

Traditionally, winter is the season of storms and disorder, though for Thomson, it is not without its beauty and joy. The disorder, moreover, is of a special kind; it is a disorder in which normal danger becomes deceptive, in which stable objects lose their shapes, in which the physical and sometimes the moral environment becomes buried or concealed by transformation. Thomson refers to the season with the Horatian term 'inverted Year' (43), and E. E. Morris remarks that it is the time 'when the usual order of things is reversed.'[4] Thus the rays of the sun shoot in 'horizontal' not vertical lines. The hyperbole of nature's influence upon man at this time is a

typical—though inartistic—example of Thomson's use of generalization: 'The Soul of Man dies in him, loathing Life,/And black
with more than melancholy Views' (61–62). As *Winter* develops,
men are joyous as well as oppressed, and the generalization indicates
that there are instances at this time in which some men become more
than merely melancholy, but although such instances could become
frequent, they do not—as is obvious—prevent moments of happiness.
The cattle droop and spread without control—'untended spreading'
(65)—but, nevertheless, they do find 'the wholesome Root' (65),
and the deforming of nature—'the loose disjointed Cliffs./And
fractur'd Mountains wild' (68–69)—is not without its warnings.

The opening storms exemplify Thomson's transformational nature;
in each of the three variations the mountains, fields and waters appear
different at different moments in time.

> THEN comes the Father of the Tempest forth,
> Wrapt in black Glooms. First joyless Rains obscure
> Drive thro the mingling Skies with Vapour foul;
> Dash on the Mountain's Brow, and shake the Woods,
> That grumbling wave below.
>
> (72–76)

> Then issues forth the Storm with sudden Burst,
> And hurls the whole precipitated Air,
> Down, in a Torrent.
>
> (153–55)

> THE keener Tempests come: and fuming dun
> From all the livid East, or piercing North,
> Thick Clouds ascend; in whose capacious Womb
> A vapoury Deluge lies, to Snow congeal'd.
>
> (223–26)

Each storm exemplifies one aspect of *Winter*'s violence, yet the
three storms, one following upon the other, stress the unruly element
of air. Showers and storms exist in each season, but in no season
do they follow so frequently upon each other as in *Winter*. Each
Winter storm undergoes a progress in time, although all are violent
and continue into the night. The difference between the first and
second storm can be noted, for example, by comparing the effects
upon the trees. In the first the rains 'shake the Woods,/That grumbling
wave below' (75–76). In the second, the branches are torn and scattered:

254

Low waves the rooted Forest, vex'd, and sheds
What of its tarnish'd Honours yet remain;
Dash'd down, and scatter'd, by the tearing Wind's
Assiduous Fury, its gigantic Limbs.

(181–84)

Paradoxically, the third storm—the snowstorm—called the 'keener Tempests (223) is beautiful as well as destructive. It creates an inverse image of harmony, 'one wild dazzling Waste, that buries wide/ The Works of Man' (239–40), dislocating the shepherd in his own fields.

One purpose of these temporal distinctions is to reveal the particularly vivid and momentary changes that take place in nature. By describing the effects of the storm upon man and other creatures as well as upon nature, Thomson achieves a simultaneity of occurrences. This awareness of associative time permits him to see positive as well as negative effects in a broad range of space. It also explains, from a temporal point of view, one reason for the mixture of personification with natural description. By simultaneously attributing human as well as non-human qualities to nature, he provides a religious justification for all that takes place in the world: just as God must be accepted despite His causing man hardships, so, too, nature must be accepted as an instrument of God. When Thomson writes 'THEN comes the Father of the Tempest forth' (72), he gives a parental interpretation to the violence of the storm, God the 'Father' being described in lordly terms. The storm which wildly 'issues forth' is the unconstrained descendant, and the violence needs no apology because it has been made part of the accepted view of God's powers.

To compare the torrential flow in *Winter* (94–105) with the *Summer* waterfall, is to reveal the differences in effect and technique. The *Summer* waterfall wakes every sense (587–88): the passage describes the blended motion, sight, sound, color, feel of the waterfall as it moves from the 'shelving Brink' to the 'Mazes of the quiet Vale.' But the *Winter* torrent is described as the breaking of restraint. When the torrent floats over the sanded valley, it 'spreads,' it becomes 'Calm, sluggish, silent' (101)—and it regains its force and violence and life only as it bursts through the constraint imposed by the hills.

The *Summer* torrent is seen in terms of its changing colors, its shifting movements, its impetuosity and subsidence. The *Winter* river overruns its banks, takes on new shapes resulting from bursting its boundaries:

it bursts a Way,
Where Rocks and Woods o'erhang the turbid Stream;
There gathering triple Force, rapid, and deep,
It boils, and wheels, and foams, and thunders thro.

(102-5)

The verbs in mixed images emphasize the sheer wild disorder of the action. The spatial uncontrol, the 'mix'd Ruin,' the power and violence of nature are, despite the disastrous consequences, seen as the work of God.

How mighty, how majestic, are thy Works!
With what a pleasing Dread they swell the Soul!
That sees astonish'd! and astonish'd sings!

(108-10)

In this rhetorical invocation to nature, the speaker admires the 'pleasing Dread' that swells the soul, but it is 'pleasing' only in so far as man remains safe. When the disastered swain is lost in his own fields, not pleasing dread, but 'Horror fills his Heart' (289). The rhetoric describing the overflowing river and that describing the invocation to nature differ in sentence structure and vocabulary. The first evokes a nature uncontrolled by normal order with adjectives—'Resistless, roaring, dreadful' and 'Calm, sluggish, silent'—suggesting a hyperactive responsiveness or extraordinary sluggishness. The second is governed by a repetitive structure that reinforces the surprise and astonishment of unexplainable power by means of fragmentary exclamations and unanswered questions.

But perhaps one should point here to the paradoxical relationship of 'Wanderer,' 'Tenant,' and 'Stranger.' *Winter* began with the childhood pleasures of wandering in nature's 'rough Domain' and, indeed, the wanderers of heaven are also playful and 'careless.' But the 'Tenants' who belong in the sky are driven from it, and the stranger, together with the tenant, is mistreated by the storm. 'Oft let me wander o'er the dewy Fields' speaks the poet in *Spring* (103), and in *Autumn* he writes, 'THUS solitary, and in pensive Guise/Oft let me wander o'er the russet Mead' (970-71). The wanderer as the observer and spectator is the typical unengaged speaker. The fancy that 'wanders,' for example, is incapable of being dispossessed because it does not possess the place over which it wanders. In this sense, the idea of wandering is related to the idea of free and infinite space; the 'Tenant' or 'Stranger' belongs or is alien, though in neither

256

situation has he the freedom possessed by the wanderer. If the 'wanderer' is understood as one not guided by a 'fixed' course, as one who roams or rambles, as one who strolls, saunters or meanders, then the idea of the wanderer becomes characteristic of the poem as a whole. A 'wanderer,' such as the swain, can find himself endlessly 'wandering' in the storm deceived by a false sense of infinity. The absence of 'fixedness' is exemplified in the unfixed course of the wanderer, in the associations or roamings of the mind. The Augustan wanderer is sometimes seen as the pilgrim, the figure who begins in disobedience, undergoes punishment, then by suffering and expiation is redeemed.[5] But Thomson's wanderer is neither a disobedient Christian nor a Wordsworthian solitary in search of himself. He moves in a social orbit, pursuing knowledge and defining himself by the knowledge he gathers of nature and man.

The wandering speaker is not the only wanderer in *The Seasons*. The wandering waters of *Summer* and *Autumn*, the migrating swallows and storks also take voyages. Such become part of the cyclical pattern of nature; their journeys are part of their order, part of the cycle of nature. For man, this cycle is the result of inner forces of curiosity and discovery; for streams and birds it becomes part of nature's order. But as streams overflow and birds are destroyed, so man finds that wandering can become a form of disorder. The 'disastered swain' of *Winter* 'wanders on/From Hill to Dale, still more and more astray' (283–84).

Wandering can become a response to dislocation, and instead of gaining knowledge, the wanderer can himself be lost and destroyed. The idea of wandering, as the poem develops it, becomes part of the general conception of control and loss of control, of order and disorder, of harmony and disharmony. The wanderer, despite his quest for knowing, realizes that the ultimate power of God is unknowable. The shifting space which creates dislocation has, despite its dreadfulness, a beauty and awe that create admiration, but not understanding.

In this view Thomson takes conventional themes and figures and places them within a typical Augustan context. The wanderer-narrator of *The Seasons*, like Robinson Crusoe and Joseph Andrews, leaves home only to return to it again with knowledge and wisdom of the external world. Whereas in *Gulliver's Travels* the wanderer discovers the possibilities of life that have ceased to be choices in England and Joseph Andrews discovers the choices that are still available and the idyllic possibilities that still exist, Thomson's speaker, moving through the torrid and frigid zones, finds that the temperate zone contains the choices under which man and animal operate even in the extreme climates. By implication, therefore, the temperate zone provides the natural arena of benevolence and responsible obligation for swains, shepherds, and aristocrats. Yet the temperate and the extreme zones indicate the need for faith, since the complicated and often secret power of life is beyond man's comprehension.

The spatial wandering characteristic of *The Seasons* must be seen as a unifying aspect by its double view of exploration and dislocation; but a parallel procedure is to be found in the idea of rest or absence of wandering. In *Spring*, in *Summer* and in *Autumn* as the speaker reclines after contention or wandering, he finds a soothing harmony. But it is also in *Spring* that the lover

> sinks awhile to Rest,
> Still interrupted by distracted Dreams,
> That o'er the sick Imagination rise
> And in black Colours paint the mimick Scene.
>
> (1053–56)

The absence of motion can give peace, but also sick dreams; the deep retirement of *Winter* gives peace, too, but there is a peace in stiffness and silence that is death, unwished and unprepared for.

Thomson touches the storms with personification so that, for example, the literal, natural sounds are also human cries:

> Along the Woods, along the moorish Fens,
> Sighs the sad *Genius* of the coming Storm;
> And up among the loose disjointed Cliffs,
> And fractur'd Mountains wild, the brawling Brook
> And Cave, presageful, send a hollow Moan,
> Resounding long in listening Fancy's Ear.
>
> (66–71)

The mingling of natural description with personification closely identified with the storm sounds treats nature as subject to powers beyond itself but addressing warnings to man. In the second storm, while cormorants scream and herons shriek, an allegorical voice speaks:

> from the Shore,
> Eat into Caverns by the restless Wave,

> And Forest-rustling Mountain, comes a Voice,
> That solemn-sounding bids the World prepare.
>
> (149–52)

And as the tempest roars, strange sounds are heard:

> Then too, they say, thro all the burthen'd Air,
> Long Groans are heard, shrill Sounds, and distant Sighs,
> That, utter'd by the Demon of the Night,
> Warn the devoted Wretch of Woe and Death.
>
> (191–94)

These examples move between metaphorical or allegorical personification and direct statement in which man and nature both are
subject to God's power. Although Thomson tries to naturalize
allegory by interrelating it with actual nature, he does accept the
direct intimation and intervention of God. For God calms nature
when it reels:

> All Nature reels. Till Nature's KING, who oft
> Amid tempestuous Darkness dwells alone,
> And on the Wings of the careening Wind
> Walks dreadfully serene, commands a Calm;
> Then straight Air Sea and Earth are hush'd at once.
>
> (197–201)

There are, also, positive and comforting supernatural voices heard
by the poet in the deep shades—the seraphic, mantic voices that urge
him to attain the holy, heavenly calm (*Summer*, 540–63). It is to
these shades that the poet begs to be taken in *Autumn* (1033–36).
This genuine belief is, throughout the poem, contrasted with comic
superstitions. The lower classes accept the superstitions about fairy
people, about goblins, about ghosts (*Summer*, 1671–81). In *Winter*,
the villagers frighten themselves with ghost stories:

> MEAN-TIME the Village rouzes up the Fire;
> While well attested, and as well believ'd,
> Heard solemn, goes the Goblin-Story round;
> Till superstitious Horror creeps o'er all.
>
> (617–20)

There appears in the ironic 'well attested' and 'as well believ'd' a
certain condescension toward the villagers. There is a playfulness in
treating the goblin tales with an awareness that they are harmless

pastimes. The single attempt to use these superstitions to heighten disorder or to create terror leads to the grotesque scene in which the wolves dig up the graves, 'o'er which,/Mix'd with foul Shades, and frighted Ghosts, they howl' (412–13).

Just as Thomson develops techniques to suggest that illusionary space is beautiful but dangerous, so he treats superstitious beliefs as games that can become dangerous. In the dark night of *Autumn* the luckless man 'bewilder'd, wanders thro the Dark,/Full of pale Fancies, and Chimeras huge" (1146–47). Even known scientific phenomena, like the comet in *Summer* or the meteors in *Autumn*, become imbued for the 'fond sequacious Herd, to mystic Faith/ And blind Amazement prone' (1713–14) with supernatural powers. Thomson attributes superstition to the 'Croud,' the 'Herd,' the lower classes, and compares these with the enlightened who can distinguish between mystic voices and superstitious sounds. In this respect, the rural folk become a social stereotype of ignorant country bumpkins.

The second storm belongs with those passages of destruction discussed earlier in *Summer*. The bending trees, described as the mountain's 'sturdy Sons' (176), become one with the bent and falling wayfaring stranger, the personification functioning to equate them:

> Lone on the midnight Steep, and all aghast,
> The dark way-faring Stranger breathless toils,
> And, often falling, climbs against the Blast.
>
> (178–80)

With the 'Limbs' (184) of the trees dashed and scattered, the personification becomes traditional and consistent—'struggling' (185), 'raving' (186), 'shaking' (188), 'howling' (190). In the first storm, the 'Cottage-Hind' disregarded the storm, but here the cottage is shaken and 'Sleep frighted flies' (189). The second storm is more violent, wilder and more chaotic than the first and its disorder is stressed by the fact that its sounds warn 'the devoted Wretch' (194) of woe and death.

The storm in its wreckage provides an occasion for contemplation, illustrating the futility of man's delusions and vanities without, however, convincing all men of the need for faith rather than vanity:

> and yet deluded Man,
> A Scene of crude disjointed Visions past,
> And broken Slumbers, rises still resolv'd,
> With new-flush'd Hopes, to run the giddy Round.
>
> (213–16)

In *Autumn* the poet commented upon the thoughtlessness of the country people in their rejoicing over the harvest that merely meant another beginning (1232–34), but in *Winter* it is the deluding, cheating vanities to which he points.

The third storm moves from its origin in the clouds to the burial of the 'Works of Man' (240). Like the burial imagery in *Summer*, it, too, moves from the womb to the tomb. The depth of the snow buries the customary shapes and locations in nature, and the result is 'one wild dazzling Waste' (239), a nature beautiful, white, and deadly. The storm description stresses the purity, the whiteness of the flakes that paradoxically 'dim' the day. But the whiteness and dazzling beauty 'buries wide/The Works of Man' (239–40).

Throughout *The Seasons* there is an aesthetic quality, beautiful or sublime, attributed to natural forms: the blending of the flowers, wind, sun and water in *Spring*, or the sensual delightful or awesome power of light and heat in *Summer*. *Autumn* presents forms as they are in the process of change, but in so far as these changes are precise and varied, they convey the transformational beauty of nature. The three seasons express changes in the forms of beauty that are changes in degree—the forms retain their identity. But the sublimity (in contrast to the occasional beauty) of *Winter* buries or conceals known forms and places. In *Winter*, actual, literal space is converted into apparent, deceptive beauty: mountains rise, but they are snow mountains, false though dazzling. Valleys disappear, because they are temporarily filled, not because they are objects of the fancy. There can be beautiful objects of the fancy, frozen and harmless, but there are also the men who become statues, and who, although they *appear* as living forms, have lost their true shapes and life. In the satiric poem, this procedure is used to enact grace while paradoxically indicating the false use of grace—as in the rites of Belinda. Or it can be used by Swift to parody false social benevolence in *A Modest Proposal*. But in *Winter* the Augustan paradoxical procedure is actualized: literal space is *actually* transformed. The spatial norm of the other seasons is deformed to establish the norm of *Winter*, though underlying both there is the consistency of God's harmony and wisdom. In the description of the wilds of *Winter* the idealized formal garden lies submerged, and the hunted hare seeks the forbidden garden because he is urged on by fearless want. The garden of the colorful *Spring* country estate or of wild nature in the torrid zone— 'Another *Flora* these, of bolder Hues,/And richer Sweets, beyond our Garden's Pride' (*Summer*, 694-95)—is a harmony image, whether arranged by man or God. But the garden view disappears from *Winter*, where nature prohibits the floral harmony and provides instead the inharmonious wilds or the substitution of beautiful and awesome frozen shapes for living forms.

In the preceding seasons Thomson described the collapse of form as chaos or sickness or plague, forms of warring nature that resulted in extreme disorder. But the snows that mislead the shepherd are beautiful, although they make it impossible for him to locate his home. The literal changes in space that distort normal extension create false limits or prevent recognition of familiar limits. Thomson can thus be seen extending the techniques developed throughout the poem: dislocation leads to false forms, but it is a dislocation of the actual. The solid, frozen shapes are appropriate to *Winter*, which can create new delicately-shaped forms, but in so far as the frost deprives objects of their motion by burying or by freezing them, it can only be considered as deforming, removing form from or distorting them. Even the seeds that are preserved by burial are deformed because they are prevented from attaining their proper forms.

This deforming in the temperate zone has its necessary counterpart—the invigoration of man and nature, the renewal of form. And what is dislocation in the temperate zone, is home in the frigid. The elks who sleep 'in the white Abyss' are at ease with the icy shapeless masses, as are also the tribes of the frigid zone, who can approximate an ideal order. Yet the keynote of *Winter*, despite occasional joys, is pain and endurance. What begins as a recollection of innocence becomes an observation of suffering and storms. The snows may still be 'dazzling,' but they are also deadly.

The ox and the fowls make 'demands' (241) of and 'claims' (244) upon man since the storm conceals their food supply. But only the red-breast seeks to become part of the human household. The section on the red-breast was added to the second edition of the poem in June, 1726, removed from the 1730 quarto and reinserted in the 1730 octavo and all editions thereafter. The bird is fearful and hesitant at first (250), beginning with a sense of dislocation—'wonders where he is'—then comes to feel a welcome guest in the human family:

> then, hopping o'er the Floor,
> Eyes all the smiling Family askance,
> And pecks, and starts, and wonders where he is:

> Till more familiar grown, the Table-Crumbs
> Attracts his slender Feet.

(252–56)

Trusted man becomes a substitute for the untrustworthy or unpleasant environment. The bird is described with a daintiness of movement, with a sense of joy in the slightness of the creature that contrasts with the heaviness and density of the storm. Its sense of curiosity and uneasiness in this strange location becomes a basis for contrast with the other dislocated and disordered animals. The joyful obligation of the family to welcome the slight creature ought also to be extended to man's 'helpless Charge' (265). Here, then, dislocation does not lead to disharmony, to destruction, and man's hospitality and benevolence exemplify God's familial care.

But the other creatures, the hare and the cattle, remain isolated from, though completely dependent upon, man's kindness and sympathy. If one compares the *Spring* passage in which the herds and flocks eye the rain with the *Winter* reaction of the cattle to the snow, the conception of Thomson becomes clear.

> Herds and Flocks
> Drop the dry Sprig, and mute-imploring eye
> The falling Verdure.

(*Spring*, 162–64)

> The bleating Kind
> Eye the bleak Heaven, and next the glistening Earth,
> With Looks of dumb Despair; then, sad-dispers'd,
> Dig for the wither'd Herb thro Heaps of Snow.

(*Winter*, 261–64)

In *Spring* the shower is, indeed, an answer to the 'imploring' of the animals; in *Winter* heaven is eyed but it is 'bleak,' and the snow which glistens is no answer to the looks of dumb despair. The cattle are 'sad-dispers'd,' disordered from the unity they possess in *Spring*; they dig without assurance in 'Heaps of Snow' that have buried the places they once knew.

Winter's snow creates new shapes in space, and by dislocating actual nature disorders the world, brings the cycle of the seasons to its end. If we consider that *Spring* establishes a harmony by concording diverse elements, using devices like synaethesia, cataloging, blending, progression to suggest such concert, then *Winter* provides not accord but discord, using the imagery of shapelessness and deception to suggest covering, entombing and burying. Both seasons retain features opposite to these dominant ones, and there is, in *Winter*, hope of renewal of the cycle, of rebirth.

The poet's public injunction to be kind to the 'helpless Charge' (265) concludes with the possibility of their submergence by the snow. 'Watch them strict' (268) warns the speaker, because valleys can become mountains:

> The Valley to a shining Mountain swells,
> Tipt with a Wreath, high-curling in the Sky.
>
> (274–75)

The 'shining' appearance of the false mountain must be distinguished from the *Summer* description:

> And glittering Towns, and gilded Streams, till all
> The stretching Landskip into Smoke decays!
>
> (1440–41)

The landscape of *Summer* (and of *Spring*, too,) is actually gilded by the rays of the sun; and its imagined extension is not a threat. But although the valley swells into a mountain, the mountain will treacherously disappear. There is a shining beauty in this transformation, but it can wreak destruction. The injunction to the shepherd to guard his sheep contains, therefore, an irony directed against the power of God in the universe. For the shepherd whose carelessness can lead to the burial of his flocks is himself buried. But who guards and guides the shepherd? Was there not in *Autumn* a shepherd who, 'a black Abyss of Drink' (566), retired from his 'bury'd' flock?

In an important essay in 1916, Cecil Moore called Thomson 'the first important humanitarian poet in English.'[6] He argued that Thomson was 'continually pleading, not merely for the spirit of benevolence, but for every special humane movement of his day.' Most of such comment in *The Seasons* is in passages supplementary 'to the original content of the poem, the chief additions being made to *Winter*: the first edition, the second, and the final contain, respectively, 405, 781 and 1,069 lines, and the increase is due principally to the insertion of humanitarian passages'. Although I do not find the increase to be primarily due to the insertion of humanitarian passages, such passages do figure importantly in the poem. Thomson does support humanitarian movements, but not for the reasons Moore gives. The difficulty lies, I believe, in the assumption that Thomson borrowed Shaftesbury's ideas, a statement that disregards Thomson's conception in the poem as a whole. Moore writes:

> In strict accord with Shaftesbury's theory of natural virtue, Thomson urges as the sole persuasive of all humanitarian conduct the 'moral beauty' of goodness. He makes even slighter concession to the orthodox notion of future reward and punishment than Shaftesbury does; the conclusion of *Winter*, altered as it now stands, allows a life of bliss to compensate the evils endured by the virtuous of this world, but Thomson makes no attempt to enforce morality by reference to a future life.[7]

But Thomson does not urge 'moral beauty' as the sole persuasive of all humanitarian conduct; in fact, it plays no part in his 'urging.' In *Autumn*, when Thomson urges the husbandman to be charitable to the gleaner, he writes:

> Think, oh grateful think!
> How good the GOD OF HARVEST is to you;
> Who pours Abundance o'er your flowing Fields;
> While these unhappy Partners of your Kind
> Wide-hover round you, like the Fowls of Heaven,
> And as their humble Dole. The various Turns
> Of Fortune ponder; that your Sons may want
> What now, with hard Reluctance, faint, ye give.
>
> (169–76)

The reason for charity is not 'moral beauty,' but the recognition of man's dependence upon fortune, the inevitable uncertainty of man's temporal condition. And Thomson, in describing the plague in *Summer*, emphasizes that the 'feeling Heart' (1082) can under such conditions forget all tender ties:

> Dependents, Friends, Relations, Love himself,
> Savag'd by Woe, forget the tender Tie,
> The sweet Engagement of the feeling Heart.
>
> (1080–82)

In urging the shepherd in *Winter* to be kind to his charges, the poet indicates that this behavior is consistent with his own self-interest in keeping the sheep alive:

> Now, Shepherds, to your helpless Charge be kind,
> Baffle the raging Year, and fill their Pens

265

With Food at Will; lodge them below the Storm,
And watch them strict: for from the bellowing East,
In this dire Season, oft the Whirlwind's Wing
Sweeps up the Burthen of the whole country Plains
In one wide Waft, and o'er the hapless Flocks,
Hid in the Hollow of two neighbouring Hills,
The billowy Tempest whelms; till, upward urg'd,
The Valley to a shining Mountain swells,
Tipt with a Wreath, high-curling in the Sky.

(265–75)

Moore assumed that Thomson believed in natural virtue[8] and that his
benevolence could be explained by the deistical 'replacing of the old
prudential argument by a more disinterested motive that lent itself
to the sentimental belief in natural goodness.'[9] He quotes a pertinent
passage from *Summer*:

After upbraiding the cruelty of those who neglect charitable offices,
he [Thomson] adds:

But to the generous still-improving mind,
That gives the hopeless heart to sing for joy,
Diffusing kind beneficence around,
Boastless, as now descends the silent dew—
To him the long review of ordered life
Is inward rapture only to be felt.[10]

(1641–46)

If a 'motive' lends itself to interpretation, it does not itself offer such
an interpretation. 'Inward rapture' is not a reference to natural goodness, but to an inner peace that the generous man achieves; it
is neither the possession of the 'impassion'd Soul' (1633) nor of the
selfishly 'cruel Wretch' (1636). If the entire passage is quoted it
becomes apparent that 'inward rapture' is not a natural phenomenon
but a way of life preferred because it is harmoniously ordered and
provides satisfaction in this life and the next:

FOR ever running an enchanted Round,
Passes the Day, deceitful, vain, and void;
As fleets the Vision o'er the formful Brain,
This moment hurrying wild th' impassion'd Soul,
The next in nothing lost. 'Tis so to him,
The Dreamer of this Earth, an idle Blank:

A Sight of Horror to the cruel Wretch,
Who all day long in sordid Pleasure roll'd,
Himself an useless Load, has squander'd vile,
Upon his scoundrel Train, what might have chear'd
A drooping Family of modest Worth.

(1630–40)

Thomson's moral attitudes are derived from *Job* rather than Shaftesbury, and they present no simple equation of rewards and punishments. At the conclusion of *Spring*, the virtuous and harmonious lovers fly 'To scenes where Love and Bliss immortal reign' (1176), but the tortur'd youth 'leads a Life/Of fever'd Rapture, or of cruel Care' (1109–10). In *Summer*, however, the men who flutter from 'Vanity to Vice' (349) do not reach blessed immortality:

Till, blown away by Death, Oblivion comes
Behind, and strikes them from the Book of Life.

(350–51)

In *Summer* Celadon, like Job's comforters, speaks of a simple world of rewards and punishments:

'that very Voice,
Which thunders Terror thro the guilty Heart,
With Tongues of Seraphs whispers Peace to thine.'

(1210–12)

But he is immediately proved wrong, and the poet exclaims, 'Mysterious Heaven!' (1215). The rewards of the good are in the future, and the very conclusion to *Winter* that, according to Moore, makes 'no attempt to enforce morality by reference to a future life' includes a reference to the second coming:

And see!
'Tis come, the glorious Morn! the second Birth
Of Heaven, and Earth!

(1041–43)

When Moore quotes the passage concluding, 'Sacred, substantial, never-fading Bliss' (*Winter*, 217–22), he writes that Thomson's 'belief in the sufficiency of virtue is contained in this prayer' (21), though Thomson's next line is 'The keener Tempests come,' an irony necessary to understand Thomson's doubts about the sufficiency of virtue.

In finding 'benevolence' and 'deistic piety' as part of the rhetorical ends of *The Seasons*, R. S. Crane, following upon Cecil Moore's essay, drew the poem within the orbit of the eighteenth-century man of feeling, despite Thomson's indebtedness to Job, Virgil and Milton. The poem surely urges benevolence, charity, humanitarianism upon its readers, but the reasons for Thomson's views are not adequately explained by reference to deism. In his essay, 'Suggestions toward a Genealogy of the "Man of Feeling,"' published in 1934,[11] R. S. Crane proposed four 'principal aspects of the ethical and psychological teachings of late seventeenth- and early eighteenth-century divines': 1. *Virtue as universal benevolence*;[12] 2. *Benevolence as feeling*;[13] 3. *Benevolent feelings as 'natural' to man*;[14] and 4. The *'Self-approving Joy.'*[15] These teachings of Latitudinarian divines supported Moore's position from new evidence.

The evidence is persuasive that Thomson knew of such currents and that he supported the need for kindness to man and animals. But these opinions are consistent with his orthodox view that earthly searchings for happiness are 'unsolid Hopes' (*Winter*, 1034). At the close of *Winter* he writes in a traditional *'ubi sunt'* vein:

> Ah! whither now are fled,
> Those Dreams of Greatness? those unsolid Hopes
> Of Happiness? those Longings after Fame?
> Those restless Cares? those busy bustling Days?
> Those gay-spent, festive Nights? those veering Thoughts,
> Lost between Good and Ill, that shar'd thy Life?
> All now are vanish'd! VIRTUE sole survives,
> Immortal, never-failing Friend of Man,
> His Guide to Happiness on high.
>
> (1033–41)

The 'VIRTUE' that is an immortal friend of man and his guide to heavenly happiness is belief in and love of God. Shaftesbury, to whom Thomson refers as a 'Friend of Man' (*Summer*, 1551) is no immortal guide but a brother who seeks to raise the aims and morals of the family of man.

Benevolence, charity, and kindness are virtues, and the reasons for them can be found in the familial life of man and nature, but not all men are benevolent and the early death of good men implies that in man's imperfect knowledge God can act in ways that appear the opposite of benevolent. 'Benevolence' (with one of its uses, 'benevolent') appears four times in the poem, three of which are in *Spring*. The induction refers to the Countess of Hertford as 'blooming and benevolent' (10) as the season, and the other uses (*Spring*, 257, 258, *Winter*, 355) do not identify 'benevolent' with 'universal benevolence'; the formal religious terms of the Latitudinarians, 'benevolence' and 'charity', occur rarely in *The Seasons*; 'charity' occurs in *Summer*, 1606, and *Winter*, 354, and 'charitable' in *Autumn*, 168. 'Kind' as a synonym for 'helpful' is more common with thirty instances, although 'helpful' is not in the poem but 'helpless' is.

In Thomson's practice of varied contexts there are numerous uses of 'virtue', and 'benevolence' is but one. Thomson refers to sexual virtue in 'Ye Prudes in Virtue' (*Summer*, 1298), to 'public Virtue' (*Autumn*, 18), and to 'heroic Virtue' (*Autumn*, 1338). In *Summer* when he addresses God to send forth 'the saving Virtues' around Britain, he lists these as peace, social love, charity, truth, dignity of mind, courage, temperance, chastity, industry and public zeal. Since they stem from an appeal to God, they presuppose a belief in His power as starting-point.

Thomson shares the view of the Latitudinarians that the passions 'are neither good nor evil in themselves; they may, however, be ordered to virtue, and when so ordered they have a positive value,'[16] but he does not believe that it is 'they and not our weak reason [that] are the forces which make it possible for us to act at all.'[17] Thomson argues that 'thought' is not weak, but a necessary control upon passion, for thought and feeling must harmonize.[18]

Thomson, in these doctrines, is following his customary practice of absorbing current ideas into his own version of experience— natural, human and supernatural. *Winter*, by insisting on the need to endure to possess a bear-like stoical resistance as well as a reindeer-like sympathy, shows Thomson absorbing the two doctrines that R. S. Crane finds at odds in this period.

Although Thomson urges goodness upon men, he does not advocate a doctrine of natural goodness which R. S. Crane summarizes as

the idea that man is essentially a gentle and sympathetic creature, naturally inclined to society not merely by his intellect, which tells him that kindness to others is the best means to the end of his own private happiness, but still more by 'those passions and inclinations that are common to him with other Creatures,' and which, like everything in his nature have 'a vehement tendency to acts of love and good-will.'[19]

This again, is a position which Thomson revises, for although he presents a Golden Age before the fall when men and animals and nature were reflective of God's love and goodness, men were after this ideal period ended,

> by Nature cast,
> Naked, and helpless, out amid the Woods,
> And Wilds, to rude inclement Elements,
>
> (*Autumn*, 47–49)

or cast out amidst a 'wondrous Waste of Wealth' (*Summer*, 860) without 'the softening Arts of Peace,/Whate'er the humanizing Muses teach' (875–76). Even if there are peaceful and happy savages, they can never attain the humanizing arts and feelings without civilization. In these circumstances, reason, truth, science, belief are the basis for man becoming humanized. Even the animals are not inherently kind; if there is a kind and wise elephant, there are also the vicious tiger and the leopard. In the same season, the poet addresses 'Philosophy' and asks, 'Without thee what were unenlighten'd Man?/ A Savage roaming through the Woods and Wilds,/In quest of Prey' (1758–60).

The divines frequently exhorted 'hearers and readers to consider how enjoyable the benevolent emotions may be to the individual who allows himself to feel them.'[20] But in *The Seasons* there is the 'smiling God' who, if he smiles on his soft scenes in *Spring*, in *Winter* he

> Looks down with Pity on the feeble Toil
> Of Mortals lost to Hope, and lights them safe,
> Thro all this dreary Labyrinth of Fate.
>
> (1021–23)

The 'enlightened Few' may in 'their Powers exult' (1717), but Celadon's benevolent reassurance of Amelia brings him no joy; the housewife's 'Force divine' does not preserve her, and sympathy for Hammond leads to thoughts of human vanity, not 'self-approving Joy.'

Man is surrounded by and subjected to forces beyond his knowledge and understanding, and although benevolence and kindness are desirable, they are not always extended to him, either by other men or by God. And there are many men who kill the harmless creatures, placing themselves in positions which disregard benevolence and its associated virtues.

The death of the shepherd presents a good man dislocated and destroyed in a world that does not seem benevolent. The 1744 additions to the shepherd passage include the idea of 'loose-revolving Fields' (278), and *'formless Wild'* [my italics] (283). The stable, friendly and recognizable fields of the swain become altered and dislocated in the storm:

> In his own loose-revolving Fields, the Swain
> Disaster'd stands; sees other Hills ascend,
> Of unknown joyless Brow; and other Scenes,
> Of horrid Prospect, shag the trackless Plain:
> Nor finds the River, nor the Forest, hid
> Beneath the formless Wild.
>
> (278–83)

The swain 'wanders' (283) astray, not because wandering is a misfortune, but because his wandering is made deceptive. It is no longer a willing act, but the consequence of estrangement. As nature becomes shapeless and unrecognizable, the swain sinks exhausted 'Beneath the Shelter of the shapeless Drift' (306). But such 'Shelter' is disastrous. In *Spring*, Thomson had written of 'The Negligence of Nature, wide and wild' (505), that was a sight of beauty. Its wildness became part of an encompassing harmony, but the formless wild becomes part of nature's apparent chaos. For shapelessness and the stiff and lifeless shape are consequences of disharmony. In Thomson's theory of the imagination, statuesque stiffness need not imply life; here it can be seen clearly related to the consequence of shapelessness or false shape: stiffness appears lifelike but is without life or motion.

This scene is followed by a diatribe against moral wantonness or aimlessness. But in contrast to the episode of man dislocated in the shifting scenes of nature, the admonition to think of 'all the sad Variety of Pain' (328) remains a series of rhetorical flourishes. It is possible to infer what Thomson sought to do: in the face of the consequences of nature's wantonness in *Winter*, its 'formless Wild' in which man is trapped, man, who is not naturally inclined to benevolence but to 'heedless rambling Impulse,' ought to exercise benevolence for his own interest, ought to give comfort to others, considering the suffering and hardships of existence.

> Thought fond Man
> Of These, and all the thousand nameless Ills,
> That one incessant Struggle render Life,
> One Scene of Toil, of Suffering, and of Fate,
> Vice in his high Career would stand appall'd,

And heedless rambling Impulse learn to think;
The conscious Heart of Charity would warm,
And her wide Wish Benevolence dilate;
The social Tear would rise, the social Sigh;
And into clear Perfection, gradual Bliss,
Refining still, the social Passions work.

(348–58)

This is one of several passages in which Thomson deals with the origin and development of the 'social Passions' (358). The argument here is that the man given to vice would be appalled by the misery and suffering of human existence if he considered it, though such proud and irresponsible men do not think:

AH little think the gay licentious Proud,
Whom Pleasure, Power, and Affluence surround;
They, who their thoughtless Hours in giddy Mirth,
And wanton, often cruel, Riot waste.

(322–25)

Such men do not give their attention to human suffering because, if they did, they would begin to cultivate the social passions of charity and benevolence. Thomson's interpretation is that such feelings are not innate; they must be developed; for this reason, he writes of the 'conscious' Heart of Charity. Their best soil is the temperate zone; in his description of the torrid zone, he points out that neither government, religion nor the social passions dwell there:

Love dwells not there,
The soft Regards, the Tenderness of Life,
The Heart-shed Tear, the ineffable Delight
Of sweet Humanity: These court the Beam
Of milder Climes; in selfish fierce Desire,
And the wild Fury of voluptuous Sense,
There lost.

(890–96)

Although this implies a climatic theory of the passions, with the wilder passions developed in extreme heat (though not extreme cold), the social passions are identified, in *Autumn*, with the founding of society. The benevolent feelings are not only not universal, they must be developed under special conditions.

HENCE every Form of cultivated Life
In Order set, protected, and inspir'd,
Into Perfection wrought. Uniting all,
Society grew numerous, high, polite,
And happy.

(Autumn, 109–13)

The social passions and society are identified with conditions of struggle, industry and suffering so that philosophic melancholy can call them forth. In other words, the social passions arise from an awareness of man's pain and suffering in two contexts: the family and state, but these do not cause social passions in all men, only in the enlightened few. The social passions in the ideal family arise from love as harmony, that rare phenomenon 'Sympathy of Soul.'

'Tis not the coarser Tie of human Laws,
Unnatural oft, and foreign to the Mind,
That binds their Peace, but Harmony itself,
Attuning all their Passions into Love;
Where Friendship full-exerts her softest Power,
Perfect Esteem enliven'd by Desire
Ineffable, and Sympathy of Soul;
Thought meeting Thought, and Will preventing Will,
With boundless Confidence: for nought but Love
Can answer Love, and render Bliss secure.

(Spring, 1116–25)

Such love is rare and indeed such passions are rare, and they explain why social sympathy is not a common phenomenon. But because Thomson sees the state as a family the exercise of social sympathy, of benevolence and pity, is desirable for the harmony of the classes within the state. The need to pity 'suffering Worth' results from the painful and anxious lives people lead. Sympathy for the less fortunate is desirable, for man cannot tell when he himself may become one of the less fortunate.

This analysis of the social passions leads inevitably into Thomson's sentimentalism, a feature of his poem that frequently annoys modern readers as it pleased many earlier ones. Douglas Grant identifies this sentimentalism with Thomson's effort to 'rouse "the tender emotions," '[21] and he gives as examples Thomson's passages about marriage, hunting, jails, etc. But Thomson's sentimentalism needs, I believe, to be distinguished from his concern for the social or tender passions, from his 'sentiment.'

When Thomson argues for marriage based on love rather than purchase, his argument is that mercenary matches do not create harmonious families, that instead of possessing the advantages of a family, they create, wherever they occur, selfish and exploitative responses. Tyrants take possession of a 'lifeless, violated form':

> Let him, ungenerous, who, alone intent
> To bliss himself, from sordid Parents buys
> The loathing Virgin, in eternal Care,
> Well-merited, consume his Nights and Days:
> Let barbarous Nations, whose inhuman Love
> Is wild Desire, fierce as the Suns they feel;
> Let Eastern Tyrants from the Light of Heaven
> Seclude their Bosom-slaves, meanly possess'd
> Of a meer, lifeless, violated Form:
> While Those whom Love cements in holy Faith,
> And equal Transport, free as Nature live,
> Disdaining Fear.
>
> *(Spring*, 1126–37)

Thomson's defense of reciprocal love is not based on any innate tendencies. Human love involves consideration for others; it involves living with a 'holy Faith,' feeling and reflecting God's blessing. Clearly such a match, involving friendship, esteem, sympathy, wealth, is not easy to achieve, but it is not sentimental; it is, rather, the goal or ideal of human love.

Thomson's sentimentalism occurs when he describes the family in extreme situations, focusing upon children or animals, and deliberately making demands upon our sympathy. Thus in the *Winter* scene of sad presage the wife and children prepare for the husband and father who will never return. Thomson adds:

> In vain for him th' officious Wife prepares
> The Fire fair-blazing, and the Vestment warm;
> In vain his little Children, peeping out
> Into the mingling Storm, demand their Sire,
> With Tears of artless Innocence. Alas!
> Nor Wife, nor Children, more shall he behold,
> Nor Friends, nor sacred Home.
>
> (311–17)

Thomson turns to the wife and especially the little children to exact our sympathy. In a world of anxiety and unexpected situations in which the father can suddenly disappear for ever, the need to be kind to helpless beings becomes an imperative of familial behavior:

> Ye Masters, then,
> Be mindful of the rough laborious Hand,
> That sinks you soft in Elegance and Ease.

(Autumn, 350–52)

And in that same season, Thomson writes of man's cruelty to animals. Thomson sees man capable of goodness but also of cruelty, and his humanitarianism is not based on man's innate goodness, but rather on man's need to distinguish the use of power for pleasure from power for harmony. Killing of animals by other animals is understandable, for they are driven by hunger and 'lawless Want.' It is in the nature of things for the fish to eat the fly, though not for man to kill the worm.

Thomson recognizes man's capacity for evil as he recognizes his capacity for good. His argument against hunting is that it is a 'falsely cheerful barbarous Game of Death' (384), a 'wanton Rage' (396). Thomson sees games as forms of joyful contention that end in concord, and this includes the ambiguous fishing episode. But the barbarous games are those in which no contest exists, and man or animals destroy the objects they sport with. Thomson points out that beasts of prey are urged on by necessity (388) and they kill and plunder in the dark, as if ashamed even of their instinctual need.

> Not so the steady Tyrant Man,
> Who with the thoughtless Insolence of Power
> Inflam'd, beyond the most infuriate Wrath
> Of the worst Monster that e'er roam'd the Waste,
> For Sport alone pursues the cruel Chace,
> Amid the Beamings of the gentle Days.
> Upraid, ye ravening Tribes, our wanton Rage,
> For Hunger kindles you, and lawless Want;
> But lavish fed, in Nature's Bounty roll'd,
> To joy at Anguish, and delight in Blood,
> Is what your horrid Bosoms never knew.

(390–400)

Although it is possible to see Thomson's humanitarianism as a consistent development of his view of man, his sentimentalism with its excessive emphasis on tears and children still remains a fault. Thus the hunted stag is described, in a Shakespearian allusion, as weeping: 'The big round Tears run down his dappled Face;/He groans in Anguish' (454–55). Tears become the consequence of helpless frustration. Thomson writes of the fox, 'dying hard,/Without Complaint, tho by an hundred Mouths/Relentless torn' (490–92). By sentimentalizing the stag and not the fox, Thomson uses the first to bemoan the fate of innocents, like children and Amelia, frightened and unable to control their distress.

Thomson exaggerates this distress and minimizes its importance by confining it to the weak and helpless, though in describing philosophic melancholy's approach, he refers to the 'sudden-starting Tear' (*Autumn*, 1006) and 'the Sigh for suffering Worth' (*Autumn*, 1022). The philosophic contemplation of man's fate leads the poet to the tears of things, but it also leads the contemplative man to seek understanding and endurance.[22]

In the *Winter* address to the 'gay licentious Proud' (322) Thomson seems to imply that sympathetic action is contingent upon thought. Thinking is no mere matter of reasoning, but of reasoning that has its anchor in faith and love and thus is guided by the concept of human limitation, by man's need to sympathize with and aid others in a world which is often full of pain. Thus individuals are, in Thomson's sense, incapable of 'thinking' when pride or cruelty rather than faith dominates their actions, and the jailers are identified as just such 'Tyrants' (367) who

> Snatch'd the lean Morsel from the starving Mouth;
> Tore from cold wintry Limbs the tatter'd Weed;
> Even robb'd them of the last of Comforts, Sleep;
> The free-born BRITON to the Dungeon chain'd.
> Or, as the Lust of Cruelty prevail'd,
> At Pleasure mark'd him with inglorious Stripes;
> And crush'd out Lives, by secret barbarous Ways,
> That for their Country would have toil'd, or bled.

> (368–75)

The Jail Committee, the 'generous Band' (359), is composed of those aristocrats in whom benevolence does operate. Thomson added (1730–44) this passage, another inclusion of actual humanitarian facts, after the appointment of the Jail Committee in 1729. Thomson supported its inquiry into the needed improvement of the prisons, and placed the passage in the poem as an instance of the 'Horrors' (361) of confinement.

He attributes the viciousness of the jailers—the 'little Tyrants' (367)—to their 'Lust of Cruelty' (372). The jailers and other 'dark insidious Men' are dominated by wild, cruel and uncontrolled forces. Thus society sometimes gives authority and power to men hostile to patriotic and to benevolent feelings, men who convert the law into self-interest. But Thomson refuses to pursue the causes of this disaster, just as he may have assumed that a moralistic reference to contemporary events would provide its own poetic justification. If *Winter* deals with nature's dislocation in space, then the jail is—for the poor, the sick, the non-criminals—an unjustly confining, deceptive place. Thomson suggests but does not develop these distinctions. Instead, he concludes the passage with a conventionalized hope for 'every Man [to be] within the Reach of Right' (388). But in order to connect this section with the one following, he added in 1744 a connective between the wanton horror of the merciless jailers and the horror of the raging wolves caused by the 'wintry Famine' (389).

The second 1726 edition and the 1730 edition placed the Russian bear passage directly after that of the Jail Committee, and in 1730 the following connective was added:

> Yet more outragious is the season still,
> A deeper horror, in Siberian wilds.
>
> (*Winter*, C, 365–66)

It was an arbitrary connection, re-emphasizing the depth of *Winter*'s horror. The 'Wintry Famine' passage then followed upon the conclusion of this verse paragraph with the following lines:

> Or from the cloudy Alps, and Appenine,
> Capt with grey mists, and everlasting snows;
> Where nature in stupendous ruin lies,
> And from the leaning rock, on either side,
> Gush out those streams that classic song renowns:
> Cruel as death, and hungry as the grave!
> Burning for blood! bony, and ghaunt, and grim!
> Assembling wolves in torrent troops descend.
>
> (*Winter*, C, 381–88)

This passage was revised in 1744 as follows (the revised Russian bear paragraph was placed at lines 799–833):

By wintry Famine rous'd, from all the Tract
Of horrid Mountains which the shining Alps,
And wavy Appenines, and Pyrenees,
Branch out stupendous into distant Lands;
Cruel as death, . . .

(Winter, E, 389–92)

The revision established a consistency of tone, and the spatial imagery of misshaped nature becomes consistent with the view of dislocation and of the cruelty of the animals roused by famine. The 'horrid' spine-like mountains, with their icy glistening and wavy appearance, grow astonishingly into far spaces, like the branches of a huge tree; from this awesome shape the wolves descend. But the syntax suggests that 'Cruel as death, and hungry as the grave' can modify 'Mountains' as well as wolves, for indeed the mountains do become cruel, and like the 'grave,' because they bury the food. The wolves are described now as 'raging Troops' whereas in 1730 they were 'torrent Troops' (388), and the jailers are described as tyrants who 'rag'd.' The wolves are seen, in the image of motion as 'pouring,' as 'bearing along' the glossy snow, as a kind of avalanche that drives, reshapes, and alters the 'glossy' (beautifully shining surface of) nature, as 'murdering Savages' (401) attacking animals and man, the living and the dead. Thomson retained this grotesque passage of extreme violence, heightened by the animals' disregard of beauty as 'Force divine' (405). This disregard implies a world in which gentleness is no longer a shield against evil. If 'Beauty' can become the 'Prey' of raging wolves, the disorder of the season is obvious. In the *Hymn,* when Thomson again refers to 'Force divine,' he means the turning of the seasons themselves, an aspect of 'Force' not so vulnerable as beauty. The wolves carry on the inhumanity of the jailers, proceeding even to the violation of the dead. But the wolves are, perhaps, less heinous than the jailers, for the animals are driven by hunger and loss of home, the jailers by viciousness and greed. In *Spring,* Thomson had made a similar point about man's inhumanity to animals, compared with the wolf:

The Wolf, who from the nightly Fold
Fierce-drags the bleating Prey, ne'er drunk her Milk,
Nor wore her warming Fleece.

(342–44)

In grotesquely digging up 'The shrouded Body from the Grave' (412) the wolves invade and disorder the world of man. It is a gruesome and extravagant scene. Thomson did not eliminate it; he added another that contrasted with the violent vocal imagery of raging, screaming and howling. Thus he inserted another avalanche in which the shifting snows fall in thunder upon a peaceful scene, establishing a correspondence among the shapeless, avalanching snow, the wolves and the tyrants.

In 1744, revising the catalog of freedom-loving humanists, he declared of Socrates that he 'Against the Rage of Tyrants *single* stood' (441), alluding specifically to the image of the jailers who like 'little Tyrants rag'd' (367). This provides a clue to the function of the historical catalog in *Winter*: it is a list of individual leaders who 'stood' (411), guided by the ideal of justice in resisting public tyranny. Thus, refusing to bend becomes a form of inner resistance, and stiffness that is a 'form' of death becomes, in this context, the position of liberty.

The 'high Converse' which the speaker holds with the 'MIGHTY DEAD' is *Winter*'s version of the prophetic voices in *Summer*. These had held 'high Converse' with the poet:

> 'Once some of us, like thee, thro stormy Life,
> Toil'd, Tempest-beaten, ere we could attain
> This holy Calm, this Harmony of Mind,
> Where Purity and Peace immingle Charms.'
>
> (*Summer*, 548–51)

In *Winter*, the storms lead the poet to retreat from life to seek the calm of 'a rural, sheltered, solitary Scene' (429), where he beholds

> Sages of antient Time, as Gods rever'd,
> As Gods beneficent, who blest Mankind
> With Arts, and Arms, and humaniz'd a World.
>
> (433–35)

As these figures rise before the eyes of the sheltered poet, they represent the heroic men who lived unsheltered lives amidst the storms and tumult of political and military violence and corruption. Because they all defend virtues, Thomson's catalog stresses the fact that in society some good men always exist, but he neglects the sacrifices they make and he neglects the differences among their virtues, even with regard to defending the state. By idealizing what the state ought

279

to stand for, he blurs the distinctions between those who oppose
it and those who defend it. Thus Socrates who opposed the state and
Solon who represented it are explained by the same values. He writes
of the decline of Greece:

> Then the last Worthies of declining GREECE,
> Late-call'd to Glory, in *unequal* Times,
> Pensive, appear.
>
> (471–73)

The dilemma of many of these worthies is that they led a state in
which virtue, honor and liberty were met by vice, dishonor and
luxurious pomp.

The account of the Roman heroes begins with humanizing feats:

> Her *better Founder* first, the Light of ROME,
> NUMA, who soften'd her rapacious Sons.
> SERVIUS the *King*, who laid the solid Base
> On which o'er Earth the *vast Republic* spread.
>
> (502–5)

But in time Rome, too, became corrupted, and Cicero's eloquence
merely 'Restrain'd the *rapid* Fate of rushing Rome' (522). In *Autumn*
the man in retreat had no interest in or regard for the fall of states:

> The Fall of Kings,
> The Rage of Nations, and the Crush of States,
> Move not the Man, who, from the World escap'd,
> In still Retreats, and flowery Solitudes,
> To Nature's Voice attends.
>
> (1302–6)

But in *Winter* the poet pays tribute to the public heroes, even while
he himself retreats from the storms, because they represent firm and
active resistance to disintegration, the deforming of the state. For
although the poet may prefer private life to clashing interests of states
in decay, he realizes that public action is essential. Since Thomson
concludes the section on the past with the present, it is appropriate
here to summarize his contexts of history.

Thomson's interpretation of social, political and literary history
is similar to and consistent with his interpretation of nature. The
particular moments in political history become absorbed in the rise
and fall of states and the virtuous leaders have a simultaneous life

with virtuous leaders in the present. In *Coriolanus*, Thomson's last play, Veturia tells the hero that the whole community that forms his 'ever-sacred country'

> . . . consists
> Not of coeval citizens alone:
> It knows no bounds; it has a retrospect
> To ages past, it looks on those to come.[23]

But states change as seasons change. Rome rose and fell, Greece rose and fell, and although Russia and Britain have risen, there is already an indication that Britain's arts and virtue are declining.

Thomson touches on the political and literary past in each season, and, in consequence, the passages about history belong in different seasonal contexts; they are fragments and should be considered as such. The statement about the 'Historic Muse' (*Winter*, 587) makes very clear his view that states decline as well as progress, that states fall as well as rise:

> The sage Historic Muse
> Should next conduct us thro the Deeps of Time:
> Shew us how Empire grew, declin'd, and fell,
> In scatter'd States; what makes the Nations smile,
> Improves their Soil, and gives them double Suns;
> And why they pine beneath the brightest Skies,
> In Nature's richest Lap.
>
> (587–93)

This enquiry leaves unanswered the question why some nations prosper under nature's blessings and others pine, and this puzzle resembles that in which some virtuous men prosper and others are destroyed, and it is followed soon after by an elegy to the virtuous young aristocrat, Hammond.

The views of history in *Spring* begin with the pre-lapsarian period of the Golden Age that was destroyed by man and thus led to the fragmented seasons and the effort on the part of a few to re-establish the virtuous life. This life when it is approximated in the present involves a disengagement from the anxious and painful actualities of experience. It is, in fact, a needed corrective to these. Man's retreats, of which the landed estates form one instance, provide a separation from the vicious and mean aspects of existence; they encourage a dream of the past in which heroes and martyrs are divorced from

281

their suffering. In this respect, the prospect view, beginning at the retreat-estate of the landed gentry, looks out upon the towns, mountains and clouds, forming a harmony in the distance by which the dream quality is maintained because it keeps the spectator removed from the details of pain and poverty that he discovers when he leaves the estate.

Thus the view of history involves a progression and a cycle, a rise and fall (though the arts and military or political power need not rise or fall at the same time), while the dream quality removes the actualities of the past from immediate scrutiny. Thus in his retreat in Hagley Park, Lyttelton walks in his landscaped garden and begins to 'tread the long Extent of backward Time' and plan for the future:

> And oft, conducted by Historic Truth,
> You tread the long Extent of backward Time:
> Planning, with warm Benevolence of Mind,
> And honest Zeal unwarp'd by Party-Rage,
> BRITANNIA's Weal; how from the venal Gulph
> To raise her Virtue, and her Arts revive.

> (*Spring*, 926–31)

This passage, added in 1744, indicates Thomson's sense of the decline —temporary or not—of Britain's virtue and arts, and it is apparent that the hero or model plays a shaping role in history, but only in so far as he leaves his retreat for the political arena.

The views of history in *Summer* belong with the torrid and the temperate zone. Thomson indicates the pagan virtues of some contemporary primitive tribes, while recognizing their shortcomings, and in the temperate zone he describes the retreat afforded by Pelham's estate at Claremont, 'Where in the sweetest Solitude, embrac'd/By the soft Windings of the silent *Mole.*/From Courts and Senates PELHAM finds Repose' (1430–32). From the present prospect the poet looks abroad and bursts into a panegyric of Britain's soul, climate, workers, youth, heroic past and beautiful women.

Not only is there a simultaneity of past and present in this context, but the political and military power of England is related to its natural virtues by the establishment of a history appropriate to *Summer*. There is no contradiction between the need for Lyttelton to oppose the decline of Britain's virtue and arts and the praise of Britain, because the passages have reference to different aspects of the society. Just as Thomson's absolute terms need to be understood in limited

282

contexts, so, too, must the apparently unrestricted praise of Britain in one passage and the attack upon its shortcomings in another. The harmony in the society must be judged against those who are vain (*Summer*, 1630–40), who are unenlightened (1702–16), against those who do not share or cannot afford this dream.

The *Autumn* account of British life depicted as a harvest must be compared with the decline of Scotland and its forthcoming regeneration. And so, too, in *Winter*, the contrasting history of the northern barbarians who have declined from their former military greatness must be compared with that of the Laplanders who live in harmony with nature:

> They ask no more than simple Nature gives,
> They love their Mountains and enjoy their Storms.
> No false Desires, no Pride-created Wants,
> Disturb the peaceful Current of their Time;
> And thro the restless ever-tortur'd Maze
> Of Pleasure, or Ambition, bid it rage.
>
> (845–50)

The Laplanders maintain an ideal family, but they do not represent a state and are thus no proper model for man, though they do illustrate the possibility of a retreat which, in rejecting history altogether, survives in its private ways. The *Winter* progress is that of Peter, who from a 'mighty Shadow of unreal Power' (965) created a country of arts, arms, and trade.

In so far as states rise in power, there is a progress. But, as critics have pointed out, Thomson in *Spring* describes a Golden Age 'Of uncorrupted Man' (*Spring*, 243), a paradisial view of man's past in a mythical pre-history period, when there were neither seasons nor punishments, a period that can never be repeated in this life; but there do exist groups, primitive and civilized, whose life is without the crimes and cruelty that have become a part of man's history even under Christian civilization.

In *Summer*, referring to the South American rivers, the poet writes:

> O'er peopled Plains they fair-diffusive flow,
> And many a Nation feed, and circle safe,
> In their soft Bosom, many a happy Isle;
> The Seat of blameless *Pan*, yet undisturb'd
> By christian Crimes and *Europe*'s cruel Sons.
>
> (851–55)

Thomson's point is that in the post-lapsarian world, there can be no complete harmony and virtue, and although such societies in the torrid zone have no Christian crimes and cruelty, they do not possess Christian humanism.

> But what avails this wondrous Waste of Wealth?
> This gay Profusion of luxurious Bliss?
> The Pomp of Nature? what their balmy Meads,
> Their powerful Herbs, and *Ceres* void of Pain?
>
> (*Summer*, 860–63)

Although nature wide and wild provides for these primitive peoples, they lack the arts, knowledge and Christian revelation that can lead them to a government of laws, to knowledge, and to true religious belief.

> Ill-fated Race! the softening Arts of Peace.
> Whate'er the humanizing Muses teach;
> The godlike Wisdom of the temper'd Breast;
> Progressive Truth, the patient Force of Thought;
> Investigation calm, whose silent Powers
> Command the World; the Light that leads to Heaven;
> Kind equal Rule, the Government of Laws,
> And all-protecting Freedom, which alone
> Sustains the Name and Dignity of Man:
> These are not theirs . . .
> Love dwells not there.
> The soft Regards, the Tenderness of Life,
> The Heart-shed Tear, th' ineffable Delight
> Of sweet Humanity: These court the Beam
> Of milder Climes; in selfish fierce Desire,
> And the wild Fury of voluptuous Sense,
> There lost.
>
> (*Summer*, 875–84, 890–96)

These primitive people reveal a disharmony between their blessings of nature and their sentiments. The barbarians of *Autumn* are similar to those of *Summer*; they, too, are without the humanizing sentiments. But if, in *Summer*, nature is profuse and rewarding without providing the dignity of civilized man, in *Autumn* nature is rude and the barbarians equally so, cast out by nature 'amid the Woods/And Wilds to rude inclement Elements' (48–49). But in the typical manner of the

season, Thomson begins with barrenness and deals with man's fulfillment, his progress resulting from effort. Since nature makes the
resources available, man's use of them depends upon his awakening
to his powers; once man becomes industrious, progress in every form
of cultivated life follows. But this is an idealized view of man's estate
and must be compared with other contexts in the poem and elsewhere
in his work. In a letter to Aaron Hill in 1732 Thomson explains that
when rewards do not crown industry, indolence follows: 'men fall
into indolence when they receive little or no advantage from their
industry.'[24] In the same season in which Thomson praises industry
he describes a husbandman whose harvest and home are destroyed.
And the first canto of *The Castle of Indolence* addresses man and
urges him not to complain of his hard lot because it is God's 'sad
Sentence,' not a progress:

> O mortal Man, who livest here by Toil,
> Do not complain of this thy hard Estate;
> That like an Emmet thou must ever moil
> In a sad Sentence of an ancient Date:
> And, certes, there is for it Reason great;
> For, though sometimes it makes thee weep and wail,
> And curse thy Stars, and early drudge and late,
> Withouten that would come an heavier bale,
> Loose Life, unruly Passions, and Diseases pale.

Even in the *Autumn* harvest, the gleaners form no part of the
progress, and Lavinia becomes wealthy by an accident of fate.
British progress, in other words, is primarily defined by a change
from barbarism to civilization, but not all share in the wealth of the
country, nor in its justice. In fact, the catalog of English heroes in
Summer proceeds by illustrating not progress in virtue but simultaneity, for heroic figures have existed since Alfred's time and they
constitute a continuing line of virtuous men, whether political figures,
philosophers or literary men. Against this continuity must be placed
that of the proud, the ungenerous, the vicious—who number more
than the good, the 'favour'd Few.' In one of his letters in 1730
(October 27). Thomson expressed himself as sharing Pope's view of
the 'Millenium of Authors' in his time.

All is as dull here as Wit had never been; and the great platonic
year predicted by the Dunciad in the following six fine lines, the
Millenium of Authors, seems to be fast approaching.

As one by one, at dread Medea's strain,
The sickening stars fade off th' etherial plain;
As Argus' eyes, by Hermes' Rod opprest,
Clos'd one by one to everlasting rest:
So at his fell approach and secret might,
Art after art goes out, and all is Night.

[III, 341–46]

Happy he! who can comfort himself amidst this general night; and in some rural retirement, by his own intellectual fire and candle as well as natural, may cultivate the muses, inlarge his internal views, harmonize his passions, and let his heart hear the voice of peace and nature.[25]

This view of intellectual dullness he still held on May 11, 1736, when he wrote to Aaron Hill regarding contemporary political corruption:

Your Observation, with regard to political Corruption, like natural, when come to a Crisis, producing more exalted Scenes of Animation, is fine, and pleases by the Prospect it opens; but it awakens at the same time, a sentiment no less mortifying, should we find our Lot cast in the Times of Putrefaction; should we find ourselves devoted, in an anti-heroic Manner, for the Good of Posterity. I wish, heartily, that I could refute what you likewise observe with regard to the Cause of this Corruption. Certainly the kind Exchanger of the Super-abundance for the Sweets and Elegancies of Life, is itself corrupted, and its Gifts abus'd, from the Want of Taste; For whence is it, save the Want of Taste, that the continual Tide of Riches, pour'd in upon this Nation by Commerce, have been lost again in a Gulph of ungraceful, inelegant, inglorious Luxury? But whence, you will say, this want of Taste? Whence this sordid Turn to cautious Time-serving, Money-making, sneaking Prudence, instead of regardless, unfetter'd Virtue? To private Jobs, instead of public Works? To profitable, instead of fine Arts? To Gain, instead of Glory? In a Word, to the whole venal System of modern Administration? And to those gross perishing Luxuries, that reconcile, at once, Avarice and Profusion, centering all in Self, and even in the meanest, the material Part of Self. This Disquisition, I am afraid, would very near lead me back again to your Observation. It must be own'd, however, that the better Genius of this Nation has often nobly exerted itself, and will struggle hard before it expire. With regard to Arts and Learning, one may venture to say, that they might yet stand their Ground, were they but merely protected.[26]

This letter and the previous one throw a good deal of light on how to read Thomson's view of British history. Both letters make plain that his generalizing praise, like his use of the terms 'boundless,' 'pure,' 'perfect,' is meant in a limited sense. 'Inglorious' luxury and self-interest lead, as they do in the poem, to political corruption and a time of putrefaction. The implication is not of progress but of decline, and Thomson very clearly wishes to distinguish between political and social decline and that of the arts. In the earlier letter he felt a decline in the arts was prevalent; in the later, he believes that art and learning might yet manage to avoid the political decline. And although it is not clear how this decline is measured, it is clear that Thomson believes that individual, virtuous acts, what he calls 'the better Genius of this Nation,' can possibly prevent the rise to power of those who lead to corruption. But since even the 'better Genius' can expire, there is no necessary progress.[27] And in the *Summer* passage, Thomson sees God's hand as the final cause of the rise and fall of states: 'O Thou, by whose almighty *Nod* the Scale/Of Empire rises, or alternate falls' (1602–3).

The rise and fall of empires pertain to political power; literature and the arts can still be at their height as the state totters. Thus Cicero 'Restrain'd the rapid Fate of *rushing* Rome' (*Winter*, 522), while Virgil, born at the time of this decline, is held up as the model poet: ''Tis Phoebus' self, or else, the 'Mantuan Swain' (*Winter*, 532). But in *Spring*, Virgil is described as singing to imperial Rome at its height of elegance and taste:

> Such Themes as these the *rural* Maro sung
> To wide-imperial *Rome*, in the full Height
> Of Elegance and Ease, by *Greece* refin'd.
>
> (*Spring* 55–57)

It is possible that Thomson thought that Rome was rushing to its collapse at its political height, but there is no evidence, poetic or otherwise, to confirm this. It appears rather that his failure to be clear about historical periods is indicative of Thomson's vagueness as commentator. In support of the theory of cycles, his patriotism leads him to unmitigated exaggeration, so that More, for example, is compared with Cato, Aristides and Cincinnatus, heroes who figure in the Greek and Roman heroic catalogs. Bacon is found to have 'in one rich Soul/PLATO, the STAGYRITE, and TULLY joined' (*Summer*, 1541–42). These great heroes have a simultaneous existence in the mind of the poet, just as Homer, Virgil and Milton (*Winter*, 532–35) are seen 'join'd Hand in Hand' (*Winter*, 535).

Their heroic virtues, which provide a model for man in diverse societies, correspond with the view that despite the changes in the seasons, certain harmonies and values persist and must be maintained, even though the heroes who maintain them are defeated. Thus there is no uniform progression in the life of man: the possibilities for progress exist, and man may ultimately use his resources, apply 'industry' to knowledge, but at one and the same time there exist the decency of primitive behavior and the corruption of civilized man. The good man may look forward to unending progress in heaven, but on earth there is no such assurance. In the cyclical pattern of human events neither the world as a whole nor countries as wholes progress uniformly. The world is composed of different zones, and countries of different classes, political as well as social and intellectual. In the rise and decline of states there seems an analogy with cyclical nature.

If the pre-lapsarian world is accepted, then the fall and the seasons are imperfect fragments; man's progress in different countries and climates does not proceed at the same pace. And in order to make progress there must be a conjunction among knowledge, industry, leadership and innate possibilities. Some men remain unenlightened while others, the enlightened, can lead, but power is sometimes given to or seized by men who exploit others because of evil or selfish motives, whatever the source of these may be. Thus at any moment in history there may be jailer-tyrants and a counteracting benevolent jail committee, peaceful pagans and cruel Christians.

In the broad view of human experience the greatest vanity is to place hope in temporal matters, for man is dislocated and impermanent in the actual world. In consequence, the safest temporal life is to live in retirement participating in the gentler rural pleasures and pondering ultimate questions: the origin, meaning and moral significance of the world. In dealing with such questions, Thomson is aware that the rise and fall of states cannot be now fully understood.

The elegy to Hammond was added in 1744 and can be compared with the elegy to Elizabeth Stanley added to *Summer* (564–84) in the same year, an elegy that is part of the poet's personal vision of the angelic future. The image of the bright sun and heavenly beams controls the *Summer* vision of immortal virtue—but the elegy in *Winter* finds the public loss irremediable. And although Hammond is a friend of the narrator, his death and his virtues are treated as cosmic irony: "Ah! only shew'd, to check our fond Pursuits,/And teach our humbled Hopes that Life is vain' (570–71). And as if in obedience to this teaching, the poet envisions himself out of the active life, and in some deep retirement (572) with a few chosen friends. The concept behind this passage is the idealized hope and dream of withdrawal.

As a hope or dream—'THUS in some deep Retirement would I pass,/The Winter-Glooms' (572–73)—it is not quite a parody of the Virgilian passage in *Autumn*, but it approaches parody, perhaps because of the allusions. In this hope of withdrawal, the speaker and his friends search the sublime questions, move to rural peace and conclude with comic relief. Surrounded as these sentiments are by passages of engagement, of heroic raptures, it is difficult to treat seriously the conversation of the poet and his friends in which their heroic virtues and patriotism take fire from their talk. Thomson may have wished to provide an example of Longinus's claim that even those little inclined to greatness become possessed by the greatness of others. But, poetically, he substitutes inflation for inspiration.

> As thus we talk'd,
> Our Hearts would burn within us, would inhale
> That Portion of Divinity, that Ray
> Of purest Heaven, which lights the Public Soul
> Of Patriots, and of Heroes.
> But if doom'd,
> In powerless humble Fortune, to express
> These ardent Risings of the kindling Soul;
> Then, even superior to Ambition, we
> Would learn the private Virtues; how to glide
> Thro Shades and Plains, along the smoothest Stream
> Of rural Life.
>
> (593–603)

There is an idealizing, a patronizing of poverty that is a stranger to suffering as it glides through shades and plains; poverty even becomes a virtue in the references to Aristides, 'In pure majestic Poverty rever'd' (462), and to the Laplanders: 'by Poverty secur'd/from legal

Plunder and rapacious Power.' Hammond's life reveals the vanity
of human ambitions, but it certainly does not reveal the satisfactions
of poverty, and when Thomson describes the gleaners, he understands this. But the humble fortune he describes here is, of course,
the swains playing at shepherds. Thomson's peasants do not glide,
nor do they let their minds play upon futurity. The above quotation
continues:

> or snatch'd away by Hope,
> Thro the dim Spaces of Futurity,
> With earnest Eye anticipate those Scenes
> Of Happiness, and Wonder; where the Mind,
> In endless Growth and infinite Ascent,
> Rises from State to State, and World to World.
>
> (603-8)

The aristocratic idealizing continues with a disregard for the depriva-
tions of humble fortune; these are learned squires who anticipate the
infinite ascent of man in the world to come. Once again, the retreat
becomes a look-out point, here intellectually, upon the past and future
while the inquirers remain safe and comfortable in their speculations.
But such idealized solemnity is, fortunately, often foiled. And the
retreat offers, finally, the 'Shapes/Of frolic Fancy' (610-11). If the
solemn ideas of the retreat can be considered a form of imaginative
dislocation, of pure, unrealizable, fictive fancy, then the associative
wit 'Of fleet Ideas, never join'd before' creates new forms. The
winds of the fancy make a comedy of dislocation. Thus the two
aspects—'Or blithe, or solemn, as the Theme inspir'd' (574)—are
played out with a consistency that I do not think Thomson intended.

The retreat represents a removal, a deliberate withdrawal from the
threats of the season, but the village and the city live amid the storms.
When the poet begins his retreat he writes:

> Now, all amid the Rigours of the Year,
> In the wild Depth of Winter, while without
> The ceaseless Winds blow Ice, be my Retreat,
> Between the groaning Forest and the Shore,
> Beat by the boundless Multitude of Waves,
> A rural, shelter'd, solitary, Scene;
> Where ruddy Fires and beaming Tapers join,
> To chear the Gloom.
>
> (424-31)

The reference to the villagers begins, 'MEAN-TIME the Village rouzes up the Fire' (617). The actions are simultaneous: in rousing the fire, the country people engage in mild carousing, reflecting their disregard of the external storms. Their 'solemn' (619) thoughts are confined to superstitious tales and their frolic fancy is not of wit but of the 'simple Joke' (623) and the snatched kiss; their pleasures belong on a lower plane than those of the poet and his selected friends, but their responsive relation to each other creates a joyful harmony that provides an alternative to the dislocating storms and the idealized retreat.

The urban *Winter* scene, on the other hand, though it 'swarms intense' (630) and thus appears aroused and heated as are the villagers, reflects the disorder and dislocation of the storm scenes. In a series of images that echo scenes of dislocation in previous seasons, the city becomes an exaggerated center of chaos. And in an ironic paragraph, the description of tragedy and comedy overlooking the scene implies that the artistic illusion is, for once, more moral and amiable and ordered than the lives of the *Winter* audience.

Thus Chesterfield, the urban aristocrat, is introduced into the poem by the '*Rural Muse*' (663) in order to show that there is no necessary connection between urban life and corruption:

> permit the *Rural Muse*,
> O CHESTERFIELD, to grace with Thee her Song!
> Ere to the Shades again she humbly flies,
> Indulge her fond Ambition, in thy Train,
> (For every Muse has in Thy Train a Place)
> To mark thy various full-accomplish'd Mind.
>
> (663–68)

Thomson's effusive praise of Chesterfield, with its imagery of motion and nature, concludes by attributing to him the God-like power of moving not only neutral listeners, but even the members of the reluctant opposition:

> And even reluctant Party feels a while
> Thy gracious Power: as thro the varied Maze
> Of Eloquence, now smooth, now quick, now strong,
> Profound and clear, you roll the copious Flood.
>
> (687–90)

Chesterfield's eloquence is contrasted with the constricting *Winter*

291

floods, for his 'Flood' remains copious. Such copiousness reflects one of the dangers of Thomson's use of natural imagery. The language, instead of establishing needed distinctions, eliminates any responsiveness other than the merely formal. Thus Chesterfield's copiousness becomes an ambiguous compliment despite Thomson's effort to allude to Denham's famous lines.

iii. Renovation and Rigidity (691–793)

After the dislocating storms the poet turns in time to 'the joyous Winter-Days' (692):

> To thy lov'd Haunt return, my happy Muse:
> For now, behold, the joyous Winter-Days,
> Frosty, succeed.
>
> (691–93)

These are the days in which the 'shining Atmosphere' (697) 'binds/ Our strength'd Bodies' (697–98). In *Spring*, the unbinding of the earth (33) was the act of love and relenting nature, but in *Winter* the binding of the bodies becomes an act of renovation. In the corrupted city, *Winter* looseness or corruption is described in terms of movement— 'flow' (632), 'falls' (635), 'sink' (637), effuses' (640); but joyful *Winter* is 'constringent' (698).

> All Nature feels the renovating Force
> Of Winter, only to the thoughtless Eye
> In Ruin seen.
>
> (704–6)

In this context 'Nature' refers to the elements: the earth gathers strength and vigor; the fire grows brighter, the rivers purer. And a few lines above the air itself was stored afresh with 'elemental Life' (696).

The storms are not a renovating force, so that Thomson here characteristically offers a different perspective on frost and its possibilities. One aspect of *Winter* imposes itself upon the others: the icy gale arrests 'the bickering Stream' (725). This example of the 'Rage of Winter' (722), like the rage of the jail tyrants, results in the imprisonment of the river. What man does to man, nature can do to nature:

292

> The loosen'd Ice,
> Let down the Flood, and half dissolv'd by Day,
> Rustles no more; but to the sedgy Bank
> Fast grows, or gathers round the pointed Stone,
> A crystal Pavement, by the Breath of Heaven
> Cemented firm; till, seiz'd from Shore to Shore,
> The whole imprison'd River growls below.
>
> (725–31)

Although the river is prevented from flowing normally, it becomes a 'crystal Pavement,' an object of visual beauty, the submerged 'growls' of which mingle with the *Winter* sounds on the surface. The frost, however, is not without its tyrannical implication. The series of dog, heifer, waterfall and traveller create extended distant sounds contrasted with spatial contraction, leading to a sense of infinity, to the shining stars that appear as a harmonious world:

> The full ethereal Round,
> Infinite Worlds disclosing to the View,
> Shines out intensely keen; and, all one Cope
> Of starry Glitter, glows from Pole to Pole.
>
> (738–41)

As the snow falls throughout the evening, the poet remarks that it 'seizes Nature fast' (744). But in the earlier passage 'Nature' (704) referred to the elements that felt the renovating force 'of Winter' (705), and this included the air and clouds. 'Nature' in this passage refers to the rural landscape—trees, hills, cascades, mountains. The earlier snowfall was 'one wild dazzling Waste' (239), and its beauty was destructive. In this snowfall followed by frost, the poet descends to particular aspects of nature that have been covered by ice to illustrate their playfulness, not their destructiveness.

> Then appears
> The various Labour of the silent Night:
> Prone from the dripping Eave, and dumb Cascade,
> Whose idle Torrents only seem to roar,
> The pendent Icicle; the Frost-Work fair,
> Where transient Hues, and fancy'd Figures rise;
> Wide-spouted o'er the Hill, the frozen Brook,
> A livid Tract, cold-gleaming on the Morn;
> The Forest bent beneath the plumy Wave;

And by the Frost refin'd the whiter Snow,
Incrusted hard, and sounding to the Tread
Of early Shepherd, as he pensive seeks
His pining Flock, or from the Mountain-top,
Pleas'd with the slippery Surface, swift descends.

(746–59)

Throughout the typical construction of phrases and subordinate clauses, varied in word order to suggest the playful labor involved, the frozen shapes are treated paradoxically: the 'dumb Cascade,' 'idle Torrents,' the frozen brook 'a livid Tract,' the forest bending beneath 'the plumy Wave.' Here, as in the coquetry episode in *Spring*, one finds a sense of nature's playfulness—contrasted in *Winter* with the grotesque scene of the men and ship frozen into statues. This playful quality that creates new and beautiful shapes exists because action is not destroyed, merely submerged or temporarily restrained and constricted.

Nature can be seen at play in making motion motionless; in contrast, man's frolics are full of motion and movement. The cold creates stiffness in nature but looseness in man, so that here they complement one another, whereas a non-harmonious relation exists in the cold that deprives man of life instead of regenerating him. The contrary contexts can be traced in the arrested stream and the youths, unarrested, rushing and swarming over the ice.

The loosen'd Ice,
Let down the Flood, and half dissolv'd by Day,
Rustles no more.

(725–27)

The youthful swains, 'in various Sport/And Revelry *dissolv'd* [my italics] (762–63), are simultaneously the Batavian skaters, the glowing Scandinavian girls, and '*Russia*'s buxom Daughters' (778). The sense of harmony by blending reappears in the relation of the sexes, for the charms of the girls are invigorated and heightened by the season; they 'glow around' (their cheeks become flushed, red) and their fire, aroused by the frost, creates a heightened response in the youths who 'on rapid Sleds' (773) ride over the ice in 'bold Contention' (777). The process of pleasant striving, of harmony by arousing hidden desires, creates a sense of the different *Winter* joys that are, however, short-lived.

The bright and powerful sun of *Summer* proves ineffectual in *Winter*. There are bright moments as a different element momentarily seeks to assert itself; the sun strikes the cliff, but its power is weak. Still, the hunters retain their power. The youthful swains engaged without destruction 'in various Sport' (762), but the hunters' 'Sport' (789) brings death and desolation. With this return to disorder, to rigidity as death, the joys are over.

iv. The Aweful Sublime (794-1069)

Just as the very long section in *Summer* dealing with the descent to the equatorial regions was, except for a very few lines, composed for the 1744 edition (*Summer, C,* 629-1094), so most of the view of the frigid zone in *Winter* was added to this edition (*Winter, E,* 799-903, 950-88). The transition from the temperate to the frigid zone is an imaginative flight to a seasonal extreme, as was the flight to the torrid zone. In *Winter* the observant narrator declares:

> BUT what is This? Our infant Winter sinks,
> Divested of his Grandeur, should our Eye
> Astonish'd shoot into the *Frigid Zone*;
> Where, for relentless Months, continual Night,
> Holds o'er the glittering Waste her starry Reign.
>
> (794-98)

In *Summer*, the narrator begins his flight while in the midst of pleasure (the summer shade); in *Winter*, it follows the renewal of destruction. If *Summer* in the torrid zone can become a hell of fire (*Summer*'s 'glittering Waste' (963) was the burning sand), then the frigid zone must be seen as an illusionary icy world of death (a frigid 'glittering Waste' (798)) in which only occasionally there lies buried the living, renovating force.

Thomson develops throughout *The Seasons* the view that man and nature are involved in growth and destruction of which the only predictable and controllable behavior is man's relation to other men and animals; trust in the future is an act of faith in God's love and wisdom. The self-appointed retreat becomes a form of ideal life, but when such retreat is forced upon man, it becomes a form of suffering. The continuity of attitude toward involuntary solitude can be seen by examining the forsaken man in *Summer* (retained from the 1727 edition, *Summer, A,* 686-97) and the exile in *Winter*.

UNHAPPY he! who from the first of Joys,
Society, cut off, is left alone
Amid this World of Death. Day after Day,
Sad on the jutting Eminence he sits,
And views the Main that ever toils below;
Still fondly forming in the farthest Verge,
Where the round Ether mixes with the Wave,
Ships, dim-discovered, dropping from the Clouds.
At Evening, to the setting Sun he turns
A mournful Eye, and down his dying Heart
Sinks helpless; while the wonted Roar is up,
And Hiss continual thro the tedious Night.

(Summer, 939–50)

The *Winter* passage reads:

THERE, thro the Prison of unbounded Wilds,
Barr'd by the Hand of Nature from Escape,
Wide-roams the *Russian* Exile. Nought around
Strikes his sad Eye, but Desarts lost in Snow;
And heavy-loaded Groves; and solid Floods,
That stretch, athwart the solitary Vast,
Their icy Horrors to the frozen Main;
And chearless Towns far distant, never bless'd,
Save when its annual Course the Caravan
Bends to the golden Coast of rich *Cathay*,
With News of Human-kind.

(799–809)

In the *Summer* passage the abandoned mariner sees visions of ships that never come. The mirage of ships dropping from the clouds is followed by the 'setting' sun and the corresponding 'sinking' of his heart. The clouds become an illusory world of redemption and when his heart sinks,

the wonted Roar is up.
And Hiss continual thro the tedious Night.

(949–50)

The sounds of the sea rise as he sinks and he is, metaphorically engulfed by these sounds. In this posture of man sitting on the 'jutting Eminence,' he is not only cut off from the joys of society, but ironically seen as the man defeated by nature. The entire passage underlines in a quite different but nevertheless equally successful way the 'Prison' of nature shared by the *Winter* exile. For his is a prison of 'unbounded' wilds, and all his movement is futile. For the sad exile sees even deserts 'lost in Snow' and 'Floods' that are solid; nature is for him a prison without gates. He is not the deluded shepherd deceived by the snow nor the prisoner punished by human cruelty, but a lonely and isolated figure in a shapeless world shared by the bristling ('horrid,' 829) bear who 'with stern Patience, scorning weak Complaint,/Hardens his Heart against assailing Want' (832–33).

The solitaries of Thomson are men cut off from society—the forsaken mariner, the lost shepherd, the Russian exile. They are not, like Wordsworthian solitaries, men blessed and self-contained. They are 'imprisoned,' detached from the sources of vital energy and life. They are, therefore, connected with the view that blending creates harmony and, being dislocated from society, they live in dread and sorrow. Their retreats are prisons, not prospects of harmony.

Winter began with a statement of the speaker's 'chearful Morn of Life' (7), but the view of the frigid zone suggests not infant grandeur but dreariness and loneliness and shapelessness. The Russian exile is confined by the 'unbounded Wilds' (799) and although he 'wide-roams' (801), he cannot free himself from the 'icy Horrors' (805).

> Nought around
> Strikes his sad Eye, but Desarts lost in Snow;
> And heavy-loaded Groves; and solid Floods,
> That stretch, athwart the solitary Vast,
> Their icy Horrors to the frozen Main.
>
> (801–5)

The 'Labour of the silent Night' (747), visible in the morning daylight, gave a playful beauty to the works of darkness. But in the frigid zone where darkness continues, the frost-work is serious; heavy-loaded white groves are not bird-like and paradoxically plumy-dark, and 'solid' rivers lie endless and cheerless 'icy Horrors' (805). Yet even here are found happy animals; one of the most colorful passages describes the life beneath the 'shining Waste,' a contrast to the dreadful 'glittering Waste' (798) and the 'Works of Man' (240) buried beneath the 'dazzling Waste' (239). Even in the most remote areas there exist living things that can be happy.

> Yet there Life glows;
> Yet cherish'd there, beneath the shining Waste,

The furry Nations harbour: tipt with Jet,
Fair Ermines, spotless as the Snows they press;
Sables, of glossy Black; and dark-embrown'd,
Or beauteous freakt with many a mingled Hue,
Thousands besides, the costly Pride of Courts.
There, warm together press'd, the trooping Deer
Sleep on the new fallen Snows; and, scarce his Head
Rais'd o'er the heapy Wreath, the branching Elk
Lies slumbering sullen in the white Abyss.

(809–19)

The poet describes the happiness these animals share as they lie on the new fallen snow or 'in the white Abyss' (819), unjoined only by the 'ruthless Hunter' (820) and the 'shapeless bear' (828). What is homeless for man of the temperate zone can be a place of rest and solace for the polar animals and tribes. It is man, however, as 'ruthless Hunter' (820) who clubs these animals to death in the 'ensanguin'd Snows' (825)—once white and joyful, now bloody. Man's rapacious beauty-destroying behavior occurs in every part of the world, despite the beauty of surrounding nature. Contrariwise, in that environment, the 'shapeless Bear,' resembling the piny forest with 'dangling Ice all horrid' ('bristling'), resembles also the shapeless environment without exploiting it or succumbing to it.

There thro the piny Forest half-absorpt,
Rough Tenant of these Shades, the shapeless Bear,
With dangling Ice all horrid, stalks forlorn;
Slow-pac'd, and sourer as the Storms increase,
He makes his Bed beneath th' inclement Drift,
And, with stern Patience, scorning weak Complaint,
Hardens his Heart against assailing Want.

(827–33)

The bear passage underwent three revisions. It was first inserted in the second edition (1726):

the Bear
Rough tenant of these Shades! Shaggy with Ice,
And dangling Snow, stalks thro' the Woods, forlorn.
Slow-pac'd and sowrer, as the Storms increase,
He makes his Bed beneath th' inclement Wreath,
And, scorning the Complainings of Distress,
Hardens his Heart against assailing Want.

(*B*, [272–78])

The 1730 text read:

> *There thro' the ragged woods absorpt in snow,*
> *Sole tenant of these shades, the shaggy bear,*
> *With dangling ice all horrid, stalks forlorn;*
> Slow-pac'd, and sowrer as the storms increase,
> He makes his bed beneath *the drifted snow*;
> And, scorning the complainings of distress,
> Hardens his heart against assailing want.
> *While tempted vigorous o'er the marble waste,*
> *On sleds reclin'd, the furry Russian sits;*
> *And by his rain-deer drawn, behind him throws*
> *A shining kingdom in a winter's day.*

(C, 370–80)

The final version created a correspondence between the shapeless environment and the origin of the bear. It established a distinction between those animals who formed part of beauteous nature and the bear who endured the hardship without reflecting the beauty. The bear and the forest are piny and 'half-absorpt' by the snow; and the problem of identification becomes one of resignation, yet belonging. The bear accepts his environment and his 'assailing Want.' Between the first and last versions, Thomson wisely altered the word order to avoid a straightforward sentence. Thus the 'Bear' which begins the sentence in 1726 is placed at the end of the second line, and the line 'scorning the Complainings of Distress' is changed into a typical example of paradoxical agreement. The line is divided into two contrasting phrases introduced by 'with' and 'scorning' (implying 'without'), but both are stoical phrases of endurance. If changes such as 'piny' for 'ragged' and 'shapeless' for 'shaggy' are artistically coherent, then it seems likely that the omitted last three lines of the 1730 version were governed by the same type of decision.

The 'furry Russian' altered the tone of the passage and gave it a lively and happy ending quite inconsistent with the effect of the bear's patience. Its removal made possible the ironic connection between the withdrawing animal in his dark bed beneath the snow and the barbarians swarming 'WIDE o'er the spacious Regions of the North' (834). The 'marble waste' and 'shining kingdom' became, in the revision, the 'shining Waste' (810), and in the section on the Laplanders, 'one Expanse/Of marbled Snow' (856–57), a spectrum image.

The relation between exile and bear (the Russian, the furry nations, and the swarming race (836–38)) demonstrates one of Thomson's

299

organizational maneuvers in *The Seasons*. In *Liberty*, Part III, 1735, the following passage about the distant north appeared:

> seized by frost,
> Lakes, headlong streams, and floods, and oceans sleep.
> Yet there life glows; the furry millions there
> Deep-dig their dens beneath the sheltering snows:
> And there a race of man prolific swarms,
> To various pain, to little pleasure used,
> On whom keen-parching beat Riphaean winds,
> Hard like their soil, and like their climate fierce,
> The nursery of nations!—These I roused,
> Drove land on land, on people people poured,
> Till from almost perpetual night they broke
> As if in search of day, and o'er the banks
> Of yielding empire, only slave-sustained,
> Resistless raged—in vengeance urged by me.
>
> (525–38)

This passage describes the motionlessness of frozen nature and the activity of the animals beneath the snow. Their activity and their multiplicity joins them with the swarms of men. In the sense that the men become hard like the climate and seek no shelter, they are inferior to the animals, and Liberty uses them as a river that it roused to overflowing. The characteristic epic figure, 'Drove land on land, on people people poured,' suggests a brutality and cruelty strangely justified by Liberty's claim of vengeance. The relationship between the 'furry Nations' (811) in *Winter* and the 'boisterous Race' is artistically wiser and more justifiable. For the animals are described at length not merely in terms of color but of beauty, of the value of their lives ('cherish'd there'). They are part of a beautiful world of color, shapes, textures. The ruthless hunter is a destroyer of such forms and the bear is the animal that represents the stoical shapelessness of the season. The northern barbarians are another instance of the prolific swarming, but without an order or a beauty found in the animals. They are also unlike the urban swarms of riotous merrymakers (630 ff.). They are not superior to them; they are men who 'bear' and who are like bears, 'who little Pleasure know and fear no Pain' (837).

There is, in the following passage, a typical Thomsonian transition of actuality to image. From the patient bear, the poet moves to a description of the 'boisterous Race' (836), with 'boisterous' a synonym for 'rough'—the bear had just been called 'Rough Tenant of these Shades' (828). The bears and the 'Last of Men' are 'rough', rugged in appearance, disordered, though the men are also harsh. At the opening of *Winter* the poet referred to the season's 'rough Domain,' its tempestuousness, though the child-poet was pleased to wander in it. But the relation between season, bear and man includes another implication, for 'rough' is applied to 'Industry' and to 'Power.' It is characteristic of the laborer, and although roughness is not necessarily gross, it is always identified with the laboring classes. The squires and the aristocrats are elegant. The rough and fearless barbarians have neither joy nor vision, but they act; they 'relum'd the Flame/Of lost Mankind' (838–39) and gave the vanquished world 'another' not a better 'Form' (842). With them are contrasted the 'Last of Men' (937), who resemble bears in grossness, not in roughness:

> Immers'd in Furs,
> Doze the gross Race. Nor sprightly Jest, nor Song,
> Nor Tenderness they know; nor aught of Life,
> Beyond the kindred Bears that stalk without.
>
> (943–46)

Between these two bear-related passages dealing with implied wrong form or shape and the surrender to violent or dull existence, there is the celebration of the Laplanders and their reindeer. The reindeer and the bear become, therefore, in their forms and actions two versions of polar animal life. The elk and the deer had earlier been seen as peaceful, happy animals clubbed to death by the vicious hunter. For the Laplanders the 'fearful flying Race' (822) yield their necks to the sled and give their lives in sacrificial harmony.

The reindeer satisfy all the needs of the Laplanders just as the trees did for the *Summer* native: 'Life-sufficing trees,/At once his Dome, his Robe, his Food, and Arms' (836–37).

> Their Rain-Deer form their Riches. These their Tents,
> Their Robes, their Beds, and all their homely Wealth
> Supply, their wholesome Fare, and chearful Cups.
>
> (851–53)

The 'form' of the reindeer, the fleet, gentle, responsive animal, branching out in beauty, becomes a model of interrelation with man.

Having mixed features of trees and animals, they accept the polar dislocations as the norm (which, of course, they are for the polar region) and lead man over the white prospect.

> Obsequious at their Call, the docile Tribe
> Yield to the Sled their Necks, and whirl them swift
> O'er Hill and Dale, heap'd into one Expanse
> Of marbled Snow, or far as Eye can sweep
> With a blue Crust of Ice unbounded glaz'd.
> By dancing Meteors then, that ceaseless shake
> A waving Blaze refracted o'er the Heavens,
> And vivid Moons, and Stars that keener play
> With doubled Lustre from the radiant Waste,
> Even in the Depth of *Polar Night*, they find
> A wondrous Day: enough to light the Chace,
> Or guide their daring Steps to *Finland*-Fairs.
>
> (854-65)

Hills and dale are one expanse, meteors dance in the sky, the stars shine reflected from the ice and the waste is 'radiant.' Night becomes like day, and spatial change or transformation creates a vision of beauty. The reindeer 'yield' their necks to the sleds, yet they 'whirl' them, and in this passive and active relation they move over the 'unbounded' expanse. This expanse is for them not a prison but a home, and the snow becomes smooth as marble, glazed with blue. Earlier, the icy gale 'breathed' over the pool 'a blue Film' (724), silencing the bickering stream, but here the blue crust glazes all the marbled ice and unifies hill and dale.

In describing the Golden Age in *Spring*, the poet wrote:

> an even Calm
> Perpetual reign'd, save what the Zephyrs bland
> Breath'd o'er the blue Expanse.
>
> (323-25)

The 'blue Expanse' represented the infinity of heaven displayed on earth, and the bland zephyrs provided the motions 'That waken, not disturb the tranquil Mind' (*Spring*, 466). The blue-glazed *Winter* ice is part of the infinite prospect that can exist even in the season of tempests. The description of the 'dancing' meteors (859), the 'waving' blaze (860), the 'vivid Moons' (961), the stars that 'keener play' (861) evoke for the Laplanders the playfulness of nature, making

'*Polar Night*' (863) into 'wondrous Day' (864). Just as the white snow on the earth provides a reflection of the unseen day, so the sky itself becomes lighted with the blazes of meteors, moon and stars. The raging fury of the wind froze the waters and imprisoned them, but it is possible for winter to create frozen waters that are beautiful and dark skies that play, not threaten or destroy.

If these are the dual possibilities of *Winter*, the coming of spring in these regions must create a somewhat different kind of joy. And it does. The description of the sun, with its 'swelling Curve,' its 'rising and dipping,' returns to the mingling sexual imagery of *Spring*. The mountains rise, the river and water imagery appear. The ideal 'by Poverty secur'd' (881) insured that these

> spotless Swains ne'er knew
> Injurious Deed, nor, blasted by the Breath
> Of faithless Love, their blooming Daughters Woe.
>
> (884–86)

The reference to the idealized Laplanders as 'spotless Swains' (884) with 'unblemish'd Wives' suggests that they belong with the other idealized figures throughout *The Seasons*. They are untouched by 'legal Plunder' (882), 'rapacious Power' (882), or 'fell Interest' (883). In lines that Gray was to imitate, the speaker describes their content:

> No false Desires, no Pride-created Wants,
> Disturb the peaceful Current of their Time.
>
> (847–48)

The reintroduction of spring illustrates here the continuity of Laplander harmony, the change of seasons bringing different but equally harmonious joys. Night and day, winter and spring, these among the Laplanders are the occasion for ideal life, and yet this earthly ideal does not conclude *Winter*; it precedes the most dreadful scenes. The implication is that, in *Winter*, such harmony is a form of wished illusion, a form of displacement, of accidental pleasures that are preceded and followed by dreadful dislocation. In *Winter* disharmony is the norm and harmony the exception, and the collocation of *Spring* in *Winter* presses this upon our attention.

The return to spring precedes the allegorical figure of misrule. If the blue glaze of ice represents the possibilities of pleasure and speed, of the remaking of the day, in the court of allegorical *Winter* the blue returns to its unrejoicing implication of death.

Thron'd in his Palace of cerulean Ice,
Here WINTER holds his unrejoicing Court;
And thro his airy Hall the loud Misrule
Of driving Tempest is for ever heard.

(894-97)

These lines, with the revision of 'holds' for 'keeps' and 'thro' for 'in,'
were identical with lines originally added in 1726, second edition,
and retained in 1730. But in 1744, 'WINTER' was given a 'Palace'
instead of 'Russia's wide, unmeasurable, Moors' (*B*, 267) or 'Siberian
wilds' (*C*, 366); the allegorical figure was originally identified with
shapeless space but was revised to create a place of beauty and
power that was an ironic deception. Winter was a grim tyrant and in
his palace were to be heard the wild, misruling tempests, not the
rule of justice or beauty. This revision is consistent with the 'wild
dazzling Waste,' with the introduction of the beautiful 'furry Nations'
contrasted with the shapeless bear; they all develop the paradoxical
quality of deceptive space or contrasting forces of beauty and ugli-
ness as characteristic of the season resulting from tempests. Thus in
this passage 'Winter' 'arms' the winds, 'Moulds' his hail, 'treasures'
his snows, and these shaping and controlling images are used to
oppress (rest upon) 'half the Globe' (901).

As the muse hovers over the North Pole where Winter holds court,
Thomson describes the sight as a 'wild stupendous Scene' (893). The
negligence of nature wide and wild is not to be identified with this
scene 'Where failing gradual Life at length goes out' (890). In *Spring*,
nature's negligence is characteristic of life and force and harmony,
but this scene, with its absence of life, is disharmonious and chaotic.

The season began with a conventionalized personification quite
like that of the previous seasons. But at this point, *Winter* is seen in
terms of its misrule, not 'rule,' and the tyrant is no 'kindred'—he
only appears to be. Thomson's perspectival view of the season leads
him to begin again, this time describing the scene in terms of chaos.
As the muse approaches the '*Tartar's* Coast' (902), snows appear
'Shapeless and white' rising to the sky. In a grotesque image,
the mountains cease to be what they appear, and alps disintegrate
into an avalanche. The shapeless, frozen, deceptive mass which
rises and then collapses becomes a form of chaos, the emergence or
collision of deceptive and violently conflicting forces. Even the
ocean is suddenly but deceptively enchained in a new form by this
furious tempest:

Ocean itself no longer can resist
The binding Fury; but, in all its Rage
Of Tempest taken by the boundless Frost,
Is many a Fathom to the Bottom chain'd,
And bid to roar no more.

(913–17)

And a consequence of this 'binding Fury' is the conversion of men into icy statues (920–35).

This description forms a characteristic pattern of man's defeat by nature, of the overwhelming, violent, unruly, uncontrollable, and incomprehensible forces. There were moments in the other seasons in which disorder reigned. But such disorder was an elemental war, a disruption or an overwhelming of normal forms. The idea of 'shapeless' mass is not the absence of shape, for this would indeed be a contradiction. It is rather the distortion of known forms. Form in *The Seasons* is identified with the conventional or known shape of objects, and harmony is the blending of elements or the blending of shapes, sounds, and colors. In this respect, the opposition or destruction of shapes becomes shapeless or chaotic, a loss of proper form.

In place of proper form there can be false and dangerous forms. This conception of form derives from the Augustan view of harmony, from the view of false grace and true grace. The life of forms persists in appropriate transformations and, as Thomson's view of the imagination indicates, when such forms are dead, cold or lifeless, even though they possess elegance, they are forms of disorder.

The movement of the earlier seasons ceases in the 'binding' (914) fury of *Winter*. The ocean is tyrannically chained for 'many a Fathom' (916) to the bottom:

a bleak Expanse,
Shagg'd o'er with wavy Rocks, chearless, and void
Of every Life.

(917–19)

The shapeless expanse has no longer the appearance of an ocean but becomes a dark object of awe. Sir Hugh Willoughby and his men become part of this imprisonment. Overwhelmed as the men are by the freezing tempest, they become themselves figures that have only the appearance of life, not life. Setting forth as explorers of nature, their path was barred, seemingly, 'by jealous Nature' (929). In *Winter*, therefore, frosty and tempestuous nature overpowers all other

305

elements, and, with the appearance of life, gives death. Nature analogically becomes the tyrant jailer.

Gone are the 'emphatic silences.' They are replaced by rigidity, motionlessness, imprisonment. If the silences of the earlier seasons were provocative moments of power and, if even in *Winter* such provocation still finds a place in the secret-working of God preparing for *Spring*, the formless sullen silences result from suppression.

The creation of false beauty, of deceptive appearances, was developed more overtly in the 1730–38 versions. There the following passage preceded the bound ocean:

> *Whence heap'd abrupt along the howling shore,*
> *And in various shapes (as fancy leans)*
> *Work'd by the wave, the crystal pillars heave,*
> *Swells the blue portico, the gothic dome*
> *Shoots fretted up; and birds, and beasts, and men,*
> *Rise into mimic life, and sink by turns.*

(C, 659–64)

In the passage can be seen the rising and sinking made implicit in the 1744 version through the bound ocean and the ships and men sealed in it. The shapes that 'heave,' 'swell,' 'shoot up' create motions far more active than the stasis of the frozen north. Moreover, the pillars, portico and dome imply a civilized wild inconsistent with the 'bleak expanse' (*C*, 669).

As the poet moves to the 'wild *Oby*' (937), he comes to 'the Last of Men' (937), savages, sunk in caves, and hibernating like the shapeless bears. When day finally comes, they take their quivers to resume the murderous hunt.

The dislocation of space calls into question the assurance with which the other seasons reveal the transformation of elements, for even if the change is present in all seasons, in *Winter* the very physical shapes are changed by the storms. Anxiety in the other seasons is not due to the questioning of the physical forms of nature, but *Winter*'s anxiety is based on just such unrecognizable objects. Moreover, the speaker moves to the frigid zone and remains there.

All such passages are bound to be followed, immediately or shortly, in Thomson's procedure, by appeals to or assertions of God's goodness or man's power as indicative of God's goodness. Thus the *Spring* passage leads to statements of ideal love 'BUT happy they! the happiest of their Kind!' (1113); that in *Summer* is immediately followed by

Vasco da Gama's triumph over the 'mad Seas' (1001); the *Autumn*
death is followed by the possibility that there is a 'better *Genius* of
the Night' (1160); and in *Winter* there is the prospect of a great
leader (Peter) 'New-moulding Man' (951).

> WHAT cannot active Government perform,
> New-moulding Man? Wide-stretching from these Shores,
> A People savage from remotest Time,
> A huge neglected Empire ONE VAST MIND,
> By HEAVEN inspir'd, from the Gothic Darkness call'd.
>
> (950–54)

Peter is implicitly compared with the grim tyrant, personified
Winter, who 'Moulds his fierce Hail, and treasures up his Snows,/
With which he now oppresses half the Globe'(900–1).'New-moulding'
is a physical and moral shape or form term, and Thomson uses it in
this sense in *Spring* (681) to imply moral shape—'form'd of generous
Mould'—and in *Autumn* to imply physical form—'the Layers then/
Of mingled Moulds' (814–15). Even in wildest Siberia, it is possible
for man to be drawn from his lethargy and bear-like sleep and be
'new-moulded.'

The Peter passage (950–87) was added in 1744 and expresses the
value of virtuous public action. It presents Thomson's view of a
benevolent monarch, one of his few successes in the use of public
praise. Peter's creation of a new order is narrated throughout in terms
of related space and morals. He 'tam'd' the country and the 'ill-
submitting' (957). The sons are both barbarians and men; he subdued one, raised the other. He sought to build his country not by
operating within its courts, but by courting external skills and engag-
ing himself to bring them back to Russia. The kind of quality the
passage needs to create is made clear by its conclusions:

> For what his Wisdom plann'd, and Power enforc'd,
> More potent still, his great *Example* shew'd.
>
> (986–87)

The success of the passage depends upon Thomson creating a sense
of order (form) governed by authority. To achieve this he begins by
suggesting the new-shaping power, and by illustrating in sentence
structure the 'wide-stretching' order that originally existed. Connecting the darkness of winter night with the long 'Gothic Darkness'
(954) and the power which controls it as 'A mighty Shadow of unreal

Power' (965), Thomson uses the physical description of the frigid winter to lead to the moral light that Peter brings. The passage develops by transformation images and scenes, indicating the new moulded upon the old. Peter substitutes the 'mechanic Tool' (969) for the sceptre and gathers the seeds of commerce and art, of peace and war. Even the order of 'gathering' suggests new unions which did not exist.

> Then Cities rise amid the illumin'd Waste;
> O'er joyless Desarts smiles the rural Reign;
> Far-distant Flood to Flood is social join'd;
> Th' astonish'd *Euxine* hears the *Baltic* roar;
> Proud Navies ride on Seas that never foam'd
> With daring Keel before; and Armies stretch
> Each Way their dazzling Files, repressing here
> The frantic *Alexander* of the North,
> And awing there stern *Othman*'s shrinking Sons.
> *Sloth* flies the Land, and *Ignorance*, and *Vice*,
> Of old Dishonour proud: it glows around,
> Taught by the ROYAL HAND that rous'd the Whole,
> One Scene of Arts, of Arms, of rising Trade.
>
> (973–85)

Past and present coexist, as 'Cities' now 'rise' amid 'Waste,' and in reference to the 'unjoyous Chear' (942) of the dull savages, the rural reign smiles 'O'er joyless Desarts' representing a paradoxical triumph in difficulty. The newly formed social harmony is further insisted upon by the Horatian reference (Ode I, iii, 22) to the social meeting of the waters, the new forms of nature. Returning again to the physical distance, 'stretching' becomes a sign of power, for 'Armies stretch/ Each way their dazzling Files.' And the tyrant Winter who 'oppresses' half the globe is now replaced by a monarch who does not oppress the just but represses the overly ambitious: 'repressing here/The frantic *Alexander*.' Thus what began in darkness has now been replaced by the glowing image: the conclusion to elemental harmony of deserts, waters and glowing industriousness in the frigid zone. If the villagers who send mirth round and rouse the fire represent the working life of pleasure, Peter represents the king who gives to the kingdom the lively and valuable qualities of the rural folk. This is a strongly prejudiced view of Peter, but it does convey the transformation, the new physical and moral location, that Thomson wished to make central.

One can, perhaps, be forgiven for referring again to the ironic juxtaposition that introduces the *Winter* thaw which, instead of freeing imprisoned nature, merely creates a different form of wintry oppression. If Peter is his own great example, then the blowing winds provide the example of nature's power. It is, therefore, a strangely unenlightened nature that is introduced: 'MUTTERING, the Winds at Eve, with blunted Point,/Blow hollow-blustering from the South' (988–89). The subduing (989) of the frost does not lead, as does Peter's of the fierce barbarian, to a nature better moulded, rather to a new but equally deceptive form—the flood. The thaw is a release of power, but this force remains wild and uncontrolled.

> The Rivers swell,
> Of Bonds impatient. Sudden from the Hills,
> O'er Rocks and Woods, in broad brown Cataracts,
> A thousand snow-fed Torrents shoot at once;
> And, where they rush, the wide-resounding Plain
> Is left one slimy Waste. Those sullen Seas,
> That wash th' ungenial Pole, will rest no more
> Beneath the Shackles of the mighty North;
> But, rousing all their Waves, resistless heave—.
>
> (992–1000)

Peter took a waste and made cities rise upon it; the torrents overflow a plain and leave it a 'slimy Waste.' The 'sullen Seas' have been freed, as Peter freed his people; but they do not rouse the waves to control or smoothness: the 'roused' waves 'resistless heave'—thrash about wildly. The thaw leads to a typical chaos scene of the 'rifted Deep' (1002), the lengthening roar, the bursting deep and the mountains piled to the clouds (1003). In the second *Winter* storm, the poet had described a scene equally chaotic:

> Meantime the Mountain-Billows, to the Clouds
> In dreadful Tumult swell'd, Surge above Surge,
> Burst into Chaos with tremendous Roar,
> And anchor'd Navies from their Stations drive,
> Wild as the Winds across the howling Waste
> Of mighty Waters: now th' inflated Wave
> Straining they scale, and now impetuous shoot
> Into the secret Chambers of the Deep,
> The wintry *Baltick* thundering o'er their Head.

Emerging thence again, before the Breath
Of full-exerted Heaven they wing their Course,
And dart on distant Coasts; if some sharp Rock,
Or Shoal insidious break not their Career,
And in loose Fragments fling them floating round.

(161-74)

There the chaos was described in terms of the varied elements, the
false mingling of fire, air, earth (rocks) and water. The waves become
'Mountain-Billows' that swell to the clouds, and the disorder results
in dispersion in an apparent mingling that is a false kind of harmony.
The thaw that follows the frost is no storm; it is a mingling of all the
released snow and waters 'shackled' by the frost, of waves, seen as
'Mountains' piled to the sky, in scenes of distruption. In the storm,
the ships are driven over the waters, sometimes even shattered into
fragments. In the thaw the rivers themselves carry their own fragments, and these attack the ships, the released waters 'shoot' down the
mountain. In the implication of freedom, liberty or release, the ships
in the storm may appear released but they are driven over the waters.
When they 'shoot' into the deep, necessity has driven them.

In the line that Goldsmith was to imitate, 'Ill fares the Bark with
trembling Wretches charg'd' (1004), the poet returns to the theme of
anxiety that has been recurrent in the poem. In a world in which man
constantly finds himself beset by natural forces beyond his control,
'tost amid the floating Fragments,' he finds no security, mooring the
vessel 'Beneath the Shelter of an icy Isle,' in which the 'Shelter' is
itself menacing because of the thawing ice. To the dying shepherd,
the tempest rendered 'the savage Wilderness more wild' (296); to
the trembling wretches at nightfall, 'Horror looks/More horrible'
(1007-8).

Can human force endure
Th' assembled Mischiefs that besiege them round?

(1008-9)

Who are the 'trembling Wretches' besieged by evils? I discussed above
the paradoxical figure of the 'devoted Wretch,' but in *Spring* (392)
the 'weak helpless uncomplaining Wretch' is the fish hooked by the
fisherman, and now the 'wretch' is the fisherman himself who hears
'the hungry Howl/Of famish'd Monsters' (1018-19). The 'Wretch'
is the fly destroyed by the spider (*Summer*, 277), the escaped prisoner
threatened by the wild animals (*Summer*, 936), the plague-smitten

man (*Summer*, 1074, 1091), or the shivering barbarian battling the animals for his food (*Autumn*, 59). The term describes those creatures who are overcome by forces beyond their control or who are menaced by such forces—man or animal. The suffering and anxiety of the 'trembling Wretches' 'besiege them round.'

The Jobian monsters of the deep engage in a sport that threatens the life of man (1015–16). 'Leviathan' and his 'Train' (1014–15) become like the hunter in his sporting inhumanity, who 'For Sport alone pursues the cruel Chace' (*Autumn*, 394). Thus the crush of ice, the roaring winds and the sea monsters play with the life of man. And this scene returns again to the theme of life as struggle, as 'One Scene of Toil, of Suffering, and of Fate' (*Winter*, 351).

> Yet PROVIDENCE, that *ever-waking Eye*,
> Looks down with Pity on the feeble Toil
> Of Mortals lost to Hope, and lights them safe,
> Thro all this dreary Labyrinth of Fate.
>
> (1020–23)

How is one to interpret this statement of faith and hope, since, clearly, the terrible wretches feel the pains they endure. The '*ever-waking Eye*' looks and man endures, and before and after death it 'lights' him with the vision of immortality. Life has its joys, but it is also a 'dreary Labyrinth,' and in the conventional Augustan terms, the maze must be accepted on faith, and the clue through it is the Christian vision of immortality. God looks from heaven, and in looking, he makes man awake to His power; in His looking He is a light. God's passive role is also an active one; in this respect man requires two roles, each distinct from the other, but God is active and passive at the same time. Thus although winter falls and all is gloom, to have faith is to have vision.

At this point in time, 'Winter' is no cogenial horror (6): 'Horror wide extends/His desolate Domain' (1027–28). The comparison of the seasons to the life of man seems trivial here compared to the implications that have been developed in the poem. The series of questions asserting the vanity of human wishes reaffirms the primacy of virtue, leading, however, to the vision of paradise, not, as in *Autumn*, to the life of retirement. For it must be remembered that the muse has not returned from the frigid zone. It has remained constricted in the stiffness of the frost. And the relief is not in nature but in God, in faith. *Winter* is the finality of human suffering, and for its relief no

311

earthly approximation of paradise can replace the apocalyptic vision itself.

> And see!
> 'Tis come, the glorious Morn! the second Birth
> Of Heaven, and Earth! Awakening Nature hears
> The *new-creating Word*, and starts to Life,
> In every heighten'd Form, from Pain and Death
> For ever free. *The great eternal Scheme*
> Involving All, and in a *perfect Whole*
> Uniting, as the Prospect wider spreads,
> To Reason's Eye refin'd clears up apace.
>
> (1041–49)

It is necessary to recognize that in this vision, nature starts to life 'In every heighten'd Form.' *Winter* has been the season of burial of form, of shapelessness, and the new birth provides newly moulded and truly freed forms, not false and disruptive freedom, but release from death and pain. The vision is seen by 'Reason's Eye refin'd' because in the 'second Birth,' faith will lead to the refinement of reason as it leads to the refinement of forms. As the poet calls upon the reader to 'see' the glorious morning, 'see' means to transcend sight. In the prophetic language of the conclusion, seeing and hearing the new-creating word are parts of one process. With prophetic bitterness, the poet attacks those who have dared to question. The 'now' suggests that the visionary future and the present are mixed together and the truth of the vision is in the present. Syntactically, he wishes to merge future and present, and he proceeds in a series of elliptical clauses beginning: 'see now the Cause.' Neglect of virtue, the bitterness of goodness, the triumph of superstition and unjust power—all these appear paradoxes in life. In the vision of the future, virtue is rewarded. The enumeration of individual pain and suffering presents the reader with the bases of human anxiety. In the last lines of *Winter*, Thomson's traditional Christian view and the artistic means he devised to express it are once again triumphant. For in these it is the 'upright' man who suffers, 'upright' because stiffness and rigidity are the characteristics of *Winter*. And it must be remembered that the parallel with *Job* is pressed very hard here, since Job is repeatedly called 'upright' (i, 1, 8; ii, 3; iv, 6; viii, 6). But at least, by this posture, the good man sees a part of the future. In the new-recreated world, he will be able to bend without corruption and see all. The faith of man, therefore, demands a position of endurance.

Thomson achieved this view in the following manner: The concluding lines of *Winter* (March, 1726) read:

> Ye Good Distrest!
> Ye Noble Few, that, here, unbending, stand
> Beneath Life's Pressures ... yet a little while,
> And all your Woes are past. Time swiftly fleets,
> And wish'd Eternity, approaching, brings
> Life undecaying, Love without Allay,
> Pure flowing Joy, and Happiness sincere.
>
> <div align="right">(<i>A</i>, 399–405)</div>

The revisions with the dates of the revised passages are as follows:

> Ye good Distrest!
> Ye noble Few! who here unbending stand
> Beneath Life's Pressure [1730], yet bear up a While [1746],
> *And what your bounded View, which only saw
> A little Part, deem'd *Evil* [1744] is no more:
> The Storms of WINTRY TIME will quickly pass,
> And one unbounded SPRING encircle All [1730].

Both versions make clear that the good who suffer but endure in this life find a life without suffering in eternity. A study of the 1746 lines reveals the fact that Thomson is restating Pope's 'partial evil, universal good'—the noble few have in life only a limited, a 'bounded' view, whereas in eternal spring the view is unlimited, 'unbounded.' One might indeed say that the 'spring of eternity,' by ending the seasons, concludes the poem by envisioning a time when seasons shall cease to exist. The terms 'bounded' and 'unbounded,' 'part' and 'all,' form the basis for the limited cyclical view of change in limited human understanding and for the realization that in the eternal view all changes will bring continual bliss.

But there is a positional interpretation, a statement about shape and form that is necessary to conclude the analysis. For here Thomson reasserted the need for a proper form, a proper shape in withstanding the shapelessness of winter's reality. The 'unbending,' which is retained in all revisions, is gradually supported by 'bear *up*,' by 'View,' and 'saw,' all of which join with the 1730 version of 'unbounded Spring encircle all.'

---

* 1730–38. These two lines were compressed into one: 'And what you reckon evil is no more.'

In the season of hope, *Spring*, 'erect' is accompanied by 'sweet Smiles' and is an easy position to maintain; 'stooping' becomes an obvious form of corruption:

> shall he, fair Form!
> Who wears sweet Smiles, and looks *erect* on Heaven,
> E'er *stoop* to mingle with the prowling Herd,
> And dip his Tongue in Gore?

(Spring, 354–57: my italics)

But in *Summer* unbending—'erect'—is a physical and moral position which one makes sacrifices to maintain. Praising Thomas More, the poet writes:

> A dauntless Soul erect, who smil'd on Death.

(Summer, 1493)

The insight which this gives to the *Winter* lines is that the unbending, the bearing 'up' of the good men who suffer, creates a courage in pain that binds them, while they accept their limited view; yet by being upright, they see more than those who are bent or who do not 'bear up.' The revision insists upon the metaphor of morals and form. In the mortal world, virtue is not free from limitations; it demands endurance in accepting God's mysterious ways; only in eternity can virtue become encircling—for where the virtuous man looks or bends in heaven 'one unbounded Spring encircles all.' And thus, while appearing to be subdued by *Winter*, appearing stiff and unbending, the good man, in an ultimate transformation, acts to conquer it.

NOTES

[1] See Zippel, pp. 248–340.

[2] For a discussion of some of the revisions see *The Art of Discrimination*, Chap. I.

[3] *Ibid.*, pp. 27-29.

[4] E. E. Morris, *Seasons*, I, 126.

[5] For Robinson Crusoe as pilgrim, see J. Paul Hunter, *The Reluctant Pilgrim*, Baltimore, 1966.

[6] Cecil Moore, 'Shaftesbury and the Ethical Poets in England,' *PMLA*, XXXI (1916) republished in *Backgrounds of English Literature* 1700-1760, Minneapolis, 1953, p. 16. Erik Erämetsä, *A Study of the Word 'Sentimental.' and of other Linguistic Characteristics of Eighteenth Century Sentimentalism*

in England, Helsinki, 1951, pp. 142–4, also finds the growing trend of sentimentalism manifest in Thomson's alterations. His generalization is based on a few instances, and does not take account of contrary examples or of Thomson's extensive revisions. Thomson's reasons for revising are ignored and the covering generalization about sentimentalism is offered in its stead.

[7] *Ibid.*, p. 21.

[8] *Idem.*

[9] *Ibid.*, p. 16.

[10] *Idem.*

[11] 'Suggestions toward a Genealogy of the "Man of Feeling," reprinted in *The Idea of the Humanities*, Chicago, 1967, I, 188-213.

[12] *Ibid.*, p. 191.

[13] *Ibid.*, p. 197.

[14] *Ibid.*, p. 203.

[15] *Ibid.*, p. 210.

[16] *Ibid.*, p. 197.

[17] *Ibid.*, pp. 197-98.

[18] See *Autumn*, above, fn. 3.

[19] Crane, p. 205.

[20] *Ibid.*, p. 211.

[21] Grant, *Thomson*, p. 104.

[22] See Chapter III, iv, above.

[23] Act V, i, quoted by Bonamy Dobrée, 'The Theme of Patriotism in the Poetry of the Early Eighteenth Century,' *Proceedings of the British Academy*, XXXV, 1949, p. iv.

[24] *Letters*, p. 82.

[25] *Letters*, p. 76.

[26] *Letters*, pp. 115-16.

[27] John Chalker, 'Thomson's *Seasons* and Virgil's *Georgics*: The Problem of Primitivism and Progress,' *Studia Neophilologica*, XXXV (1963), 55-56, declares that 'the blend of idealization natural description and nationalistic enthusiasm that one finds in *The Seasons* is entirely characteristic of the [Georgic] "kind" that Thomson is imitating.'

V

A HYMN

THE ADORATION OF GOD

A Hymn is Thomson's song of praise to God, and, since it is a
hymn, it is a public declaration, an overt statement of the speaker's
love and faith. Leslie Stephen writes that the 'descriptions of nature
are supposed to suggest the commentary embodied in the hymn.'[1]
I find this a mistake. In the *Hymn* the poet sings of God's beauty
and sublimity, not of human suffering or nature's destruction; thus
the changing seasons themselves become a harmonious whole:

> MYSTERIOUS Round! what Skill, what Force divine
> Deep-felt in These appear! a simple Train,
> Yet so delightful mix'd, with such kind Art,
> Such Beauty and Beneficence combin'd;
> Shade, unperceiv'd, so softening into Shade;
> And all so forming an harmonious Whole;
> That, as they still succeed, they ravish still.
>
> (21–27)

These are not the seasons that took their origin in *Spring* from the
fall of man and operated with 'severer Sway':

> THE Seasons since have, with severer Sway,
> Oppress'd a broken World: the Winter keen
> Shook forth his Waste of Snows; and Summer shot
> His pestilential Heats.
>
> (317–20)

At the conclusion of *Winter*, the poet addressed the 'good Distrest,'
for he accepted the actuality that the good can be distressed, and he
urged them to endure, for in Paradise their bounded view that led
them to consider certain sufferings as evil would be seen as an error.
The seasons then will disappear:

316

> The Storms of WINTRY TIME will quickly pass,
> And one unbounded SPRING encircle All.
>
> (1068–69)

This view of the changing seasons as punishment, as oppression, disappears from the *Hymn*: it belongs to the other aspect of Thomson's world, the observation of suffering and disharmony. The *'varied God'* (2) of the *Hymn* does not include among His variations the death of Hammond or the husbandman's loss of his fields; God is 'varied' in the sense that the seasonal changes form a harmony. In the age before the fall, when music held all in perfect peace, 'the tender Voice was heard,/Warbling the vary'd Heart' (*Spring*, 268–69), and the poet, about to sing the passion of the groves, asks that his 'varied' verse reveal true harmony—the soul of melody:

> Lend me your Song, ye Nightingales! oh pour
> The mazy-running Soul of Melody
> Into my varied Verse!
>
> (*Spring*, 576–78)

Thomson's hymn has considerable affinity with the 148th Psalm and with the hymn sung by Adam and Eve in paradise:

> These are thy glorious works, Parent of Good,
> Almighty, thine this universal Frame,
> Thus wondrous fair; thy self how wondrous then!
> Unspeakable, who sitst above these Heavens
> To us invisible or dimly seen
> In these thy lowest works, yet these declare
> Thy goodness beyond thought, and Power Divine.
>
> (*Paradise Lost*, V, 153–59)

Milton's idealized sublime is appropriate to Paradise, and the 'glorious works' include the variety of nature. In *A Hymn* it is the change and the variety in the change that becomes characteristic of God: 'THESE, as they change, ALMIGHTY FATHER, these/Are but the *varied* GOD' (1–2).

Thomson's *Hymn* is the idealized voice of the poet not describing the world but praising God's love, beauty and power in it. Man is rebuked for not noting the secret-working hand of God throughout the seasons, though the mighty hand is seen as bringing only grateful changes:

317

> But wandering oft, with brute unconscious Gaze,
> Man marks not THEE, marks not the mighty Hand,
> That, ever-busy, wheels the silent Spheres;
> Works in the secret Deep; shoots, steaming, Thence
> The fair Profusion that o'erspreads the Spring:
> Flings from the Sun direct the flaming Day;
> Feeds every Creature; hurls the Tempest forth;
> And, as on Earth this grateful Change revolves,
> With Transport touches all the Springs of Life.
>
> (28–36)

These rhetorical assertions of change are not Thomson's best poetry. His most effective presentation of change is not found in mere variations, but in his version of the unexpected transformations that relate the seen to the unseen by imagery, spatial distance, puns, reciprocity of response—by linguistic means that themselves partially conceal their meaning. The hymns to God in the poem often follow descriptions of suffering and anxiety that define the mystery of God's action—as nature's calm and the rebuke to man for not giving thanks follow the death of Amelia and praise of God follows the *Winter* exclamation on deluded and vain men. The *Hymn* is an extended poem without the varied texture of the individual seasons; and what it gains in consistency it loses in allusive implications. In *Summer*, for example, the seasons are seen, as in the *Hymn*, as harmoniously blended. Referring to the sun, the poet writes:

> round thy beaming Car,
> High-seen, the *Seasons* lead, in sprightly Dance
> Harmonious knit, the rosy-finger'd *Hours*,
> The *Zephyrs* floating loose, the timely *Rains*,
> Of Bloom etherial the light-footed *Dews*,
> And soften'd into Joy the surly *Storms*,
> These, in successive Turn, with lavish Hand,
> Shower every Beauty, every Fragrance shower,
> Herbs, Flowers, and Fruits; till, kindling at thy Touch,
> From Land to Land is flush'd the vernal Year.
>
> (*Summer*, 120–29)

This allegorical pagan version of the seasons belongs to a tradition that Thomson successfully absorbs only when he can combine it with scientific or Biblical language to convey the relation between allegorical powers and natural description. This is apparent when one

318

compares the last four lines of this quotation with the similar lines from *Spring*:

> But who can hold the Shade, while Heaven descends
> In universal Bounty, shedding Herbs,
> And Fruits, and Flowers, on Nature's ample Lap?
> Swift Fancy fir'd anticipates their Growth;
> And, while the milky Nutriment distills,
> Beholds the kindling Country colour round.
>
> (180–85)

The *Hymn* is a song in which nature is asked to join man in adoration.

> NATURE, attend! join every living Soul,
> Beneath the spacious Temple of the Sky,
> In Adoration join.
>
> (37–40)

Although the *Hymn* is a public poem, the poet introduces himself at the end of the fourth stanza in allusion to Psalm 137—'If I forget thee, O Jerusalem'—

> For me, when I forget the darling Theme,
> Whether the Blossom blows, the Summer-Ray
> Russets the Plain, *inspiring* Autumn gleams,
> Or Winter rises in the blackening East;
> Be my Tongue mute, may Fancy paint no more,
> And, dead to Joy, forget my Heart to beat!
>
> (94–99)

The 'darling Theme' is praise of 'the God of Seasons' (93), and the poet suddenly particularizes what had been a general hymn. The introduction of the first person in a third person address is one of the characteristic procedures of Thomson and it operates with sudden vividness here. The conventionalized figure of the poet-walker in *Spring* and *Winter* is brought into a third-person narrative to give a precision to the statements about man and to relate the movement of the poet to that of nature. It also serves to place the poet-singer in the tradition of the Biblical Psalmist or, in *Autumn*, of Spenser and Pope, who also sought to moralize their song. The introduction of the first person places the poet in continuity with the past and makes it possible for him to describe the changing present because he is, himself, a part of it. Just as he praises the 'majestic Main'

319

in the *Hymn*—'and thou, majestic Main/A secret World of Wonders in thyself' (52–53)—so, too, he speaks in his own person of a secret world of wonders.

In the *Hymn*, the 'I' identifies praise of God with the poet's song of joy about each season, and he first refers to himself as catching his praise from nature:

> His Praise, ye Brooks, attune, ye trembling Rills;
> And let me catch it as I muse along.
>
> (48–49)

In the reciprocity that characterizes Thomson's harmonious view of nature, God gives nature breath, growth, beauty, and it, in turn, displays these capacities as a form of adoration:

> Soft-roll your Incense, Herbs, and Fruits, and Flowers,
> In mingled Clouds to HIM; whose Sun exalts,
> Whose Breath perfumes you, and whose Pencil paints.
>
> (56–58)

This reciprocity exists between nature and man, for the forests' harvests breathe their still song into the reaper's heart:

> Ye Forests, bend: ye Harvests wave to HIM;
> Breathe your still Song into the Reaper's Heart
> As Home he goes beneath the joyous Moon.
>
> (59–61)

Referring to the song of Wordsworth's 'The Solitary Reaper,' A. A. Mendilow finds that 'The song so thrills the traveller that he is plunged into a trance, into what elsewhere Wordsworth calls an "idealistic abyss" (Preface to *Intimations of Immortality*); he is raised "to a higher mark than song can reach" (*Excursion, Works*, V, 231). Thereafter he is haunted by the echo of the strain of music in his heart.'² In the *Hymn* the bending and waving forests and harvests 'breathe' by their odour and movement a 'still Song' into the reaper's heart. It is not the epiphany of sound or motion that interests Thomson but the manner in which movement in nature creates a kindred harmony in man. The equally significant fact that such harmony is as often not created has no place in the *Hymn*, though it has a place in the poem.

Thomson's *Hymn* was apparently meant to crown the poem, to praise God as the ultimate cause of the beauty, sublimity and pain in the world. If this is so, the *Hymn* cannot be taken as a summary of the poem; it is rather an exclamation of adoration of God's love, wisdom and power. And it urges prayer and submission to God as the proper role of man. Because of its optimism, its emphasis on nature, it gives the impression that the whole poem is deistic, that God is to be understood from His works. But the different seasons again and again imply that, for all the beauty and sublimity of nature, there are many of God's ways that man cannot understand. Despite this ignorance and despite all his misfortunes, man must love and trust in God. The *Hymn* can, therefore, be understood as a reassertion of God's blessedness, despite the actual pain and suffering in the world.

Men sing God's sublime praise in the cities or his gentle praise in the 'rural Shade,' but the poet sings both the sublime and the beautiful. For the poet in the *Hymn*, the prophetic song of the 'darling Theme' is identified with the moral value of life itself! 'When I forget the darling Theme... forget my Heart to beat!'

In the responsive, repetitive harmony of the *Hymn* the elements give praise to God: the 'vocal Gales' (40), the 'Brooks' (48), 'Torrents' (50), 'Floods' (51), the sun with its 'every Beam' (69), the 'Hills' (72), 'Rocks' (72), 'Valleys' (73), 'Woodlands' (76). The air, water, fire, earth—each in its diverse manifestations blends to form a harmony. And when the poet speaks in the first person, he sees his spatial wandering as controlled by an inevitable joy in God's presence:

> SHOULD Fate command me to the farthest Verge
> Of the green Earth, to distant barbarous Climes,
> Rivers unknown to Song; where first the Sun
> Gilds *Indian* Mountains, or his setting Beam
> Flames on th' *Atlantic* Isles; 'tis nought to me:
> Since GOD is ever present, ever felt,
> In the void Waste as in the City full;
> And where HE vital spreads there must be Joy.
>
> (100–7)

The spatial wandering which leads the poet to the most distant places, barbarous airs, unknown rivers, burning suns—all become subsidiary to praise of God for his omnipresence. Thus the *Hymn* in its praise leads the poet to transcend the world, to disregard the suffering that he has described and, in a sense, to minimize and then falsify the immediacy of pain. It is a transcendent state, one indeed that becomes him more in the future world to which he finally turns than in the one in which he lives.

This distinction between the present and future world did not exist in the original *Hymn* (1730). There God was found to be in all 'apparent' as well as 'wise and good,' and the revision removes this deistic note that is inconsistent with Thomson's position. The original read:

> Since God is ever present, ever felt,
> In the void waste, as in the city full;
> Rolls the same kindred Seasons round the world,
> In all apparent, wise and good in all;
> Since He sustains, and animates the whole;
> From seeming evil still educes good,
> And better thence again, and better still,
> In infinite progression.

(A, 112–19)

The original implies that the poet can know and understand God's actions in the present. In *Summer* he had declared that it was 'Enough for us to know that this dark State' (1800) 'cannot prove/The final Issue of the Works of GOD' (1802–3). The 'ever rising Mind' (1796) was reserved for the future world, for man in his eternal state, not in his 'dark State,' and the final version of the *Hymn* makes this clear.

> When even at last the solemn Hour shall come,
> And wing my mystic Flight to future Worlds,
> I chearful will obey, There, with new Powers,
> Will rising Wonders sing: I cannot go
> Where UNIVERSAL LOVE not smiles around,
> Sustaining all yon Orbs and all their Sons,
> From *seeming Evil* still educing *Good*,
> And *Better* thence again, and *Better* still,
> In infinite Progression.

(108–16)

The revision supports the view that in future worlds, and these only, will the poet possess new powers and see the rising wonders in infinite progression. Then and then only will he see and understand how '*seeming Evil*' educes good, and from 'Good' will move to higher and higher virtues in an infinite progression. In answering a letter from William Cranstoun (October 20, 1735) who had written of

Thomson's brother's death, Thomson wrote of his belief in an increasing succession of future states:

> This, I think, we may be sure of: that a future State must be
> better than this: and so on thro the never-ceasing Succession of
> future States; every one rising upon the last, an everlasting new
> Display of infinite Goodness!

and he quotes in this letter some lines from his not very effective
elegy on the death of his friend, Mr. Talbot:

> Children of Nature! let us not reject,
> Froward, the God we have, for what we want.
> Since all, by Turns, must spread the sable Sail,
> Driven to the Coast that never makes Return.
> But where we happy hope to meet again
> Sooner or later, a few anxious Years,
> Still fluttering on the Wing, not much imparts.
> ETERNAL GOODNESS reigns: be this our Story;
> A Subject for the past of grateful Song,
> And for the Future of undrooping Hope.[3]

What began as a song, a hymn, ends in silence. God's power
throughout nature is and can be celebrated only as long as the particular voices separate themselves from the totality of God. But as the
poet loses himself in love for God, he ceases to be able to maintain
his own identity, and when this happens, silent prayer is his true song.
Earlier the poet had called down death upon himself, if he forgot
his 'darling Theme,' for singing this theme was identified with life.
But in the conclusion, not to sing becomes more expressive of love
of God than singing itself. For if one loses himself in God, belief
itself becomes a more endearing song than poetry, becomes, indeed,
that silent sublimity more expressive than words:

> But I lose
> Myself in HIM, in LIGHT INEFFABLE!
> Come then, expressive Silence, muse his Praise.

NOTES

[1] Leslie Stephen, *English Literature and Society in the Eighteenth Century*,
London, 1904, p. 131.

[2] A. A. Mendilow, '*The Solitary Reaper* and the Growth of a Poet's
Mind,' *Scripta Hierosolymitana*, X, Jerusalem, 1962, 91.

[3] *Letters*, pp. 99-101.

VI

CONCLUSION
THE ARTISTRY OF *THE SEASONS*

In this study I have sought to provide an interpretation and evaluation of *The Seasons*, urging its reconsideration as a major Augustan poem. I have argued that Thomson's unity, diction and thought are entwined with a conception of man, nature and God poetically tenable and distinctive. The case for *The Seasons* as an important work of art depends upon its effectiveness as a moving vision of human experience. Many critics have not felt this effectiveness because they have misconceived Thomson's vision and misunderstood his idiom. I hope that my study will persuade them to return to the poem and to examine it within the context of Augustan traditions.

Thomson's great achievement is to have fashioned a conception which, by bringing nature to the forefront of his poem, became a new poetic way of defining human experience. Thomson was not the first nature poet to write in English,[1] but he was the first to provide an effective idiom in which science, religion, natural description and classical allusion blended to describe the glory, baseness and uncertainty of man's earthly environment, holding forth the hope of heavenly love and wisdom.

Thomson did not deny the actuality of wickedness, the hunter-killers, the wealthy aristocrats disregarding human need and squandering their wealth, the religious exploiters and the brutal executors of injustice. Nor did he deny that aspects of nature seemed, at times, jealous and vindictive, destroying good men and sparing the wicked. But these aspects existed simultaneously with others, with the comic, exhilarating, joyful transformations. This double view he accepted, but he did not accept any simple moral arithmetic in nature and he did not believe that virtue or benevolence was directly rewarded on earth.

Thomson did not have these considerations in view when he composed *Winter* in 1726, and the final work is all the more impressive if one attends to its modest inception. In a famous letter to William Cranstoun [*c*. October 1, 1725] Thomson wrote: 'Nature delights me in every form, I am just now painting her in her most lugubrious dress; for my own amusement, describing winter as it presents it self.' And in the same letter he explained the source of *Winter*: 'Mr. Rickelton's poem on winter, which I still have, first put the design into my head.'[2] When he published his 'Preface' in the second edition of *Winter* (1726), he announced his intent of composing poems on the other seasons, but he was now cognizant that he was working on a 'great' subject formerly treated by the 'best' poets.[3]

The seasons provided Thomson with a naturalistic basis for change which, by its cyclical pattern, permitted limited progression in any one season while relating the whole to God's power. But the cycle of the seasons is not the circle of perfection, and in the poem the cyclical repetition, like the confrontation of opposites, does not lead to a whole. It leads to a temporary completion that introduces a new beginning. Scientifically, change was explained by the traditional assumptions of the transformability of the four elements, but Thomson mixes this view with a description of observed natural changes. The speaker absorbs the scientific explanation by mixing natural description with personification, by using the same term in a literal and metaphoric sense. A knowledge of science can assist man in understanding nature, but such knowledge cannot provide answers to ultimate questions.

Pope and Swift saw much of the present as a rejection of the humanistic views of the past, but Thomson, while sharing many of these objections, found approximations of the ideal past in the society of the present. This recognition was in no sense a support of all current institutions, but neither he nor the satirists were revolutionaries. Change came by degrees, and the history of states was the history of rising and falling empires, and only God's wisdom could explain the ultimate reasons for such change.

For us, Thomson's patriotism and his flattery of his aristocratic friends and patrons is reprehensible. Yet it is consistent with his interpretation of the state as a responsible institution in the family of nations. Britain, by creating necessary commerce and putting down disorderly nations, becomes the father of an international family, even though in its own local family there are proud, vicious and unruly members. Since Britain is the poet's country, set in the temperate zone, the mean between extremes, it possesses the features of a model.

Thomson's own move from Scotland to London was a personal instance of the more general movement taking place in his society. His poetry describes commercial expansion, the movements of geographical exploration and inquiry. Such movement could be harmonious or disharmonious, but it explains why a rural estate could be interpreted as a retreat that was not an escape but a model. In so far as man sought to incorporate into his estate a sense of the past with a prospect for the future, he rested content within his limited world. It was Thomson's conception that the world could not and should not remain confined within man's private domain. His poem, therefore, reveals the need to explore, to inquire, to leave the comfortable shelter. Man had to experience the nature that God created, though it might merely lead him back to the temperate zone.

Marshall McLuhan has suggested that 'landscape offered a broader and less exacting course for those who were preoccupied with the new psychological interests on the one hand and with the means of evading the new insistence on non-metaphorical and mathematical statement as the mode of poetry, on the other hand.'[4] But this interpretation, with its assumption that Pope's poetry was a poetry of statement and its claim that 'landscape' poetry provided an alternative to it, merely perpetuates fictions about Pope's and Thomson's poetry. Pope's poetry was no more a poetry of statement than Thomson's was anti-mathematical. Nor was it a less exacting course.

Thomson's artistry must be understood in terms of the scope and ends that I have been outlining. Whatever his conscious sources were in 1726, the poem gradually became a palimpsest, the ends of which were to evoke the varied sentiments towards nature, man and God and to urge that as a consequence of man's fragmentary understanding the joy, beauty, pain and puzzle of the world demanded endurance and belief.

The poem, with its cyclical pattern and progressive moments, with religious exclamations preceded and followed by empirical description, deliberately avoided rational connections. It was composed of diverse fragments, the purpose of which was to establish links and contrasts among nature, animals, man and God. Thus Thomson created a world of simultaneous occurrences in space, but these only occasionally led to harmonious blending. The world being perceivable only in fragments, it was inevitable that no view of the whole could exist without an act of belief.

In so far as the past existed in the present, it could be found in an ideal retreat, in those isolated moments in man's life when the virtues of the past, the deeds of virtuous men and the writings of genius lived for those who appreciated them and sought to bring their values into the living present. For it is in the living, changing, joyous and uneasy present that Thomson's poem has its vitality.

There is no single narrative development, but there are varied narratives and scenes of 'sad Presage.' There is no single 'nature,' but there are varied interpretations of nature at different places and times. Yet all of these are controlled by a concept of natural change governed by a God who for all His variations is timeless and omnipresent. In the organization of *The Seasons* even organically unified parts are merely another aspect of fragmentation, held together by the principles of repetition and transformation.

The unifying imagery in each season and the stylistic and thematic unity of the whole prevent the poem from collapsing into a heap of fragments. Not only is there an underlying rhythm in the succession of the seasons and an order of elements, but within each season the fragments are juxtaposed to blend or clash. These reveal, in the very order of the seasons, a world in which man, while rejoicing in and competing with nature, is surrounded and often engulfed by it. Man may be superior to the animals in consciousness, but he can be their prey, as they can be his. It is possible to establish coherence and organic interrelatedness in some areas of Thomson's world, but the world as a whole remains a maze, the plan of which is hidden from mortal eye. It is, however, the poet's privilege, because of the eminences on which he stands (emblematic of his philosophical and spiritual elevation), occasionally to see and to speak with prophetic, with more than mortal, vision.

The repetitive themes, images, words become a means for inter-connecting the whole. Thomson's unifying procedure makes demands upon the reader to construct distinctions within the poem, a demand that has all too often been rejected. It is now a commonplace that terms like 'wit' and 'nature' carry multiple meanings in the *Essay on Criticism* or the *Essay on Man*, and critics no longer deny to this repetition a valuable artistic function. Thomson's procedure is a variant of this Augustan practice, but he has not been granted the same consideration and understanding. Yet in *The Seasons* the development of varied and contrary contexts, the use of illusive allusion, the use of participles, of deliberately altered parts of speech, is Thomson's artistic signature. His general terms must be understood as incorporating many individual possibilities, exactly as God is to be apprehended in and through variations that are, nevertheless, one. This conception of general terms is inherent in the conception of Thomson's language. His terms are not mythopoeic, but rather inclusive terms for a varied group of references, since the same act or event can be interpreted from different perspectives. It is for this reason that metonymy is a frequent figure in the poem; in it, the whole represents a part, the general is used for the specific, the effect for the cause.

The other types of imagery in the poem—personification, periphrasis, metaphor, etc.—are all instances of Thomson's conversion of literary conventions to his own artistry. For these images, fluctuating as they do between the literal and the metaphoric, the allegorical and the natural, the human and the non-human, exemplify Thomson's world. In it the imaginative is interpreted by reference to the known. The natural environment becomes the basis for the magic changes and transformations that take place, and Thomson celebrates the beauty, sublimity, wonder and menace of the known world.

One aspect of nature can show cruelty or love to another—the sun to flowers, the breeze to the seeds, the fish to the flies—just as nature can show love or cruelty to man. There is no necessary harmony between nature and man or within nature. Moments of harmony exist, but in no particular instance can imperfect man presume to understand perfect God. The imagery of change that enacts this view is a Thomsonian innovation and neither Milton nor Wordsworth uses the conventions for such purposes.

The language of the poem is unmistakably directed toward expressing Thomson's thought and feeling. It is the result of his experience of the world, and the prose language of his letters and his 'Preface' find their way into his poetry in demonstration of the fact that his poetry springs from his view of the world. The language, indeed, provides a unifying force in the sense that, for all its variations of tone—burlesque, comic, eulogistic, elegiac, beautiful or sublime—it incorporates Biblical, classical and scientific meanings with current usage. To this extent illusive allusions, Latinate words, periphrases and personifications, participles and hyphenated terms belong to the procedure of making the past simultaneous with the present or adding present implications to past meanings and acts. Yet such words and procedure are selective, for not all fragments of the past function effectively.

The language and thought incorporate not only external traditions but personal feelings and events. The Latinate and scientific constructions serve to create an aesthetic distance between the narrator and his private feelings. Thomson's personal involvement in the poem is concealed by these techniques at the same time that they convey his views of human experience. Thus he can talk about sex while describing flowers or about his own feelings of the pain of love by describing the ideal. These techniques are methods so convert and conceal his private feelings though critics have naïvely assumed that his language was 'objective' rather than an artistic instrument for disguising but not disregarding the personal sources.

Thomson uses the third-person speaker so that the reader can place himself in the position of the speaker. When Thomson shifts to the first person or to the vocative, he does so to indicate that the speaker's private perspective is another instance of the general voice. In this, it becomes a model for responding to the environment and God. The different tones—the comic, burlesque, mock-heroic, elegiac, etc.— provide perspectives on the different classes and on the literary conventions appropriate to them. For the tones are referred to and tested by the naturalistic environment which, traditionally, they have allegorized and idealized. Thomson's poem may, therefore, be understood as seeking to fuse the allegorical with the natural and to use allusions to Virgil and the Bible to support his own vision of the world.

Thomson's defects are of two kinds: he is limited in his knowledge of man and in the range of his understanding of human behavior; and, within the range to which he confines himself, he sometimes uses techniques formalistically to conceal his inadequate grasp of a situation or to cajole the reader by flattery or sentimentality. The poem can become overly scientific and excessively formal or overly sentimental, the types of dangers that Thomson risks by using the mixed form and scientific or abstract terms. There is always the risk, too, that repetition will rub off the rough individual edges of a general term and make it vague and indefinite. Thomson tries to avoid succumbing to such faults by employing a fragmentary structure which prevents any readily accepted generalization, and in this he is overwhelmingly successful, even when he introduces scientific explanations and terminology.

Thomson related nature's transformations to the familial, commercial, political and social world of man. The unity, thought, diction, grammar of the poem offered an interpretation of Augustan society, that, for all its similarity to the views of Pope, presented a novel poetic vision. When Wordsworth came to write of nature in the *Lyrical Ballads* and *The Prelude*, he was writing of a different nature and a different world. Thomson's third-person speaker-poet, his interpolated narratives, his shuttling between description and metaphor, his preferred epithets and individual diction were not idiosyncrasies; they were related to a view of poetry that sought an idiom for the fragmentary, yet beautiful and aweful, firmament of space in which man and nature were subject to the transient moments of beauty, awe and destruction. For Thomson there was the need to collect as many fragmentary views as possible so that they became an ordered disorder. For Wordsworth the symbolic language envisioned a wholeness and a unity through the poet's consciousness, so that his fragments imply a whole. But Thomson's order demands of the reader a rejection of completion, a constant and unending discrimination of distinctions. He recognized then what we recognize now, that what man understands is only a perspective, and that although some of these may fortunately combine to give a momentary harmony, too much occurs that is inharmonious to permit a reasoned answer. Thomson saw and felt and knew a world for which he found a personal idiom and he believed unfailingly in another world that he neither saw nor knew. For both these worlds he created an artistic vision, and *The Seasons* is its unfolding.

NOTES

[1]Grant, *Thomson*, p. 100. See also Maren-Sofie Röstvig, *The Happy Man*, Oslo, 1958, II, 285: 'Thomson's true originality consisted in creating a new poetic form for already well-known poetic themes.'

[2]*Letters*, pp. 16, 17.

[3]In his 1726 'Preface' Thomson referred to 'great and serious Subjects' and the 'best' poets; see Zippel, p. 241.

[4] *The Gutenberg Galaxy*, Toronto, 1962, p. 269.

INDEX

Names, *Selected* Titles, Key Words, and Concepts